. . . .

The
World
of Our
Mothers

Sydney
Stahl
Weinberg

· ·

The
Lives of
Jewish
Immigrant
Women

The
World
of Our
Mothers

Schocken Books

New York

Library of Congress Cataloging-in-Publication Data

Weinberg, Sydney Stahl.
    The world of our mothers : the lives of Jewish immigrant women /
Sydney Stahl Weinberg.
        p.   cm.
    Includes bibliographical references.
    ISBN 0-8052-0967-0
    1. Women, Jewish—United States—Social conditions.   2. Women,
Jewish—United States—Interviews.   3. Jews, East European—United
States—Social conditions.   4. Jews, East European—United States—
Interviews.   5. Immigrants—United States—Social conditions.
6. Immigrants—United States—Interviews.   I. Title.
E184.J5W43   1990
305.8′924073—dc20   89-43237

Manufactured in the United States of America

First Schocken Edition

FOR MICHAEL

Contents

· ·

Illustrations

Acknowledgments

. . . .

Many people have helped me in this attempt to distill the day-to-day lives of Jewish immigrant women. First, of course, are the women themselves, who gave so willingly of their time and memories. Without them, this book could not have been written. I owe much particularly to Nina and Tanya for sharing their lives in more ways than one. Thanks also to the staffs of the Katharine Engle Center for Older Citizens, Project Ezra, and the West Bronx Jewish Community Council, who put their resources at my disposal and thus enabled me to meet many of the women I interviewed.

Numerous friends and colleagues have read all or parts of the manuscript, pointed the way to relevant material, and made important suggestions. Among these are Paula Hyman, the pathfinder in writing about Jewish immigrant women; Yolanda Prieto; Laura Anker Schwartz; Betty Boyd Caroli; Maxine Seller; Stephan Brumberg; Judith Friedlander; Carole Campana; and my friends from the Women's Study Group of the Institute for Research in History. Hasia Diner, Corinne Azen Krause, Sherna Gluck, Leonard Dinnerstein, and Ruth Miller Elson read the entire manuscript and gave me the benefit of their expertise. Leonard Dinnerstein has been, as ever, a constant source of sound advice. Thanks also go to Jim Shenton for his encouragement when this book was little more than an idea. Beatrice Silverman Weinreich acted as a sounding board whose knowledge and caution have corrected misconceptions more than once. She generously suggested sources, helped with Yiddish translation, and shared with me her considerable knowledge of Jewish life in Eastern Europe. Barbara Myerhoff's enthusiasm for this project in its early stages gave me the confidence to continue, and the encouragement of my editor, Iris Tillman Hill, helped to complete it. Rosalie West copyedited the manuscript with great skill, and Sandra Eisdorfer guided it through the process of publication with impressive efficiency. Vivian Bergman transcribed hundreds of pages from tapes with speed and intelligence. Diana Bowstead, Ida Fireman, Jack Olshen, Rita Riman, Ruth Schreiber, Audrey Kobrin Weinberg, Beatrice Silverman Weinreich, and Ann Weissman generously shared family photographs with me. I also owe a debt of gratitude to William E. Leuchtenburg, who taught me the craft of writing history, and to Oscar Handlin, whom I have never met, but from whose work I learned that history is really about people.

Ramapo College has given generously of funding and time released from teaching duties to enable me to develop this manuscript. A fellowship from the National Endowment for the Humanities made the initial research possible, and the Memorial Foundation for Jewish Culture helped with a grant to transcribe tapes of interviews. Henry Bischoff and the Garden State Immigration History Consortium assisted with funds to reproduce photographs. All these organizations have my gratitude.

My family has been a continuous source of support and pleasure. I want to thank my daughters Deborah and Elisa for communicating their enthusiasm and their questions, which challenged a few of my own assumptions, and for valuing and carrying on some of our family's traditions; my parents, Berenice and David Stahl, for their interest; and my mother-in-law, Sylvia Weinberg, whose food nourished us while I was writing. Most of all I owe thanks to Michael Weinberg, my oldest and dearest friend and intellectual colleague. He never lost faith in this project even when my own self-confidence ebbed, and with sensitivity and infinite patience, he read and analyzed more drafts than he or I would care to remember. Throughout the ten years of sharing a home with these oral histories, his constant concern and understanding eased the strain of research and writing.

Introduction

. . . .

Several years ago, often over a cup of tea, I listened to my elderly neighbor tell stories of her childhood in Russia and her early life in America. Tanya's memories reminded me of my own grandmother, who had left a village in Galicia alone at a young age for a new life in the United States. Sarah Kirschner was poor and illiterate, yet she encouraged one of her sons to attend college while she cooked and kept the books for the catering business she operated with her husband. She died when I was five, so I had only fragmentary memories of my slight, wrinkled *bubbe*. These were inextricably connected with a sense of Jewishness that seemed exotic yet compelling to a child of assimilated parents. I remember the savory smell of chicken soup simmering on the stove, and my grandmother, with covered head, lighting the candles and extending her arms to welcome in the Sabbath.

The memories awakened by Tanya's stories stirred a latent desire to learn more about my grandmother and women like her. I wondered how they felt about their lives, so different from my own. What compelled them to leave their homes in Eastern Europe? In what ways did immigration alter their lives? How did their background affect adjustment to the United States? Did this country fulfill their expectations? What ambitions did they have for their children? What role did they play in their families? How did the process of "Americanization" affect them and their families? What kinds of satisfactions did they seek and find in this country?

It is difficult to retrieve a sense of the lives of ordinary women in cultures that have changed or disappeared. In most societies, the vast majority of women like my grandmother were too busy with day-to-day tasks to leave such records as memoirs or diaries, even if they had all been literate. Most were not joiners or activists and seldom entered the written record or history books. Statistics can tell us where women settled or what jobs they held, but little about how they viewed their own lives. Thus, until recently, the history of immigration has been the story of men, with the role of women emerging, if at all, only peripherally. During the past few years, however, a number of anthropologists, sociologists, and historians have been studying the lives of immigrant women using imaginative source material and, for groups where this is still feasible, oral history.[1]

I decided to use oral history to explore the lives of Jewish immigrant women from Eastern Europe to get a sense of how these women perceived their lives and coped with the transition from one society to another. The forty-six women I interviewed came to the United States as part of the great migration that ended in the mid-1920s when restrictive laws effectively shut the gates to what was called the "Golden Land" (*di goldene medina*). Although the narrative that developed from this quest explores the collective lives of these women, it will be helpful to examine a single life history to understand the themes that emerged from the interviews.

Nina S. was born in a small town in the Ukraine on March 23, 1897, the third child and oldest daughter of six children. Her parents owned a grocery store and the family was prosperous enough to have its own cow. Nina's father died when she was about fourteen, and her mother supported the family by running the store alone after his death.

"I don't know why," Nina observed,

> but I always wanted to know about the world. We went to *cheder* [religious school] with the boys, but that was Jewish education. It was a time of turmoil [the Russo-Japanese War of 1904 and the abortive revolution of 1905]. I wanted to understand, to learn about geography, algebra, Russian, the history of the world. My mother understood me. I didn't have to explain much. In our town there was no *gimnazye* [high school]. When I was about sixteen, I told her I wanted to go to Odessa, to the *gimnazye*. She tells me, "Child, I understand, but where is the money? And a pretty young girl should go away alone?" What I did was go around to all the Jewish families in town. The Jewish families wanted education for their children. They respected me, and I offered to teach the children. I did this all the time, and after a year, I had saved up two hundred rubles—it was a lot of money. I remembered how proud I was when I went to my mother with the two hundred rubles. And I said, "Now, you have to let me go."

There was another reason her mother might let her go to Odessa. "I had a boyfriend," Nina recalled. "He lived next door, and he loved me and I loved him. But my mother didn't like him, and he didn't know how to cherish me right. So I told my mother, 'If you want me to forget David, let me go to the *gimnazye* in Odessa.'"

Despite her reluctance to permit her sixteen-year-old daughter to leave home, Nina's mother had encouraged the girl's desire for education. She herself had been permitted little schooling and was betrothed at sixteen to a boy she had only seen once. "A blind person is always blind," she would tell her daughter. She had taken the town's library into her home free of charge, and Nina worked herself through all the classics in Yiddish and Russian. Her mother had her read aloud each night so that she, too, could learn.

From her mother's example, Nina understood how to cope with adversity. Her mother had gone from the wealthy house of her parents into a poor one, to a strange young man she had not wanted to marry. And then her husband had died after twenty years of marriage, leaving her with four children to support. (Their two oldest sons had already been sent to America to avoid the draft.) Yet despite her trials, she gained the respect of both Jewish and Russian neighbors by operating the grocery shop and earning enough to keep her family together. "She spoke a beautiful Ukrainian," Nina recalled. She remembered her mother's instilling the lesson of optimism that guided her own life. "Everyone has a *pekl tsores* [pack of troubles]," her mother would say. "But if people had to lay their *pekl* in a row and then pick up one, each would choose his own. Things could always be worse. Learn!" she exhorted her daughter.

While Nina was in Odessa, life was difficult for her mother. World War I had begun and effective government no longer existed. Many people in their town, including all the prosperous Jews, were killed in pogroms by Cossacks or bandits in the anarchy that prevailed before the Bolshevik government managed to establish order. When she finished her second year at school, Nina joined a group of young people attempting to get back to their families in the Ukraine. She would never return to complete her education. After a trying train trip of almost a month—it should have taken only three days—Nina arrived home, only to have her mother exclaim, "I thought you were safe in Odessa—now I have another daughter to hide." Nina was a beautiful young girl, and her mother was fearful that she would be raped by the marauding bands. That night, Nina recalled, she slept in the basement with the local pigs who wandered in. During this period of trial, her mother insisted that her children sleep in different areas of the house—one in the cellar, one on the oven—so that if bandits did break in, they would not find them all, and some would survive. Yet her mother was so respected among the local peasants that before an attack on the Jews one would invariably warn her, and immediately after a pogrom a neighbor would come by to make sure that she was unharmed.

Although she was now past twenty, Nina was not anxious to marry. "When a woman married, she sold herself," she observed. "Then she had to worry about having children, supporting her family." But during the Civil War in Russia times were even more difficult than they had been in World War I. Her mother wanted to see Nina settled and persuaded her to marry a second cousin who loved her dearly. He was never a strong young man, weakened, Nina thought, by his years of fear and hiding to avoid being drafted into the Russian army. Before their marriage she had gone with him for a day trip to his nearby town, and came down with typhoid fever; although she recovered, her fiancé contracted the illness from nursing her and never fully regained his strength. His poor health meant that Nina would have to assume increasingly more of the burden of supporting them and their children.

About a year after their marriage, when Nina discovered that she was pregnant, she insisted that they had to leave. It was no place to have children. "Mothers had the strength to kill their babies," she recalled, remembering a time of hiding in a cellar when a mother kept her hand over her infant's mouth to prevent it from crying out and giving them away to the rampaging Cossacks. There was no food, no safety. When her mother's uncle sent his address and a money order from the United States, she clung to them as her only hope. She decided that she and her husband had to leave immediately, and a sister-in-law who had traveled to a distant town had to be left behind.

This was not the first time Nina had tried to leave for America. Once, in her early teens, when she and her father were escorting an older brother out of town to send him to the United States, she had asked if she could go with him. With tears in his eyes, Nina remembered, her father told her, "No, my child, he has to go now, but you don't. When a child leaves, it's like a piece of your heart torn out. Stay a while." Nina didn't ask again, and her father died soon after.

Now, she felt that there was no longer any choice. With the help of a kindly Polish officer billeted in her house, Nina was able to get herself, her husband, and a young cousin from the Ukraine into Poland. There she went for aid to the Hebrew Immigrant Aid Society (HIAS), which the officer had told her about. She and her family had to wait for four months in Poland because they had no papers. Her husband earned some money by buying bread from a bakery and peddling it to other immigrants waiting in line to try to get entry visas. Nina learned to use whatever resources were available to her. She managed to get passage ahead of other refugees by thrusting forward her growing stomach with determination. When the official asked her why there were no affidavits to explain why the young cousin was with them, she was prepared to answer that she could not understand the language of the document and thought that he had been included.

Nina's ability to manage extended to her life in New York. She and her husband arrived on March 4, 1921, and their child was born on March 11. Life was harsh. Her husband was ashamed that he had to peddle and that his wife, a former *gimnazye* student, had to see him tending a pushcart. Yet she knew that her family had to be cared for, and she was able to help him with his peddling. She had the real business sense in the family. When her husband purchased a cartload of tiny corsets to sell to the large women in the Italian neighborhoods, Nina got out her sewing machine and stitched three together to make fewer but ampler corsets that sold easily. From a relative with a dry-goods store she bought remnants of lace and stayed up until two in the morning making petticoats for her husband to peddle. For years, she saved to bring over her mother and a younger brother and sister, a frail girl who never married and remained emotionally dependent on Nina her whole life.

Because of their poverty, she intended never to have a second child. Whatever advantages Nina and her husband could manage, she hoped to shower on their daughter, for she did not want to make the difficult choices she remembered from her early life that resulted from having more children than a family could afford. And since her husband's health made him a poor provider, she knew that the task of supporting the children would eventually fall on her shoulders. But when her mother arrived in this country, she told Nina, "Only one eye is not good," and urged her to have another baby. Seven years after Rose's birth, Bella arrived. Although Nina had hoped for a son, she knew that this would be her last child.

As her husband's health deteriorated, Nina took on more of the burden of earning a living. Because a younger brother and sister, as well as her mother, now lived with them (the two older brothers did not contribute to their upkeep), she decided to move to the Bronx and take two apartments in the same building. A neighbor had told her that the schools were better there, and Nina wanted the children to get a good education. To support her family, she rented a defunct fish store, and after a month of cleaning, scrubbing, and painting, she turned it into a dry-goods shop, which she operated. On the day it opened, her husband had a stroke and subsequently had to give up peddling. When he recovered, he helped out in the shop and cared for the home. Rose also worked in the store after school.

Although Nina was delighted that her older daughter was an excellent student, it did not occur to her that they could afford a college education. The family surely needed the added income Rose might bring in by taking a job after graduating from Monroe High School. Yet when one of Rose's teachers stopped by to urge Nina to let the girl continue her schooling and told her that there were free colleges in New York, Nina felt that by sending her daughter to school, she could help to achieve her own frustrated ambition. Although her husband thought it was sufficient for their daughter to graduate from high school and get a job—in the height of the depression this was no small accomplishment—Nina determined that her daughter would be given the opportunity to attend college.

Nina took pride in the fact that both her daughters earned advanced degrees and became professionals. As hard as life was in America, she loved it for the freedom it offered and the opportunities it provided for the children. She also expressed satisfaction that she was able to bring her mother over and make her last years easier. Like her mother, she had to deal with the wrenching premature deaths of a husband and a daughter. Yet—also like her mother—she knew that whatever trials life inflicted on her, they could have been worse. "I guess when you suffer, it makes you stronger," she reflected on her ability to endure repeated tragedies during her ninety years.

Despite these losses, despite the feeling that she has lived too long, despite the physical weakness that frustrates an active mind, Nina looks forward as well as back. Until recently, she lived with her daughter but cherished her independent ways. Still an avid reader, Nina delights in learning about the world. Forgetting her arthritic hands, she promises to knit one of her famous afghans for an admiring neighbor. And there is always the family—a grandchild to see married or a new great-grandchild to await with anticipation. Life has not been easy, but it has been rich, and the love and esteem of her family and friends are the harvest of her later years.

Like Nina, the other forty-five women interviewed for this book were Jews who emigrated from Eastern Europe to New York City before 1925. They differed from one another in many ways. Some, like Nina, decided to leave on their own as young adults, while most departed for America either as children with their parents or as teenagers going to live with a relative. Geographically, they came from areas ranging from Hungary or Austria to Poland and Russia. Some had lived in thatched huts in small villages; others spent their childhood years in large houses or apartments in towns or cosmopolitan urban centers like Vilna or Budapest. Most came from orthodox religious families where Yiddish was spoken, although a few remember their parents as modern "free-thinkers" who spoke Russian, Polish, or Hungarian in their homes. There were women who cherished a childhood of middle-class comfort, with servants and other luxuries, and there were those whose early years evoked memories of hunger and poverty. Many lived through the horrors of war or pogroms, while a fortunate minority seemed insulated from such troubles. Some women remembered their parents as loving and supportive, but several were orphaned or deprived of affection.

Their lives took differing paths in this country as well. One woman worked her way through medical school and became a doctor, while another never managed to learn to read. Some came young enough to go through the public school system and attend high school, while for others who came at an older age, education remained an elusive dream, and work was the reality. Those who emigrated as children became Americanized with relative ease, while older teenagers never succeeded in shedding a sense of foreignness and often felt as if they were hovering between two worlds. Most married and had children, although a few remained single or childless, only three by choice. All worked at some time during their lives, although individual economic circumstances varied enormously. About half of them eventually achieved comfortable, middle-class lives, while the rest managed to make ends meet by working either continuously or temporarily, as family needs determined. Their jobs ranged from domestic servant, garment worker, and shopkeeper to bookkeeper, tax auditor, and opera singer, with most of the less affluent women working in small factories or shops. Many expressed satisfaction with their lives, although a few regretted the opportunities missed and the roads not taken. (See the Appendix for a more complete description of their lives.)

Despite these differences, common threads weave through their lives. All were Jewish, all were women, all had to deal with the problems involved in uprooting themselves from Eastern Europe and emigrating to the United States. And all, regardless of religious differences, shared a cultural heritage that affected their lives in this country. One element of that heritage was a reverence for education. Another was an acceptance of married women's working to support their families. And yet a third, more difficult to demonstrate, was the strong position of women within the family. These young women, who emigrated between 1896 and 1925, were growing up during a period of intense social and economic change. How their old-world cultural traits, absorbed in the home, were unconsciously utilized or modified to meet the needs and opportunities of this new urban, industrial society provides a theme for this book.

This theme emerged only after many interviews, for initially, I had little idea of what the oral histories would reveal. The free-flowing interview style I had adopted enabled women to concentrate on what was most meaningful in their lives rather than simply respond to a predetermined agenda.[2] When certain patterns seemed to develop, I altered my loose list of questions to reflect their perceptions and often returned to talk with women several times if issues brought up by others had not been raised in a particular interview. Though each person had her own story to tell, I came to believe that a limited number of oral histories could give a good sense of what life was like for these women as a group if the same features and attitudes turned up regularly.[3] For example, if forty-one out of forty-six women most regretted not having more schooling, this desire for education could be described as a common characteristic.

Much of what I learned in this way was unanticipated. I had expected to find great changes resulting from emigration to the United States and was surprised to discover that a sense of continuity from one generation to the next pervaded many of these women's lives. I had assumed that immigrant daughters with different experiences had little to learn from their mothers, but one woman after another told me of the influence her parents, and particularly her mother, had upon her life. My narrative reflects this influence by delving into the lives of the mothers of immigrant women, whether or not they left Eastern Europe. Many women also emphasized the importance of the age at which they emigrated and their position of birth in the family, so these factors, too, assume a prominent place. And although I had originally planned only a brief summary of the European past, attitudes shaped in Eastern Europe loomed so large that this background expanded to fill four chapters.

Thus this book considers these women's lives as they themselves viewed them. It deals with attitudes toward what they considered most important—namely, family, work, and education. And it attempts to differentiate their perceptions from those of Jewish men, with whom they shared a class and an ethnic background, but not a center of interest. For like most males, Jewish immigrant men focused on the world outside the home—the synagogue or workplace—while women defined themselves within the domestic sphere regardless of whether or not they worked for wages.[4] In this sense, their interests were more similar to those of women in other ethnic groups whose concerns and satisfactions were connected with activities revolving about the home and relationships with people rather than with external accomplishments.

Yet although women of all ethnic groups may have shared basic interests, differences in their cultures created or reinforced differences in attitudes toward aspects of their lives. It is the purpose of this book to explore how Jewish immigrant women sought and found meaning for their lives within the framework of their own system of values and culture. As E. P. Thompson observed of early British industrial workers, "They lived through these times of acute social disturbance and we did not. Their aspirations were valid in terms of their own experience."[5] And although we live in different times from these women, we must also attempt to understand their attitudes and aspirations in the context of their own experience.

A Note on Sources

. . . .

These oral history interviews took place between 1978 and 1986, when the women ranged in age from seventy to ninety-four. Taping averaged four hours, with the shortest lasting two hours and the longest sixteen. The first fifteen women interviewed were selected on the basis of their availability. The second group of twenty-six were chosen in an attempt to achieve more balance in the following areas: place of birth, social class, circumstances of emigration (for example, whether they emigrated alone or with parents), age at time of emigration, number of children in the family, and birth order of the informant.

Although some women were willing to have their full names used, others were not, and so to maintain consistency, I used only the first names and last initials of informants (I changed one last initial from K. to N. because there were two women with the name of Fannie K., and I changed a second Anna R. to Anna S.). The one exception, Anna Kahan Safran, agreed to the use of her complete name because material from her interview is used interchangeably with information from a diary—since published—that she kept as a girl, and it seemed confusing to cite a name in one instance and an initial in another. Although the published diary uses the name "Anne," she was called "Anna," and I have continued to use this form of her name as well as her original surname of Kahan. None of the oral history interviews is footnoted, although the diary is. Last names are used only in quotations from published sources or material open to the public, like the Tamiment Oral History interviews or the YIVO Manuscript Autobiography Collection.

Because material from other sources is interspersed with evidence from the interviews, I make no claims for scientific methodology and avoid using percentages of the women interviewed to support a particular attitude. I do attempt to indicate whether an attitude or pattern of behavior was one shared by many women or exhibited by only a few.

When transliterating whole phrases in Yiddish, I have relied upon the standard scholarly spellings provided by YIVO Institute for Jewish Research. For commonly used Yiddish words, however, I have generally adopted American spellings, such as those found in the unabridged *Random House Dictionary of the English Language*. It seemed reasonable to call the Sabbath bread *challah* rather than *khale*, since that spelling would be more recognizable to American readers. Yiddish words in cited published sources retain their original spelling.

The
World
of Our
Mothers

Eastern Europe in the Late Nineteenth Century

⌒ Boundary of the Pale of Settlement

From *The Promised City*, by Moses Rischin (Harvard University Press, 1962).

1

. . . .

Women of the Shtetl

Cobblers' wives must make the thread . . .
Tailors' wives must sit up late . . .
Coachmen's wives must tar the axle . . .
Butchers' wives must carry the meat . . .
Weavers' wives must throw the spindle . . .
Filers' wives must turn the wheel . . .
Painters' wives must mix the paint . . .
Carpenters' wives must saw the boards . . .

—*popular Yiddish song*[1]

1. A feather plucker and her daughter.
Photographer: Alter Kacyzne. YIVO Institute for Jewish Research

By the late nineteenth century, disturbing currents of change had already begun to agitate the apparent stability of Jewish life in Eastern Europe. Jews lived in a wide area controlled by Russia and Austria-Hungary, and their experience extended along a broad spectrum from the illiterate poverty of villages in Galicia to the urban sophistication of cities like Vilna and Odessa. Although most Jews were orthodox in religious practice, many responded to the joyous, semimystical appeal of the Hasidim, with their ecstatic vision of life; others were attracted to the *Haskalah*, or enlightenment, which came from the West and urged Jews to abandon old ways in order to play a fuller part in the intellectual and cultural life of their country. They had to cope with changing policies of the Russian government, which in midcentury opened educational opportunities for Jews and then later reversed itself to close off possibilities of secular education as well as many ways of making a living.[2] Narrowing economic opportunity in the countryside and government decrees were also forcing Jews from small towns into the larger urban centers where the factory bell rather than the rising and setting sun determined the pace of work.[3]

Despite this agitation and differences in background, a sense of a shared heritage, religion, and culture bound together the Jews of Eastern Europe. Gentile neighbors perceived Jews as different and sometimes discriminated against them—which in turn fostered a feeling of apartness. During most of the century, the great majority of these Jews lived in small towns, or shtetlach, and traditional ways in those towns deeply affected their subsequent experience. What they brought with them to their new urban environment, and later to America, were the culture and values developed in the shtetl—altered, perhaps, to meet a new situation and a different need.

Meanwhile, in the late nineteenth and early twentieth centuries, Jews in many shtetlach lived much the same way as had their parents or grandparents. In small towns like Swislocz, where 2,000 out of 3,000 inhabitants were Jewish,[4] they had relatively little to do with Christians who inhabited the outskirts.[5] The one small-scale industry, leather goods, employed most of Swislocz's Jews and was run by prosperous merchants who traveled to the nearby city of Bialystok to sell their goods. But for many Jews, the world was bounded by the shtetl limits. Mary Antin recalled, "the world was divided into two parts, namely Polotsk, the place where I lived, and a strange land called Russia   Russia was . . . far off, and . . . many bad things happened there."[6] Much of the time, however, the Russia of worrisome officials seemed far away. Apart from collecting taxes and gathering recruits for the army, the government generally let Jews run their own affairs. Jews were better-than-average taxpayers, and it was easier and cheaper to collect taxes through local community organizations. Until midcentury, a community council regulated all aspects of shtetl life. Voluntary associations, ranging from artisan guilds to mutual benefit societies, melded the community together.[7]

Although most Jews were town dwellers,[8] a few lived in villages so small that, as Dora G. remembered, "on the one side was the houses and on the other side was trees"—places where wild animals would peer through the windows after it snowed and drag chickens and geese from the coops. In such communities, everything had to be done by hand. "Wood was cut, water had to be carried in—not even from a well, but from a river near the house," recalled Ethel B. Her grandfather fished in the local river. The father of Frieda M. made a business of fishing by buying the concession on the local lake. In their village, the eight or nine other Jewish families, all related, performed skilled services for each other and for the peasants. "There was a dressmaker, a blacksmith and a shoemaker," Frieda observed, "one of a kind." Such settlements had few Jews. Bessie Kriegsberg and her parents lived in a village where there was only one other Jewish family, and their situation was no better than that of the surrounding peasants.[9]

Even in larger towns, if one was poor, conditions were primitive at best. The house Dora W. was born in had burlap sacks tacked onto the walls, with straw and hay between the sacks and walls for insulation. The roof was thatched and the floors "earthen, that were pounded down and reworked every few years. The only place we had boards were under the beds, to give them a little warmth." In her native Serbia, Marie Jastrow remembered that toilets were nonexistent, with outhouses used in towns as well as villages.[10] Even in urban Pinsk, Miriam Zunser observed, "the mud puddles of our yard as well as those of all other yards . . . were the happy hunting grounds of the pigs of the city."[11] Sanitary conditions were rudimentary and medical service was in short supply. Disease could spread quickly, as it did during the cholera epidemic of 1868. "Conditions were terrible," recalled Jeanne S. of her parents' village, which she left after World War I. "There was a stable with the urine from the cows. Nearby was a well, and I'm sure it was seeping in. There was a lot of typhoid as long as I can remember."

Others were fortunate enough to live on the right side of town, for this was a society in which class was of major importance. Even lower-middle-class families would employ a servant, usually a local peasant girl, to help with the cooking, cleaning, and young children. Some women remember their families as living more comfortably still, with parents having fur coats, shoes imported from Vienna, gold watches, and silver candlesticks and samovars. Members of this privileged group of Jews might speak Russian or

Polish in the home rather than Yiddish,[12] and a few, emulating the Russian aristocracy, preferred French.[13] In such middle-class families, women generally did not work outside the home. Fannie C. observed, "my grandfather would have killed himself before he would have seen my mother go to work. It would have been horrible!" Nor did a girl marry a boy whose family status was lower than that of her own parents. Fannie's mother fell in love with a man whose grandfather was a shoemaker, and her father refused to permit the match. The poor but scholarly family of Frieda M. felt disgraced when a cousin fell in love with a blacksmith's son and married him. "Her sister cried so bad and wouldn't talk to her again," Frieda recalled. "You wouldn't believe the snobbery in a small village—you couldn't have anything to do with them." The classes did not mingle, except at the synagogue and possibly at some limited social affairs. Fannie C., a tailor's daughter, was forbidden to play with children from lower-class families. "And that made a big impression on me," she remembered. "For some reason, the child I couldn't play with I always liked the best."

But money was not the only mark of prestige, or even the most important one. This was above all a religious society, where the talmudic scholar achieved the highest degree of status, or *yikhes*.[14] Although very few attained such glory, and most men worked to make a living for their families,[15] a young man who showed scholarly promise proved a rare prize for a prospective father-in-law, who would bid for him with promises of *kest*, or keep, for several years, thereby helping assure his own place in the hereafter. A girl could marry well only if her father had status in the community by virtue of his learning or wealth. But a boy could rise above his status by religious scholarship. As one grandmother's saying goes, "A boy stuffed with learning is worth more than a girl stuffed with banknotes."[16] Scholarly ability transcended class lines, for all Jews valued learning.

Once the period of *kest* was over, the wife of a scholar often would make a living for the family if her own parents could no longer afford to support them. Thus, the ability to earn money was a desirable characteristic for potential brides. Kalya Rivkin, who described herself as a "very homely, fat and husky girl," was chosen to marry a promising young man because her future in-laws considered her a good risk—she had started her own dressmaking business.[17] In her town, Frieda M. observed, "the man studied unless he had an exceptional business head. Usually the women maneuvered." "The women worked," agreed another woman. "The men sat in shul and davened [prayed]. You couldn't make a living from that." A woman generally considered it a privilege to support a scholarly husband, while he reciprocated by preparing a place for her in the world to come. I. J. Singer, for example, remembers his paternal grandmother as "a saintly woman who never assumed that it was her husband's duty to support her. She left him to his beloved Torah and Kabala and herself traveled to Warsaw to buy goods and earn a living for her family since her husband's wages [as a rabbi] could not keep a bird alive. . . . It never occurred to her that one day her precious son would be expected to earn a living. She always considered this a wife's responsibility."[18]

Thus, although the great majority of men worked, helping to earn a livelihood was frequently considered a woman's job and an extension of her work in the home. This meant that working for money was not a source of shame for Jewish women as it would be among cultures where a man's status depended upon his ability to support his family. Throughout most of preindustrial Europe, non-Jewish women also shared this burden with their husbands,[19] but only among the Jews of Eastern Europe was it accepted practice that some women would provide the sole means of support.[20]

Earning a living, whether for men or women, was frequently a haphazard undertaking. Since government regulation prevented Jews from owning land or sources of raw material, many served as middlemen. Ruth R. remembered the ups and downs of this kind of life. "In the summer," she recalled, "my father did all kinds of things, whatever was in season. Sometimes he had orchards and dried prunes and would sell them. Then sometimes he would rent farms and then sell the wheat. Another time he had plantations of beets he'd transport to where they would brew whiskey. There was times where he got rich and made out very well. There was hundreds on the table when he sold the prunes. And next year it was raining and they couldn't pick the prunes in time. They opened up and could not be dried, and then we were broke." Still other Jewish men were skilled workers, but much work was seasonal and people often had to live "by their wits."[21] Peasants bought boots from the shoemaker or a jacket from the tailor only before the onset of winter. Blacksmiths shod horses for work in the fields in spring and summer and had little to do when the snows fell. Carpenters worked mostly in the warm months, and logging also had its season.[22]

Because of this precarious existence, frequently the added income a wife could bring in was helpful if not essential for the family. In rural areas, women sometimes grew cucumbers, cabbages, and carrots and sold what they did not need in the market. Managing the orchards of a local landlord was more often than not a family enterprise, with wives taking charge when their husbands were away marketing the produce. Many women brought in a low but steady income if their husband's earnings were seasonal or insufficient to support the children. When the cattle business of Jeanne S.'s father was slow, the family was sustained by the grandmother's grocery. Sarah Reznikoff's mother ran a tavern because her father was unable to make an adequate living as a glazier.[23] Frieda M.'s aunt made liquor from beets and sour bread—kvass—and sold it illicitly to the peasants when times were hard. Rose G. remembered the ritual care with which her grandmother baked the town's passover matzoh, with all the girls joining in to roll it out. Another common way of making a living was by baking bread or fattening geese to sell. Basya Saroff slaughtered geese she had bought from farmers and cut them up to sell to families unable to afford a whole bird.[24] Many Jewish women also kept cows or goats and made butter and cheese to sell along with milk either in the local market or door-to-door.[25] Both the mother and grandmother of Jennie H. purchased milk from farmers and sold it in town each morning.

Particularly for impoverished families, this contribution sometimes made the difference between subsistence and hunger, as it did for poor families throughout Europe.[26] Gussie M. remembered the perceptible change in her family's standard of living after her mother died. "My father became very poor," she recalled, "because my mother used to help him. She had a cow, so she had milk and cheese and butter. She had geese and chickens to sell—not much, but that helped out. But after she died, all this was gone and we were poor."

Women often used the skills they learned as children to help provide a living. Many Jewish girls were taught how to sew and knit. In Minnie Fischer's town, all young girls knitted their own socks and gloves by the time they were six.[27] Once the family's needs were met, the rest could be sold. Sometimes, women would sell or barter their handmade garments to neighbors or other family members. Louise C.'s mother sewed her family's underwear and outer clothing and then earned money doing the same for her sister's family. While Frieda M.'s grandfather studied Torah, her grandmother was "sewing for the peasants, trading and managing to make a living." Dora W.'s mother also used this skill to eke out a living, embroidering needlework on overblouses to sell to the peasants. "I remember as a little girl," Dora recalled, "I used to watch her needle go back and forth in the cloth like a machine working—so tiny were her stitches." One tailor's daughter wrote that as soon as girls were able to hold a needle, they were taught to use it. When her father left home to avoid conscription into the Czar's army, the women supported themselves by this ability: the mother sewed, the blind grandmother knitted stockings, and the young girl mended the dropped stitches.[28]

The type of work a girl did depended upon the availability of jobs and her parents' financial situation. For a young woman to seek employment herself was considered almost shameful.[29] A comfortable family might pay for an apprenticeship for its girls, but for the daughters of the poor, there was always unskilled domestic work.[30] At the age of twelve, Morris Raphael Cohen's eldest sister was sent into service in a distant town and lost touch with her parents until a chance meeting many years later.[31] For girls without money, an apprenticeship usually *meant* domestic work, for as Mollie Linker observed, "You were supposedly going to learn a trade, but . . . you had to take care of a flock of children and do other things before you learned how to thread a needle."[32] At twelve, Jennie H. experienced this kind of frustration in her attempt to learn dressmaking. With no money for a proper apprenticeship, the training promised to her was little more than unpaid servitude. When Jennie went to her first "apprenticeship," she recalled, "They used to tell me to wash the floor, to clean the windows, to rock the baby. And during the day they would give me a needle and thread and some cotton to sew up maybe a pocket. So I came one day, two days, three days and I go home to my grandmother and say 'I don't want to do that. If I have to go and clean, I can go and work and get money for it, but not for nothing.'" The same thing happened with three other potential employers, and Jennie had to come to the United States before she learned to sew.

If they could afford it, many mothers made sure that their daughters were trained in a marketable skill. Although all women hoped their daughters would marry well and not have to work for a living, their own experience had taught them to prepare their girls to earn their own way if necessary. "My mother had a philosophy," recalled Yetta Brier, "everyone should have a trade. If you're rich you won't practice the trade—if you're poor you'll make a living by it." Bella Farkas planned to emigrate to the United States, and her parents paid a woman a ruble a month to teach her how to sew "because they knew that the needle trade was big in America and that's the kind of job I would get."[33]

In villages with few Jewish families, where poverty was the rule rather than the exception, all family members worked at whatever they could do to bring in money. The mother of Bessie Turner Kriegel knitted socks for the peasants while her father was the blacksmith.[34] The only other Jewish couple in their village were a brickmaker and his wife, a wool dyer. In another poor hamlet, women made a living "by carrying water from the brook, or they wash clothes, or they work in the rich people's houses. The men help them along, but there was no real work." Planting, weeding, and digging potatoes was the only job available for Sara Plotkin in her impoverished village, and when she was only eleven, the mother of Morris Raphael Cohen was also hired out by her father to dig potatoes.[35]

Larger or more prosperous shtetlach usually had more opportunities for women to earn a living. One town had a cottage industry that provided young girls with work making hairnets. But even without industry, there were many ways a clever woman might turn a ruble. In the small town of Sonik, there were a matchmaker, folkdoctor, bath-house attendant, an advisor to those cursed by the evil eye, a chicken seller, pearl stringer, baker, pretzelmaker, knitters, girdlemaker, sausagemaker, yeast seller, pickle vendor, herb vendor, sellers of rags, honey and date sellers, a sponge vendor, crackermaker, and finally, "the Holy One," an enterprising woman who sold crosses and prayer beads to the peasants.[36]

Since there was limited industry in small towns, most women thus "earned their living by services, one to the other. Peasants lived in the surrounding areas, and every few weeks there would be a farmer's market on the main square," Dora W. recalled. "They would bring their livestock and their fruit and their vegetables and set up stalls, and the little shopkeepers would buy their produce so they could sell them afterwards. Mainly the women were the shopkeepers, because the men were scholarly. They were learners, not earners, and the women would keep shop and do the buying and selling." Sholem Aleichem remembered these markets of his childhood as a scene of controlled chaos: "Peasants were strolling with their wives and children," he wrote. "Gypsies loitered here and there. Horses neighed, cows mooed, pigs squealed . . . and above all this din, one heard the voices of the Jews. There were Jews of all kinds: Jews marketing furs, Jews selling hats, Jews dealing in cloth, Jews selling bread and cakes and buns and cider and anything else you could think of. . . . And the Jewish women! They elbowed their way through the confusion, carrying baskets, selling chicken and fried fish and pickled apples and buttons and thread. The noise was enormous."[37]

Some women performed services that gave them a certain status within the community. The mother of Jeanne S. was such a woman. Although she never knew how to read, "she was very smart. In her small village, she was the healer—she was called in for whatever ailed them. She was a very important personality." Her knowledge of herbal cures gained the appreciation of poor people with little access to medical care. Rachel Leah, the grandmother of Mary Antin, had a great reputation for practical wisdom,

2. *A market in Kuzmir, about 1920.*
Photographer: Alter Kacyzne. YIVO Institute for Jewish Research

and people in their village consulted her for advice.[38] Rose Chernin's mother, when she wasn't busy cooking, baking, or sewing, would write letters for illiterate women whose husbands were in America.[39] Other women with some education might give lessons to girls in Hebrew, Yiddish or Russian, arithmetic, and other subjects.[40] Some women operated their own shops, selling food, fabrics, and whatever might bring in customers. In one town, women ran twelve out of sixty shops themselves.[41]

But most of the ways in which women earned a living won them little in the way of status or financial rewards, which was true of most work associated with women throughout Europe.[42] When Frieda M.'s mother became pregnant soon after marriage, the poor woman who took care of the *mikvah*, or ritual bath, in their village "was very upset. She said that finally she got somebody who needed a *mikvah* and here she got knocked up! So that was the end of that!"

If one's family had a business, daughters were expected to help out as a matter of course. These skills often came in handy once they were married. Louise C.'s grandfather saw to it that each of his eight daughters had a different specialty to contribute to his grocery and fabric business. They learned about materials, lace, ribbons, embroidery; they learned how to knit, buy, and sell wool. This early training bore fruit. "My aunt," Louise recalled, "was a businesswoman. She kept the store, even though her husband was also in the business." To augment her own husband's skimpy living, Louise's mother "decided that she would buy ready-made goods like socks and handkerchiefs and she'd peddle. And my father agreed to help. So she used to go to the marketplace every week. And she knew most of the business people because my grandfather dealt with them. Then when they had a fair once a year in towns, she'd go with my brother to sell her stuff." Mary Antin's grandfather only permitted his daughter to get some education once he saw how well she could manage his business when he was away. After she married and her husband showed no interest in store-keeping, the shop prospered under her guidance. Antin's mother kept the books and got on well with her Russian and Polish customers.[43] One contemporary observer noted with approval that Jewish wives always assisted their husbands at their trades.[44]

When women married, whether in the shtetl or the city, they often played a role in running the family enterprise, and if their husbands traveled frequently, left for America, or died, these women might take charge. Even for middle- and upper-class wives, this kind of work was accepted, although working for others would be shunned. As early as the middle of the nineteenth century, when the owner of an international freight business died, his wife took over, learning several languages to deal better with customers. Under her guidance, the firm prospered. More than sixty years later, after Frieda M.'s father emigrated to the United States, her mother took his place in their fish business. Although she lacked prior experience, "she held her own. The partners would send her to make the contracts because Russians were softer towards a woman."

Some men, raised to believe that earning a living was less important than religious study, were content to leave much of the work to their wives. In the inn run by the parents of Pauline H., her mother "used to bake rolls, bagels, and bread, and she tended the customers. My father didn't do anything. He used to go to shul and in the evenings he'd sit down and read a book." To Janet A.'s father, "the paper and the book were always more important than the business. My mother ran the business—he was in it, but she did it. He was always the scholar." The same was true in the food shop of Bella Hyman's parents, where "mother worked and father studied."[45] Louise C.'s mother started peddling because her father could not support them. A bookbinder by trade, "if he'd get hold of a good book, he'd stop in the middle of his work to read the book. So he was not a breadwinner." In the city of Vitebsk, Bella Chagall's parents owned a shop selling mirrors, clocks, and jewelry, but Bella remembered, "Everything was on my mother's shoulders. . . . She hardly even slept at night. . . . It was she who worried about paying the day's bills, while father was often lost in contemplation praying. . . . The hustle and bustle of the shop didn't interest him at all."[46] Anna Kahan's grandmother arranged for her family to move from their town to the city of Siedlce where she could work to support them. Her husband "was so absorbed in the study of Talmud that earthly matters did not concern him much." His wife "was the breadwinner—she carried the burden."[47] While the father of Ruth Katz attended to his largely unpaid duties as a rabbi, Ruth's mother earned a living by running a small grocery store and a factory where seeds were pressed to yield their oil.[48] The grandfather of I. J. and I. B. Singer was also "a visionary with a total dependence on God. He hated responsibilities of all kind and gave no thought to practical matters." On one business trip, his wife gave birth to a son in the wagon. It was a woman's accepted lot, Singer observed, to "bear children, cook, run the household and earn a living—while the man studied Torah." Rather than complain, Singer asserted, these women praised God for giving them husbands who were scholars.[49]

Occasionally, a daughter remembered her father as inept as well as uninterested in earning a living. Fannie Edelman's mother was the shrewd businessperson in her family. With his wife's dowry, Fannie's father opened a store selling flour, barley, and the like. "At first," Fannie recalled,

> my mother alone conducted the business as the customers in general were gentile, and my father was unable to speak their language.[50] But the work was too hard . . . and she tried to get him to assist her. . . . Well, you can imagine what happened! Once, my mother went up to the attic to get something. Just then a gentile woman came into the store and asked for a pound of flour. My father told her the price and apparently the woman felt it was far too high. Like a common peasant, she said in her vulgar way, "I will give you manure!" My father yelled to my mother, "Esther, this gentile woman is giving me manure for a pound of flour. Shall I take it?" Because he thought that manure was a small amount of money![51]

Doubtless, few husbands were this obtuse, and most took the major role in supporting their families. However, in this society that placed a premium on scholarship and learning, it was no shame for a man to lack interest in business, and no embarrassment for a woman to earn a living for her family. Despite assimilationist pressures, this traditional life would continue for the many nonurbanized Jews in Poland until it was snuffed out by the

Holocaust.[52] In the 1920s, in Czestochowa, for example, "Dvoyre-Miriam arose early and went about the hamlets and peasant houses, buying whatever was available: a chicken, a calf, a little milk, a quart of berries, a slab of butter or cheese; later she would sell it to the summer people at their dachas, or to her regular customers in town. . . . She took care of every aspect of her business at once, buying, selling, bartering and doing a little matchmaking on the side." In other towns, one woman delivered milk and another was a coachwoman who "might as well have been a man."[53]

Regardless of any other kinds of work they did, the needs of the home came first, and here the women were indisputably in charge. "All the women knitted and spun yarn and cooked," recalled Ethel B. "On Monday, mother baked the bread for the week. Friday she did the cooking and cleaning for *Shabbes*. We made our own butter, our own cheese, everything." If a woman worked outside the home as well, a full night's sleep became an infrequent luxury. The mother of Rita S. "would get up around three in the morning on Friday to bake the *challah* and the little cookies, and everything for *Shabbes*. And by seven or eight, she was in the store and everything was done." Making bread sometimes also meant bringing wheat to the mill and waiting while the miller ground it into flour. Frieda M. remembered those trips and the smell of the starter her mother saved to leaven the next week's batch of bread.

If a family lived in a rural area and could not afford a servant, there was even more work to be done. Morris Raphael Cohen observed that in addition to ordinary household work, women in his village "had to chop wood for the oven, . . . go considerable distances to draw water from some well, and carry it uphill even when the streets were covered with slippery ice. Worst of all, underwear, linen sheets, tablecloths, and the like had to be washed in the river nearly a mile away, even in the wintry months when the washing had to be done through a hole in the ice. To press the water out of the wet things a kind of wooden hammer had to be carried, in addition to the wooden board. It was indeed a heavy load to carry home."[54] Mariam Nirenberg remembered beating her wash at the lake with a wooden *pratsh* until it was "white and clean."[55] The clothing then had to be dried and pressed with heavy irons heated repeatedly on the wood stove.

Although much of women's work was repeated anew every week, some tasks were seasonal. In the fall, food had to be canned or stored for the winter. Tanya N. remembered climbing down a ladder to the deep cellar where her grandmother "had all kinds of vegetables, potatoes, carrots, beets, and cabbages, and different kinds of beans. But mostly I liked the pickles—half sour and fully sour." The cellar was also filled with dairy products—sweet cream, sour cream, butter, and cheeses that her grandmother prepared herself. During the summer, there were berries to be picked and made into jam, mushrooms to gather, beans to pick over and clean. When it grew cold, Mary Antin recalled, "I liked to sit with the women at the long, bare table picking feathers for new featherbeds. . . . Sometimes we played cards or checkers, munching frost-bitten apples between moves. Sometimes the women sewed, and we children would wind yarn or worsted for grandmother's knitting."[56]

On festive occasions, most women put forth great efforts to make the food special, despite their limited means. Louise C. remembered that although her family ate poorly most of the week, somehow her mother "was able to put together a Sabbath fit for a king." For weddings or bar mitzvahs, while men performed the ceremonies, the women's authority was unquestioned over all other activities. Sholem Aleichem remembered that "endless hands were busy preparing, all under the command of Grandma Minde, who, in her Sabbath frock and headband, really looked like the head of a regiment. It was she who had decided whom to invite and whom to pass over; who was to sit in the places of honor and who in more humble places; what dishes were to be served as well as what kind of brandy and wines."[57]

If the role of women was wider than it seems at first glance, it nevertheless had strict boundaries that could be crossed only at great risk, for the pressures to conform were strong.[58] The shtetl was a closed society that enforced its own rules. A woman who violated the community's sense of propriety was made to suffer or was cast out. In *The Agunah*, a novel by Chaim Grade set in postwar Vilna, an irreligious woman is driven to hang herself because she has committed the unpardonable sin of remarrying fifteen years after her husband has disappeared in the maelstrom of war. Because no one had seen him die, in Jewish law she is still considered married to him, and the community joins ranks to persecute and drive this "bigamist" to suicide.[59]

The worlds of public leadership and religious learning were reserved for males alone, and although men could choose whether to follow these elevated paths or adhere to more humble callings, for women to seek such honors was considered unnatural and unseemly, even blasphemous.[60] Fortunately, a woman could sublimate such unacceptable desires, as did Bathsheba, the grandmother of I. B. and I. J. Singer, "a gifted scholar . . . [who] knew the Scriptures almost by heart." Bathsheba sought a learned rabbi for a husband and spent her life supporting him and inculcating her love for learning into her sons. Singer's mother was less successful and less happy. She disliked housekeeping and cooking and loved to read the sacred books, but her husband failed to live up to her scholarly expectations, and because "she was only a female . . . her quick intelligence was more a detriment than a virtue."[61] I. B. Singer wrote of a girl who was considered a dybbuk. Among the indications of her soul's possession were the facts that "she spoke in a man's voice . . . sang like a cantor . . . [and] knew all the prayers by heart." Even his own sister suffered from transgressing the limitations of the female world. "Had she lived in another era," Singer wrote, "she might have been a female saint. Hers was a life of holidays, hymns, hope and exultation. She was a hasid in skirts; but she suffered from hysteria. . . . My father ignored her because she was a girl, and my mother could not understand her."[62] Not incidentally, the girl later became a radical.

Orthodox life was thus divided into the religious and the secular, with females at best segregated in the religious realm or at worst relegated by men to the secular world. Women could be a potential source of danger for pious men—not because they themselves lacked virtue, but because they could arouse in men desires that might lead them from the paths of righteousness.[63] Fear of female sensuality emerges frequently in folklore, Talmudic legends, and literature,[64] and probably the laws regulating a strict separation of the lives of men and women developed from this apprehension. A woman or girl breaking the rigid taboos would pay a penalty: Sholem Aleichem remembered a girl in his hometown who played with boys, going so far as to kiss them, and was thereafter given the nickname "Feigeleh the Witch," a name that stayed with her even after she became an exemplary wife.[65] These fears of women as temptress were generally strongest among young, unmarried men. In Opatow, for example, Yeshiva students believed that if they looked too much at a woman, they would be hung by the eyebrows in Hell.[66] To minimize such dangers, religious young men were often married at an early age, so that sexuality could be channeled by the insistence that girls be virtuous and seek their destiny as proper wives and mothers.

Despite the importance of their economic role, in this religious, patriarchal society, women had no accepted public role outside the home besides collecting for charity and caring for the sick. Male opinion was valued far above the female voice, regardless of the sense it made.[67] Men perceived women's spiritual life as less important than their own, and some sages debated whether women even had souls. If they attended the synagogue at all, women sat separately from men, in the balcony or behind a curtain, and did not count as part of the congregation before God. Even their prayers differed from those of their husbands: although the men chanted in Hebrew in the shul and most of their prayers praised God, women prayed more often at home and in Yiddish, the common language, and their prayers expressed concern with the daily problems of making a living and good health for their families.[68] A woman's specific religious role was to observe three mitzvoth, or commandments—to purify herself in a ritual bath after menstruation to avoid polluting her husband, to light the Sabbath candles on Friday night to usher in the holy day, and to burn a piece of dough when baking *challah* as a sacrifice to God.[69] Apart from these duties, a Jewish woman was expected to pray, but separately from men. She was responsible for running a harmonious, ritually kosher home, for bringing up the children, and, if her husband was a learned man, for lifting from his shoulders the worldly cares of life. Her piety was to be based upon faith rather than learning, and her greatest pleasure was to come from encouraging a learned husband or seeing a son become a scholar. Ideally, Jewish women were shy, submissive, docile, self-sacrificing, and completely devoted to their families.[70] If they stayed within the parameters of this supportive role, they could win great esteem. Yiddish folklore and literature abound with stories of women who made great sacrifices for their scholarly husbands or sons—a view reflected in the latter-day stories of I. B. Singer, whose only praiseworthy women are those who devote themselves to the care of husbands and children regardless of the cost.[71]

The important position of women in the shtetl made this idealized image a half-truth at best. Although women generally did, in fact, defer to husbands as the heads of their families and achieve satisfaction from their roles as wives and mothers, the skills they learned in managing a household and helping to earn a living also reinforced a sense of their own importance and were in many ways antithetical to the traits of the idealized wife. To buy and sell in the market, to devise ways to "help out" often required assertiveness, shrewdness, and the ability to get by in several languages. "Yes," they might say, "Men think we don't count, but they're stupid—what could they do without us? Could they get married? Could they bear children? Could they even be fed and clothed and housed decently?" They dealt with men's assumptions of superiority in the same down-to-earth way they dealt with prayers and daily life: "Although men have the *recognized* souls," one woman observed, "women have the real souls."[72]

One reason why many women avoided internalizing the notion that they were inferior to men was the support they received from others of their sex.[73] In this society where a pious man would not even glance at a woman lest he be diverted from righteousness, whatever time wives spent apart from their families was passed in the company of women who shared most of their concerns.[74] A child's illness, fears of the evil eye, or a husband's inattentiveness would be discussed with friends.[75] Praying, trading in the market, making featherbeds for the winter, bathing in the river, cooking jam from the summer's fruits and berries—all were done amidst the companionship of other women. "One fall, when the plums and cherries were ripe," reminisced Dora W., "we went down to the river's edge and built huge fires and had tripods with pots hanging over them to boil the fruit. And it was picnic time. The younger children went wading; the older children swam. And our mothers talked and made jam that they could use for the rest of the winter." The most intimate affairs—the ritual bath at the *mikvah*, preparation for weddings, births, illness, death—all were attended by women. I. J. Singer remembered his grandmother's holding her own court for the women who had come to consult his grandfather, the famed Bilgoray rabbi, on legal matters. While the rabbi tended to the legalities of the issue, his wife would minister to the emotional needs of the visitors. "Many women . . . gathered in my grandmother's domain," Singer recalled. They would "pour out their troubles and joys, voice their problems and difficulties. . . . She exercised her authority with immense dignity."[76] If her husband was sought for his spiritual and legal knowledge, she was valued for her warmth, emotion, and friendly concern. Women thus shared a world, composed, as one anthropologist has observed, "of smaller and commoner materials . . . as complex and compelling as the external, male dominated realm."[77]

An important part of this everyday world of Jewish women was the unique role piety played in their lives. Some women, like Vella Grade, were so devout that they constantly reproached themselves for not being even more pious.[78] But because religion was intertwined with their daily functions, most wives were bound to be more aware than men of the minor compromises that sometimes had to be made with purity. Was a chicken kosher if it had a bloodspot? What if a child spilled a drop of milk into the meat soup that was the evening's dinner? Or emptied his pockets of a crust of bread after the kitchen had been ritually purified for passover? Although rabbis were consulted when possible, if the choice was between a hungry family and a strict interpretation of the rules, the family's needs might well win out. The God the women prayed to in the kitchen seemed to have a more personal nature than the deity the men invoked in shul. Because their religious concepts were minimally related to a body of dogma, a place of worship, or even a religious leader—for women did not seek out the great rabbis except in emergencies—the essence of their faith might be retained regardless of the degree of conscious religiosity. The literature is filled with examples of men who discovered the lure of secular learning and subsequently abandoned all aspects of Judaism. Women, possibly because of their different concept of religion, seemed more resistant to this kind of radical transformation. Thus, they could surrender a custom like wearing a *sheitel*, or wig, yet not consider themselves any the less pious because of it.

Women's religion differed from men's in its context as well as its content. For example, Rachel, an elderly woman, told the anthropologist Barbara Myerhoff what religion meant to her. "It comes into you through the rituals," she began.

> We had a grandmother who gathered us seven girls around. The two boys went off early in the morning to pray. For us, we had to say the morning prayers. I couldn't understand the Hebrew words, the meanings of it, because we were girls and we never went to school. But I understood the expression of the little grandmother. She was so beautiful, so tiny and white. . . .
>
> Now, I knew the Hebrew words already by heart. I knew about the washing of hands, the prayer for the bread, keeping separate the meat and milk, all these things Grandmother taught us. But not what anything means. But it was our habit and it was beautiful. God wants it so, that's all.

For Rachel, religion was even tied up with wiping the dishes, with all of everyday life. "I think the boys didn't have it that way," she observed. "They knew what the sacred words meant so they could argue and doubt. But with us girls, we couldn't doubt because what we knew came without understanding. These things were injected into you in childhood and chained together with that beautiful grandmother, so ever since infancy you can't know life without it. The boys in cheder could learn the words and forget them, but in this domestic religion, you could never get rid of it."[79] Like Rachel, Jennie H. absorbed her religion from her grandmother, who told her biblical stories and taught her how to keep a home kosher. Jennie accepted without knowing reasons: "This you're allowed," her grandmother would tell her, "and this you're not allowed." This explanation was sufficient.

Such rituals in the home were always connected with a mother or grandmother and were more enduring in women's memory than occasional, infrequent attendance at the male-dominated shul. While the men and boys were praying in the synagogue on Yom Kippur Eve, Bella Chagall remembered her mother pulling out skeins of thread before the large wax candles that were to burn in the shul at the cantor's reading stand. She drew out a thread for each person she wished to bless, "sprinkle[d] it with tears, and passe[d] a big piece of wax over it, as though trying to rub it full of good wishes."[80] Another woman, Basha, described how such childhood associations continued to affect her. When called to light the candles at her senior citizens center on Friday night, she remembered that when she was a child, "I would stand this way, beside my mother when she would light the candles for shabbat. We were alone in the house, everything warm and clean and quiet with all the good smells of cooking food coming in around us. We were still warm from the mikvah. My braids very tight, to last through Shabbes, made with my best ribbons. . . . To this day, when the heat of the candles is on my face, I circle the flame and cover my eyes, and then I feel again my mother's hands on my smooth cheeks." This "domestic religion," associated with childhood and the home, with feeling rather than understanding, permeated women's lives. Myerhoff explained that it provided "a sacredness that issues from its being thoroughly embedded in a culture . . . completely internalized within the psyche of a people."[81]

Thus, in the shtetl in the late nineteenth and early twentieth centuries, wives were central to the family's emotional and economic well-being. All women performed the traditional female roles of keeping a family together—caring for children, cleaning, sewing, and seeing to the religious atmosphere of the home. But in addition, a Jewish wife often contributed to the family's living by working outside the home if her husband was a scholar or made little money at his trade. Middle-class women, while they seldom worked for others, frequently played an active role in their husbands' businesses. Such women had considerable freedom of movement, for even a market stall might require traveling to purchase goods. To some extent, this differentiated them from most European women at this time, who had little secular life outside their families.[82] The only avenues that were closed to Jewish women were those of public leadership and religious scholarship, the most prestigious positions in the shtetl.

However, despite the fact that women were barred from these activities, a society that enforces separation between the spheres of men and women also provides different kinds of satisfactions for each sex. While women could never achieve the status of Talmudic scholars, their world offered the possibility of its own kind of fulfillment. Keeping a proper Jewish home, the sense of "domestic religion," and the ability to help provide for their families obviously endowed many women with a sense of competence, if not satisfaction. The Book of Proverbs emphasized this important role by praising "a woman of valour" who was industrious and productive and who cared for and enriched her family. For such a woman, "her price is far above rubies."[83] This feeling of competence was strengthened by the authority wives possessed within the home and by concerns shared with other women. One Jewish saying goes "*A mineg brekht a din*"—"A custom is stronger than a law." Although women held an inferior place in Jewish law, customary practices in the shtetl—women's economic activities and central role in the home—often provided them with a source of strength and self-respect.

2

Family Relations in the Shtetl

Maybe I got that from my mother, to have a feeling for other people. To be with people, to touch them, to talk to them, to help them.

—Jeanne S.

Trouble is, the parents did not have the time. There was a lot of work. Already they had three smaller children than I. My mother was always cursing and angry and she was frustrated—working very hard. You have to let it out on somebody, so she always let it out on me. They expected a lot, and there was so much work.

—Ruth R.

3. A shtetl family.
Jewish Daily Forward

In traditional Jewish society before the late nineteenth century, marriage was too important a matter to be left to the young. Men and women were considered incomplete without a spouse and children, so marriage was an essential arrangement involving mutual duties and obligations whose main purpose was raising a family. Betrothals were arranged by parents, usually with the assistance of a marriage broker—a *shadkhen*—with an eye to improving or at least maintaining the family's prestige and prosperity. Young men were sought after if they displayed scholarly potential or if their families had a high degree of *yikhes* due to their learning or wealth. Girls were prized for the dowries they brought and for their domestic virtues. Romantic love played no role in the process, and usually, the young people were not permitted to see each other before their formal betrothal.[1] "First you marry," parents told them, "then you love."[2]

This system probably produced no more unhappy matches than today's freer choices and different expectations of relations between husband and wife. If parents were middle-class and enlightened, their home might resemble the harmonious haven remembered by Sophie A., where parents "had tremendous respect for each other and passed this trait on to their children." Few mothers were formally educated, but even in poor families, many could speak several languages, and differences in education or temperament between husband and wife could produce a complementary relationship, particularly when a husband admired his wife's qualities. Hannah F.'s father, for example, was a learned man, whereas her mother was barely literate. Although they had their differences, their daughter recalled, he never made his wife feel inferior, for "in some odd way, she filled in for him what he needed." Sara B.'s father was also a yeshiva student who married an uneducated girl whom he came to appreciate. "My mother was a very calm and collected person," Sara observed, "and my father was a very excitable man with a temper, so to a degree they balanced each other." The parents of Morris Raphael Cohen also achieved a kind of equilibrium despite their conflicting temperaments and lived together peacefully for sixty-seven years. From this relationship their son came to value "the love that grows out of devotedly living together in common efforts" as opposed to simple romantic attraction.[3]

Not all marriages between opposites led to an affectionate tie. I. J. Singer was particularly sensitive to the gulf that could develop between a highly educated, religious man and a woman brought up to be a traditional wife. His own grandmother, a plain, semiliterate woman, "felt challenged by her husband's erudition and masculine severity. . . . For years at a time he barely exchanged a superfluous word with the woman who had borne him a half dozen children. Beginning with their marriage, she at fourteen, he at fifteen, they had gone their own ways, having nothing in common."[4] But at least his grandmother had the company and respect of the many women who came to consult her husband. Singer's aunt provided a more poignant example of the possible effects of such marital differences. A simple woman with simple interests, Singer remembered her "as forever cooking . . . leaning over the stove. . . . She always exuded the smell of the kitchen. Her husband would growl 'Hey, you cow, a glass of tea!' She never took offense at this. She knew that he meant nothing malicious by it; that he was merely expressing his general attitude toward females." "Like most married couples in scholarly households," Singer concluded, "they had at best little to do with each other."[5] Florence B. considered the mismatch between her own "fanatical" father and ignorant mother equally demeaning for her mother and disastrous for the children. "She did not want to marry that man," Florence observed, "and that was the great tragedy of all our lives." Rae K.'s parents were similarly mismated. Her mother had reached the advanced age of twenty-three when her father married her to a yeshiva student. "My mother was such a gentle thing," Rae recalled, "such an angel in heaven, and she wanted love and affection. But my mother had a miserable life with him because he was such a fanatic; he was stubborn, he had the audacity, the character. And my mother was a lovely daisy flower. She could be broken like anything. So she had a miserable life."

Most marriages fell somewhere between the extremes of happiness and misery. Expectations of marriage were limited, and women generally accepted their lot for better or worse. The mother of Louise C., for example, remained with her husband despite a difficult relationship. Louise recalled that "she was willing to go through all the hardship and endure it for the sake of keeping the family together." Both she and her mother also came in time to value her father for his good qualities. Yet several of Louise's mother's sisters, supported by their father, had left their spouses. "My grandfather," she remembered, "he used to make the matches, and if they didn't work out, he'd say, 'So you'll get another husband.' And they got divorced." Divorce was undesirable, but it was always a possibility.[6]

Although children were encouraged to view their father as the head of the family, mothers often made the important decisions.[7] Formally, the father's word was law, but usually men were content to leave day-to-day cares to their wives. Janet A. remembers her mother as "the hub in the family," the focus of great respect. "My father always felt that my mother could come up with a decision. In fact, if we'd go to my father, he'd say, 'Go to mama.' She was very, very clever, could reason things out, and generally, her advice was good." Anna R.'s parents had a similar relationship. "My mother was a little more aggressive than my father," she recalled. "He was a gentle soul and loved my mother very much. It was a love affair. And either it was a course of least resistance that he took, or he knew he'd have to give in anyway. So he took the shortcut and gave in right away. Whatever she did, whatever she wanted, that was it. There had to be peace, there was no chance for argument. It was good for him, it was good for her, it was good for everybody. That's why they didn't argue." Rose S. remembered her mother as "the center of the family," making all the important decisions. Katya Govsky's mother, a university graduate with a strong character, was also the acknowledged head of her family. "Mama wanted somebody who would look up to her," Katya recalled, "and Pa thought she was God herself. Whatever she said, whatever she did, was law. . . . Papa was very happy. He thought that he got the golden egg from heaven."[8]

Warmth and gentleness were considered positive characteristics for both sexes, and in many families, fathers were perceived to have softer natures than their wives. Many women who felt burdened by the responsibility of seeing that a family business prospered, or who had to manage to feed a family on too little money, could spare no time for sentiment. Rita S., for example, remembered her mother as always being busy in the family store. When Rita returned home one day after a long visit with an aunt, she recalled that her father told her with delight, "My child, it's so good to have you back." Her mother was more restrained in her greeting. "So the wonderful feeling," she reminisced, "was with my father." Anna S.'s mother, who also ran a shop, was described by her daughter as "a good woman, all around, but with a strong character." Her father, on the other hand, "was softer," and cried frequently. These strong women would also be guardians of propriety in the home. When Dora W.'s grandfather came home tipsy from synagogue on Purim, a happy holiday, and began to dance on the kitchen table, his wife stopped him swiftly with a sharply worded "Stop that! It isn't becoming to you!"

Since fathers bore no responsibility for the training of daughters, as they did for sons, the relationship between father and daughter could be an easier one than that between father and son, or between mother and daughter.[9] Although most fathers were expected to act as disciplinarians, some daughters remember their treating this duty lightly. When Ruth R. misbehaved, for example, her mother would threaten, "'I'll tell your father when he'll come home.' And the way she said it," Ruth recalled, "you'd think he'd kill you. But the most that he would do is say, 'Oh, Ruthele, you were so bad, how terrible you were.' He had to please her a little bit, but in the next minute he'd forget it." Fathers made no serious intellectual demands on daughters as they sometimes did on sons, and thus might more easily spoil a girl than a boy.[10] Rita S. explained this kind of relationship: "My father, I had him under my little finger, because he was very easy going, but he was especially easy going with me. I was his little girl, and I was not afraid of him; I never had any fear from my father, never. I mean, if he got mad, I'd start laughing and he'd laugh with me. But my mother was the strict one. I had to ask, 'Could I go out? Could I go play with this girl or that?' She loved me, but she was the one that took over."

Not that all fathers displayed affection openly or indulged their daughters. Minnie Fischer remembered that her father and uncles even seemed ashamed to have fathered girls.[11] Louise C. also recalled her father as "not a very lovable guy. If he patted you on the head you were very lucky. My father kissed me twice a year. He kissed me on Pesach at the Seder, because my birthday was on Passover, and my father kissed me at Yom Kippur when he blessed me. But I never remember my father cuddling me or kissing me, or putting his arm around me until I left for America, when I was seventeen years old." But Louise's mother compensated for her husband's coldness by a warm relationship with her daughter.

Sometimes, fathers were called "fanatical," a word that seemed to combine extreme religiosity with prohibitions on the activities of other family members, particularly their children. Interestingly, mothers, no matter how religious, were never called "fanatics," possibly because their piety seldom manifested itself in the form of restrictions on their daughters' lives. Often such fathers sought to maintain traditional ways, while daughters wanted to be "modern," a tension one can see reflected in the fiction of I. L. Peretz.[12] Louise C.'s father, for example, forbade his daughters from associating with young men or girls who were "keeping company." Young women from liberal families were also considered a bad influence and were proscribed. Rae K. ultimately left home because of her father's strictness in these matters. But she realized that the situation was even worse for her brother, who was active in a radical group and fought constantly with his father, who wanted him to concentrate on religious studies. "And so," concluded Rae, "there was always struggle in the house." To keep the peace in such families, often mothers would attempt to mediate between husbands and children.

Fathers and mothers played different roles in their daughters' lives, and relations with them differed accordingly. Fathers were often portrayed in dramatic or romanticized terms and emerged in their daughters' memories as less than three-dimensional figures. They could be fanatical tyrants like those delineated by Rae K. or Anzia Yezierska in her novel *Bread Givers*, or warm and loving parents who gave freely of love and made no demands in return. The role of a father in a daughter's life was important but limited: he could give or withhold affection, be strict or lenient, and be either a good or a poor "provider," although her relationship with him did not depend on his ability to make a good living.

Relations with mothers tended to be more complicated, and they stand out in daughters' memories with more clarity and complexity.[13] From either fathers or mothers, girls might learn such individual, abstract values as honesty; but mothers also had to teach their daughters how to perform the myriad daily chores and fulfill the obligations of women. This required the assimilation of a whole system of values and skills, from selflessness to managing a home and family. Fathers could not provide such role models for daughters or supervise their domestic apprenticeship.[14] And because mothers had sole responsibility for training daughters for adult functions and duties, they were likely to be more demanding than fathers.[15]

Even when daughters were too young for conscious instruction, they often learned from their mothers' example. "I was very attached to my mother," Gussie M. reminisced, "and I did everything she did. Like if we had a milk dish for supper after having meat for lunch, I wouldn't eat it even though the children were allowed to eat before the six hours. But I had to wait until my mother ate something, then I know it's right." Mothers also instructed their children how to behave outside as well as inside the home. Sara B.'s mother, a proud woman, told her daughter that no matter how little money one had, even if there was no food on the table, "when you left the house, none of this was to show. If she had to stay up half the night laundering and mending, she did it because she always wanted us to be presentable. She used to say to me, 'the cheeks, the color should be there.' In other words, put up a good front."

Self-sacrifice and helpfulness were other important lessons, common to women of all ethnic groups. Florence B. believed that her mother remained married to a husband she disliked for the children's sake, and she sought to be equally selfless. "There was absolutely no one like her," Florence insisted, "and I always prayed that I would grow up to be like my mother." Girls learned the obligation to perform *tsedakah*—helping others in need— from their mothers' behavior.[16] Anna R. absorbed this value from her grandmother, transmitted by her mother. "I was the oldest of four children," she began,

And all I knew was *to help*. But there's something that's always with me, through my whole life, since I can remember—personal things, my own gems, my own treasures.

My mother's mother died in childbirth when she was forty-one years old. My mother was left with six children and she was only seventeen years old. . . . My mother's mother was such a person that when she died, in came people that fell on her body, one person on top of the other. And they cried.

My mother didn't know those people. Then each one told their story, how charitable my grandmother was. In Europe, you have to go to the temple before you get married. And this young girl would say, "who is going to give me the dress to go to shul with?" And my grandmother, sometimes she didn't go to shul because she knew that there is a bride who needs her good dress to make a showing of herself. And then another girl says, "who's going to give me potatoes, who's going to give me corn, who's going to give me onions?" And other needs she filled.

Nobody ever knew that she did anything. And those people came in and mourned more than the family because she was so good and charitable.

Anna's mother followed the example she learned at the funeral: "Whatever she got," Anna recalled, "she got from her mother. That you just have to do things and you *are* your brother's keeper." Anna did the same, which became a source of great satisfaction. "I have peace of mind," she observed, "because since I'm the oldest one in the family, I've always been taking my mother's place of responsibility. I believe that my strength is from my grandmother. Because all I heard are the things she did and how she did it."

Mothers who had yearned for an education usually passed this characteristic on to their daughters as well. The mothers of Anna Kahan and Miriam M., who had been denied the opportunity to attend school, supported their daughters' desires for an education. The mother of Katya Govsky, a strong-willed and intelligent woman, had been one of the lucky few to attend a university, and her daughter sought to follow in her footsteps. "I wanted to accomplish the same as she did," Katya recalled. "I wanted to educate myself to be somebody in this world, so I would be independent."[17] Jeanne S., whose mother was the village healer, and who herself became a doctor, credited her mother with stimulating her own ambitions. "Maybe I got that from my mother," she mused, "to have a feeling for other people. To be with people, to touch them, to talk to them, to help them. As little as I was, I never felt that I was not capable. I always had a feeling I want to be somebody, and I think I became somebody."

Other women could also become role models for girls conscious of wanting lives different from their mothers'. Louise C. chose the youngest of her mother's seven sisters as an example because she married a "modern" man who supported his family, as her father and other uncles failed to do. Louise also learned about different ways of life from friends. "On Saturday," she related,

> we played mother. Because each child came from a different family, they could tell each other, "You are not a good mother. My mother doesn't do that." So you found out whether your mother was good, what she was good in. And the same thing—when I used to ask them, "Does your father learn with your brothers," my friends would answer, "No, my father gets up at five in the morning and goes away to work." But my father was home, trying to run his home like my grandfather ran it. To keep the girls home, send the boys to yeshivas, and the girls will learn how to be wives and how to be mothers and how to be maids.

The difference between her friends' homes and her own further convinced her of the advantages of "the modern way."

Because mothers and daughters were in almost constant contact, a close bond often developed. Just as mothers frequently showed their love by performing small services like cooking a favorite dish, young girls learned to demonstrate their feelings by trying to ease their mothers' burdens. Jennie S. remembered her delight in this reciprocal relationship. "I was so good to her. I used to do everything; I used to wash clothes and I used to iron and fix. And she was a very good mother—the best." Louise C. also derived great pleasure in helping her mother. "I loved my mother so much," she mused, "that when she wasn't home, I was unfortunate."

Sometimes, the cares of an impoverished home or numerous children rendered women incapable of showing love. Mothers struggling to make a living or stretch a few kopecks far enough to feed their families often lacked time or energy to devote to the children.[18] "I never had that feeling that I could talk to my mother," recalled Rita S. regretfully. "She was so busy in the store that she wasn't around much—she had a lot to do," Miriam Zunser's grandmother, Yentl, bore twenty-four children but displayed affection only for one. Even when a family was more comfortable, women's responsibilities left little time to indulge children. "Like most Jewish children in Eastern Europe," wrote Elie Wiesel, "I had two mothers—an everyday one absorbed by her work in the store and the kitchen and the one on Sabbath, transfigured, radiant, and inaccessible; a princess full of beauty and grace. Neither one encouraged my confidence."[19]

Other female family members, usually an oldest daughter or a grandmother, could serve as surrogate mother and give younger children the affection they craved.[20] Rose Chernin told her own daughter that she never had the kind of care given to her older sisters. When she was born, her prematurely aged mother "had nothing to give me. By the time I came along, it was all used up."[21] Rose's older sister, though, gave her the love her mother was incapable of. Gussie M. and Beatrice Pollock[22] were nurtured by older sisters after the death of a mother, and Frieda M.'s aunt, childless herself, took the place of an affectionate parent. The grandmother of Jennie H. similarly replaced a working mother. "I had very little from my mother," Jennie recalled. "I had more love from my gradmother. My mother never handled me. Because she used to go out at three in the morning to pick up milk from the farms. Then she used to bring it into the city. And she would come home late. My grandmother used to feed us and care for us."

If no surrogate mother existed, the results could be devastating. Ruth R. remembered that her mother "liked me at the beginning, and my younger sister too. But when the third girl—maybe if it was a boy it would be different—but it was a third girl and she protested very loudly, 'I don't love her, I don't like her.' She didn't want her and she neglected her. And I was five years old. I took care of her, and after her there was another girl born. And all right, she nursed them, she took care of them when they were babies. But once they started to talk, she had no time." Ruth looked after the younger children, but had no one to give her the loving concern she provided for them. "I was so anxious for affection," she recalled, "that I wanted to make myself sick. You know, only when you got sick you got a little attention. So I knew that when you drink a lot of water, you get sick. We had a jar with a handle that you used to take water from—it was eight quarts of water. I picked it up and I drank and I drank and I drank, so maybe I'll get sick and get a little affection." "But I didn't get sick," she observed ruefully, "and I didn't get affection."

Despite such deprivation, Ruth later understood why her mother had no love to give her. "Trouble is," she explained,

the parents did not have the time. There was a lot of work. There was cows and chickens and they baked their own bread and made butter and cheese. Already they had three smaller children than I, and the smaller ones were always crying. And it was such a pity—my mother was always cursing and angry, and she was frustrated—working very hard. And my father was free. He did not feel anything the way they now teach men to share, to help.

And I was still young. I couldn't understand. My mother complained a lot and when you're frustrated, you have to let it out to somebody, so she always let it out on me. I was punished plenty of times. I know now I didn't deserve it—I didn't do anything wrong. But they expected a lot, and there was so much work.

In *A Girl Marries*, a story by I. L. Peretz, Leah, the eldest of several children, was treated as harshly as Ruth, with a mother never satisfied by her exertions. But like Ruth, Leah also excused her mother even as she condemned her behavior. "My heart knew that it was not my mother beating me," Leah thought, "but her ill fortune."[23]

For such unhappy girls, alienated from their families, mothers could become negative rather than positive role models—images of what they hoped to escape or determined not to be. Remembering her mother laboring in the kitchen at dawn, Ruth asked herself, "Will I have to do that too when I get married?" She decided that such a life was not for her. "Everything that my mother did," she vowed, "I would do the opposite."

Thus, sex was not the only determinant of a child's role in the family; an oldest daughter would be given more responsibilities than the younger ones. As the oldest daughter, Ruth felt more heavily than her siblings the dual burden of lack of affection and greater parental expectations. Another first-born daughter, Sarah Reznikoff, could not attend school because her father told her, "You were born the eldest and the family needs your help badly."[24] Younger daughters were often aware of their privileged position in the family. Rebecca Berg, a youngest child, wrote, "Life was bitter around me and I knew nothing about it."[25] Naomi L. remembered that her older sister did most of the housework while she lived a pampered life, and Rita S., also a younger daughter, observed, "I had lots of love because I was a nice little girl so everybody was always shleping [carrying] me around." Miriam G., similarly favored, even traced bad feelings between her two older sisters to a time after her own birth, when her mother was ill and her nine-year-old sister had to care for the house and younger children. Anuta Sharrow, the youngest of four children, was permitted to attend school while her older sister did the housekeeping and "gave up her life for all of us and for my mother."[26] This difference in expectations based upon age was poignantly described by Mary Antin, whose sister "learned to bow to the yoke, to lift burdens, to do more for others than she could ever hope to have done for her in turn. She learned to see sugar plums lie around without asking for her share . . . while I sat warm and watched over at home, untouched by any discipline. . . . It was my good luck . . . to be born after, instead of before. . . . The lot of the firstborn is not necessarily to be envied."[27] Particularly, she might have added, if the firstborn was a female.

Like Mary Antin, younger daughters sometimes seemed to develop a self-confidence, even a brashness, absent in their more responsible older sisters. Anna Kahan got to attend her town's elementary school at the young age of five or six by going along with her older sister, sneaking into the classroom, and impressing the teacher enough to get her to agree to let her remain. Frieda M. recalled, "I was smarter than my older sister, and I thought that I was special. I had a doting aunt who built me up and gave me gifts and all the relatives liked me. Everything I said was repeated. And I really felt very important." Such early memories of being appreciated seem to have had a significant effect in developing a sense of self-confidence. Naomi L., for example, remembers a story her parents told: "I was sleeping with an older sister, and suddenly I got up and began to make noise and cry. And they say I saved the whole household because something happened with the coal stove and smoke was filling the house. And my waking up woke them all and they were saved." Several women recalled similarly being made much of for precocious acts that helped the family. During World War I, Ethel B. was the heroine of an incident that occurred when she and her mother and grandparents were on the way to her uncles' town with their cow. "We were stopped by Cossacks on the way, and they wanted to take the cow from us. And I knew how to speak Ukrainian," she explained, "because of the peasants who worked for us. And I talked them out of taking that cow! They simply did not take the cow. And I was only five years old!" Ethel concluded, with obvious pride, "My mother always talked about it."

Despite such examples, there were limits on activities and attitudes acceptable for girls, who were generally expected to be "good," obedient, and lacking in ambitions considered inappropriate to their sex. I. J. Singer remembered that his mother expected *him* to become a rabbi, but when his sister asked what *she* could be when she grew up, "Mother answered her question with another: 'What can a girl be?'" His sister, he observed ironically, had been jealous of her brothers since childhood, and "couldn't accept the fact that her talents weren't appreciated."[28] Bella Chagall also thought her brothers were lucky because they were boys. "I envied them," she wrote. "They could go wherever they liked and mother would never scold them. But I? Where could I go? Into the kitchen?"[29] Ruth R. echoed the same complaint: she was chastised for behavior improper for girls, but not for boys. Once, when she climbed over a fence to pick some strawberries, she was chased home by the watchman of the estate. He "came and told my parents," she recalled, "and my parents were very embarrassed. My father said if I was a boy he wouldn't mind so much, but that a girl should do that! Jump over a fence! Oh, I paid for that!"

Many women remembered the boys in their families as being favored in such ways. As children, they could deal with these inequities by simply deciding that boys were luckier than girls and accepting the limitations on their sex,[30] or they might seek an education so they could be more like their brothers. Another way was to internalize the values of their society, as their mothers had done, and shift their own unacceptable ambitions to a favored brother. Kate Simon discovered that by caring for her brother, she learned that "one could intensely love and as intensely hate the being who was both core and pit of one's life."[31] Transference did not always work.

In the shtetl, boys and girls were treated differently from birth. Male children were valued more and were celebrated with rituals when they were born and at thirteen, but girls generally had no ceremonies to mark their way from birth to marriage.[32] Pregnant women prayed for sons but asked that, if the child had to be a daughter, she be "tidy and not impudent and accept reproof from all who instruct her."[33] Girls also cost parents more than boys, for each had to be provided with a dowry or face spinsterhood. They were a poor religious investment as well: girls could not say the Kaddish, the prayer for the dead that parents counted on to assure a kind of immortal continuity.[34]

Personal accounts and literature reflect this attitude. Miriam Zunser's uncle, Mayshe, was always referred to as her grandmother's firstborn, although there had been several girls born before him. But they had died young, and "the loss of females did not matter much." As she was a girl, Miriam's own mother was considered "an empty nutshell."[35] Anzia Yezierska's fictionalized father in the novel *Bread Givers* was always throwing up to his wife that she had given him only daughters, but no sons—bearing only girl children usually was considered a woman's fault.[36] Lucy Lang remembered that her grandfather never forgave her for being a girl, and she was told that he had refused to speak to her mother for a long time after her birth because she had not produced a son.[37] Fathering girls seemed also to reflect on a man's virility. When I. J. Singer's mother gave birth to a girl, he recalled, "the Hasidim snickered. Surely fathering a female child was an act for which they occasionally flogged a young father with their belts. Naturally, the birth wasn't celebrated at our house."[38]

Girls were thus little valued by this society. Singer wrote of a neighbor who had borne many children. When she "gave birth to a boy," he recalled, "she would stay in bed until after the circumcision. But if it was a girl, she would be up and about by the third day, washing and cooking as if nothing had happened to disrupt her routine."[39] Fannie G.'s mother told her that her father was on his way home for the Sabbath when a neighbor informed him that his wife had just given birth to a girl. "And I was the third girl born," she related. "He says, 'A girl? I'm not going home!' They didn't want me, but I came." One Yiddish proverb encapsulates this attitude. It goes, "Many daughters, many troubles, many sons, many honors." Another similarly observes, "If you have daughters, you have no use for laughter."[40]

Despite this attitude, once a daughter was born, she was not necessarily loved less than a son. For a woman who had several boys, she might be particularly welcomed as a potential helper in housekeeping chores, something never expected of male children, for from a young age, girls' lives followed a different path from their brothers'. A girl's life centered about the home, while a boy was expected to focus on religious study. At the same time as a daughter began an early apprenticeship at her mother's elbow, her brother would be thrust out of the home into the men's world of learning.

A boy was removed from his mother's care as young as three and was taken, with much fanfare, to religious school, where he would spend most of his time. His long hours in cheder were often tedious and demanding, and were sometimes punctuated with beatings from the teacher or rabbi when a performance was not up to snuff. The warm environment of his mother's kitchen became an occasional, comfortable refuge. And although mothers were always beguiling their young sons to remain close,[41] boys learned quickly that they did not belong in the female world. Women's work was not for them: when Ruth Katz's brother tried to help his sisters by fetching water from the well, her mother told him it was not appropriate for a rabbi's son.[42] I. B. Singer learned the same lesson as a child. During a visit to his grandfather's home, he wrote, "I wanted to remain in the kitchen, listening to the gossip and nibbling on goodies, but grandfather dragged me away to his study, to the Torah, and to Jewishness. 'A boy's place is not in the kitchen,' he stated, and I didn't dare oppose him."[43]

Girls, on the other hand, had no other accepted place. They were initiated early into the mysteries of their future role. "A girl's real school-room," observed Mary Antin, "was her mother's kitchen. There she learned to bake and cook, and manage, to knit, sew and embroider; also to spin and weave, in country places. And while her hands were busy, her mother instructed her in the laws regulating a pious Jewish household and in the conduct proper for a Jewish wife; for, of course, every girl hoped to be a wife. A girl was born for no other purpose."[44] From the time a girl was old enough to dry a dish, she was expected to assist her mother and even take over in her absence. Louise C. was six years old when she learned how to scrub a floor. "I used to do the floors," she recalled, "so that my mother shouldn't have to do it. And as I was growing, I was learning more and more and I was the maid in the house." Fathers were expected to be inept in the kitchen if they cooked at all. When Louise's mother was away selling her wares at a fair or purchasing new goods, her young daughter did most of the cooking. "My father could cook cornmeal in buttermilk, or mashed potatoes with scrambled eggs," she related, "but he couldn't cook a meal. So I learned how to make noodles when I wasn't high enough yet to stand at the board. When I was about eight years old, I used to make all the noodles in the house."

Regardless of any outside work they did, girls were still expected to help with housework. Anna Kahan went to work for a milliner at the age of ten, but she also had to clean house on her day off. "I worked very hard yesterday," she complained in her diary, "scrubbing the floors, polishing the furniture, polishing the brass hoops of our water barrel and the copper frying pans till they shone like a mirror. I also helped Broche [her sister] with the cooking. . . . By the time my mother lit the candles, I could hardly stand on my feet."[45] Like Anna, Louise C. had to combine a paying job with housework once she convinced her parents to apprentice her to a dressmaker.

If a mother had an outside job, her daughters were usually pressed into service in some capacity, for in every country, children in families with modest means were expected to contribute to the family economy.[46] Sarah Reznikoff kneaded dough for the rolls her mother marketed in Warsaw; Sophie Saroff helped cut up the geese her mother sold and often collected the milk she purchased from farmers; Sonia Farber sold the cakes her mother baked.[47] Girls were not only expected to help out, they were expected to know what had to be done almost without being told. Janet A. observed, "My sister and I always felt sensitive about my mother's needs for help. And I don't even remember if my mother had to ask. We just knew it had to be done. Maybe we grew up with responsibility."

Because boys and girls played vastly different roles in their mothers' kitchens, their memories of its atmosphere differ sharply as well. Sons remembered and romanticized the comfortable place where they were fed and petted and had no responsibilities.[48] Girls' memories of the kitchen, on the other hand, often emphasized in great detail their mothers' constant drudgery. The mother of Rose L., for example, "worked so hard," her daughter recalled. "She worked on a grinder that made matzoh meal and matzoh farfel. It had a sifter in the middle so the matzoh meal used to fall down and the farfel went into the other compartments. How she ever did it I don't know." Ida Richter also remembered the hardships of her mother's life: "She had so much work, my poor mother," Ida observed. "We had two cows, and she had to feed them. And to wash clothes by the pond or in the house for nine or ten people—the people that worked for my father, she had to wash their clothes too—and cook for them three meals a day. And before a holiday, we used to rejoice, and when I used to say to her, 'We like holidays so,' she said, 'Not me; when a holiday used to come, I was tired before it came.' To do all the work for all the cooking for all the people."[49] Many young girls, particularly those from poor families, saw their mothers living lives of unremitting toil. Ruth R. realized that her mother was so busy that "she wasn't thinking of happiness. She was always working. You could see her day and night. Maybe she had a few hours of sleep. I opened up my eyes about six or seven in the morning and could already smell the aroma of potato soup. How and when did she do that? When did she peel those potatoes?"

These girls were conscious of the stratagems their mothers used to make ends meet. When there was no food left or money to buy it, Ruth's mother kept her family from going hungry. "She was from the country so she knew how to pick stuff, salad greens," Ruth recalled. "She would go to the outskirts of town and pick leaves that grow in the wild. And she would make a soup from them in a big pot, and maybe she put an egg in it." Louise C.'s mother never turned away any man her husband brought home with him from the synagogue on Friday evening. "She managed," Louise observed, "and everybody got a smaller piece of chicken, so I ate the grease and the *gorgl* [neck]. That was my part of the chicken." When there was poverty, choices had to be made by mothers that often left daughters feeling deprived. Hilda S. still remembers,

My mother had nothing to give us. She wanted everything for her children, but she had nothing to offer. One example—we went to a Jewish school. We wore brown dresses. And during the week we wore blue-black aprons, but for the holidays, we had to have white aprons. So when my mother went out of town one day to buy merchandise, I said to her, "Ma, I could use a half a yard of material for a new apron." She says, "All right, my child." She never said no. She went away. She brought back my sister three yards of material, but nothing for me. I was a child; I was hurt, I was stunned. But she didn't have any more money. And my sister was a big girl already, so she came first. Can you blame my mother? But still, I had bad feelings.

Such girls eventually understood their mother's dilemma, just as they understood the inability of some of them to display affection. Hilda brought up the incident of the apron fabric after she and her mother had come to America. "I said, 'Ma, how could you,'" she recalled. "She said, 'Child, I only had so much money. And it was more important that Cora should have a decent dress to wear than that you should have an apron.' So," Hilda concluded, "she had no choice." Ruth R., though feeling intensely deprived as a girl, realized as an adult why her mother had been unable to express love. "When I was very young, maybe seven," she began hesitantly,

I would come over and want to embrace her and have a little affection. She would say, "Love you have to buy. You have to be so good to earn it. If you don't earn it, you can't have it!" That's the way she felt. So when you have to earn love, you kill it.

But later, when you grow up, you know the reason why she was like that. It is not only my mother. It is a lot of women that suffered, and their life is such that they have to take it out on somebody.

She did everything else. She would take a blanket and sew around a white sheet, a cover, that you can wash out. That she would do after she was through with the dinner and everything else and maybe about midnight she would bring it over to the bed. She couldn't do it during the day, only after she was through with her work. It was taking maybe two hours to sew all around it.

You remember these little things. She did everything to make you comfortable. The way she was washing your hair. The best beauty parlor was not doing such a job the way she did it. She would massage it, she would wash it, she would set it. And then everybody would say, "What is your mother doing to your hair that it looks so beautiful?"

She didn't do any harm. She just didn't give any affection. Maybe because she was angry at my father that he made her always pregnant, that she took it out on the children.

Because their mothers' experiences gave them, in a sense, a foretaste of what their own lives might be like, many of these girls seemed particularly aware of the vicissitudes of childbirth and the trials of child-rearing. Frieda M.'s earliest memory, at two, was of her mother giving birth. "I don't remember their faces," she recalled, "but I remember the women and a big tub and the screaming, and finally they took me out of the room." Among poor families in villages, an older daughter sometimes assisted in her mother's childbirth. Rebecca August, whose mother had experienced seven miscarriages, occasionally had to act as midwife in emergencies, while Bessie Kriegsberg's mother, at ten years of age, assisted the midwife when her stepmother gave birth.[50] Anna Kahan's mother inherited a large brood at a young age when her own mother died in childbirth with her sixteenth child. Louise C. remembered that her mother became a peddler when she temporarily freed herself from bearing children by banishing her husband from her bed. After the birth of her sixth child, a doctor had warned that another pregnancy could mean her death. Also at an early age, Ruth R. understood the sorrow caused by constant childbearing. "When I was about five years old," she related, "my mother had already three children and she was pregnant with another baby. So I understood her life was very bitter. And there was always a tear in her eyes after she was finished lighting the candles. And I realize her prayer must have been only that God shouldn't make her so fertile, because she suffered so much."

Poor women with many children aged rapidly. "I do think my mother had a wasted life," Ruth observed sadly. At thirty-eight, her mother had borne eleven children and lost six of them to illness and accidents. The trials of constant childbirth and child-rearing drained her energies and ruined her health. Fannie K. echoed Ruth's story. Her own mother had given birth to fourteen children, of which only three survived to adulthood. When Fannie left her mother in Russia, she recalled, "she was forty and she was an old woman. I never remember my mother young."

Apart from the effect upon their mothers, there was an additional reason that the babies were so important to these girls: one of their major responsibilities was caring for younger siblings. When Louise C. was seven or eight, she reminisced, "I was already the whole *balabusteh* [housekeeper]. I was taking care of the younger one and the baby. That was my baby—he did not go to my mother. He used to come to me. I didn't have much of a bed—I had a couch—but he slept with me. When he slept with me, he slept. When I put him in the crib, he cried." Rita S. was also held responsible for her brother, even though he was older than she, and Sophie Saroff, before she was six, cared for a baby brother while her mother was at work delivering milk.[51] If a mother died in childbirth, or was sickly—not an unusual occurrence—the oldest daughter often had to become a second mother to the younger children, as did Gussie M. and Rebecca August, who "had to be the midwife, nurse, housekeeper and everything else that has to do with running a home."[52] When her stepmother died at thirty-eight, eleven-year-old Mariam Nirenberg had to raise five younger children.[53] In some families, responsibilities were divided. The sisters of Rachel R. went to work to help the family, while Rachel remained at home to care for younger brothers and sisters. Kate Simon also had complete charge of a younger brother. By the time he was two and a half, she wrote, "I was four, grown silent and very capable. I could lift him to the pot, clean him and take him off. I could carry him to bed and mash his potato. I knew where he might bump his head, where he might topple, how to divert him when he began to blubber. . . . I had my first baby at not quite four."[54]

The grandmother of Sholem Aleichem recognized the importance of this function in the lives of her own granddaughters. After their mother died and her husband remarried, the grandmother, who had been caring for the children, sent the boys home but kept the girls. "How can you compare boys to girls?" she asked. "What's a stepmother to boys? A boy spends his whole day in cheder, but a girl stays home and nurses the stepmother's babies."[55] "We were grown-ups at a very early age," observed Etta Byer. "Our childhood was short."[56]

From a young age, then, Jewish daughters, particularly those from the working class and lower middle class, were expected to take on serious responsibilities within the home and sometimes in the workplace as well. In some cases, their efforts were appreciated by parents; in other instances they were simply taken for granted. But the experience of assuming obligations early in life gave many of these young women a sense of competence that would stand them in good stead as adults.

Family relations therefore depended on a number of variables, apart from individual differences. Not the least of these was social class, for as one might expect, harmony in families was more easily achieved when the corrosive effect of poverty was absent. Poverty seemed to affect daughters' relations with mothers to a greater degree than their relations with fathers, for women in poor families usually had more work than they could manage, and they depended heavily upon their girls for assistance. Tension with fathers was frequently caused by a girl's desire to be more "modern" than a religious parent was willing to permit. But unless a family was "enlightened"—i.e. less religious—traditional ways would be maintained with better consistency among upper- and middle-class parents than they would among the working class.[57] In families of all classes, however, mothers often served as role models for daughters and were praised for their skill at "managing" and their ability to mediate differences. A girl's role within the family was also determined by her position of birth, for older daughters generally had greater responsibilities than younger ones. Many girls believed that boys, in general, had an easier time of it, and even in the shtetl, they were less accepting of this difference than their mothers had been at their age. All of these factors helped shape the perceptions and attitudes of young Jewish women in Eastern Europe at the turn of the century, and would exert a major influence on their subsequent lives in the United States.

3

· ·

Changing Times

Rich people would send their children to the next city, to high school and then to the college, and . . . to the university. When they were rich they could do it, but me, I didn't have anything and I wanted the same things.

—Rae K.

· · · · · · · · · · · · · ·

A woman has just as much desire as a man. Of course, we are still young. We need awakening.

—Anna Kahan, age 13[1]

· · · · · · · · · · · · ·

We went back to our hometown and we didn't find nothing. Our house was burnt. No parents. Then we got up and walked from one town to another. We walked and lived like that until 1918. Many times we didn't have food to eat. . . . Was really tough. Now I can never get enough to eat to make up for those years.

—Frieda W.

4. *Different generations of a family. Traditional parents pose with their
"modern" children and grandchildren.*

Collection of Rita Riman

By the beginning of the twentieth century, the world of many Eastern European Jews was changing irrevocably. In Russia, while pressured by the government to urbanize and Russify, Jews faced increasing impoverishment as factories multiplied and a native middle class preempted traditional Jewish occupations. Agitated from within by liberal trends and the new possibility of emigrating to the United States or Palestine, Jews even in remote villages became aware that their traditional ways were threatened.

Many old methods of making a living in the countryside and small towns now were closed off.[2] After the assassination of Czar Alexander II in 1881, a series of repressive laws had made it more difficult for Jews to enter the professions, attend universities, or practice skilled trades. By 1888, hundreds of decrees further circumscribed the lives of Jews. They were forbidden to buy or lease land, and after the government took over the liquor monopoly in 1897 and prohibited Jews from participating, over a hundred thousand Jewish families who owned inns were forced to close their doors.[3] Industrialization had also displaced large numbers of Jewish artisans, and the development of the railroad did away with the need for transport workers, a largely Jewish trade.[4] In 1907, thousands were evicted from Kiev and cities outside the Pale,[5] while in 1910, yet another decree forced many Jews out of villages and towns into the increasingly crowded cities of western Russia.[6] At the same time, in Rumania, Jews were subjected to laws even more discriminatory than those in Russia, and in Galicia, where the Austrian government treated Jews benignly, they suffered the wrath of peasants and townspeople in the face of a rising nationalism.[7] German-Jewish sources estimated that one-third of all Galician Jews lived on the edge of starvation.[8] Thus, in Eastern Europe, as in the United States—at the same time but for different reasons—great masses of people were moving from the countryside to the cities.[9]

Yet in the midst of such adversity, the economic turmoil and increasing urbanization of Jews paradoxically helped to create new opportunities, particularly for young people seeking to alter their lives. Attitudes toward education, for example, changed dramatically.

Before the middle of the nineteenth century, a secular education had been considered inappropriate in the Jewish community and was in any case unattainable because of restrictions on Jews. Despite the traditional Jewish emphasis on learning, religious training alone won approval, and then only for males. Secular subjects were mistrusted as a first step toward conversion, an avowed goal of the Russian government.[10] When Miriam Zunser's grandfather was discovered at sixteen to be secretly reading "profane literature" in the attic, his father threw him out of the house for deserting the faith of his ancestors. The boy's father then "tore his garments, put ashes on his head and sat on the floor reciting the prayer for the dead. He had lost his son."[11]

Fifty years later, the situation had changed. In the 1860s, the Russians had enlarged the possibilities of secular education for Jews, and the *Haskalah* sought to make such education acceptable.[12] Now, in addition to studying the Bible and Talmud, many boys learned arithmetic and became literate in Russian or Polish.[13] Some could hope to go on to a *gimnazye* if one were available locally and had not filled its quota of Jews. For a privileged few, a university education was also a possibility, for universities and professional schools had begun opening their doors—if only a crack— to Jews. By the 1880s and 1890s, secular education thus seemed to offer opportunities for advancement in the non-Jewish world at the very time when, paradoxically, a new regime was reversing the policy of assimilation and cutting off those opportunities.

These changes had important effects on the education of girls. Throughout most of the century, young women in Europe were thought to need no book learning, and apart from a smattering of written Yiddish to enable them to read the women's bible, the *Tsene-Urena*, Jewish girls were no different in this respect.[14] Too much education might reduce their desirability as brides or prevent them from concentrating on domestic duties.[15] Rebecca Berg's mother, for example, was well-read in her youth, but it was thought best that she conceal this ability.[16] Although some girls from cultured families, like Rebecca, could read and write Russian, Polish, or German, for the most part they were usually little more than semiliterate.[17] In some towns, observed Gussie M., "you could hardly find a woman who could sign her name. Women only had to take care of the children and the house." Mary Antin, who was critical of this treatment, remarked that if a young woman "could sign her name in Russian, do a little figuring, and write a letter in Yiddish to the parents of her betrothed, she was called wohl-gelehrnt—well-educated."[18]

Despite this attitude, because education generally was valued so highly in the Jewish culture, many women growing up in the 1880s and 1890s who had absorbed a reverence for the written word sought such knowledge for themselves. They knew the proverb, "If you have learning, you'll never lose your way,"[19] and many saw no reason why such knowledge should be restricted to their brothers. Some managed to learn to read and write by listening in when a teacher instructed the boys or by convincing a brother to tutor her secretly. Others, usually from wealthier and more "modern" families, were permitted to attend state or Jewish schools that expanded educational opportunities for girls in the 1870s and early 1880s.[20] Just a few years after the St. Petersburg Medical Academy opened its Women's Medical Courses in 1872 to train young women in obstetrics, fully one-third of those attending were Jewish.[21] But most girls had to do without even an elementary education. The mother of Mary Antin, for example, learned her prayers from a teacher and writing from her own mother. "My mother was quick to learn," Antin wrote, "and expressed an ambition to study Russian. She teased and coaxed, and her mother pleaded for her, til my grandfather was persuaded to send her to a tutor. But the fates were opposed to my mother's education. On the first day at school, a sudden inflammation of the eyes blinded her temporarily . . . and it was taken as an omen, and my mother was not allowed to return to her lessons."[22] Miriam Zunser's mother also unsuccessfully begged her father to permit her to learn Russian or Hebrew, and she bitterly resented the meagerness of her education.[23]

Mothers who were thwarted in their longing for education often transferred these desires to their children. Some determined that daughters in particular would have the opportunities that were denied to them. Anna Kahan's mother, an orphan who had pleaded uselessly with her grandmother to let her learn to read and write, resolved that her own daughters would have all the education they wanted.[24] When times were hard, some women managed to save money for their daughters' lessons by skimping on food. The mother of Ethel B., who could herself read and write German as well as Yiddish, paid a student to tutor her daughter in high school subjects. Jennie S. did not want to attend school and went only at her mother's insistence. Basya Saroff rented a room to a young woman teacher to enable her daughter to learn Russian and arithmetic, and Sophie always remembered her mother's conviction that knowledge was more important than riches.[25] Rose Schneiderman was also sent to Hebrew school largely because of her mother's determination.[26] The mother of Rita S. took her daughter to live in the nearby town of Kamenesk, where there was a high school, and engaged a tutor to assure her of passing the entrance examination in mathematics. It was her mother's goal, Rita explained, that she get an education. The same ambition motivated the mother of Fannie K., who swallowed her pride and begged her wealthier brothers to permit her daughters to be tutored along with their own children. "In the beginning," Fannie recalled, "they didn't let us in. And my mother said, 'My children must have education.' She actually begged them. She made us go there, though my aunts used to be very rude to us. But my mother says, 'My children have to go to school!'"

During the dislocations of World War I, some women resorted to extraordinary stratagems to continue their daughters' educations. With her husband gone to America, Florence B.'s mother "took off her *sheitel*, and after she began to think about a livelihood, how to feed us, she began to think of education for us. And so the two girls, my sister and I, were sent to a Catholic convent." This unconventional way of assuring her daughters an education almost had serious consequences: "I immediately became so enamored of these nuns that I wanted to be a nun." Her father was told of neither her "schooling" nor of her unacceptable ambition.

In some families, both parents or the father alone provided the impetus for a daughter's schooling, particularly if there were no sons. Both of Mary Antin's parents sought an education for their daughters, with the ideal of a modern education as "the priceless ware" her father brought back with him from his travels beyond the Pale. Her mother readily acquiesced to his desire for their daughters' education, which was "less common than gold earrings in Polotzk."[27] If parents themselves had an advanced secular education, like those of Rose G., they were usually in favor of the same for their daughters. Janet A., the daughter of an urban, secularized family, recalled childhood memories of her father's reading to her mother in German from Schiller's *Mary Stuart* on Saturday afternoons. Even among poorly educated, rural Jews, however, parents sometimes supported their daughters' desire for education. The greatest pride of Frieda W.'s semiliterate father was showing visitors her *gimnazye* diploma, and Jeanne S., who grew up in a small village in Galicia, credited her illiterate parents with "the ambition to make something of their girls." Some fathers even compromised religious beliefs to enable their daughters to attend school. When Sophie Saroff enrolled at the local Russian school, she was forced to attend classes on the Sabbath. After her education was completed, her pious father asked if she had had to write when she was in school on Saturday. When she asked why he hadn't questioned her before, he replied, "I didn't want you to sin twice: once to tell me a lie, and once in the actual writing."[28]

For the most part, though, fathers were not anxious to have their daughters educated,[29] apart from learning how to read and write—which was still more than their own fathers had thought necessary for daughters. Some simply felt it was useless, and possibly even unsuitable. When Gussie M. told her father she wanted to go to school like the boys, he told her that "the Jewish boys they have to learn the Bible. But the girls don't have to.

5. *Young Jewish women attending a secondary school in Odessa.*
Collection of B. S. W.

And you're a pretty girl. You'll get married." "And this," she sighed, "was the answer." Etta Byer's father went one step further. He taught her to pray and read the Bible. "He said that I could become a fine scholar if I were a boy," she recalled. But this was as far as he would go. He told Etta that she had enough education for a girl.[30] Anna Kahan's father, "who was otherwise the most wonderful man in the world," thought it was enough that his daughters could read and write in Yiddish and follow the prayers in Hebrew. He opposed Anna's desire to go to *gimnazye* because attendance was mandatory on the Sabbath.[31] But Anna's mother hired a tutor to prepare her and talked her husband into permitting his daughter to attend when she discovered that the local Polish school tacitly permitted Jewish children to cut Saturday classes. Rae K.'s father also opposed a *gimnazye* education for religious reasons. "He thought I'll go too far," Rae recalled, "that I'll turn Christian. So there was a limit. He used to help me with arithmetic and Russian, everything, because he was very brilliant. I got from him what I could, but I couldn't stand his restrictions."

Although most fathers seemed at least to approve a limited education, some even opposed their daughters' picking up what they could at home. Louise C. remembered that when she was seven or eight, her father "used to stay up with my brothers, and he used to teach them Polish, Russian, Hebrew, the Talmud. And he could argue with them, and it was so fascinating. Girls weren't allowed. We weren't supposed to learn. But by laying there at night listening, it was so fascinating you could learn without reading a book."

These young girls' attitudes toward education seem to have been shaped by the traditional Jewish reverence for learning, now shifted from the religious to the secular sphere. Some young women doubtless resented their brothers' access to a religious education, like Mary Antin, who wrote, "There was nothing in what the boys did in heder that I could not have done—if I had not been a girl."[32] Sarah Reznikoff also complained to her mother of this double standard. "Do you remember when Grandfather Fivel gave me the Tree of Life to read and memorize?" she asked her mother. "'In that it said, "He who does not know how to read is blind."' 'A man is meant,' Mother answered, 'I don't believe intelligent people think a woman is not as good as a man.' And I made up my mind not to listen to Mother or Grandmother and learn as much as I could."[33] But the sphere of religious scholarship was closed to girls in a way that secular learning was not. Females were expected to be pious, but not learned. So girls concentrated their desires on attaining a secular education—at the very least to learn to read and write in Russian, Polish, or German as well as Yiddish.

Many hoped to go on to *gimnazye*, and some even cherished the hope of attending a university, open at the end of the century to few Jews, male or female. Even in small towns, girls were no longer satisfied if they could simply read the Bible and write a plain letter. They wanted to be able to read books in Russian, and some wanted to learn Hebrew as well.[34]

For some, this desire to learn represented a mild rebellion against the favoritism their society seemed to shower upon men and boys. Anna Kahan recalled that the *melamed*, or teacher, who taught her Hebrew prayers, had remarked that it was "too bad she wasn't born a boy—she could have been a rabbi." Anna reacted by actively pursuing a secular education all her life. Women in an earlier generation may have chafed occasionally under the restrictions defining their lives, but there was little that they had felt was appropriate to do about what was perceived as a God-given order. Younger women seemed more willing to question the treatment of females. I. J. Singer, for example, remembered his grandmother's resentment at having to retire to eat in the kitchen after serving the Sabbath meal when her husband had invited male guests for dinner, for he considered it improper for women to sit at the table with strange men. But she was annoyed only when the guests were beggars, and gladly made the sacrifice when they were "respectable men."[35] Women considered it "natural" to give men the best food, to do all the work for holidays while sharing only peripherally in the actual celebration.[36] Bella Chagall, born into a Hasidic family, also remembered being forbidden to eat in the family sukkah[37] after serving the holiday meal. When she asked her mother why females were treated like servants while males were favored, the older woman told her sadly, but with resignation, "Ah, my child, they're men."[38] Bella, on the other hand, was pleased when it began to rain and spoiled dinner for the privileged men and boys.

Thus, by the beginning of the twentieth century, young Jewish women wanted more schooling than their mothers and expected at least to learn how to read and write.[39] "Who didn't want an education?" recalled Ruth R. "I was writing a letter for a girl that was twenty-one years old," she went on, "and was engaged to a fellow from another town. And she had two sisters, and nobody knew how to write. I was nine years old, and I could see that the girl was embarrassed and she couldn't write through me, a child, what she wanted to tell her sweetheart."

Despite these dreams, economic hardship required many young women to put aside their desire for education and go to work to help their parents. Anna Kahan had to give up *gimnazye* when her father's business reverses made the small amount she could earn a necessity. But, she recalled, "I never gave up the hope of continuing my education. I studied in snatches," she recalled, "between seasons or when I was out of work. It only increased my hunger for knowledge, it did not satisfy it." "I was precocious," she recorded in her diary, "but I had no choice. Conditions were against me."[40] Sarah Reznikoff also had to give up her dream of an education because of family needs. She had overheard her mother tell her father, "What can we do? I need her at home. I have no other help."[41]

Even if parents were willing to have their daughters educated, often there were no schools available for Jewish children where they lived, and it took money to finance studies away from home. As Rae K. remembered, "Rich people would send their children to the next city, to high school and then to the college, and to Kharkov, to the university. When they were rich they could do it, but me, I didn't have anything and I wanted the same things." To get her cherished education, Rae moved to a university town where she could get free tutoring. Rae remembered one girl who had registered as a prostitute to stay in Moscow and attend the university. Jews were permitted to live there as prostitutes, but not as students. In some villages, there was no school at all, and in others, the only school might be run by the local church. Mary Antin remembered her keen sense of deprivation. "I used to stand in the doorway of my father's store," she wrote, "munching an apple that did not taste good anymore, and watch the pupils going home from school in two's and three's: The girls in neat brown dresses and black aprons and little stiff hats, the boys in trim uniforms with many buttons. They had ever so many books in the satchels on their backs. They would take them out at home, and read and write, and learn all sorts of interesting things. They looked to me," she concluded, "like beings from another world than mine."[42]

The desire for an education was accompanied by equally liberal ideas about relations between young men and women. Even in small towns, some members of the younger generation in the late nineteenth century had reacted against the attitudes of their elders. Folk songs of the period reflect the conflict between parents who were trying to arrange appropriate marriages for their daughters and the young women themselves, who sought a "pure, true love."[43] For as little as three kopecks to buy or only one to rent, wandering peddlars provided young women with Yiddish novels whose themes vindicated the principle of romantic love.[44] The growing acceptance of secular education and the influence of the Worker's Bund[45] led many boys to break with the orthodoxy of their fathers. A few young people were even deciding to marry the mate of their choice and only then seeking parents' approval, although this probably happened more in working-class than middle-class families.[46] In the 1890s, one middle-class son, Frieda M.'s father, was betrothed to a girl but fell in love with an orphan without a dowry. "That was a terrible slap to my grandma," Frieda explained, but her grandmother adjusted to changing ways and accepted her son's choice. Even earlier, in the 1860s, Miriam Zunser's parents' betrothal was arranged traditionally, but both her father and mother refused to marry unless they could see each other before the ceremony. Several of her mother's younger brothers and a sister went a step further and married spouses they chose without consulting their father.[47]

The overwhelming majority of young people did not flout tradition, but certainly the daughters of this earlier generation, growing up at the turn of the century, often expected to have a greater voice in the selection of their husbands.[48] Sarah Rothman insisted on marrying a young cousin her father disliked because he refused to attend religious services. Instead of disowning his rebellious daughter, Sarah's father attended the wedding but showed his dissatisfaction in a mainly ceremonial way: "At the wedding, my father didn't say 'mazel tov' [good luck] to my mother-in-law. She didn't talk to him and he didn't talk to her."[49] Sarah Reznikoff broke one engagement when her betrothed could not be persuaded to move away from their village, and she refused to consider other potential husbands selected by her parents.[50] Although this kind of freedom was more likely to exist in working-class homes, even among the poor, fathers generally did not willingly surrender the traditional right to arrange their children's marriages. Sholem Aleichem's Tevye stories, written between 1892 and 1907, reflect the conflicts between father and daughters and highlight his diminishing authority and their increasing assertiveness.[51]

Poverty helped erode a father's ability to select his daughter's groom. When a father lacked money for a dowry, he could not go to a matchmaker, and a girl had more leverage to choose her own husband. "Only the poor can afford to marry for love," went one proverb.[52] In the White Russian town of Maitchet, Fay R. remembered, most young people married for love. Because the girls were good-looking, they had no trouble attracting suitors, and fathers agreed to the matches because they were too poor to provide their daughters with dowries.[53]

Young girls of this generation also had more liberty with the opposite sex than their mothers had as young women, particularly in the freer atmosphere of the larger towns and cities.[54] Sarah Reznikoff had gone as far as dancing with gentile boys at a party given by non-Jewish neighbors, although she did not participate in kissing games.[55] Bella Chagall's best friend was less shy. She liked boys and "would kiss them unabashedly right on the lips." With more braggadocio than real intent, she even suggested that they assist a young artist by posing for him in the nude.[56] Less atypically, Anna Kahan and her friend opposed traditional sexual mores by reading books that opposed conventions and criticized parents who educated their sons while marrying off daughters, as they put it, "to the highest bidder."[57] As a young teenager, Anna was permitted to walk or play alone with boys, and she and her girlfriend often discussed romantic love, a subject stimulated by reading such books as Tolstoy's *Kreutzer Sonata*.[58]

Parents sometimes approved of greater freedom for their daughters and could smooth the way with stricter relatives. Hilda S., for example, recalled,

> I was a very outgoing girl and I was a happy child, and I wanted to live my own life. Now I went to school, and going out of school, I had to pass some of my relatives' houses. And they came complaining to my mother, "Look at this, we had a pogrom, we lost a relative, and she walks out of school—one boys carries her books, the other boy carries her bag, and she sings, she's so happy. Who knows what's going to become of her?!"
>
> So my mother says, "She's a child. What do you want from her? Let her enjoy herself. She'll have plenty to worry about in her life." Every day my mother had to make up a defense. So one day she came to me and she said, "Do me a favor. When you leave school, when you pass Uncle Silas' house, don't walk with the boys, make the sourest face that you can, don't be happy. As soon as you pass it, you can do what you like."

The father of Ruth Katz was even more permissive. Although he was a rabbi, he permitted his daughters' suitors to visit and sing and dance with the girls. Beatrice Pollock was also allowed to have unchaperoned dates with her boyfriend, and when her father came upon them kissing, he only told her, "I don't mind, don't worry about it, but don't stay out late."[59]

Even sex was a fit subject for discussion among girls from more liberal families, although their mothers were usually as reticent as traditional women in this respect.[60] Just before twenty-year-old Frieda M. left alone for the United States, her mother tried, with some difficulty, to tell her about "the facts of life." Frieda recalled with some amusement that she "would have been in plenty of trouble if [she] hadn't known by then." The diary of the then thirteen-year-old Anna Kahan records a friend's assertion that "a woman has just as much desire as a man. Of course, we are still young. We need awakening."[61] The veneer of sophistication, however, still concealed a basic factual ignorance. When Anna's friend was sixteen, a yeshiva student was bedded down by her parents in her room, an unusual occurrence, and she believed that his presence would make her pregnant. Only the discovery of a book on sex written by a doctor convinced her otherwise. In the book, intercourse was described graphically, "almost as if it was rape." "When I read this book," Anna recalled, "I kept saying 'Pigs! *Chazere* [Pigs]!' And I hated all boys."

Despite this ignorance about the particulars of sex, girls were aware of it indirectly. Because a religious man was prohibited from sleeping with or even touching a menstruating woman until she had been ritually cleansed at the *mikvah*, young girls could frequently put two and two together. Louise C. remembered how she had learned. "When I saw my father come home from shul towards evening and give my mother a little package, and I would see my mother take it and sit down and eat that delicatessen that he brought for her, as young as I was, I had an idea that she was pregnant! Either that or he brought it as a reward because I knew she went to the *mikvah*, that there is going to be a relationship—as young as I was. One Saturday morning, I went to my mother's room, and my father was in the bed. Then I had something to worry about, that she's going to be pregnant—without having any idea what sex is." A quick learner, when Louise went to the United States and stayed with relatives, she observed her aunt putting her arms around her husband and thought, "Tonight it'll be like after the *mikvah*!" Frieda M. epitomized this combination of knowledge and ignorance by saying, "I saw sex all around me not knowing it was sex!"

Thus, by the turn of the century, the traditional world of many Jews was giving way before the forces of modernization. Stimulated by rural poverty and government decree, masses of people were moving from the countryside to the city. As a result of this migration, by 1898, 51 percent of all Jews lived in urban areas. Jews constituted between one-fifth and one-third of all factory workers in the Pale,[62] and although there were jobs available in the new industries, such work may have slowed, but did not stop, the plunge of many families into poverty. In 1898, almost a fifth of all Jewish families were forced to apply for Passover charity.[63]

Families with middle-class status but no money now frequently had to rely upon the work of all members, including daughters and sometimes wives,[64] although married women seldom took jobs in the factories. Ruth R., as a young woman from a "good" but impoverished family, was forced to go to work. "When I came the first day to the seamstress," she recalled, a neighbor came in and saw her working. "In a small town, they notice right away a new hand, an apprentice. They say, 'Who's this girl? It's Moishe

Dekovitza's *eynikl* [granddaughter].' They said, 'Oh, Moishe Dekovitza's *eynikl*? What a time. Even they already try to learn a trade.' Yes, times were changing."

By the end of the century, 15 percent of all artisans in Russia were women, mainly dressmakers, milliners, and flowermakers—all traditional Jewish women's jobs.[65] Twenty-four percent of all workers were female, and in the textile mills of St. Petersburg, this number rose to 42.6 percent.[66] Many unmarried women worked as operatives in the factories. Other girls and many married women were able to earn their living at home. The sewing machine had created new opportunities—women could buy sewing or knitting machines on time and work in their own homes for independent contractors.[67] Sarah Reznikoff, before she was twenty, had purchased four sewing machines and employed eight women sewing for her.[68] Yetta Brier, who learned dressmaking in her native Galicia, had started her own shop at sixteen and became the chief support of her family.[69] Young women could also work in small factories or sweatshops in the clothing trades and tobacco industries.

Although conditions were hard and pay was poor,[70] for young women there were some advantages to working in the cities. Most obviously, they could for the first time count on earning a steady living and thus becoming wage earners independent of their parents.[71] Few young women, however, expected to keep their jobs once they were married. Etta Byer, for example, decided to work in a cigarette factory rather than become a dressmaker as her parents wanted. She reasoned, "All dressmakers work forever for their husbands and families, but there are no married women at the cigarette factory. I shall never work for a husband. It is enough to give him a dowry to marry me."[72] Rose Chernin's mother also realized that skills could lead as readily to a life of toil as to independence. This unusual woman told her daughter not to learn to sew or even to cook. "You'll marry a rich man," she told her, "then you won't need it. If he's a poor man, better you don't know how to become his slave."[73] Clearly, in the city, such women had adopted the middle-class attitude that married women should not work outside the home,[74] and Byer viewed her entry into the factory as a means of saving money for a dowry and lasting only until she had found a husband. Among Jews in the United States, this attitude would become even more prevalent, but it originated in the cities of Eastern Europe.

Another attitude that would be transplanted was a working-class consciousness, also fostered in the cities of Russia and Poland. There, often for the first time, young women came into contact with the radicalism swirling through prerevolutionary Russia. The Jewish Socialist Labor Bund, or the

General League of Jewish Workers, established in Vilna in 1897, proved particularly attractive to young Jewish working women. Two of its seven founders were women, and the movement promised equality to their sex and the opportunity for leadership denied by the traditional community. In Russia, over 64 percent of women imprisoned for political activity in one twenty-month period were Jewish, although Jews were only 4 percent of the Russian population.[75] Within the Socialist Revolutionary Party between 1901 and 1916, 14 percent of the members were women, and a full 25 percent of these were Jewish.[76] The successes of the Bund in calling and winning strikes excited many young people.[77] Jewish students in the cities could scarcely avoid learning about radical ideas: Anuta Sharrow remembered a reading circle among the girls in her *gimnazye* discussing Zionism and revolution.[78] Rose Cohen, who became a union organizer in the United States, had become a radical after studying in a Russian school with socialist teachers.[79] Sonia Farber participated in the revolutionary movement in Kiev and took part in a general strike.[80]

This ferment spread from the cities to towns and villages. Little Swislocz resounded to debates among Zionists, Bundists, and Anarchists. In 1900, the Bund concluded successful strikes in leather factories, demonstrating to young people in particular the power of concerted action.[81] In her village of Kletsk, Ida Richter remembered hearing about the Zion-Laborites, Social Democrats, Socialists, Anarchists, and the Bund.[82] After Russia lost the Russo-Japanese war of 1905 and many soldiers returned home with a heightened political consciousness, few Jews were unaware of such radical ideas.[83] Anna Kahan, as a child, wrote in her diary with enthusiasm about hearing of Zionism, the Bund, and other issues affecting Jews. A cousin recently returned from London excited Anna and her sister with talk of the burgeoning Socialist movement.[84] Sara Plotkin learned about radicalism during World War I when speakers roused her village. At first their speeches were confusing. "We didn't know who or what the proletariat was. When they said workers, we understood, but not proletariat. They spoke of the capitalist market. To me, Bobroisk was a big market and Minsk was a large market; we didn't understand the world market of capitalists." But Sara and her friends soon learned the difference. "When the Socialists sent a speaker," she recalled, "he spoke our language."[85]

Sometimes, parents shared their children's enthusiasm for these new movements. Frieda M.'s mother told her daughter that as a young woman, she had belonged to a secret society dedicated to overthrowing the Czar. Basya Saroff housed a young revolutionary and helped the movement by transmitting messages. Although her daughter Sophie was only twelve, she learned from her mother that "class struggle was part of everyday life."[86] Ida Richter's mother, who usually tried to avoid trouble, nevertheless helped to smuggle out of town—one step ahead of the police—a radical young man who had worked for her husband.[87] Yetta Altman was born while her father was involved in a strike in the factory where he worked. While she was growing up, her parents and their friends held secret political meetings in their home. By the time she left for the United States at twelve years of age, Yetta had a well-developed class consciousness.[88]

More often than not, however, the political sympathies and activities of young people created friction with more conservative parents. The German-Jewish feminist reformer Bertha Pappenheim observed of Galician Jews in 1909 that radical politics helped to undermine traditional family solidarity. "The generations," she wrote, "do not understand each other any more; parental authority and power have almost disappeared; religious, cultural and political contrasts heap themselves up between them."[89] Some young people, like Rae K.'s radical brother, left home because of conflicts with a religious father. Louise C., who emigrated to Palestine, learned to oppose her father's conservatism after she came into contact with revolutionary Polish immigrants.

At the same time as radical ideas were agitating many communities, the religious practices of the shtetl were also undergoing a transformation. Earlier, in the 1860s, a relatively few Jewish families—perhaps 3 percent—had been beguiled by the Czar's promise of full participation in Russian society to go further than simply "bending" the rules of traditional Judaism.[90] Pauline Wengeroff, a wealthy, upper-middle-class woman, bemoaned the transformation of her family. Departing from the ways of her "godfearing" and "deeply pious" parents, Wengeroff reluctantly followed her husband in abandoning one by one the customs of Judaism in return for the promise of assimilation. Looking about her at the Russified Jewish communities in St. Petersburg and Minsk, Wengeroff asserted with understandable exaggeration that "no group but the Jews so swiftly and irrevocably abandoned everything for West European culture, discarded its religion, and divested itself of its historical past and its traditions." Wengeroff, to her sorrow, saw the results of this decision: after a short-term effort to Russify Jews, the government reversed its policy in the 1880s and closed off educational and career opportunities to those who refused to convert to Christianity. Her own sons, considering such advantages preferable to the vestiges of Judaism that remained with them, chose to be baptised rather than "renounce everything that had become indispensable."[91]

The vast majority of Jews, however, stopped far short of apostasy, and many instead attempted to blend the old ways with the new. They hoped, as did Moses Leib Lilienblum, an influential writer, to remove the "encumbrances and customs that make Judaism difficult to practice and unattractive" to those who sought to reconcile a degree of secularism with religious tradition.[92] For many families, this might mean seeing that their daughters as well as their sons had a good secular education. It might mean spending Saturday afternoons reading Goethe or Schiller as a family rather than observing the Sabbath in prayer.

For women, who often had to weigh the practicalities of life against the letter of the law, this transition may have been easier than it was for men. For Anna Kahan, a sign of her mother's enlightenment was her willingness to reheat the Sabbath meal on a *mashinka*, a small kerosene burner, instead of keeping it in the oven overnight.[93] The mother of Lucy Robins Lang seemed to her daughter to be a pioneer. "Because she had lived in a big city for a number of years," Lang recalled, "our house became the center of rebellion against the stringent rules that forbade all joy of living." While her father was in America, her mothers' sisters, brothers, and cousins would gather at their house to dance every Saturday afternoon.[94] One contemporary observer bemoaned the change he observed in Jewish women: "They are the children of our period and therefore quick in accepting modern ideas." Children were permitted to do as they pleased and women "strive no more for the lofty ideals of their foremothers. . . . Their ambitions," he complained, "are luxurious dwellings, costly garments . . . and festivities."[95]

The city certainly accelerated such "modern" trends. Although the middle class clearly was not immune, social change tended to take place most rapidly among the working class, possibly because they often had to migrate to urban areas to find jobs.[96] Tanya N. credited her mother's cleverness and freethinking ways to her frequent visits to the city of Vilna as a young girl. The mother of Sophie Abrams-Flint, also raised in a city, belonged to what her daughter called "the doubting generation."[97] What it meant for her was a loose construction of religious restrictions and a refusal to wear the *sheitel*, or wig, prescribed for married women. Even daughters of rabbinical families, I. B. Singer observed, read modern books openly, dressed stylishly, and went about without chaperones. But these young women, as well as Tanya's and Sophie's mothers, nevertheless maintained kosher homes and kept the Sabbath. Since women's role in Judaism was based less upon doctrine than men's, it may have been easier for them to discard peripheral elements yet feel they had retained the essence of a proper Jewish home. This flexibility may also have eased their transition to the even newer culture they would find in the United States.

The outbreak of World War I increased the pressures upon Jews. Russian forces suspected them of favoring the Germans, and the Germans of favoring the Russians. Fueled by the passions of war, anti-Semitism took a virulent form, and the Russian government began to forcibly expel Jews from border provinces at the approach of the enemy.[98] After the armistice, when the Bolsheviks and Poles began to fight over disputed territory, Janet A.'s family felt buffeted between these opposing forces. Situated in a strategic area, their city was "occupied first by the Poles, then by the Russians, back to the Poles, then the Russians again. And generally, the Jews suffered. The Russians accused the Jews of being anti-Communist. And then when the Poles reentered they accused the Jews of being pro-Communist and anti-Polish. So many people whom my parents knew were shot. It was a childhood of constant war." Anna Kahan remembered the Germans as being more friendly to Jews than the Russians, but she asserted that "they robbed Poland," taking what food they needed and leaving nothing for the townspeople to buy.[99] If one lived away from the front, life was easier. In Budapest, the mother of Elsie F. took in homework making nightgowns, with her children helping by threading ribbon through the lace and delivering the finished products to the contractor. War seemed far away.

In Russia and Poland, however, the war caused grave dislocations regardless of economic status. Fannie C., who came from a middle-class family, remembered her childhood as a time of fear. Her favorite aunt was killed in a pogrom, and Fannie's own life was filled with memories of war and revolution: "I remember going to school one day, and a bomb bursting right in front of me. And my mother running around to look for me to make sure I was alive. Many a time my mother would go out when the wounded soldiers were coming in from the front to see whether they wanted some water, and they would die right in front of her eyes. I really feel as I grow older that I had no childhood."

War was especially frightening for girls and women who, unlike their brothers, had to worry about the possibility of rape. The military director of Siedlce even tried to allay the fears of townspeople by telling them that when the army passed through, "the stores may be plundered and girls violated. Otherwise the town will remain intact."[100] Minna S. remembered that at the approach of troops, all the women dressed up to appear old and unattractive, and they hid their young daughters in the woods. Rose Soskin's mother tried to conceal her beauty by keeping her hair uncombed.

She stayed in the house when soldiers were in town and sent her daughters out to scrounge for food. On one of their forays, a friend was raped and subsequently gave birth to a child.[101] The aunt of Shirley Harris was shot by soldiers, and her sister and a maid only escaped rape by running into the woods.[102] Several women also remember being hidden in the cellar to escape this indignity, and one who was not so fortunate never married after her traumatic experience with Polish soldiers. So in addition to caring for their families, women had to be concerned about protecting themselves and their daughters from this atrocity particularly feared by females.

On a day-to-day level, women had to use ingenuity to get food and care for their families. Louise C.'s father couldn't get work as a bookbinder, so, as Louise recalled, "My mother used to bake *kikhlakh* [cookies] and my father went to the *besmidrash* [place for prayer] and he used to sell tea and *kikhlakh* and we sort of had an income out of that. And my mother helped out by selling merchandise in the market." Anna Kahan remembered vividly one example of her mother's bravery to protect her children.

It was hard to get food. There was a shortage everywhere. But on Rosh Hashanah [the Jewish New Year] my mother managed to get three *challahs*. They were sour! But we were glad to get them. I remember it was on Saturday, a holiday, and my father had gone to the synagogue and we were home. And suddenly, a whole big crowd collected and came up on our porch. My mother, of course, had all the windows closed. And the first thing she said was, "You girls, down in the basement, down in the basement!" They were always hiding the girls, because you know what happens.

And one man came to the window and knocked on the window. He said, "Give us bread!" My mother was a brave woman and very, very clever. So, she told us to run down to the basement. But I peeped. And I listened. And I saw him come over, and she said, "Look, we are refugees too. We have little enough. How can I give you bread?" And the crowd was growing and growing on that little porch. It was filled, and they started yelling, "Give bread! The Jews give us bread! Give us to eat! You have everything. We have nothing!"

And she was alone. My father wasn't there. But maybe it was better that he wasn't there. And she said to this man, "You look like an intelligent man." He was the leader. "How can I feed you? I have children." She didn't say what kind of children. She was afraid they would go and look for us. She says, "How can I feed a crowd like this? I have only one bread." She spoke to him very nicely. So he says, "Give me that bread. I'll take them away." Imagine! She brought out one *challah* and she gave him. And he said to them, "Come on, there's nothing here."

And this stuck in my mind.

A middle-class, "modern" woman, Anna's mother learned how to make do. Her husband bought a cow, and she made cheese and even baked bread, something she was not accustomed to doing. Trying to escape from the fighting, they traveled from one town to another, with Anna's mother getting other refugees to help her and her five children. Even before they fled their native Siedlce, times were hard. Money was worthless, for there was little food to be bought, and "often we used to go to the fields outside the city to dig potatoes because that was the only food available. We had money, but no food." The Poles were taking all able-bodied men they found to work camps or into the army, so her father remained in hiding for weeks in the attic, and her mother had to tend their store alone and find food for the family. But her father had seldom been an effective provider. Once, when he had collected a debt, on the way home he gave the money to a friend who seemed to need it more. Her mother was furious, for she needed the money to buy food. But "that was the sort of man my father was," Anna recalled. "My mother was more practical—she had to feed her children."

Many women, though, were not fortunate enough to have a husband at home to help provide for them and their children. Under the best of circumstances, families wishing to emigrate before World War I had left together. But circumstances were seldom ideal. Given the increasing hardship in Russia, relatively few had the resources to finance a mass exodus. More often than not, a father or older child would leave first and save enough to bring over other members one or two at a time. If things went poorly in America, or if the father had departed shortly before the war began, it might be years before the family was reunited. This meant that thousands of women spent years without husbands, that thousands of children grew up with few or no memories of fathers. Often babies too young to remember their fathers were sung to sleep with a lullaby Lucy Robins Lang remembered:

> Sleep, my baby, sleep. Your father is in America.
> In that wonderful country he eats white bread every day.
> When there is a sound at the door, he does not flinch;
> It is not the officers of the Czar but only the wind.
> Sleep, baby, soon you will join him.[103]

Such songs were inadequate recompense for an absent parent. Kate Simon, whose father had left when she was a baby, wrote, "I missed my father and looked for him constantly, behind doors, under tables, in the street."[104] Fannie C. also remembered feeling keen deprivation. "My childhood days were not happy ones, because my father was not with us. I always knew that I was lacking something that so many of my friends had—both their mother and father. And during the revolution, it was horrible!"

If husbands were in the United States, women had to use great resourcefulness to care for their families and often became more self-reliant in the process.[105] Hilda S. remembered that, in the postwar struggle between Russia and Poland, her "mother used to get up every single morning and go out in the market place to find out, what are we today? Are we Polish or are we Russian?" Unless they had parents or other relatives to rely upon, wives had to make a living themselves, even if they had never worked before, because their husbands' remittances could not get through to them. Some had the foresight to learn a trade. When Riva P.'s father was taken into the army, her mother worried about how to support her children and parents, Riva recalled, "so she went to millinery school and learned how to make hats." Others used their wits. With a husband and two sons in America, Fannie S.'s mother was stuck in Odessa when war erupted. Although she was untrained and had never worked, she joined forces with another woman to buy sweaters and other knit goods and sold them in the market.

Traditional skills enabled many women to make at least a meager living. Mollie Linker's mother, the pampered daughter of a middle-class family, was too proud to ask her parents for help and took up sewing to support her four children.[106] Some took in boarders, who sometimes bartered for their keep. The mother of Hilda S. also cared for lodgers, but hers were uninvited. After the revolution began, Red Army soldiers had requisitioned her house and wanted her to cook for them. With kosher meat all but unavailable, when they asked her to roast a pig they had killed, she swallowed her religious scruples and agreed to cook it if they gave some meat to her children, although she would take none for herself. The soldiers also gave her salt and other commodities to sell and sometimes drove her into the nearby city of Kiev to buy merchandise to peddle in town. Hilda was fifteen at the time and helped by operating a switchboard for the Red Army officers. The mother of Fannie K. moved to her brother's village and managed to feed her four small children by knitting socks and gloves and exchanging them with the peasants for food. When Fannie was only five, she made a shawl for which a peasant woman gave her mother forty pounds of wheat. "So we ate for a while on what I made," Fannie recalled, "but most of the time we were hungry." Frieda M.'s mother sewed aprons and bartered them to peasants for flour, and she also took her husband's place in his fish marketing business. The mother of Florence B. fled to Silesia with her six children, none older than ten, where she took shelter in an abandoned barracks and "earned a living at most anything she could get hold of. She picked raspberries and had us go around from house to house and sell baskets of berries. And sometimes she would mash and cook them to make jam. Sometimes she bought sugar on the black market to resell." Florence's evaluation of her mother's role during the war was equally true for many Jewish women who had to make do on their own: "She was very innovative, and she was determined to keep us together. Many families separated, but we stayed together."

Some young women were separated from their families during the war and thus had neither mother nor father to rely on. In 1914, at the age of ten, Jeanne S. and several of her friends fled from a group of Cossacks who came riding through her town. She recalled vividly that "they were right behind us in the woods on their horses." The children reached the nearby border of Austria-Hungary and were put on a train to Vienna where Jeanne's older sisters already lived. Because her sisters had no room for her, she spent the war years in a shelter for homeless girls. Frieda W., then seventeen, and her sister were working in Vilna when the war broke out, and they tried to make their way back home. With the little money they had, they bought such notions as combs, needles, and buttons and exchanged them with farmers along the way for bread. "And so we went back to our hometown," she recalled, "and we didn't find nothing. Our house was burnt. No parents. Then we got up and walked from one town to another. We walked and lived like that until 1918. Many times we didn't have food to eat. We used to try to get a couple of potatoes to eat and then we would walk further. Was really tough. Now I can never get enough to eat to make up for those years."

Despite the dislocations of war, daily life had to go on. Anna Kahan noted with surprise in her diary that despite an order posted on the city hall drafting all men younger than thirty-five, "some customers come in and order hats. And I thought the world was coming to an end. An hour ago I thought no one would think of such nonsense as buying hats."[107] Although many girls raised during the war had little real education, some mothers made sure that their children continued to learn, either from a tutor, or in school, if one was available. Ethel B.'s mother insisted that her daughters attend the local school, which managed to remain open during the war. Minna S. went to school for a while in her small town of Buczacz, but left because of the anti-Semitic taunts of Polish children and was tutored at home. Anna R. started school in the border city of Bialystok, but then, as she recalled, "they started to fight again, and the shells came over. So then when it was safe to go back again, after two or three months, there was no sign saying '*Russka Schola*,' [Russian School]—now it was '*Polska Schola*' [Polish School]. Then again they start to fight, and again the Germans take over the town. So no more '*Polska Schola*' but '*Deutsche Schule*' [German School]. Believe me, if we grew up, it's a miracle, what we got through in our life, our childhood. A miracle!"

Young Jewish girls and women who lived in Eastern Europe were thus growing up in a society in rapid flux. By the time of World War I, it was suitable, as it had not been a generation earlier, for even girls of a religious family to seek a secular education. Many daughters of working-class or enlightened middle-class families now expected to choose or at least have a voice in the selection of their husbands. Furthermore, the possibility of industrial work in the cities made it feasible for poor girls to work before marriage to enable them to save money for their dowries. From their mothers, who often managed to care for their children alone during the war, as well as from other women, daughters knew that women without men were not necessarily helpless. This, no doubt, aided the self-confidence of many. However, the desires awakened in the villages, shtetlach, and cities of Eastern Europe could not always be fulfilled there. The dislocations of war and hostility to Jews often made it difficult to get an education or a good job. The intellectual life some longed for was seldom available in a small town. Along with their husbands, brothers, and fathers, many young women and girls resolutely turned their faces toward the west to America, the "Golden Land," where they hoped to achieve their dream.

4

Leaving Home

I saw my father could not make a living. . . . And I was a big, robust girl, and I couldn't go out and work and earn a living there. I figured coming here, I'll be able to go to work and help the family, which I did.

—Louise C.

I will not bury my best years here. I must go to the big, wide world where I can learn and experience life. . . . I see myself in the United States, dressed neatly, walking to school with books in my hand.

—Anna Kahan[1]

That was our dream—in the small towns, almost everyone wanted to go. . . . All I could do was read books and dream, that's all. We didn't go to get rich, but we wanted to have a more rich life. We wanted to be on our own, to come to a big life, a big world.

—Fannie K.

*6. Awaiting money to join her husband in America,
a woman poses with her daughter.*

Collection of Diana Shapiro Bowstead

After the war ended in 1918, migration became a possibility once again. In addition to the poverty and economic discrimination of the prewar period, there were new reasons why Eastern Europe provided an unfriendly environment for Jews. The rising nationalism in Poland and the nations newly created out of the former Hapsburg Empire often manifested itself as anti-Semitism.[2] This was particularly true in areas of Eastern Europe where Jews had operated as middlemen between aristocracy and peasantry. In Russia, where the Bolshevik revolution might have been expected to improve the situation of Jews, civil war made life difficult, and the increased animosity toward Jews during the world conflict had convinced many that they had no future there.

Despite these hardships, the decision to leave, whether before or after the war, was almost always a painful one. Those who emigrated believed they had no alternative. Ties to their homes were strong—the father of Morris Raphael Cohen had gone to America several times in the 1880s, hoping to save enough to set up a business in his native Minsk. He finally gave up the struggle and had his family join him in New York.[3] Many of these early immigrants did, in fact, return to Russia.[4] Even when a young person longed to go to America, even among families who could afford to emigrate together, the sense of uprootedness was keen. Usually there were close relatives, often a father or mother, who could not or would not leave, and then the parting was particularly poignant, for chances of meeting again were slight. The father of Sophie Saroff, who attempted unsuccessfully to deter his daughter from emigrating, begged her at least to wait until he died before leaving. But Sophie refused; she knew that if she postponed her departure, she "would just be sitting there waiting for his death."[5] Tanya N., as a five-year-old child, remembered her mother and the family nursemaid, Maryushka, who had raised her mother and then Tanya—kissing and crying on each other's shoulders as they parted at the border. Ten-year-old Pearl Moscowitz was forced to remain behind for close to a year, her eyes infected with trachoma, when her parents and brothers and sisters left Poland for the United States. Shunted from relative to relative, she feared she would never see her family again. Unlike Tanya and Sophie, Pearl was eventually reunited with her loved ones. Once her eyes were cured, a relative and an agent helped her get transit to a German port, and from there to New York. She traveled alone at eleven years of age by pretending to be sixteen, the legal age.[6]

Some families left for unusual reasons. Frances F.'s parents were ostensibly assimilated and Christianized Russians, and so had been permitted to live in Omsk, a city in Siberia ordinarily forbidden to Jews.[7] When her mother became pregnant, a serious decision had to be made. If the baby was a boy, and they had him ritually circumcized—which was essential if he was to be considered a Jew—they would risk being denounced as secret Jews and forced to move into one of the crowded cities of the Pale. There was no future, so the solution was to go to the United States.

In a few cases, the original destination of emigrants was not America.[8] Louise C. became a Zionist and first left Russia to settle in Palestine. After two years of hard work on a kibbutz, she and her fiancé decided to seek a better life in the United States. Riva P. and her parents also made a double migration. They first fled east, via China, to Kobe, Japan, because her father, who was in the reserve, was in danger of being conscripted into the Russian army. They were unhappy in this alien environment, and although her mother wanted to return home, her father could not go back without being drafted. Somehow, through a business acquaintance, they located a sister who had left years before for New York, and when they received an invitation to stay with her, the family uprooted itself a second time. The parents of Sara B. also had another destination in mind. They emigrated first to Manchester, England, where one of Sara's brothers had gone earlier. But because of the damp climate and the death of two of Sara's siblings, her parents left for the United States. The mother of Hannah F. had a similar experience. She settled first in England with her four daughters and decided after two of them died that the United Kingdom was unlucky. She and the remaining children returned to Russia, and her husband later convinced her to set out for America.

Families who were less comfortable financially—the majority of emigrants—usually sent over a father or an older brother or sister to earn the money to equip an apartment and finance the passage of the others.[9] Most men left for America to avoid conscription, to improve their economic position, or to find a better life in general. The father of Pauline H., who had spent several years in Palestine, simply could not get accustomed to living once more in a small Russian town and decided to try the United States. Some men seeking a new life left their wives behind permanently. Such "grass widows" were trapped—deserted, but unable to marry again unless their husbands could be found and agree to give them a divorce. Generally, though, men departed with their wives' support and approval.

But sometimes a husband, fearing his wife's protests, left without telling her. Anna R.'s father was dissatisfied with his business, so he collected some money owed to him, and without saying a word, left for America. "He just took the money and went off because he knew my mother wouldn't do it," Anna explained. "He told a friend what he was going to do, and that as soon as possible, he would send for us—which he did, after he was here six months." Rose Schneiderman's father departed in the same way, also sending for his wife and children once he was settled.[10] The father of Frieda M. was another who "ran away" to America for fear of being recalled into the army, leaving his wife alone with two young children and pregnant with a third.

Women's attitudes toward uprooting themselves varied with the individual. As with pioneers heading for an unknown life in the American West, many married women seemed less willing to leave than their husbands because of attachments to familiar surroundings and extended families.[11] Marie Jastrow's mother dreaded leaving a mother and father behind in Serbia when her husband sent money for her to join him in New York. Yet the parents convinced Marie that "wives belonged where their husbands settled," and she reluctantly left.[12] Once a husband had made the first step, a wife had no option but to follow. Sometimes, though, the initiative to emigrate came from the wife. Nina S. told her husband that they had to leave because of her pregnancy, for war-torn Russia was no place to bring up children. This determined woman and her husband arrived in New York a week before the birth of their daughter. The mother-in-law of Anna R. decided to make the journey after her sister was killed in a pogrom. When her husband refused to pull up stakes, she went herself, taking her five-year-old son.

Often women made the trip by themselves or accompanied only by their children, and even if the journey was made by choice, the way was not always smooth. The mother of Hattie L. disliked New York and insisted on going back to Russia, five months pregnant and with three young children in tow. When her husband set up a home more to her liking in rural Connecticut, she agreed to return. Fannie N. and her mother, who left after the imposition of restrictions on immigration in 1921, heard that the Russian quota had been filled for that year. So they traveled to Poland and managed to board a cattle boat headed for Cuba, where they lived for a year until her father was able to bring them into the United States. While they were in Cuba, all quickly learned enough Spanish to make a living: her brother peddled and the mother hired a sewing machine so that she and Fannie could make underwear for a local factory.

Some young girls convinced their families to let them go to America by themselves. At eight years of age, Naomi L. began to nag her mother to send her to her father in New York. "The wanderlust was with me," she explained. Although she had older sisters who should have emigrated first to work and send money home, her father mailed a half-price ticket and

Naomi crossed the ocean alone with the ship's captain looking out for her welfare. Rachel Goldman's parents, impoverished during the war, had only enough money to send one of their three daughters to America. They "felt that somebody should be saved," Rachel recalled. "I was the strongest of the children, and after a great deal of debate they decided that they would permit me to go, and I left home shortly after my sixteenth birthday."[13] The family of Dora G. had to make a similar choice. They were very poor and considered sending her father and an older brother to America to improve the family's situation. But most Jews were aware that while *di goldene medina* offered economic opportunities, it also provided a less religious environment for Jews than their home in Eastern Europe. "How can he go?" demanded Dora's brother, "He's so religious—how could he go and see his children smoking on *Shabbes* and not going to shul when it's time for them to daven two times a day? They can't keep kosher like we keep kosher—it will kill him quicker." So thirteen-year-old Dora left instead to get a job and live with her father's brother and sister-in-law.

Like Dora, many young women came to America to get work and send money home to help their parents. Louise C. saw no alternative to leaving: "I left home," she recalled, "because I saw my father could not make a living. I had two brothers who were Talmudic students, they went to yeshivas. My sister was seven years older, but she was not well. And I was a big, robust girl, and I couldn't go out and work and earn a living there. I figured coming here, I'll be able to go to work and help the family, which I did." Bella Hyman also emigrated alone at fifteen to earn the money to bring over her parents and younger brothers.[14] Such immigrants had no illusions of finding gold in the streets; what they sought was a job.

Motives for departing often were mixed. While Louise obviously hoped to help her parents, she also longed to get away from home. Her father had been very strict, and, she observed, "It was very hard to live in a family, with eleven children, where there was a lot of want and needs and no way to help yourself." Hilda S. also had different reasons for going to America. Leaving for a short trip, ostensibly to bring the baby of a dead cousin to the infant's grandmother in Oklahoma, she took with her only her one dress and pair of shoes, a coat, and an extra set of underwear. But Hilda never returned. She had dreamed of living in America, where she expected life to be more interesting, and she convinced her parents to let her stay and work to bring them over.

Sometimes the need to work to help the family meant that other ambitions had to be held in abeyance. When Anna Kahan was thirteen years old, she hoped to attend school in America. "My fantasy," she wrote at the time, "paints such beautiful pictures for me in America . . . I will not stay in Siedlce," she vowed. "I will not bury my best years here. I must go to the big, wide world where I can learn and experience life. . . . I see myself in the United States, dressed neatly, walking to school with books in my hand."[15] But as the family's economic fortunes declined during the war, the reality of what her life would be like asserted itself. "Two years ago when we began talking about emigration," she wrote,

> I was sure that in the new country I'll have a chance to study, to make something of myself. . . . Now all I can think of is work, work in a factory or in a shop, work hard enough or long enough to earn enough money to pull my dear ones out of the pit. Brokhe [her sister] has no trade. Although I am younger, the responsibility falls on me. . . . I must provide for her and myself and for our parents and the smaller children. When I think of the coming winter with its lack of bread and fuel, I see a bottomless abyss, and I shudder. And we, Brokhe and I, over there, their only hope. . . . How can I at this time think of myself?[16]

Unless the girls went to America, the family would have no food after another three months. "This is our only hope," her father told them. Since her sister was sickly, Anna, as the strong-minded and healthy one, knew that her dreams of education had to be put aside.

Other young women left openly to help themselves rather than to assist their families. Elizabeth Hasanovitz wanted to go to America to work and thus better herself. Her parents felt that she would be degraded by taking a job, and only a hunger strike convinced them to let her go. "I do not want to waste my life," she remembered thinking. "I am tired of being condemned to eternal limitations."[17] Ruth R. also saw no future for herself in her small town. "My mother demanded from me," she recalled.

> She needed help. She said I wasn't doing enough. And since I could not justify how much I was doing, I had to escape from the house. And I found a way to convince them that I got to learn a trade, because I would like to go to America.
>
> I already heard talk between my father and my mother. They knew there was no future for a man with five girls, that they had no money for dowries, there was no chance. So I convinced my parents that I'm grown up enough to learn a trade and I went to a seamstress to learn how to sew. And when I'll come to the United States, I'll be able to work. I was about nine and a half or ten by that time.

> Now that I'm a candidate for the United States, I was only too anxious to get away from the family. The only thing that amazes me is that I had no sympathy for the other kids. I can't understand why. No wonder my mother was angry at me. They were always crying, and I had my own selfish life to dream about.

Yet despite her "selfish" dreams, Ruth helped her family by traveling back and forth from Poland to Russia during the war to get supplies like linen and cod liver oil that were unavailable at home.

Like Ruth, other poor young women emigrated to avoid the fate of being married off and consigned to a life of poverty, or to avoid the possibility of not being able to marry at all because their families lacked money for a dowry.[18] Girls knew that in the United States, young people were free to wed for love. As one popular song went, "In America . . . when a fellow loves his girl, he marries her without a penny!"[19] Jennie S. did not want to marry the butcher's son or someone she felt was beneath her. Sarah Reznikoff also turned down all prospective bridegrooms and hoped to improve her life by emigrating to the United States.[20] Rose Pesotta decided to follow her sister to America, where "a decent, middle class girl can work without disgrace." She saw no future for herself in Russia "except to marry some young man returned from his four years of military service and be a housewife. That," she stated flatly, "is not enough."[21] Fannie Edelman, one of six daughters, watched her sisters married off, some against their will, to men their father had chosen for them. "If a sister of mine said she did not like the bridegroom," she recalled, "that meant nothing. My father was a stern man and we feared him. . . . I was nearly sixteen, and I began to fear that one fine day my father would come home with some ready-made human merchandise for me. I therefore began to think more and more frequently about America—where I saw my only refuge."[22]

A few daughters like Fannie left for America specifically because of their father's repressiveness. Rae K. ran away because she couldn't live with a father who forbade her to see "liberal" friends and opposed her desire to get an education. Etta Byer left home at thirteen when her father beat her for refusing to act as a spy among fellow workers in her sister's cigarette factory.[23]

Many young women, though, had loving families and chose to emigrate because they longed for something they believed they could find only in America. "Everyone knew about the United States," Fannie K. reminisced. "That was our dream—in the small towns, almost everyone wanted to go. In a small town, there was nothing to do. All I could do was read books and dream, that's all. We didn't go to get rich, but we wanted to have a more rich life. We wanted to be on our own, to come to a big life, a big world." Her feelings were echoed by Jennie S., who also felt stifled in her small town: "Like it came Saturday, Sunday," she recalled,

> there was no holiday in your home. Saturday you go from one neighbor to the other, and that's all you do. I sat and sat and there's nothing else to do. There was no work even for girls. Whenever I used to visit my uncle in the city, I envied the girls. They dressed up in hats, and they go out. It was a dull life, very dull.
>
> Then one day I thought to myself, "I want to go to America." I had to fight. I didn't eat, I didn't sleep. I was fighting to death for the money to go to America. I used to see the people going to the train to leave. I used to envy those people like anything. They said, "You'll get married and then you'll go to America." I says, "I need a shlepper to America? I can shlep myself!" Who didn't want to go to America?

Sonia O. summed up these feelings of longing: "Somehow there was a feeling in the air. And maybe there was a little romance in me, so I decided, whatever it is, I have to go." She persuaded her reluctant father to give his permission and set out alone at age nineteen.

Sometimes, girls had other ambitions to fulfill. If they were leaving as children, America was the land where fantasy reigned. Frieda M. looked forward to going to the fabled country where gold grew on trees, and Mildred L. expected to find money in the streets. Sometimes their dreams could be achieved: Mildred had always gone barefoot and she looked forward to getting her first pair of shoes in America. Minna S. remembered dreaming constantly of seeing her father again. Although most older girls went either to work or to try to get an education, some had more specific goals in mind. Jeanne S. had left her parents' home in a small town in Galicia when she was ten, during the war, and lived in a home for girls in Vienna. She wrote to an aunt in New York for a ticket to the United States, where she intended to achieve her dream of becoming a doctor. Frieda W.'s desires were more basic. She and her sister had been separated from their parents early in the war and spent the following years trading, begging, and scrounging for enough food to stay alive. Her dream of America was of a bountiful place where she would never be hungry again.

Despite differing reasons for deciding to leave home for America, most young women who departed alone went with parents' permission to emigrate—a vote of confidence in their daughters' ability to manage on their own in a strange new country. Some, like Anna Kahan, left with their mothers' and fathers' encouragement and blessing. Others, like Sonia O. or Sophie Saroff, had to fight to win approval, for parents were afraid they would never see their daughters again. Yet her father had confidence, Sonia recalled, that she would do the right thing and not bring shame on the family. He had just heard about the mass deaths in the fire at the Triangle Shirtwaist Company factory, and his only fear was that she might have to work in such a dangerous place. Naomi L. had convinced her mother to permit her to cross the ocean alone when she was eight to go to her father in New York, and the parents of Jeanne S. also permitted their fifteen-year-old daughter to travel by herself to live with an aunt in Brooklyn. The mother of Ruth R., who would sorely miss her assistance in their home, nevertheless encouraged her to escape their poverty-stricken existence for a new opportunity in the United States.

This confidence expressed by parents in daughters, combined with the responsibilities the young girls had fulfilled in their homes—their premature adulthood, as one woman called it—could not help but lead to a sense of self-sufficiency on the part of these young people who emigrated by themselves.[24] This characteristic was one that would stand them in good stead in the urban, industrial society they were heading for.

These women joined the 2 million Jews—men, women, and children—who left their homes in Eastern Europe between 1881 and 1924 to seek a better life in a new land. Worsening political and economic conditions, periodic waves of pogroms, and fear of a lengthy conscription had all contributed to the desire to emigrate.[25] But not all Jews wanted to leave. Religious leaders, professionals, the rich, the acculturated, and many of those who were unwilling to make the religious compromises they knew America would require remained at home. What attracted most dissatisfied Jews to America, however, was news from friends or relatives who had gone before of the opportunities available in *di goldene medina*. Thus, eight out of ten emigrants headed for the United States.[26] Those who left saw no future if they remained, and almost all of them intended to make America their permanent home, unlike some members of other national groups and even an earlier generation of Russian Jewish emigrants, who hoped to earn money in the United States and then return to their native land.[27] And just as great masses of people were making this crucial decision to leave home, cheap, improved transportation, the work of Jewish refugee committees in Germany and Russia, and easier movement across borders made the journey more feasible than it had been before.[28]

Because Jews came mainly as families and intended to remain in America, almost half of them were women, although among other immigrant

7. *Brothers and sisters who emigrated to the United States.*
Collection of Rita Riman

groups, females numbered only about a third.[29] Jews coming to Ellis Island had the largest proportion of any group reporting no occupation. This also reflected the large number of wives and children brought over, for even if married women had contributed to the family's finances, they would generally not describe themselves as having an occupation unless they held a steady job.[30] One of every four Jews was a young child, twice the rate among other immigrants,[31] so each working man or woman would have to support non-wage-earning family members to a greater extent than adults in other ethnic groups.[32]

Those who left were probably poorer than many who stayed behind, but they tended to be more literate. Young people emigrated in the greatest numbers, and this generation, growing up in mainly urban areas, had more access to schools than their elders. Eighty percent of Jewish men who entered the United States between 1908 and 1912 could read and write, although the census of 1897 indicates that only 67 percent of those in Russia could do so. While Jews generally were better educated than their Christian neighbors in Eastern Europe, Jewish women were considerably less educated than men—fully 36.8 percent of female immigrants arriving between 1908 and 1912 were illiterate, almost twice the rate for males. The large difference in literacy rates between men and women reflects the relative importance given the education of boys and girls in Jewish families. Nevertheless, women had obviously made large gains in the preceding years, for in 1897, 67.2 percent of Jewish women twenty and above had not been able to read and write.[33]

On several levels, the journey to America could be taxing, if not perilous. When the war ended, some women attempted to travel from Russia, still enmeshed in civil strife, to Poland, to try to contact their husbands and rejoin them in the United States. Florence B.'s mother went for help to a local official, and Florence remembered her uncle's asking how she had the courage to approach him. Her mother answered, "Well, I lay down on the floor and he stepped on me, but I got my request." Women leaving to join their husbands usually had to arrange to sell their homes, furniture, and whatever belongings they could not take with them. At each step of the trip, unscrupulous predators hoped to take advantage of their situation. The mother of Rose Cohen was deceived into parting with her cherished feather pillows, linens, and brass candlesticks in Hamburg for a pittance after hearing a rumor that immigrants to America could bring no luggage apart from what they could carry.[34] Fannie K.'s mother, aware of such potential dangers, "sold the house, and she took the gold and gave it to a shoemaker to put it into the heel of our shoes, that we should be able to bring it to Poland, or else they would take it away from us. They never searched us children." The mother of Frieda M., still ill from the effects of typhoid fever,[35] had the presence of mind to bake her silver cups into breads. "Though she was not well," Frieda explained, "she knew enough to escape."

Women had to be prepared to face even more serious dangers than loss of the family's belongings. When Frieda and her mother stayed overnight at a farm on the way to the border, a bandit group entered and tried to abduct an eighteen-year-old girl cousin traveling with them.[36] "And my mother stood in front of her and wouldn't let her go," Frieda recalled. "They were going to kill my mother, but just then Red Army soldiers came in." The border was another possible danger point. Rose Cohen remembered her own fear when she and her mother were driven over the Russian border in a cart as "bags of flour" once the guards had been bribed.[37] The guards were so poorly paid, Tanya N. observed, that they could be bribed to turn the other way with "a pair of socks and a couple of apples." But one never knew for certain.

Emigrants knew that the life they were heading for would be very different from the one they were leaving behind. Many were aware that it would be difficult to maintain religious practices as they could in Eastern Europe, despite the problems of life there. Rabbis warned them to stay at home lest they endanger their immortal souls.[38] One such disillusioned immigrant bluntly urged religious men to remain where they were. If they came to America, nothing would be left "save dressing in black, wrapping . . . in shrouds, and rolling from darkness to the abyss."[39] The mother and grandmother of Jennie H., like many pious people, refused to leave with her because they believed it impossible to be a proper Jew in the "Golden Land." Jennie's mother used to tell her, "In America, even the stones are *treyf* [impure]." Upon hearing that Rose Cohen and her mother were going to join Rose's father in the United States, a malicious neighbor tormented the girl with the inevitable transformation she foresaw. "You who will not break a thread on the sabbath now," she told Rose, "will eat swine in America. . . . The first thing men do in America is cut their beards," she grumbled, "and the first thing the women do is leave off their wigs."[40] "The new world is a world turned upside down," observed an orthodox immigrant. "People walk on their heads in Columbus' land, not on their feet."[41] Most who decided to emigrate knew that some compromises would have to be made. On the train going to the port city of Danzig on the way to join her husband in the United States, Anna R.'s mother threw her *sheitel* out the window. "In America, they don't wear these," she told her daughter.

For young women traveling without families, there could be more immediate dangers. Urbanization had brought with it a concomitant increase in
crime and organized prostitution. Rising profits from the business of sup-
plying young women to the brothels of urban centers in Eastern Europe,
the Near East, and Latin America had encouraged procurers to entrap
unwary young women newly arrived in the cities.[42] Many of these traffick-
ers and prostitutes were Jews, particularly from Russia, Rumania, and the
poverty-stricken province of Galicia, and fully half the prostitutes in Buenos Aires in 1909 were Jewish.[43] Folk songs warned young women of the
pitfalls awaiting them if they left their parents' homes. "You took me away
from my mother's house and promised me precious things," went one song.
"But instead, you brought me to Buenos Aires and made a loose woman out
of me."[44] While some were driven into prostitution by poverty, many others
were seduced or raped, and once "ruined," a girl had little option but to
accept her fate.

Few of these young women were as fortunate as Hilda S. and her sister,
who survived to tell of their escape from "white slavery." At the ages of
seventeen and twenty-one, they were on their way to the United States with
two other young women from their town. When they arrived at the train
station in Warsaw, they were met by a *droshky*, a carriage whose driver
agreed to take them to the address of a relative. After a long trip, they
arrived at a house, where they immediately became suspicious:

> We came in, the door is open, and there's a houseful of people, at three
> o'clock in the morning! There are mattresses all over the floors—boys,
> girls, and whatever. So we ask for our relative and they say, "He's
> asleep. You'll see him in the morning. Why wake him up? Wouldn't
> you like something to eat and drink?" We looked at each other and we
> were frightened. My sister and the other girl said, "Something is fishy
> here. Don't eat anything, don't drink anything, and don't get un-
> dressed."
>
> We huddled—all of us got into a corner. And whatever they said to
> us, we said, "We want to see that man." We never saw the relative. So
> my sister and the other girl said, "We're going to try to get away to get
> help. All of a sudden a young man comes over and takes my hands in
> his and says, "Oh, you have such beautiful hands." And I grabbed my
> hands away and said, "Don't touch me!"
>
> It got light and my sister and the other girl weren't there. Then the
> bell rings and my sister walks in with the other girl and—I'll never
> forget his name—a Mr. Rosenthal, a reporter from a daily Jewish

paper in Warsaw and a policeman. When my sister and her friend ran out of the house, they asked people where there was a Jewish organization, and they sent them to the Jewish paper. They got this reporter and they got the police and they arrested three or four of them!

It was in the papers. It was a place where they took the girls and they sent them into white slavery! This is exactly what it was. They were going to send us to South America!

Even when the trip to the port was less traumatic, the impersonal examination before embarkation[45] could prove frightening. Fannie C., only nine years old at the time, recalled this experience vividly. "We arrived in Dansk," she related,

> and the things that they subjected us to were unbelievable. At that time there was an epidemic of some sort, so they shaved all the women's heads, including my mother's. And this to me was the most awful—it was an experience I shall never forget, because I had a beautiful head of hair as a child—all curls. And when I took a look at myself in the mirror, I became hysterical. And they deloused us in the nude and did horrible things. It was just awful. And by the time we reached the boat, anything that would come along just didn't matter any more, because I was already so terribly upset.

Twelve-year-old Mary Antin described in her diary the terrors of being bathed. "No wonder," she wrote,

> if in some minds stories arose of people being captured by robbers, murderers and the like. Here we had been taken to a lonely place where only that house was to be seen; our things were taken away, our friends separated from us; a man came to inspect us . . . ; ourselves driven into a little room where a great kettle was boiling . . . : our clothes taken off, our bodies rubbed with a slippery substance that might be any bad thing; a shower of warm water let down on us without warning; again driven to another little room where we sit, wrapped in woolen blankets . . . , and we see only a cloud of steam, and hear the women's orders to dress ourselves,—"Quick! Quick!" . . . We are forced to pick out our clothes from among all the others, with the steam blinding us; we choke, cough, entreat the women to give us time; they persist, "Quick! Quick!—or you'll miss the train!"—Oh, so we really won't be murdered! They are only making us ready for the continuing of our journey, cleaning us of all suspicions of dangerous sickness. Thank God![46]

The sea journey itself, usually in steerage, could be unpleasant, or it could even be a welcome change, depending upon the age and temperament of the girl and the circumstances of the voyage. For young children traveling with their parents, the trip was often a great adventure. Some remembered with delight the constant diet of herring and potatoes that others complained of not being able to eat. Hilda S., after escaping abduction in Warsaw, also had an enjoyable passage. She and her sister were bringing a baby left with their family to its grandmother, and because of the child, they were the recipients of a dizzying array of foodstuffs from other passengers and the crew. Hilda never said no to any offer, no matter how imperfectly she understood it. One day, after saying yes to a crew member's question asked in an unknown language, she was delighted when he tossed into her lap a linen napkin containing a hot, roasted chicken, a welcome change from herring and potatoes. Her memories of the trip were not all pleasant, however. One young woman was raped by another passenger, and the night before the ship arrived at New York, a sad-looking Polish woman with two small children killed herself. Her husband had been in America for several years, and she was coming to him pregnant with another man's baby.

Anna R. remembered another potential danger of the passage. When she and her mother, along with her brother and sister, left to join their father, they encountered frightening weather conditions in midocean. "All the elements got together and had a fight," she related,

> and the captain of the ship came down to the steerage and he says, "Twenty years have I manned this ship, but never have I seen such a storm. I tell you, people of any religion, pray to your gods because we're in danger."
>
> I remember there was a bench where we were, our whole family. My mother took that bench and turned it upside down—she may have had some rope and tied it to something. She told us, "Come, my children. If we're going down, let us all go down together." And we got into that bench space and held each other. We all held each other, ready to go down, because that's what the captain of the ship said. And my brother gets sick right there and then. And someone says, "If he dies, we have to throw him in the ocean."
>
> And I remember now that all the people took out their crosses, and all the Jewish men put on their *tfiln* [prayer phylacteries], and it was one of those goodby-to-the-world scenes. We are going. So it was a disaster.

In another fierce storm, Anna Kahan was afraid that her parents' hopes for survival might sink with her on the wave-battered vessel. She remembered that she heard a great noise and woke with a jolt. Anna and her sister feared that they were sinking. "The water was over my ankles," she recalled, "and the place was filled with women and children and all the passengers from the steerage. And they were all screaming. Sailors were rushing through, and some of them helped the women dress the children. I was so exhausted I just stood there and leaned against the wall. And I prayed, 'God save us. It's not just us—it's the entire family, the entire family. We left five people behind.'" Even in the midst of such a crisis, her thought was for the responsibility she bore her parents.

Both ships obviously survived the storms, but the young women's experiences in the new world had just begun. For all those who had made the difficult decision to leave their old country, the journey was only the first step. America lay before them.

5

Reunions
and New
Beginnings

*When I came here, within a day, it was as
if we had never been separated. It was the
most amazing thing!*

—*Ethel B.*

*I just didn't know how to cope with it all. I
was unhappy because I didn't understand
the language. . . . Here, I didn't know
anything, and I was frightened. . . . When
they used to call me names like
"greenhorn," I felt that I would rather die
than hear it again. There were times I
wished that they would send me back to
my grandfather. That I would have rather
been without my parents than be here.*

—*Fannie C.*

8. Hester Street, New York.
Library of Congress

Ellis Island. The scene is etched in memory—the long-anticipated reunion of husband and wife, parents and children, brothers and sisters. The lucky ones, with some money, had been able to emigrate together, and for these, the transition to America would be less disruptive of family life. But the majority could not afford such a luxury. More often, a father or an older brother or sister had left first and sent money home for other family members to join them, sometimes one at a time, like a chain. After months or years of separation, they were together again. For many, it was a dream come true, and family life resumed as if no interruption had occurred.

For others, the reunion was a difficult one, no matter how fervently desired. Abraham Cahan, in his short story "Yekl," describes the plight of a young immigrant who prided himself on being "a real American." The wife he has reluctantly sent for after three years of separation seems dowdy and unfashionable compared to women he has met in New York. He cannot adjust to her old-country ways, or even to being a husband again, and the marriage ends in divorce.[1] This was not an uncommon problem: one man wrote for advice to the Socialist newspaper *Wahrheit*, for he feared he could no longer love the wife he had not seen for so long.[2] Wives, too, had to overcome a sense of strangeness. Hutchins Hapgood, a contemporary observer, noted that literary sketches in Jewish newspapers often told how shocked immigrant women were at the change a few years in America had made in the character of their husbands.[3]

Sometimes, women or children felt disoriented after leaving their homes and suffering the trials of the journey and the bustling impersonality of Ellis Island. Rahel Mittelstein recalled the trauma of her arrival in the United States, when she and her family had to remain on the island for several days.

> Ellis Island in Russian is called the "Island of Tears," and in every way it merited the name. We all cried. Every immigrant who was sent to the Island spent at least the first day in tears. We cried because of fear and disappointment. We had come a long way: we had sold everything we had and spent every cent, and now we were afraid of being sent back. We had much to be disappointed about. . . . We were treated like prisoners and with as much sternness and contempt. We marched to bed and we marched to eat our supper; and as we marched, we were counted by people who evidently did not know how to smile. All the way to America, we were scrubbed, cleaned, and examined by physicians and now dirt and squalor seemed everywhere. We had no sheets

of any kind and the blankets we used we found piled up on the floor
. . . there was no place to take a bath, . . . wash.

   As for the people in charge of us, they seemed to regard us as some
sort of inferior beings.[4]

Most family reunions were less dramatic than Yekl's, the trauma less
profound. But relationships were seldom the same as they had been. A
woman accustomed to a relatively stable life in Eastern Europe might be
thrust into a strange environment where she found herself totally dependent upon a husband or oldest child who appeared completely Americanized and incomprehensible. Daughters or sons who had brought their
parents over were no longer children, but the major wage earners in the
family. They would be less willing to alter their lives to accord with a
parent's desire—to stop spending some of their wages on clothing or going
out dancing with friends. A husband who had been in America for several
years, even if he had not become an irreligious playboy like Yekl, had to
become reacquainted with a wife who was often herself quite different from
the woman he had left behind. Very young children, sometimes with no
memory of their fathers, had to learn to live with a strange man. Time apart
had created differences, and only time together could determine the new
family relationships that would emerge in the United States.

   Usually, children weathered the journey well and looked forward eagerly
to being reunited with a father remembered only dimly, if at all. When Rose
G. met her father for the first time at Ellis Island, she was delighted, for she
now had the parent she had always missed. Ethel B., who had been
unhappy about leaving her grandmother and aunt behind in Europe,
nevertheless had a joyous reunion with her father. "When I came here,
within a day," she recalled, "it was as if we had never been separated. It was
the most amazing thing." In the seven years that her husband was in
America, the mother of Minna S. constantly described him as an extraordinary man, and Minna learned to love her father even before they met.
When she and her mother were finally able to rejoin him, he had not yet
received the telegram that they were arriving at Ellis Island. So he was
not there, and young Minna felt that his absence was a "great tragedy."
"Everybody's father came but not my father," she recalled, "and I cried. I
remember my mother saying that I wouldn't cry as much at her funeral,
because papa meant so much to me. And he always did."

   Members of a family sometimes had different reactions to the reunion,
depending upon their expectations. Rose W.'s father had left seven years
before, and her mother had described him as he was then—a beautiful

young man. His orthodoxy prohibited the taking of photographs, and when his wife and daughters rejoined him in America, they found a prematurely aged man, sick, with white hair and a long, white beard. Rose's mother was shocked, and her sister, anticipating seeing the young father she remembered, was devastated. Rose, however, was simply glad to have a father. And since she hadn't known him before, she had no particular preconceptions.

Being the youngest child was often an advantage. Rose's father made a great fuss over her because he had never seen her, and they could start a new relationship unencumbered by the past. Frieda M., the second of three daughters, remembered family stories that if one of the children died before they could be reunited with their father, he hoped it would be neither his oldest, most precious child, nor the youngest, who was born after he had left. "So it would have been me," recalled Frieda with amusement, "and I became his favorite."

Many fathers, however, could not live up to childhood memories or the fantasies children had created in their absence. Rose Cohen was disappointed that her pious parent had cut his earlocks and shaved his beard, and she learned to her dismay that he now carried money on the Sabbath.[5] Fannie G., an infant when her father left, could not get used to him once the family was together again. Minna S. also had great expectations of her father. While he was in the United States, she and her mother lived with a tyrannical aunt, and Minna imagined him rescuing them and showering her with affection. When he finally sent for them, he turned out to be little better than the aunt. "I was used to being disappointed fairly early," she concluded sadly.

Fathers could also be resented because of the attention they received from mothers who until the reunion had devoted themselves entirely to their children. Fannie C., whose father had been gone for six of her nine years, remembered her ambivalent feelings. Although she looked forward to having a father once more, she was fearful of seeing him again at Ellis Island. "I was not sure that I would recognize him," she recalled. "Would I like him? Would he like me? All these things which crossed my mind made me miserable." Most important, though, Fannie "was terribly jealous of the attention that my father paid to my mother. And I felt that I was going to take second place. Here I was, the light of her life, and now here was this strange man taking her attention away. I was very, very unhappy. And many times, unbeknown to my mother, I cried myself to sleep." Hannah F., who was only two weeks old when her father left Eastern Europe, described her childhood anger with him in much the same way. "I was afraid of him," she recalled. "I used to sleep with my mother when I was a baby. And here comes this strange man who took my place in bed and I'm left in the cold." Later, Hannah learned to love and appreciate her father, but at the time, she felt resentful that "he took my mother away from me, and I was on my own."

Some daughters later realized that both of their parents had a lot of adjusting to do. After living alone for years, fathers suddenly had to accommodate to the demands of a family, with children who often were like strangers to them. "My father really did not know how to manage with a family," observed Dora W., trying to explain her strife-ridden home. Fannie K. understood how hard it was for her father to deal with his teenage children and wife after twelve years of separation. He was accustomed to going out whenever and wherever he liked without telling his wife when he would return. Fannie's mother cured his bachelor habit by turning the tables. To teach him a lesson, she went out one evening and didn't have his dinner ready. "From then on," recalled Fannie, "he stuck to the house, and he liked her."

Other problems of adjustment were not as easily solved. Rose Chernin's mother found herself unable to deal with her early years in the United States. Her husband never took her out, she had no one to speak with, and she was soon overwhelmed. The country that seemed like paradise to her children was a living hell for this unfortunate woman. She suspected her husband of loving another woman and drank kerosene in an attempt to kill herself. "Nobody cared about her and papa hated her," Rose recalled. "From the time we came to this country it was unmitigated misery in our home."[6] The family of Frieda M. also proved unable to heal the breach caused by the passage of time. Frieda's mother, who had been ill with typhoid fever during the war, had metamorphosed from an attractive young woman into a prematurely old lady with emaciated limbs, a flat chest, and a big stomach. Frieda remembered getting on the train in Poland to leave for the United States and hearing relatives say of her parents, "If he lives with her, he's an angel." When she and her mother arrived at Ellis Island, her father must have been shocked at seeing his wife so transformed, but, as Frieda surmised, "He was so goddamn honorable that he stuck to his bargain." The mother was jealous, the father resentful. "It was not," she concluded, "a happy home." Many men were less "honorable." More husbands deserted their wives in America because of strains caused by the long separation than left because of the hardships of life here.[7]

Rose S. summed up the feelings of strangeness and alienation experienced by many immigrants after they joined relatives who had been here for years. When Rose and her mother arrived, she explained,

> I wanted to go home, and so did she. Oh, how we wanted to go home! She came to two sons, and she didn't know them. They were away for eleven years. At Ellis Island, these two young men came up and stood right next to us. We don't know who they are, they don't know who we are. That's a terrible thing. They spoke English, they were married, they have children, and you can't visualize those things when you think, "Oh, I haven't seen them for eleven years, but when I see them I'll recognize them." It's not always the case. It was soft living, and it was a nice home. But it was so lonely for my mother. And that made me closer to my mother than ever before because she felt that all she has is me. She was the only link that I had with my family because they were strangers to me.

For such families, the distance between those who had come first and the ones who followed years later was too great to be bridged by time. As Dora W. put it, "Our family life was disrupted in Europe, and we just couldn't get it together again."

Despite such difficulties, the family remained the major element of stability in this strange and unpredictable land. The vast majority of Jews lived in family units,[8] and regardless of the problems of adjustment many of them faced, the family was the heart of immigrant life and crucial to the survival of many of its members.[9] Even the focus of religious practice, which in Europe was the synagogue, shifted subtly from the house of worship to the home.[10] As Irving Howe recalled his own childhood, it seemed to him that "the family remained the center of life. Sometimes the family was about all that was left of Jewishness; or, more accurately, all that we had left of Jewishness had come to rest in the family. Jewishness flickered to life on Friday night, with a touch of Sabbath ceremony a few moments before dinner; it came radiantly to life during Passover, when traditional dignities shone through its ritual. Our parents clung to family life as if that was their one certainty: everything else seemed frightening, alien, incomprehensible."[11]

Letters to the "Bintel Brief," a column in the popular Yiddish newspaper the *Forward*, revealed tenacious attempts to restore family solidarity threatened by the problems assailing immigrants. Husbands worried about how taking a boarder would affect their wives,[12] how freer relations between young people would affect their daughters, and how their wives' demands for more money would affect the peace of their homes. Women complained of husbands who wore them down or deserted, who would not permit them to attend night school, who came home drunk or refused to take jobs that would support their families. Mothers and fathers complained of children too Americanized to understand their parents, of sons and daughters who abandoned the religious beliefs they cherished. Young men and women wrote of fights with parents over going out on dates or freedom to live their own lives.[13] Above all, these people sought some way to resolve the conflicts threatening to disrupt their families.

Besides the family, immigrants had few resources to help them cope with the new world around them. They wrote to the "Bintel Brief" in part because traditional sources offered little guidance. The authority of the rabbi had already eroded in sections of Eastern Europe, but in this country his influence was almost nonexistent.[14] Even the synagogue, that rock of Jewish culture, had changed when it crossed the Atlantic Ocean. Although synagogues proliferated on the Lower East Side, in this country they never became centers of learning and prestige. Instead, they served a social purpose in helping new immigrants to adapt and still maintain some sense of being Jewish.[15] Thus, the newcomers had to face great uncertainty in understanding how to live their lives here. Not only their customs and language, but even their values were in question. Instead of tradition, religion, and learning, America seemed to respect money alone, or as one contemporary observer put it, "the only thing of value in this country is almighty Mammon."[16]

Even Jews who came from the cities or towns of Eastern Europe had to adjust to a new way of living, for life in Odessa or Bialystok could hardly prepare them for New York. "It was more than a geographical transition," wrote one historian, "it was a quantum leap."[17] In sheer size—the height of its buildings and the great numbers of people living cheek by jowl on the Lower East Side—it was unlike anything they had seen. Tens of thousands of Jews settled in the densely populated tenth ward, where more than seven hundred people lived in each acre, surrounded by 60 cigar shops, 172 garment shops, 65 factories, and 34 laundries.[18] The whole area hummed with the sound of sewing machines in the shops and resounded to the clash of political debates in the meeting halls and coffee shops. It was at once exciting and frightening. The Yiddish novelist David Ignatow pictured the Lower East Side of New York as a terrible storm that threatened to engulf the new immigrants and tear them apart. "Buses and trolleys rushed through the streets with devilish force," he wrote. "Waves of people pounded the streets, their faces like foam. The immigrants came to feel a sense of fright before the weight of these massed streets. It was all wild, all inconceivable."[19]

Great contradictions seemed to exist side by side. Most striking to the newcomers was the hardship amidst wealth. When David Levinsky, newly arrived in New York, saw an evicted family on the sidewalk, he marveled at the quality of the furniture surrounding them. In Levinsky's birthplace it would have been a sign of prosperity. "But then anything was to be expected," he surmised, "of a country where the poorest devil wore a hat and starched collar."[20] America was obviously very rich, even if the streets weren't paved with gold. But while a few prospered, most worked hard and just managed to make ends meet. As Tanya N. noted, this was a place to get rich, but *her* family got poor. Here there was freedom, but little time to make use of it. Elizabeth Hasanovitz, who worked as a shopgirl, mused on this irony. "In Russia," she observed, there was "time, but no freedom; here I had freedom, but no opportunity to enjoy it . . . I was made to work hard for a mere existence. And where was there time for the free schools, for more knowledge, where was there time for the wonderful libraries, for the luxurious museums? Where was the opportunity to rejoice in all the blessings of this free country?"[21]

Life for most was difficult and uncertain. The shtetl system of bartering, the possibility of growing some of one's food, were not possible in the tenements. You had to pay for everything, as Rose Cohen's neighbor had warned her—for "the rent . . . for the light, for every potato, every grain of barley."[22] Labor in the sweatshops was arduous, and the work, relying as it did on seasonal employment, was insecure. Although most Jewish men had not worked on the Sabbath in Eastern Europe, here only 25 percent of them were able to find jobs not requiring them to work on Saturdays.[23] Sixty percent of Jewish-owned shops had to remain open to do business on this holy day.[24] Still worse, often a man's wages were insufficient to support his family. Before 1925, at least $800 a year was needed to support a family of five, while in 1915, the average wage of industrial workers was only $670. More than half of working-class families thus had to rely on the income brought in by children or wives as well as husbands.[25] With fathers, sons, and daughters all going off to work and returning at different times, family life suffered disruption because of the difficulty of coming together for even one common meal during the day.[26]

Frequently, home was a dark dumbbell tenement, where four families shared a toilet and only one in eight apartments had running water.[27] Privacy was virtually unknown, a bedroom to oneself an unthinkable luxury. Ida Richter remembered sleeping on a black couch near the stove.

"'Course I used to get a headache once in a while from the gas fumes," she recalled, "but who cared? Everybody was so busy keeping alive."[28] If a young woman emigrated alone she might find a temporary home with relatives. This gave no assurance of comfort or security. Jennie H. shared a couch with another girl in her future husband's cousin's home. They fought constantly over who would get to sleep by the wall—the other girl usually wound up on the floor. But at least Jennie had a bed. Others were less fortunate. Gussie M., who emigrated at eighteen, stayed with her brother for six months, but then had to leave to make way for another brother newly arrived from Europe. "One by one we came," she recalled. "And there was one room which had to be vacated when the green person arrived."

Young women without relatives in New York would rent a room in a boarding house, which could be equally precarious. Rose L. was dispossessed from one room because of the vanity of her landlady, who was willing enough to accept rent but didn't want the neighbors to know she had to take in a boarder. As Rose put it, "She wanted to fall and not hurt her behind." But when Rose washed her clothes at lunchtime and hung them out to dry, the landlady told her to get out, because her wet clothes made it obvious that a boarder was in the house.

There were dangers in the streets for young people frustrated with the meagerness of their lives. Some children rejected the hard work ethic of their parents in favor of the promise of easy money. One contemporary observer wrote that the Jewish ghetto on the Lower East Side was a "nursery in crime," where youngsters gained "primary instruction in pickpocketing and prostitution." For young women, particularly those without families, possibly jobless and hungry, walking the streets offered an alternative to hardship. Maimie Pinzer, a Jewish woman who had been a prostitute, explained to a friend that she "had the easy life that immoral living brings, and . . . [could not] be moral enough to see where drudgery is better than a life of lazy vice."[29]

Temptation abounded everywhere. On Canal Street, a row of brothels stood directly across from a shop selling religious articles.[30] Prostitutes plied their trade on every block, particularly Allen Street, where there seemed to be "one hundred women on every street corner." Madams like "Mother" Rosie Hertz continued to live grandly in their old neighborhoods and thus provided unsavory role models of women who had "made it." In 1912, 19 percent of the prostitutes in one major New York reformatory were Jewish.[31] There were dangers even in such popular and apparently harmless diversions as "balls." The social worker Lillian Wald observed with alarm that such dances were frequently held over saloons, and sometimes "an entirely innocent and natural desire for recreation afforded continual opportunity for the overstimulation of the senses and for dangerous exploitation."[32]

Families did not always provide a haven for young women or girls. One Jewish prostitute told investigators that she had left home and drifted into her profession because she feared her parents' anger when she lost her virginity.[33] Sometimes, girls were abused by trusted relatives or neighbors. Maimie Pinzer traced her descent into prostitution to an uncle, who, she wrote, "did me the first wrong, when I was a tiny girl."[34] Kate Simon narrowly escaped abuse by the neighbor of a friend who attempted to bribe the girl into letting him fondle her.[35] A friend's mother warned young Sophie Ruskay to stay away from "that accursed shoemaker" who evidently had molested a neighbor's daughter.[36]

Yet life in Eastern Europe had not been easy either. One toilet on a hall was at least an improvement over an outhouse, and housewives considered running water a blessing. If children might get into trouble on the streets of New York, at least they were safe from marauding Cossacks. Prostitution was no stranger to many impoverished Galician women, and economic conditions combined with government policy had denied many Russian and Polish Jews the opportunity of making a living. At least in New York one could work, and no trade was forbidden to Jews. There were ample jobs for men and women in the burgeoning factories of the city.[37] The slums in Vilna or Lvov were as bad as those of the Lower East Side, and here there were no laws sanctioning discrimination against Jews. Food was cheap, and children could go to school.

Their experiences in Eastern Europe had also given many Jews some preparation for the kind of life they found in America. Because they had lived in countries where they were not really accepted, many were accustomed to an alien environment. The radicalism of prerevolutionary Russia had led many young workers to an easy acceptance of unionism and political activity. In addition, urbanization had given Jews ready access to music and theater, a taste which could be indulged in the United States. Yet despite these experiences, the difficulty of adjusting to a new country, new customs, new language, and sometimes new values made the other hardships less bearable.

Sometimes the path of adjustment to what were perceived as American ways could take surprising turns. Often, parents' goals were not as much to become American as they were simply to fit in with people around them or do business in a Jewish area. If they had been assimilated in their native country, immigrants might discover on the Lower East Side a new awareness of being Jewish. Elsie F. and her parents, secularized Hungarian Jews from Budapest, had to learn Yiddish in New York in order to run their garment shop and communicate with others in their neighborhood. Lisa and Rose H., who came from Kiev with their "modern" parents, as well as Hilda S. and Rose G., had to learn Yiddish as well as English here, for they had spoken only Russian at home.[38] Tanya N., who left Russia at five, was taught Yiddish in America, but for a different reason. Although her parents knew Yiddish, they had always conversed in Russian to each other and their children. However, when Tanya's father heard that she had called a local shopkeeper a "dirty Jew," he took her to a Polish-Jewish family on the next block who taught her Yiddish, and he decreed that thereafter it would be the only language spoken in their home.

For married women, despite the strangeness, at least the tempo of daily life often resembled the one remembered from Eastern Europe. In both places, their concerns centered around caring for husband and children and stretching the family's money to see that they were fed, clothed, and housed. Most families settled in the midst of other Eastern European Jews, and so the language in the streets and the food in the shops were familiar to the ear and palate. The religious observances and customs of women, rooted in the home and tradition, could be practiced as easily in America as in Europe, while the obligations of men, focused on biblical texts and commentaries studied in the synagogue, found stonier soil in the United States.[39]

Since many women had been affected by modernizing trends in Eastern Europe, they were willing to surrender some customs while emphasizing others, and they considered themselves no less religious than before. As early as the 1880s, one disapproving observer condemned Jewish women who desecrated the Sabbath by shopping.[40] Forty years later, other women who lived in a neighborhood that had lost its kosher butcher shop began to use nonkosher meat.[41] Most women, though, sought a middle way. For example, Morris Raphael Cohen's mother, a pious woman, took advantage of the convenience of using gas for lighting and cooking and deftly parried her husband's religious objections against lighting matches on the Sabbath.[42] Similarly, while the *mikvah* all but disappeared from the American scene,[43] and many younger married women abandoned the *sheitel*, the great majority kept kosher homes,[44] lit candles on the Sabbath, and maintained the ritual celebrations of holidays in the home. Many were able, as their husbands were not, to observe the Sabbath by not working outside the home. Thus, fewer married women than men would face decisions as wrenching as that of Rose Cohen's pious father, who had to shave off his beard lest he be beaten up on the way to work.[45]

If life in Eastern Europe had been harsh, America easily fulfilled humble expectations. The mother of Ruth R. had led a sad and impoverished life as the wife of the miller in their Russian village. Before she was forty, her husband and six of her eleven children were dead. "When she came to the United States," Ruth recalled, "she was forty-two years old and looked like seventy. The first thing she got was dentures, so she could chew. And she was with her children and brothers and sisters. This is the first time I remember that she was happy."

Women's lives were affected enormously by their husbands' success or failure in the job market. Since few Jewish married women took work outside the home or a family store, a husband's ability to earn a decent living determined the economic well-being of the entire family. As one woman put it, "Her world, her all, began and ended in her man; if he was successful, she might be, that is, if he continued faithful—if he was a failure, she would inevitably be the same; a burden to herself and her children."[46] If a man did well financially in the United States, his family could live in one of the better neighborhoods in the Bronx or Brooklyn. His wife would never need to worry about having enough money for food or paying the rent. All their children could go to school instead of working. Even luxuries were possible. Women could have fur coats, or buy a piano for the children. The whole family might spend the summer at a resort in the Catskill Mountains.[47] These were the lucky ones. Miriam G. remembered her mother as a happy woman because her father made such a good living. Upon arrival in New York, Miriam's family was one of the fortunate ones that could bypass the Lower East Side and move immediately into one of the more desirable Jewish neighborhoods in Brownsville, Williamsburg, or Harlem.[48] "If he had brought us to the East Side," she speculated, "mother would have struggled and maybe my sisters would have had to go to work. Maybe I would have grown up without an education. We all attributed it to my father." But it took two, she concluded. "Mother made the home."

Money did not automatically make marriages happy, nor did poverty necessarily embitter them. But if two people were basically mismated, if their lives in America failed to meet their expectations, they could easily wind up blaming each other and creating a hostile home environment. The parents of Florence B. had never been happy together, their daughter observed, "but we were not aware of it until we came to America, and then it was hell!" The mother of Dora W., who had not wanted to leave her parents in Eastern Europe, nevertheless followed her husband to America where she lived a miserable life with him. He fought with her over money and with the children over religion, and barely provided a living for his family. She was not happy with him or with the little America offered her. "We were poor, very poor," Dora recalled. Her mother "worked from morning to night. And the life which she led was so meager. I feel terrible that such a beautiful, lovely person was wasted. She was angry, she was often angry. I remember she had these sparkling blue eyes and flashes of anger would come out. And towards the end," Dora observed, "she was not lovely at all."

If a family had been prosperous in Eastern Europe, the disappointment at an impoverished existence could be particularly acute. The mother of Fannie C. had to give up a comfortable home in a small town near Kiev for a crowded, third-floor walk-up and a difficult life in New York. "Saturday night, the great thing was to wash her clothes and put them out on the line early Sunday morning before anyone else." Despite her husband's devotion, Fannie recalled, "from the time [her mother] came to America, she was a disappointed woman." While the parents of Sophie Abrams-Flint also had led a comparatively easy life in their native Keltcz, in New York, her mother as well as her father had to work in low-paying, difficult jobs. In his unguarded moments, her father blamed marriage for his problems and called his wife his *imgluck* [misfortune]. Her "mother tallied with the retort, that he, in turn, was her *Malchumus* [hovering angel of death] . . . and kept moaning 'Better than to live this kind of life is the carrying of stones.'"[49] Even if there was affection between parents, when money was short, little disagreements could easily grow into big ones. The father of Tanya N. had been a prosperous fur merchant in his native Ukrainian town, but in this country, he made a poor living as a capmaker. Tanya understood that the friction between her parents was caused by poverty. "Both are upset, both are in need," she recalled, "and they quarrel, about nothing at all, nothing serious. It was bitterness, sadness. Because they were so wealthy in Russia and so poor here, in the 'Golden Land.'"

While parents coped with the problems of readjusting to each other and to a new life, young children had a different perspective. Fannie C. remembered above all the Christmas lights as the ferry boat from Ellis Island approached the tip of Manhattan at night in December 1919. Fannie had lived through a pogrom, and she couldn't believe that "here was Christmas and people were going in the streets and nothing happening and you didn't have to be afraid. And nobody told you that you killed their God." Anna R.

also recalled a happy first impression of New York. Leaving Castle Garden to take the subway uptown to their new home, she and her parents came upon an organ grinder and his monkey playing music, "and the children were dancing in the street. I just stood there and thought, what a wonderful place this must be—where you hear music and little children like me dancing!"

Not all young children immediately took to America. Despite her initial enthusiasm, Fannie C. remembered crying herself to sleep for months at the strangeness of this country. Minnie Fisher regretted leaving the beautiful forests of her native village,[50] and Rose G. was miserable because of difficulties with the language, the tough children at school, and schoolteachers who had little patience and didn't spare the rod. After her initial joy at seeing her father again, Fannie C. "was terribly unhappy." "The whole American life was strange to me," she recalled.

> My home, my school, the food, the city in itself. I just didn't know how to cope with it all. I was unhappy because I didn't understand the language. I sort of felt that I was a big shot student in Russia. And here I didn't know anything, and I was frightened. Two days after I came off the boat, my father enrolled me in school, and that was the worst time. When they used to call me names like "greenhorn," I felt that I would rather die than hear it again. There were times I wished that they would send me back to my grandfather. That I would have rather been without my parents than be here.

Frieda M. also longed to return home. In her native village, she had been a popular girl from a prosperous family. In Minneapolis, where her parents first settled, Frieda was poor and insignificant. She remembered making herself a new dress and showing it to a friend who always dressed well. "Look, Lola, I made it," she told her. The friend "looked me up and down and said, 'It looks like it!' I was somebody in Buczacz," Frieda concluded, "but I was a nobody in Minneapolis, and I guess I didn't like being a nobody." Clothing was a visible display of social class, and it also could betray a child as a new immigrant—a greenhorn. Rose Cohen wrote that her brother was so tormented by children about his village-made Russian shoes that he often came home crying, and he finally threw his hated footgear off a roof to force his parents to buy him "American" shoes.[51]

But children were generally more flexible than their parents, and problems with adjustment, with the language, with being called "greenhorns," the worst possible of insults, usually faded within a year. If they were too young to work, they attended public school, that great Americanizer, and soon many had shed their own origins enough to taunt newcomers with the rhyme that had met them upon arrival: "Greenhorn, popcorn, five cents a piece, / July, July, go to hell and die."

Unlike children, young adults who came without parents had to make their own way. Most of them had some relative—a brother or sister, aunt or uncle—who could be counted on to supply a bed for a few months at least and provide tips on where to go for a job. Sometimes these family connections proved a slender reed. Like Gussie M., some young women found that the promised room lasted only until it was needed for a higher-paying boarder or a "greener" relative just arrived from Eastern Europe. Others complained that an aunt or brother used them as unpaid servants, insisting that they care for children or help in the shop if they were too young to get a factory job. Pauline H., at the age of fourteen, kept house for her brothers and cried herself to sleep every night because she missed her mother so much.

On the other hand, relatives could prove a great comfort in the absence of parents. An aunt might take the place of a mother, encouraging her niece to attend school and make something of herself. Sophie Abrams-Flint and her brother spent every Saturday visiting relatives, where they drank tea, sang old Jewish songs, and talked about how much they missed their parents.[52] Even if they were doing well in America, many longed for their homes and families. As one song laments,

> Why did I come to America,
> And what fortune did I find there?
> Instead, I was forlorn
> Separated from my father and mother,
> So far away from my sisters and brothers.[53]

One young woman in Anzia Yezierska's short story, "Hunger," recalled, as her eyes grew misty, "How I suffered in Savel. I never had enough to eat. I never had shoes on my feet. I had to go barefoot even in the freezing winter. But still I love it. I was born there. I love the houses and the straw roofs, the mud streets, the cows, the chickens and the goats. My heart always hurts me for what is no more."[54]

Often, though, these young women who emigrated alone set their sights on the present rather than the past and sought to recreate new lives in America. They had envisioned no future for themselves in Eastern Europe and had few pleasant memories of their homes. Many had chafed at the lack of education and intellectual excitement in their childhood villages and sought the challenges of New York. Sometimes they had come to

America to escape from poverty or an oppressive father. For these young women, America promised the heady brew of freedom. Gussie M. remembered how it felt: "Here I was very free," she recalled. "No one watched over me. I felt here like a queen. I says, 'This is me,' and every burden was thrown off." Even poverty could not dampen her spirits. "The fact that I had to work, the fact that I had no rent money, the fact that my shoes were torn—that didn't matter at all. I was used to this."

For young people accustomed to living on very little, the city offered much in the way of excitement and inexpensive amusements. Movies and theater were within the reach of all. For immigrants who had not mastered English, the Yiddish theater presented plays with a wide range, from comic escapism like *Mendel from Japan* to Ansky's classic, *The Dybbuk*. Standing room tickets for a concert or the opera could be bought for very little.[55] Jeanne S., who had learned to love music from her early years in Vienna, reserved Sunday afternoons for Carnegie Hall and the Metropolitan Opera. In the line to buy standing room tickets, she recalled, a kind of camaraderie developed among the young immigrant working men and women who met there every week and saved places for one another. Janet A. and her parents also brought their love of music with them. Although they had very little money, going to the opera and to concerts was "almost as important as food." For the less culturally inclined, dance halls provided a popular place to have fun and meet young men. In the heart of the Lower East Side, there were thirty-one dance halls, one every two and a half blocks, more than in any other area of the city.[56]

And then there was the city itself. Minnie Fisher recalled "When you come from a little village, you're naturally surprised in a big city." But young people, she observed,

> have a way of getting oriented very quickly. You belonged to a cultural club, you went to school at night. You didn't feel the pressure of the city. And the city itself! Sunday we would get dressed up and for five cents on the Fifth Avenue Bus take a ride to Central Park. That was an outing. Life wasn't that pressing. I was very excited about the openness, about going to the ocean. There used to be an open trolley that went all the way out to Coney Island. Can you imagine how beautiful that was? The excitement of the city was so great, from the first day that I came, that I hardly ever realized there were any hardships.[57]

Without relatives to rely on, close friendships took their place.[58] Shared hardships molded firm bonds. As Fannie K. recalled, "When we didn't work, we couldn't afford to eat, so we lived on ten cents a day. You could buy cheese for five cents and rolls for four cents and milk, and we ate together, my friend and I. We stuck together. After the slack, when we went to work again, I paid off the landlady, because I owed her for rent. And once a week we used to eat a real dinner together—on Friday night." These friendships formed at work provided a major satisfaction and source of support.[59] Fannie Shapiro moved out of an aunt's house to live with a young woman who worked in her shop. "There I met people my own age," she recalled. "We formed a Jewish club, we played theater, and we danced. . . . Life was different."[60] For many young women, the excitement of this new way of living wove a common thread.

The multitudes of clubs and political groups these young people joined served a dual purpose: friendship and a sense of shared goals. There, a girl could meet others with similar background and interests. These friends often became a surrogate family. "My friends and I, we found a different life," mused Fannie K. "We formed a club, joined organizations. We wanted to know about life, and all kinds of things. We went to school, to lectures. Life wasn't bad, it was interesting. But very poor. We struggled very much." The experiences were new and stimulating, and the friends, who shared a common background and language, common hopes and dreams, made the poverty bearable.

These clubs fulfilled different needs. For those seeking education, there were groups like the one Tanya N. joined at eighteen—the "self-culture club." "We were Jews yearning for education," Tanya explained, "but we had to work and find some kind of cultural outlet." Dramatic clubs were another possibility. Some concentrated on the works of Yiddish authors and provided young working people with the opportunity to learn something of their own culture. Others became agents for Americanization. Elizabeth Hasanovitz enjoyed her dramatic club for acquainting her with good literature—not, as she put it, the "trash" presented by the Yiddish theaters.[61] Many clubs were formed by young people simply as a means of finding companionship. With young men and women now seeking their own mates, social clubs that sponsored dances and picnics provided an acceptable environment for young people to meet and "fall in love."[62]

The politically inclined often joined clubs and organizations extending over every part of the radical spectrum. The revolutionary activity that was shaking Russia particularly affected young people old enough to be aware of its effects when they emigrated. "We went to hear every speaker who spoke against oppression," recalled Fannie N. of her club. "And that brought life into our home." The clubs often became the focus of their lives.

Gussie M. and her brother both became mainstays of the local branch of the Socialist Party, and she met the man she would marry at a meeting. "I didn't understand the Socialist problem," observed Minnie Fisher. "So we got together a few youngsters and made a club, called the *Yiddishe Yugend* [Jewish Youth], where we discussed the problems of the world. . . . We thought we knew an awful lot," she concluded wryly.[63] For some non-Jewish men, unaccustomed to seeing women arguing and expressing political views, this activity sometimes appeared unseemly. "Where the cigarette smoke is thickest and denunciation of the present forms of government loudest," wrote one observer, "there you find women . . . who listen to the strongest language and . . . [who never] fail to make themselves heard in the heat of discussion."[64]

For married women, family obligations would limit participation in such clubs,[65] yet some form of social life offered the comfort of familiarity in the midst of strangeness. These older women generally remained within the immigrant community. Many belonged to a lodge, or a *landsmanshaft*—a mutual aid society—which helped create a sense of community with people of similar backgrounds.[66] Within the reassuring environment of the *landsmanshaftn*, men and women fearful of the many changes demanded of them in America could join with like-minded people from the same town and discuss in Yiddish the difficulties facing them all.[67] Dances and other social activities sponsored by these groups or by labor unions provided festive occasions to celebrate and forget about the daily struggle to put food on the table. Elsie F. remembered her mother singing with joy as she took time out from her constant round of cooking and cleaning to stitch up the costume she was making for the Purim Ball given by her *landsmanshaft*.

Visiting relatives was the most common way for married women to socialize. Such visits cost nothing and provided an opportunity to reminisce about family members left behind or the "old days" in Russia or Poland. It was easier if they lived in the same neighborhood. Then children could drop in frequently, and men could go over to play cards or women to chat and exchange recipes.[68] Sometimes these relationships were formalized by creating family clubs.[69] Weddings were a particular delight, and Hannah F. remembered being put to sleep during the festivities and then awakened early in the morning for the long subway ride home from Brooklyn. A streetcar trip to the nearest park on Sunday proved a welcome respite from daily work and the gray of the pavements, while the wooded areas often reawakened memories of home.

Whether these women were young or old, married or single, life in America would be different from what they were used to in Eastern Europe. For some the adjustment was easier than for others. Those who came in family groups would at least be able to rely on a ready-made support system and the continuity of family life. Women who had experience in the urban, industrial centers of Russia and Poland would be accustomed to the rapid pace of city life and work in factories. Young children who attended school would learn more quickly than their parents how to speak English and behave like "real Americans." Women or girls who emigrated at an older age, who left reluctantly, or who had dreams that clashed with the reality they found here—these would have a harder time dealing with an environment they had not sought and did not expect. But regardless of the circumstances of emigration, very few would adapt effortlessly. It took more than an ocean voyage to turn an immigrant into an American.

6

. . . .

Becoming Americans

I wanted to be an American, so therefore I was. I took it for better or worse. But there was nothing worse in America; there was just terrific.

—Frieda M.

. . . .

Because I came from the other side, I had to work harder to become American. But my growing up didn't do me any good, because I had nobody to learn from.

—Mildred L.

9. A young Americanized immigrant woman.
Collection of the author

Once immigrants had arrived in this country and made initial adjustments to their families and to new living and working conditions, the next important step was to become Americanized. Unlike many other newcomers, Jews escaping the poverty and persecution of Czarist Russia had no intention of returning. If America was to be their permanent home, they had to determine what balance to strike between adopting American ways and retaining their own language and customs. This was no simple task, for while some made the transition with relative ease, others within the same family often had a harder time or a different interpretation of what changes were necessary, of what "Americanization" meant. These differences could create friction among siblings or conflicts between parents and children.[1]

The Jewish wife had her own problems in adapting to America, for her daily life, more than that of her husband or children, began and ended in the ghetto of the Lower East Side. In Eastern Europe, middle-class wives generally had not worked, but women in poor families usually had no option but to try to earn some money. In America, early in the century, even working-class Jewish married women seldom took jobs outside the home.[2] In *The Rise of David Levinsky*, one husband bemoaned this transformation in his wife. Before they came to America, he told Levinsky, she "had a nice little business. She sold feed for horses and rejoiced in the thought that she was married to a man of learning." In this country, however, she had changed for the worse, for "instead of supporting him while he read Talmud, as she used to do at home, she persisted in sending him out to peddle. 'America is not Russia,' she said. 'A man must make a living here.'"[3] But most husbands were proud that their wives did not have to go out to work, especially in factories. As Frieda M. put it, "We were high class with low-class means. We just didn't let a woman like my mother go to work, even if she wanted to." Such wives saw little reason to leave their neighborhoods, where the people and language seemed less strange. If a married woman had to earn money, it would be by working in the home.

This housebound existence was a mixed blessing, for it made it more difficult for wives to learn the language and customs. A man could pick up English in the workplace, but how was his wife going to become more Americanized? Some married women made the effort to go to night school, despite their many household chores. Janet A.'s mother attended night school regularly and learned to speak perfect English, but, as her daughter observed, "she was not the typical immigrant." Still other women learned English and American ways from their children,[4] insisting that the youngsters teach them what they had learned in school. For women fluent only in

Yiddish, Jewish newspapers, particularly the daily *Forward*, offered advice on how to adapt to America. One reader called the *Forward* her family's "Bible," for it determined their outlook and patterns of conduct.[5] On the women's page, wives could read articles about education, child psychology, love, marriage, family life, and appropriate behavior. All aspects of American life were grist for its mill, from politics to the proper use of the handkerchief. Some mature women were determined to master the language. The mother of Riva P. went to night school with her husband and both she and Sarah Reznikoff took great pride in reading American rather than Yiddish newspapers.[6]

But for most women, there were too few opportunities to learn what it was to be a "real American." "At first it was very lonesome," Ruth R. remembered. "The man goes to work, you're alone with the baby. But I'm not Americanized, don't know the language. What do you say, 'a lollipop' or a 'lollipie'? But I survived." While her husband was at work, Gittl, the wife in Abraham Cahan's story "Yekl," lost in her strange, new surroundings, whispered fearfully, "Lord of the World, where am I?"[7] Elsie F.'s mother was so unhappy in her early days here that for months she refused to unpack her suitcases. As soon as the war ended, she told her husband, she was going back to Hungary. One Jewish woman, pleading for greater education for immigrant women in 1915, observed that while life in the old country was harder, it was also simpler. In Europe, the economic struggle to survive absorbed all the energies of husband and wife, while here, the husband could gain an education from his dealings with the outside world while the wife's horizons remained narrowly circumscribed.[8]

Many married women had no desire to become Americanized and only made the effort because of a husband's insistence or a child's embarrassment at her foreign ways.[9] Rose Cohen persuaded her mother to abandon her wig by pointing out that many husbands were ashamed to be seen with their "old-fashioned" wives.[10] If a husband and children were anxious to Americanize, a wife's inability or reluctance to change might create tensions within the family.[11] Gittl's refusal to abandon her wig—to act, as her landlady instructs her, "like edzecate peoples" in "an edzecate country," was a sign to her husband of her unacceptable foreignness.[12] Sometimes older women, like Frances F.'s mother, were too proud to speak broken English and refused to communicate in anything but Yiddish. Ida Richter's mother even forbade her children to speak English at home because, she asserted, "This is a Yiddish house and no Gentile languages are going to be spoken here." Her children were upset because they "wanted to be American very much." Ida recalled, "I saw people who looked better and dressed better and I wanted to be like that kind."[13]

However, if a mother acquiesced to the needs of her family at the expense of her own, the results might be equally unfortunate. The father of Minna S., an orthodox Jew in Poland, had become completely disillusioned with religion in America and became a Socialist. When his wife joined him here after seven years, she had great difficulty adjusting to his irreligious views. To Mary Antin's father, "Americanization" also meant the abandonment of Orthodox Judaism, and he insisted that his wife follow his example. As a loving and obedient wife, like Minna's mother, she acceded to his wishes, but at great personal cost. "My mother," wrote Antin, "gradually divested herself, at my father's bidding, of the mantle of orthodox observance, but the process cost her many a pang, because the fabric of that venerable garment was interwoven with the fabric of her soul."[14]

Most women eventually came to terms with the changes they found in America. The mother of Fannie C., who never managed to learn English or become accustomed to poverty, told her daughter that she wished they had never come. "If I would ever know what I was going to go through, if papa had spread dollars all across the Atlantic Ocean, I would never have gone to America." Yet, with no alternative, Fannie recalled that her mother began to realize "that running the house and bringing up the children was about all that she could handle. It's hard to accept the fact that life cannot be changed a great deal." But accept it she did.

What aided women like Fannie's mother in adjusting to life here was the friendship and support of others like themselves. While husbands and children were away at work and in school, women newly arrived in this country learned from neighbors how to deal with the day-to-day difficulties that sometimes seemed overwhelming. Over a cup of tea, or while hanging the wash on an outside line, they might discuss how to keep a husband from wandering or where to find the cheapest pushcart to buy herring. When she had been in New York only a week, the mother of Marie Jastrow learned from "the grocery lady" where to find an apartment with a toilet in each hall rather than three floors down. The highlight of her day was the kaffeeklatsch with neighbors, and when the family moved, it was those women she missed most. During her first few years in America, they helped ease the pangs of homesickness. "It was good to have a friend," her daughter recalled her saying, "when the struggles in the beginning were too heavy to bear alone."[15]

These friendships sometimes crossed ethnic lines. Tanya N. remembered her mother baking extra cookies for her Italian neighbor who in turn often brought over the specialties of her own kitchen as a gift. Both families lived and had small shops in the same building, so the women spent many hours together discussing ways to prepare food, raise children, and make a living. When Tanya and her family moved away, the old Italian woman was in tears because, as Tanya observed, "she loved my mother like they were mother and daughter."

Such neighbors, who had not been here long themselves, understood the frustrations of the greenhorn and were quick to offer help and advice. Fannie observed that her mother eventually reconciled herself to her lot because "she was surrounded by friends and women who had exactly the same troubles she did." Sharing burdens with neighbors who had to cope with similar problems helped ease the stress of transition.[16] In "The Fat of the Land," Anzia Yezierska describes an unfortunate woman whose children had prospered and insisted that she move away from Delancey Street to the Upper West Side of Manhattan. But her Americanized children are strange to her, and she feels isolated amidst her new luxury and misses, above all, her old neighbors. "Uptown here," she tells a friend who comes to visit, "nobody cares if the person next door is dying or going crazy from loneliness. It ain't anything like we used to have in Delancey Street, when we could walk into one another's rooms without knocking, and borrow a pinch of salt or a pot to cook in."[17] In friendship, there was comfort, and without it, women felt bereft.

Some women, particularly those with a strong personality and a good relationship with their husbands, were able to surmount the problems of adjustment more easily. Instead of being embarrassed by her lack of competence in English, Janet A.'s mother used her sense of humor to help her learn it. "She could laugh at herself when she'd go to a store, to the butcher, for example, and say 'kitchen' instead of 'chicken.' Or she'd go to a hardware store and ask for a 'pitcher.' In Yiddish it's 'kruch.' So of course, he'd say 'Kruch?! What are you talking about?' 'Oh, you know, to pour water.' 'Oh, you mean *pitcher*!' Or pitcher and picture. And we would all laugh about it, and she would laugh most of all. Eventually, she learned and could speak and write very nicely." The mother of Tanya N. also used humor and determination to overcome obstacles. "My cousin came from Philadelphia one day to see my mother," Tanya recalled.

She knocked at the door, and she heard my mother singing, "*Ikh klin vontsn, mir iz gut*" [I clean bedbugs, my life is good]. This was being sung by a woman who had been enormously wealthy under the Czar and got poorer and poorer in the United States because her husband was forced to do poorly paid work. Yet the great change that took place in her life did not change her feelings about life itself. She could take it.

She was very poor, but she sang, "I clean bedbugs. *I* am very lucky. My life is good." My mother was an optimist, not a dreamer. A realist and an optimist. She understood her hardships, and she faced them with a sense of humor.

As in Europe, sometimes mothers who were aware of their limited options transferred thwarted ambitions, particularly for an education, to their children. The mother of Rose G., after being snubbed by her own brothers as a "greener," insisted that her daughter quickly learn the English that eluded her. Mollie Linker also remembered her mother's wanting something better in life for her children, especially the girls.[18] The mother of Hattie L., who made a career out of helping other immigrants get settled, was proud when her daughter became a nurse. In Cahan's *The Rise of David Levinsky*, Dora, an illiterate immigrant woman, lived her life through her daughter, whom she viewed with a combination of pride and envy. "My own life is lost," she thought, "but she shall be educated."[19] This was not an uncommon attitude. Riva P.'s mother, like Dora, used to berate her daughter when she did poorly in school and told her how lucky she was to be able to get an education. "If I were raised in this country," she told her repeatedly, "do you imagine what I would have become?"

Fathers did not necessarily have an easy time adjusting to American ways either. They had to support their families whether or not they could speak English,[20] and the transition was particularly difficult for those who had earned a good living in Europe or been given to scholarly ways. Even in America, the great majority of these men were religious, or at least were involved in Jewish community affairs,[21] and many of them had a harder time than Mary Antin's father in adopting American values and abandoning orthodoxy. Some were unable to cope with the lower status they had to settle for in America, the land where everyone was supposed to get rich. Tanya N. recalled that she and her brother had to go to work to pay her father's debts after his business as a capmaker failed. He was not a competitor: "He loved music; he hated what he was doing. He saw himself going down, down, down—that he couldn't make a living. He saw also that he had to give up any hope of being a great cantor in the United States because he couldn't speak English." Rose G.'s father also hoped for a career as a cantor, but had to settle for making mattresses. "Whatever job he got didn't suit him—at all of them he was inept."

Such assaults on a man's pride took their toll. Most men wanted their wives to stay home and care for the children while they worked to support the family, but all too often, unemployment or illness defeated this aspiration.[22] "Being long unemployed," wrote Kate Simon, "as I had noticed among the fathers of several friends, seemed to silence and emasculate them and they became quiet, slow-moving old women."[23] "I left Europe and I was a man," Fannie Kligerman recalled her father complaining because of the poverty of their home, "and here I am a what?"[24] The father of Riva P., formerly a dashing junior officer in the czar's armies, failed in the dress business, failed in the laundry business, failed in the restaurant business, and wound up being a waiter. "He couldn't seem to really find himself," Riva recalled, "and it rankled him. He was not happy with his work; he did it because he had to. And I think he was ashamed of himself." Although he remained a good father, he consoled himself with a succession of extramarital affairs. Fannie G.'s father also cushioned his downward economic slide from furrier to tailor by seeing other women. Both men, though, remained devoted to their children.

Jewish women often suffered from their husbands' difficulty in adjusting to America. Some men, feeling trapped by their inability to support their families, abused, divorced, or deserted their wives. As early as 1887, an orthodox immigrant observed, "Bills of divorce are very common."[25] While other ethnic groups endured similar strains, their Catholicism prohibited divorce; thus, in 1903, Jews had the highest divorce rate of any ethnic group in the city.[26] And while the middle and upper classes resorted to this method of solving irreconcilable family conflicts, desertion was more often the solution of working-class men. For years, the *Forward* published "A Gallery of Vanished Men,"[27] and the National Desertion Bureau, a Jewish agency, handled about twenty-five hundred cases a year. Often, pregnancy or the birth of a child triggered a husband's desertion.[28] Frieda W. believed that her husband left her because she could no longer have sexual relations with him after their child was born. For many men, the increased responsibilities represented by a child were too much to bear. Some deserted wives managed to support themselves and their children, some turned to charity, and a few even were driven to prostitution.[29] The trauma of migration and Americanization exacted a high price.

Children who came to the United States at a young age often adapted more quickly and easily than parents or older brothers and sisters. For example, Dora W. was the third child and second of three daughters who emigrated with her parents when she was eight years old. Dora recalled, "We were once in my house, my sisters and I, having discussions of olden times. We spoke about our parents, and it was fascinating. You would think that the three of us had different parents. And maybe we did. You wouldn't recognize *my* parents from what my older sister said or what my younger sister said." Dora went on to explain why she and her sisters held such diverse impressions. Her older sister hated her father for taking her away from Russia, leaving behind school, a boyfriend, and a familiar life. A sensitive and educated girl, she was too old for school in America and had to work in a garment shop where she was miserable. As the oldest daughter, she also bore heavy responsibilities for helping her mother with house-work. When she wanted to go out with friends or keep some of her salary for herself, her father refused to permit such liberties. She never managed to "Americanize," or to do the next best thing—to marry an American man—and she blamed her father for her unfulfilled life.

Dora's younger sister, on the other hand, was born in America and shared the unfortunate trait of some American-born children—shame at having European parents. As the youngest, she was a favorite of her father and mother, but she disliked their old-world traits and refused to speak the language they knew best. This sister wanted her family to be American too, and she resented the fact that they were not like the parents of her native-born friends and felt ashamed of their home on the Lower East Side.

Dora, however, believed that she had "the best of both worlds." She remembered enough of her early life in Russia to appreciate the difficulties her parents faced in leaving and creating a new life in America. She understood that they did this for the sake of the children, and she felt that she had benefited from their decision more than her sisters. She had been able to start school here, as her older brother and sister could not, but she still had to make the effort to learn a new language and way of life, which her American-born sister could take for granted. As poor as her family was, Dora knew that life was going to be better here than it would have been in Europe; she always felt that she was "upward bound."

Thus, because of the difference in age, Dora and her sisters held different attitudes toward their parents and "led totally different lives." Her eldest sister remained within the immigrant culture. The youngest blamed her parents for preventing her from being a "real American,"—as one observer put it, she was too foreign for the schoolroom and too American for the home.[30] Dora, on the other hand, believed that she alone had successfully bridged the gap between the cultures, and she felt comfortable with both her European origins and her subsequent life in America.

While the adult generation often sought to retain many old customs, many were, at the same time, particularly proud of their Americanized children and wanted them to become real "Yankees."[31] Dora was aware of the contradictory nature of her parents' views. "It was a strange thing," she observed, "that much as they clung to their habits and restrictions from the Old Country, they were delighted with any of their children who became Americanized." Several parents refused to permit books written in any language but English into their homes. When Ethel B. brought German books home from the library, her father threatened to burn them: "You have to learn English," he would say. English rather than Yiddish was spoken in a third of Jewish immigrant homes, and once a family had been here as long as ten years, almost half had adopted the language of America.[32] Fannie C. recalled how her parents relied upon her because of her knowledge of English. Whenever her father went to the doctor, she had to come along and translate for him. "They really depended on me." In her family, Frances F. reminisced, "I was the one who conquered the language, so I became the emissary. Whatever had to be done, like getting a license or being a translator, it was I." This ability evidently conferred high status: "I became the head of the family," she observed, with understandable exaggeration. "Whatever I did was fine with my parents." Several women, who were youngest children and therefore the most Americanized, commented upon this pride and observed that in their parents' eyes, they could do no wrong.

The public schools facilitated this transformation of young immigrants into Americans. To be a "real American" seemed to require giving up the external signs of being Jewish.[33] Ethel B. remembered the pressures she faced in school. In her last year, a teacher asked her to read a passage from Shakespeare. "I must have had an accent," Ethel recalled, "because she said, 'You people come here and you don't want to learn English!' And she really made me feel like dirt." Most important was abandoning the use of Yiddish in favor of learning to speak good English. Theodore Roosevelt's credo, enshrined on the back of a Board of Education bulletin, reflected the attitudes of most educators. "We have room for but one language here," wrote the former president, "and that is the English language . . . and we have room for but one sole loyalty, and that is loyalty to the American people."[34] School superintendent Julia Richman, herself the daughter of German Jewish immigrants, forbade the use of Yiddish in the schools of the Lower East Side. Teachers were told to patrol lunchrooms, restrooms, and

10. Jewish immigrant children at school.

Collection of Ann Weissman

schoolyards, giving students demerits if they dared to speak this un-American "jargon."[35]

Regardless of the reason for the transition, teachers and social workers marveled at the speed with which Jewish children managed to pick up the language.[36] Lena Kimberg remembered following other children around and asking questions in Yiddish that they answered in English.[37] Most children learned quickly in school, in part from necessity. Rose L. came alone at fourteen and went to live with her sister in Weehawken, New Jersey, where there were few Jews. She could speak only Yiddish, so she was put in the first grade and had to endure the ridicule of other children who laughed at her and called her "dumb." Rose G. remembered the shame on her first day of having to use the toilet and not knowing what to ask. Soon after, the class was going to Central Park and the children were told to bring their lunch. "'Lunch' I knew was a couch—a 'lounge.' So I had no 'lunch,' and I couldn't wait to come the next day to see all these lounges. Where would they put them? And then I first learned what lunch was, and I had none. We went to the park and I had to be hungry."

In school children were taught English and the superiority of the "American way," which implied that their parents' values were outmoded.[38] By the early twentieth century, the public schools had consciously assumed the responsibility of weaning their charges away from foreign customs and traditions.[39] Children rapidly discovered that what they learned in the home was not a reliable guide to American tastes and attitudes. Nina S. recalled the day her daughter came home from school and tried to convince her to cook "the American way," with meat, potato, and vegetable in each dinner. Nina responded indignantly, "I've been cooking for you for twelve years, and now you tell me how to do it?" But she nevertheless altered her menus to reflect these American standards. Mary Feldman recalled how teachers even unconsciously communicated proper behavior and tastes to their students. "I saw they were a different breed," she observed, in "the way they acted, dressed and so on. . . . My Jewish background is to be outgoing and to yell and scream . . . and I think the one big thing that I learned is to behave and to be retiring, not to be pushy. I think I learned that from my teachers. I think," Mary concluded, "that's an American trait."[40]

Many young people anxious to conform quickly discarded what they could of old-world ways.[41] They happily changed the names their parents had given them to "American" names suggested by teachers or the school clerk: Paia became Pauline, Dvoirah became Dora, Rivka became Ruth, and Ruchele became Rose. Only Naomi objected to becoming "Nellie," and her parents supported her decision. But this was unusual—most children were delighted to have American names, and teachers encouraged them to be American in every possible way. For example, in the 1890s, the flag salute taught in the twenty-one industrial schools scattered throughout the tenement districts instilled this less than subtle message: "We turn to our flag as the sunflower turns to the sun," it began. Then, "We give our heads! And our hearts! To our country!" And finally, "One country, one language, one flag!" Jacob Riis observed of this ritual, "No one can hear it and doubt that the children mean every word, and will not be apt to forget that lesson soon."[42]

No wonder that some children, like Dora's younger sister, resented parents' foreign ways, which might make others question their own wholehearted Americanization. Alfred Kazin remembered the mild sense of embarrassment children had at speaking English improperly. "Our families and teachers seemed tacitly agreed that we were somehow to be a little ashamed of what we were," he wrote. "It was certainly not because we were Jews, or simply because we spoke another language at home. . . . It was rather that a 'refined,' 'correct,' 'nice' English was required of us at school that we did not naturally speak. . . . This English was peculiarly the ladder of advancement. . . . We were expected to show it off like a new pair of shoes."[43] Most immigrant groups experienced this discomfort about their origins. Leonard Covello learned in school that to be Italian was to be inferior, that the price of Americanization was abandoning one's roots. "We were becoming Americans," he recalled, "by learning how to be ashamed of our parents."[44] Riva P. always felt that teachers looked down on her parents because they didn't speak English well. And though she loved them, she remembers thinking often, "I wish they were American." Yiddish spoken outside the home was embarrassing for many youngsters who consequently did not encourage their parents to come into contact with the rarified American atmosphere of the schools.[45]

This rapid Americanization of the younger generation, with children knowing the language and customs better than parents, could alter traditional relationships within the family. Many parents were unable to transmit to their children the values of a way of life that seemed antithetical to the demands of the new society they found in America.[46] Mary Antin described her own extreme example:

> My parents knew only that they desired us to be like American children; and seeing how their neighbors gave their children boundless liberty, they turned us also loose, never doubting but that the American way was the best way. . . . In their bewilderment and uncertainty they needs must trust us children to learn from such models as the tenements afforded. More than this, they must step down from their throne of parental authority and take the law from their children's mouths; for they had no other means of finding out what was good American form. The result was that laxity of domestic organization, that inversion of normal relations which makes for friction, and which sometimes ends in breaking up a family that was formerly united and happy.[47]

With children often the teachers and parents the learners, no wonder that many immigrants called America "a godless country. All the wrong side up. The children are fathers to their fathers. The fathers children to their children."[48]

The requirements of orthodox religion also created major tensions between parents and children anxious to be "real Americans." For example, when Dora W. took a job requiring her to work on the Sabbath, she recalled, "My father would not take my money when I brought it home. He said it was tainted. My father did not speak to me for one whole year! It was simply terrible!" But Dora believed she was right. "I did it," she explained, "because I felt that I couldn't live in Europe. I had to live in the United States." If children, now the experts on this country, told their parents that Americans ate nonkosher hot dogs or went to the movies on the Sabbath, what were parents to say? If they accepted these demands, they lost an important part of their religion. If they refused, they risked the alienation of their children, to whom so much freedom had been given. "Where worldly-wise children guided their elders," wrote one historian, "adult patterns, shaken in their equilibrium, trembled beneath pitiless scrutiny, and filial affection often vanished."[49]

Parents were afraid that a daughter's desire to be American might lead her to abandon Judaism. An otherwise defenseless daughter might use such fears in the battle against a parent's attempt to exert control. Once, when the father of Tanya N. was beating her for being "a rebel," she remembered telling him, "You know, papa, if you keep on hitting me, I'm going to do something to you. One day I'll come home with a souvenir in my belly, and it's going to be a Christian one!!" The threat to take up with a Christian man was a frightening one to parents, and one never knew what American customs would lead children away from their religion. When Rose Schneiderman attended an occasional Sunday lecture, her mother feared that she was secretly on her way to church.[50] Parents often worried about the effects non-Jewish friends would have on their children.[51] When Rose Cohen sought Christian friends and read secular books, her parents thought she would leave her faith and her father tried to stop her.[52] Thus, some parents' strictness can be traced to the fear that a daughter's adoption of American ways might lead to the abandonment of Judaism.

The Yiddish theater reflected these problems that threatened to turn the generation gap into a chasm. Many plays like *Mirele Efros*, *Kreutser Sonata*, and *The Jewish King Lear* dealt with conflicts between husbands and wives, and between parents and children. In Jacob Gordin's popular version of the Shakespeare classic, the daughters who stayed within tradition and married orthodox Jews turned out to be greedy and spiteful, while the youngest daughter, rejected because she had insisted on going to St. Petersburg to study medicine and then married an atheist, remained a faithful child. Parents who sought their children's success, yet feared losing them to "modern" and foreign ways, could be reassured. Gordin was telling parents that they could trust their sons' and daughters' American dreams.[53]

Some parents attempted to solve this problem by providing children with an education emphasizing their backgrounds and thus neutralize the relentless Americanism taught in the public schools. About 25 percent of

Jewish children were enrolled in some kind of Jewish school. Boys usually attended a cheder after public school to prepare for their bar mitzvah, and in 1918, New York had about fourteen thousand pupils in these schools. But in Yiddish schools such as those run by the Workmen's Circle, which emphasized culture rather than religion, girls made up 37 percent of the student body. In Sunday Schools, generally run by the earlier generation of German Jews, girls provided a clear majority.[54] The head of the Jewish Educational Association had warned that the new set of values that children learned in the public schools had estranged them from parents and their traditions. Boys and girls who attended Yiddish schools learned to value the traditions of parents and were thus better able to blend both cultures without considering their heritage a burden.

While children usually picked up American ways without much effort, young women who emigrated in their teens often had to work harder to Americanize. Despite the difficulties of mastering a new language, they made it their business to learn English as quickly as possible.[55] Young women working in shops chattered incessantly of "clothes, styles, beaux and dances."[56] In the factories, at school, or from other young people, these girls learned that they had rights as well as obligations, and that these included self-expression, a social life, and entertainment.[57] The movies reinforced these beliefs. Many early silent films directly addressed the experiences and hopes of immigrants by portraying ordinary people who shouldered the burdens of a difficult life and emerged successful.[58] Later films of the 1920s taught young working women a different lesson about how to succeed. In the illusory world of the silver screen, women who mastered the artifices of makeup and fashion, danced well, and radiated sex appeal might rise above their class origins and marry millionaires.[59]

Daughters like Anzia Yezierska, who left home at seventeen seeking above all to become a "person,"[60] had longings alien to their parents, whose main concern was basic survival. Leisure amusements and access to consumer goods promised satisfaction that seemed particularly American and desirable.[61] Wearing fashionable clothing was second in importance only to learning English in the quest to become American.[62] Mary Antin recalled her delight at discovering that "dazzlingly beautiful palace called a 'department store,'" where she and her sister "exchanged [their] hateful home-made European costumes . . . for real American-made garments, and issued forth glorified in each other's eyes."[63] For Leah Stern, high school opened up a new world. "I wanted to dance, to play, to have fun just like the other girls in my classes," she discovered. "I didn't mean to go to work at fourteen or fifteen, marry at sixteen, be a mother at eighteen and an old woman at thirty." Above all, she sought an objective inconceivable to her parents: "I wanted a new thing—happiness."[64]

But a decision to work on the Sabbath, spend money on clothing, attend dances, movies, or union meetings in the evenings, and, in general, to seek more freedom, often caused conflicts with parents. In such families, the daughter's desire to express her individualism, a trait fostered by American society, clashed with a parent's insistence on the primary importance of family needs or a simple assertion of traditional authority.[65] In Anzia Yezierska's semiautobiographical novel *Bread Givers*, when young Sara Smolinsky asks her mother if she will be proud once her daughter becomes a teacher, the mother replies within the framework of a different value system: "I'd be happier to see you get married. What's a school teacher? Old maids—all of them. It's good enough for goyim, but not for you." Her father's reaction is even more brutal. "A woman's highest happiness is to be a man's wife, the mother of a man's children. You're not a person at all."[66] There was little guidance from home on how to behave. Mothers could not provide role models for their teenage daughters on the Lower East Side of New York any more than they could in the working-class areas of Bialystok or Odessa.[67] Urbanization and industrialization had altered life in both places, and their mothers' homebound lives offered no clues to behavior. The strains of immigration thus exacerbated the "generation gap" of modern society.

Young women who wanted to become Americans often felt as if they lived in two different worlds. Their home environment offered a stark contrast with the environment at work or at school. After Rose Cohen had recuperated from an illness at a country place run by social workers, she was unable to readjust to life with her parents. "It was all stranger than ever," she wrote, "the home, my people, their ways."[68] The immigrant girl in Anzia Yezierska's story, "Children of Loneliness," attended college to better herself by becoming a teacher. Upon returning home, she also found that the squalor, the dirt, and the eating habits of her parents repelled her, and she moved out. Yet she discovered that she did not belong in the American world either and had to endure the loneliness that denied her comfort in both spheres.[69] As early as 1905, the *Forward* discussed this problem. Many Jewish typists, it observed, "live in two distinct worlds." In the office, among well-dressed people, a typist is treated with respect and spoken to "like a countess." "But at home, living in dirty rooms, she's plain 'Beyle' or 'Khontshe.' Her parents speak crudely to her. They pounce upon her if she expresses an interest in a new hat. If she mentions a ball, they tell her to dance with the laundry."[70]

Even if the contrast was less dramatic, and a family was tightly knit, young women often had difficulty reconciling the two halves of their lives. Rita S., who had a genteel job as a salesgirl, recalled, "It was a different life in Macy's and it was a different life when I came home to the Bronx. It was a really crazy family. Our house was not nice. I would never think of inviting any of my fancy friends. In a way I felt like nothing was my home until I got married." The writer Vivian Gornick observed of this atmosphere in which she grew up that "even while one was being nourished by it, one was straining to separate from it" and become part of the larger American world.[71]

Many girls longing to resolve this division in their lives found a solution in marriage. For young women anxious to become American, marrying an Americanized, or even better, an American-born man was even more important than finding a wealthy or an educated husband. "All I wanted was to get married," recalled Frieda M., "and of course never to marry a foreigner." Rose G. dated a pleasant young man but refused to consider marrying him. "I was a real American girl," she observed, "and he wasn't as Americanized as I was." Dora W. used the example of marriage to contrast her own success in Americanization with the failure of her older sister, who came here too old to make a complete transition. "The difference came through distinctly in our marriages," she observed. "My sister wanted to marry somebody who was American—a great goal at that time. But she never could. She married somebody quite foreign." Dora, on the other hand, married a man who, like herself, immigrated young and was as Americanized as she was. Mildred L., who fought to cast off the invisible shackles of her poor, illiterate parents, saw marriage as her only way out. Even attracting American-born men was a source of pride to her. "I didn't attract immigrant types," she recalled. Her life was a heroic struggle, her daughter asserted, because she was the only one of ten children who managed to enter the mainstream of American life, and she accomplished this feat by marriage.

If mothers or fathers were unwilling or unable to understand the needs of these daughters, parents were sometimes rejected as part of the European background the girls wanted to shed.[72] Some young women working in factories found an alternative focus to family life by participating in union activities or socializing with their peers. Those who did not work lacked this option, and their lives were more restricted. Young women occasionally chose to enter the labor force because of the greater freedom this would give them; one fourteen-year-old girl decided to take a job when her mother told her that only those who worked needed new clothes and shoes.[73]

Such young people seeking a new identity as Americans often felt that others judged them by their mothers, so they tried to transform the older women into more acceptable American matrons. In one of Anzia Yezierska's short stories, a young girl works, to no avail, to modernize her dowdy, old-country mother. "I dressed her in the most stylish Paris models," she tells her brothers, "but Delancey Street sticks out from every inch of her. Whenever she opens her mouth, I'm done for. . . . I, with all my style and pep can't get a man my equal because a girl is always judged by her mother."[74] Elizabeth Hasanovitz wrote of a friend who also was ashamed of her mother. "To me, as to many," her friend told her, "my mother was only a 'greenhorn,' a foreigner, and of course, inferior to me, an Americanized girl." Hasanovitz often heard such quarrels between mothers and daughters: "I am an American—you are only a greenhorn; you don't even understand what I say."[75]

This intense rejection was shared by women like Mildred L., who sought singlemindedly to dissociate herself from her poor, illiterate mother and become a "real American." Mildred spent her money on scented soaps and fashionable clothing and chose only American-born friends whom she never brought home to meet her parents. She refused even to date immigrant men because she always wanted to "better" herself. "I didn't have what I yearned for," she recalled with effort, "to speak well and to live in a nice place that I wasn't ashamed of. I saw other people were different and I couldn't understand why I couldn't be the same way." Even the religion of her parents was discarded. After a non-Jewish friend took her to a Christian Science church, Mildred began attending services and studying to convert. Mildred's lasting memory of her mother is that she was enmeshed in the poverty, ignorance, and dirt of the Lower East Side and was someone only to escape from. "My growing up didn't do me any good," she stated, still passionate with feelings of deprivation after more than fifty years, "because I had nobody to learn from." Americanized at last, the delight of Mildred's later years was the thrill of working in that shrine of immigrant girls, the department store.[76]

Such daughters may have suffered from a kind of identity crisis, because although they rejected the behavior and personality traits of their mothers, they had also internalized them and were therefore fearful of seeing these characteristics emerge in themselves.[77] Many second-generation immigrants believed that taking full advantage of what America offered required first that they rid themselves of their parents' ethnic identities. However, they often wound up in an impossible position, consumed with unfulfilled hopes, anxiety, and self-hatred.[78] The strain of changing oneself could be fearsome. Mildred had what sounds like a nervous breakdown at sixteen. Like Mildred, Elizabeth Hasanovitz also rejected everything associated with Eastern Europe and her parents. Although her father was a Hebrew teacher, she ate ham and scorned Yiddish. She too went into a deep depression from the constant struggle to make herself into what she was not.[79]

This tension between the desire to Americanize and the psychological hold of parents and their traditions has been best described in the novels of Anzia Yezierska. In six books published between 1920 and 1932, Yezierska wrote of the squalor of ghetto life and the constant struggle against dirt, poverty, and old-world family restrictions. Her works portray the longing of a young woman for freedom and beauty, personified by the non-Jewish world, and each one ends with the realization that the source of life lies in the world that was rejected. "All these years," she wrote in *All I Could Never Be*, "I have gone about a little bit ashamed of my manners, my background. I was so eager to acquire from the Gentiles their low voices, their calm, their poise, that I lost what I had—what I was."[80] The young woman in *Children of Loneliness* observes, "I can't live with the old world, and I'm yet too green for the new."[81] Yezierska was not so much writing novels as she was autobiography, so her plots appear and reappear in scarcely changed form. She could tell no other story than her own, but she recorded that with a searing passion. The plot of *Bread Givers*, her most popular novel, she explained to producer Sam Goldwyn, "is the expiation of guilt. . . . I had to break away from my mother's cursing and my father's preaching to live my life: but without them I had no life. When you deny your parents, you deny the ground under your feet, the sky over your head. You become an outlaw, a pariah. . . . And now, here I am—lost in chaos, wandering between worlds."[82]

Quite possibly, families who were most urbanized and secular weathered this transformation best.[83] As in Eastern Europe, the attitudes of such families seemed to conflict least with the demands and opportunities of an urban, industrial society. Daughters remembered these parents as being very much in tune with the times. Tanya N., whose parents had revolutionary sympathies in Russia, recalled visits of their friends who spent the evening singing radical Russian songs. Some of those friends, she recalled, all of whom were well educated, scorned traditional marriage and lived together openly. "This was considered the more intellectual, the more esthetic kind of marriage. They didn't believe in going to a rabbi," she observed with obvious approval. Tanya's father took the whole family to Socialist Party lectures to help them learn English as well as ideology. Since the father was a "free-thinker," his daughter's religious irreverence hardly mattered, nor did her working on the Sabbath affect relations. The parents of Marie Jastrow took pride in being new Americans. One of the delights of her childhood was a daylong family excursion in 1909 to see a parade commemorating the discovery of the Hudson River. As her father gazed at the floats celebrating historical events, Marie remembered his observing "This is wonderful. . . . From one end of the world to the other we came, together, to build this country."[84] Clearly, in these families, the American-ization of children would become a source of satisfaction rather than conflict. Such parents were more likely to hold liberal views and share the aspirations of their children.

Even when a parent was religious, if his or her views were not forced upon an unwilling child, family life generally remained harmonious. The daughters in such families generally had little difficulty reconciling the values of their parents with the demands of America. Janet A. remembered the closeness of her home and the importance of music and literature to her parents. Although her father was orthodox, he believed in letting his children find their own way. The mother and father of Anna R. had similar views. "Whatever they had, they shared," she recalled, but they never insisted that the children follow their example. Anna rejected their ortho-doxy but embraced their ethics. "Who could be richer?" she asked. "They were people's people, and that's who I learned my life from." In these families, too, children could generally win the freedom they sought with-out a struggle.

In most families, however, mothers seemed more willing than fathers to let daughters live their own lives—as in Eastern Europe, the term "fanat-ical," occasionally applied to a dictatorial father, was never used to describe a mother, no matter how religious she was. Furthermore, mothers often served the function of mediator—a bridge between the old ways and the new, or simply between a rigid father and a daughter or son seeking more freedom. Elizabeth Stern wrote, "I cannot think of mother except as of one who always stood between us and . . . father. It was she who made it her task to explain us to father, to soften him to our desires."[85] Dora W.'s mother also continually urged her husband to ease his restrictions on their children. She accepted the money Dora earned when he refused even to speak to their daughter because she worked on Saturdays. This persistent woman eventually secured a reconcilation between her husband and Dora, and her constant intervention on behalf of the children was all that kept them from leaving home.

Although mothers may not have shared their daughters' attitudes toward working on the Sabbath or other signs of entry into the modern world, they nevertheless seemed to accept them better than many fathers. In much of the immigrant literature, a father's attempts to impose old-world values upon his children precipitates an upheaval in family life, while the mother holds the family together by her common sense and greater willingness to adapt to American standards.[86] Women seem to have played this role in many Jewish immigrant families. For example, the mother of Fannie N., even though she was more religious than her husband, tolerated her daughter's lesser piety and helped hide from him the dresses Fannie bought lest he object to the unnecessary expense. Possibly mothers could, through their daughters, vicariously gain a freedom they sometimes dreamed of but seldom achieved in Eastern Europe. Perhaps they believed that their own traditions might prevent the children from assimilating and thus reaping the benefits of becoming Americans.[87] Perhaps the compromises such women themselves had to make with religious practices had made them more receptive to the belief that surrendering some aspects of orthodoxy did not threaten their daughters' attachment to Judaism. Perhaps they simply wanted to keep peace within the family. Regardless of the reason, mothers seemed to accept the Americanization of their daughters with relative equanimity.[88]

When young women immigrated on their own, if all their friends were also immigrants, or if their ambitions to be American were less demanding, then the transition was easier psychologically. Frieda M., who met her husband in the same garment shop she worked in, simply asserted, "I wanted to be an American, so therefore I was—I worshipped America." Because most of her childhood was spent evading soldiers and bandits and fighting off hunger during World War I, to her, America "was wonderful in comparison." Pauline H., who came here at fourteen and kept house for her brothers and father, never spoke English with ease; nevertheless, she learned to dress well and clearly believed that this made her "just like an American girl." Fannie K. managed to surpass her friends in learning English and was proud that other immigrants thought she was native-born. To Gussie M., who came from a poverty-stricken home and worked in a garment shop here, Americanization meant discovering how to behave in the United States. She and her brother and friends all spoke Yiddish together, and English always remained difficult for her. But Gussie never strayed beyond the immigrant sphere. She joined the Workmen's Circle, founded by Eastern European working-class Jews, and served as secretary for a Socialist Party branch whose business was conducted in her native language. Gussie educated herself by reading Yiddish literature for the first time at the Workmen's Circle library and by listening to speakers, particularly those from the *Forward* who would come and lecture the young people about proper manners and customs in America. "It was wonderful," she recalled. "We enjoyed it thoroughly."

Such women came from poor backgrounds and were grateful for what the United States could give them—a job, the opportunity to learn, a secure life, like-minded friends—and they seldom measured their achievements against those of American-born women who inhabited a different world from their own. Unlike children, who grew up as Americans with minimal effort, and unlike older women, who struggled to become American, these young women generally lived and worked within the immigrant community and married men much like themselves. But although their goals and accomplishments were limited, they avoided many of the conflicts with parents and within themselves that could afflict young women who aimed higher and abandoned the values and traditions of their families to follow the lure of America.

7

. . . .

Mothers, Fathers, and Daughters

During the first years, there was always a struggle, but fortunately, it didn't warp my mind or spirit. And I think it's because of the love that we had from our parents. They were sweet people, dear people, full of love.

—Frances F.

. . . .

In our home my father made the decisions. . . . But [my mother] is a very strong-willed and determined woman, and I think that many of the decisions my father thought he made were really hers to start with.

—Fannie C.

. . . .

Mama was a very good manager—she was able to make two pennies out of one. I don't know how she did it.

Rivu P.

11. An immigrant mother and daughter.

Collection of the author

An ever-changing amalgam of Eastern European and American influences shaped the social and family roles assumed by women of the immigrant generation. While home and family remained the center of women's concern, life in New York seemed to breed a new assertiveness. As early as 1902, normally quiescent Jewish housewives took to the streets to protest the rise in the price of kosher meat. When landlords on the Lower East side raised rents during the depression of 1907–8, six hundred angry housewives marched from house to house mobilizing likeminded women to strike. The movement soon spread to other areas of Manhattan and Brooklyn.[1] Women also organized local groups to fight the influence of Jewish gangsters in their neighborhoods.[2] When the family's interests were endangered, many women took action, and they seemed to prize similar initiative in their daughters.

Although ambition to be anything but a wife and mother was not considered appropriate for young women of any ethnic background,[3] Jewish immigrant mothers sometimes reluctantly encouraged daughters' desires for education or career. For example, Marie F.'s mother opposed her daughter's going on the stage, preferring that she be "safely married," but when Marie proved adamant, her mother moved to Chicago to help with her career. More subtly, when Sophie Abrams-Flint, as a child, read until late at night, her mother would wake up and say, "The light is still on? What do you expect to be, a doctor or a lawyer? What's the use of all this reading and writing? Don't be foolish, a woman never needs to know anything!" But under her breath Sophie would hear her mutter, "A talented child has hands of gold."[4] Despite the desire that their daughters marry, such mothers encouraged in them a sense of independence, sometimes without themselves being aware of it.[5]

If mothers hoped daughters would find fulfillment in marrying and raising a family, they also followed tradition by encouraging them to prepare to support themselves if necessary. In this country, women knew that if daughters got an education, they could take a step up the economic ladder and become clerical workers or possibly teachers until they married. Few mothers, though, went as far as Kate Simon's did in advising her daughter to choose a career instead of marriage. "Study, learn. Go to college," she told her daughter. "Don't get married, at least not until you can support yourself and make a careful choice. Or don't get married at all, better still."[6] But on the other hand, few Jewish mothers would have prayed, as some Italian mothers did, that their daughters not disappoint them or disgrace the family by going to school and remaining spinsters.[7]

The way parents felt about a daughter's relationships with young men depended in large part on attitudes formed in Poland and Russia. By the end of the nineteenth century, in the cities and towns of Eastern Europe, modern ideas had already made inroads into traditional ways. Marriage as a strictly social and economic arrangement was breaking down. In Sholem Aleichem's *Tevye's Daughters*, the father's right to select his daughter's groom has been replaced, to his chagrin, by the young people's seeking his mainly ceremonial approval after they have fallen in love. Arranged marriages were giving way to a more flexible system, and especially in the cities, working girls had freer relations with young men and frequently chose their own husbands. Parents raised in this liberal atmosphere, like those of Janet A., from a city in Lithuania, or Elsie F., whose family came from Budapest, were most likely to permit daughters more freedom without a struggle.

Yet old traditions still held sway, particularly among those who grew up and married in the Old Country. Alfred Kazin recalled the disdain with which his parents considered the idea of "love," an emotion they considered appropriate only in movies. When Kazin's cousin and her friends protested to his mother that they could not marry men they did not love, she exploded into a diatribe. "Liebe! [Love] Liebe! What is this love you make a stew about? You do not like the way he holds his cigarette? Marry him first and it will all come out right in the end." Whatever his parents thought of each other, "*love* was not a word they used easily." They seemed committed to something beyond love, Kazin observed. "Their marriages were neither happy nor unhappy; they were arrangements" that resulted in a family.[8] And the harmony and stability of that family, the proper rearing of children, were the primary goals of marriage.[9] If love existed, it was a result of marriage, not a reason for it.

Although the words of romantic love were alien to many of the adult generation, a deep affection between parents shaped the attitudes of many daughters. When Sophie Ruskay asked whether her father actually proposed, her mother answered, "Maybe not in so many words. . . . But your papa has shown his love in ways that are better than words."[10] Rose G. observed that "at home, I saw love. My father adored my mother. And with love, the parents got along—it was a big thing." This feeling was usually expressed more in deeds than in words. For example, the father of Naomi L. dearly loved his young second wife. "He treated her practically like a child," Naomi recalled. "When my mother slept, he'd say, 'Shh!, Mother is sleeping.' We had to walk on tiptoes. And he would give her whatever she wanted. He would get up early to make packages for my sisters who took lunch to work. He would prepare it and mother would sleep." Similarly, the father of Hannah F. expressed affection for his wife through his behavior. A cultured man, he helped his illiterate wife learn American ways by reading articles aloud from the *Forward* and then discussing them with her. "He never made her feel that she was beneath anybody," Hannah recalled. "And he helped her so much. I still have the recipes he gave her from the paper for fish with lemon juice." Hannah believed that her parents gave her the most valuable gift possible by the example of their mutual devotion. "The most important thing in life is the love that you feel," she observed. "It gives one the security of being able to face whatever comes in life." And she credited that love with enabling her to live a richer life.

This is not to say that all marriages were harmonious. Novels and memoirs of the time reflect the weakening of the immigrant family, particularly when poverty made life bitter.[11] Etta Byer, for example, lost a child she was unable to nurse because of overwork. On the day she returned from the hospital, her husband had refused to get coal to heat their icy house. "I did not get the care a cow would get when she brought a calf into the world," she observed with bitterness.[12] Byer eventually left her husband. Generally, though, dissatisfaction with marriage was considered insufficient cause to separate or divorce. Even a husband's philandering was often ignored by women unable to manage on their own. Fannie G.'s father owned a tailor shop and had affairs with women who came in as customers. But his wife did nothing. "What could she do?" Fannie asked. "How could she leave him? She didn't speak English, she didn't know how to make a living. Where could she even go?" Such women swallowed their disappointment and devoted themselves completely to their children. "My mother wasn't happy," recalled Fannie. "She was happy with the children, and that was all."

As in Europe, most marriages fell between these extremes. Arguments were accepted as part of relationships, and certainly there were many things to argue about. The parents of Riva P. fought over her father's frequent affairs with other women. "But mom always forgave him," Riva recalled. "He always came back." Despite his infidelity, she was certain that he had loved his wife. "He used to call her his little doll." And after her father died, when her mother walked by his coffin, "she didn't say 'lover,' but she said, 'Goodbye *chaver*' [comrade]. So that with all that, she said that nobody had a husband like she had. If friends had kept their mouths shut, maybe it would have blown over." Money was a more common source of friction. Tanya N.'s parents quarreled frequently over spending, for "when there is no money, it is easy" to fight. Ethel B.'s parents argued over business matters because her father never did well and her mother felt insecure. Religious practice was another source of dissension. "If my father had been less religious," observed Dora W., "my mother would have been happier here." Yet despite the misery of her mother's day-to-day life with her husband, after he died, she told her daughter, "You know, I didn't know how much I loved your father and how much I would miss him." She outlived him by only nine months.

Often disagreements focused upon the children. Dora recalled, "My father was very restrictive with my sister and brother. And my mother used to try to defend them and argued with my father. And in turn she became the victim, so to speak. So she was not happy." Ethel's mother felt that her father was a "spendthrift" because he often spent what little money they had on their daughter. "He'd say, 'the child wants; she has to have.' And my mother's feeling was that 'when a child wants, you wait for three months and then you buy it, so you don't spoil her.'" Kate Simon fought with her father over her desire to attend high school and to lead a more independent life, but her mother defended her constantly. "She has a right to a father who encourages her, who helps her," she used to tell him. "Why do strangers, teachers in a school, praise her, push her on while you try to break her legs?"[13] Although mothers usually tried to keep peace within the family, many drew the line at what they perceived as their children's long-term interests.

Conflicts were resolved in different ways, depending upon relationships in a particular family.[14] At one extreme was the dictatorial structure, where fathers made all decisions and imposed their will upon wives and children. In such families, the mother frequently interceded, or acted as a buffer, particularly when fathers clashed with children. Dora remembered, "My mother always tried to avoid quarrels. My father wanted my brother to *lay tfiln* [put on prayer phylacteries]. And to say the morning prayer. My brother didn't really want to do it. But she would say to him, 'Do it. Let's not have a quarrel.' So he would do it hastily. Anyway, my mother would turn the pages and close the book, so that when father came home it would be all right, there would be no quarrel." The mother of Tanya N. played a similar role. When Tanya defied her father and had her long hair clipped short, her mother first sent her to a grandmother's and then mediated between the girl and her angry husband. This was a typical role for women who understood that their children's lives would differ from their own.

At the other extreme were families where mothers made all decisions concerning the home and children, an arrangement based on a division of labor. The parents of Rose S. had this kind of relationship. "My mother was dominant," Rose recalled, "because my father was always a hard-working man, and if something came up with the children, she would never tell

12. Immigrant parents and children, about 1908.
Collection of Ida Fireman

them, 'Wait until your father comes home!' She never said it and she never did it. If a child did something he shouldn't have, she dealt with it. She told me many a time, 'Daddy works hard enough and we don't want to make him feel bad when he comes home.'" Rose remembered her father as playing little part in bringing up his children. "He used to leave in the morning when we got up to go to school, and he'd come home when we were in bed." Whenever something had to be decided, even by her mother's sisters or parents, Rose recalled, "They always came to mother for advice." It was not unusual for many women to make the important decisions under the guise of freeing men from such day-to-day cares.[15]

Most family decision making, however, seemed to follow a subtler pattern. Many wives deferred to husbands publicly and before the children but played a forceful, albeit circumspect, role in determining the outcome.[16] For example, Fannie C. began by stating, "In our home my father made the decisions." But then she continued, "My mother was the type that when I was a child, I'd go to her and ask for this or that, and she would say, 'When papa comes home, I'll ask him.' That would be her typical response. But she is a very strong-willed and determined woman, and I think that many decisions my father thought he made were really hers to start with. But as children we were under the impression that it was my father's decision. Like when she would say, 'Wait until papa comes home,' I'm sure that she made a decision before he made up his mind what to say." Marie Esposito, a Jewish woman married to an Italian man, learned a similar strategy from her mother. "She lets him think he is boss," she observed, "but when anything really important comes up she usually handles it without letting him know she is doing it. When it is disposed of, he pats himself on the back and claims all the credit. And she lets him get away with it, never contradicts him. She tipped me off to that system when I got married," Marie concluded, "and I guess that is why my husband and I get along so well."[17]

Men had to *appear* to be heads of the family, making all important decisions. The reality was somewhat different, as it was among other immigrant groups where it was important to maintain the public posture of male leadership.[18] Rose G. remembered her mother as the "starter" in the family. But she would insist to the children, "Papa has to be respected." "My father was on a pedestal," Rose recalled, "and so was my husband. As a matter of fact," she went on revealingly, "I once said to my husband, 'Louis, I look up to you. Please don't ever come down from that pedestal.'" Riva P.'s mother also acted submissively before her husband. "He was the boss of the house, and he made the decisions," she recalled. But "if there was something she wanted, she would usually manage to change his mind."

In all such families, men were, as one anthropologist has described, the "ceremonial leaders," often assuming credit for decisions the women convinced them they had made on their own.[19] These husbands generally held this position less because they automatically assumed it as a right, as authoritarian men did, but more because of the respect and affection borne them by wives.[20] As Frances F. phrased it, "The women were really the silent partners. They did the thinking and helped the men. The males were supposed to be the active ones. But the women were very often the power behind the throne." These women had great influence in their families.[21] Of course, a strong role for a wife could not be assumed at the expense of a man's pride. Marie Jastrow's mother quit a desperately needed job when her husband, upon discovering she had gone to work, told his wife, "Do as you wish, but understand that when you hire out, I am shamed."[22] Many women acted in this circumspect way to help maintain the egos of husbands who had difficulty adjusting to a low status and poorly paid job.

Most daughters credited mothers with being more open to change than fathers. One of the sources of family tension was parents' uncertainty about what was right for the children, for the behavior they had assumed was appropriate no longer seemed an adequate guide. In American society, young people generally identified with peers rather than parents,[23] and while immigrant mothers and fathers might not approve, many were unsure about how to act. Mothers, though, generally seemed more willing than fathers to trust the American ways their daughters brought home. Many read a Yiddish newspaper regularly and took an interest in the world. Fannie N. believed that had her mother spoken English and been more educated, she would have become a suffragette. In fact, after gaining the vote in 1917, Jewish women in New York were among the most enthusiastic voters and registered in large numbers.[24] These mothers could be strict with their daughters, but few were incapable of compromise.

Fathers often were more rigid, and daughters of authoritarian men could either make a virtue of obedience or leave home. Anzia Yezierska was driven from her parents' home by terrible fights with her father, and she reconciled with him only in the stories she told.[25] Ella Wolff recalled how her father had taken her out of school and then refused to let her attend night school or waste precious electricity by reading after dark.[26] When a boy visited thirteen-year-old Rose Cohen, her father sent him away and, complaining that she expected too much freedom, restricted her activities rigidly.[27] Many young women had particular difficulties with fathers over their social lives. When twenty-year-old Elsie F. decided to spend a weekend with a friend at a hotel in Lakewood, her father said, "No, you're not going." So Elsie unpacked. Her friend, though, "was a rebel. She said she was going to go regardless. And she got smacked; her father punished her. She didn't go either."

Although some fathers had difficulty accepting children's behavior, many coped in a way that salvaged pride and principles. Fannie C. was one of the fortunate girls who grew up in New York and attended high school. However, when she asked her father for permission to attend the senior prom with a young man, he became angry and refused. "By that time," Fannie recalled, "I felt that he went overboard. That it was too much. Before that, all my friends, their parents were the same way, so I had nothing really to compare him with. It was so terrible. But as I grew older, I began to resent it." Although Fannie missed her prom, after graduation she began to work as a bookkeeper and met her future husband at work. Within a year, she told her father that she was going away with her fiancé for the weekend. Although he protested strongly, she told him "I'm going, and that's that." Fannie's mother calmed him down, and like Tanya's father, after making a fuss, he bowed to the inevitable and accepted what he could not change.

The reaction of Fannie's father illustrates a typical pattern of behavior. Many men, after fighting a daughter's assertions of independence, eventually acquiesced rather than force the issue at the risk of severing family ties. They almost never took the irrevocable step of telling daughters to obey or leave home. Sometimes, a father's opposition to expressions of independence could assume an almost ritualized form. For example, despite the fury of Dora W.'s father at her decision to profane the Sabbath by working, this very religious man still permitted his daughter to remain under his roof. He showed his disapproval by refusing to speak to her for a year, at which time his wife reconciled them. Such a ceremonial expression of disapproval fulfilled the requirements of pride, while the underlying acceptance of the situation validated a daughter's claim to the rights of adulthood.

Because men frequently brought home only a meager salary and were sometimes unemployed, married women often had to find a temporary way to feed their families and pay the rent.[28] Although fathers frequently suffered a loss in self-esteem when they had to accept menial jobs, mothers who had to work for money did not seem to mind this loss of status as much—it was just another form of "managing."[29] These women took jobs when they had to, but their identities were rooted in family rather than in any paid work they might be doing. Thus they may have weathered the psychological storms that buffeted so many husbands who felt degraded by low-level work.[30] As Riva observed, her mother believed that "the important thing was for her family to be taken care of." At some time in their lives, many women had to find ways to support their families or supplement a husband's inadequate income.[31] For a married Jewish woman, working in a factory was usually out of the question—husbands considered it particularly shameful, and the rigidity of working hours left little time to care for a family or run home to prepare lunch for the children. The ease with which a job could be combined with domestic duties was more important than wages or the simple availability of work.[32]

Home finishing of garments was one way of earning money that meshed with family needs, and for married Jewish women who came here in the 1880s and 1890s, this provided an important source of income. Often a whole family would work at the kitchen table sewing and pressing until late into the night to make the few cents that would put the next night's dinner on the table. But by 1907, tenement laws, mechanization, and competition from Italian women had sharply limited the number of Jewish women engaged in homework.[33]

Before restrictive laws in the early 1920s almost eliminated the flow of new immigrants, taking in boarders was the most common way to earn money and be able at the same time to keep an eye on the young ones. As the number of Jewish wives doing homework decreased, more began to take in such paying guests as a matter of course. Possibly 15 to 20 percent of all urban households included lodgers,[34] yet in New York City in 1905, one out of four married Jewish women took in at least one boarder.[35] When the mother of Marie Jastrow decided to move her family to a more expensive apartment after their arrival in 1907, she earned the additional rent money by caring for one live-in boarder from her hometown and making dinner for several others.[36] This was a common arrangement. By 1911, as the rate of boarding among other immigrant groups began to decrease, Jewish homes were becoming even more crowded with paying guests: 56 percent of Russian Jewish households had at least one boarder.[37] For a woman unaccustomed to working outside her home, it was the obvious way to supplement the family's income, or to provide one if a husband was temporarily jobless. For example, when the father of Frieda M. went bankrupt and honorably attempted to pay all his creditors, her mother made enough money for food by taking in a lodger. Rose L. observed that Jewish women did not work outside the home once they were married. "Boarders you had," she recalled. "You worked for them, you cooked for them, you cleaned for them." When times were hard, Mary Wasserman Natelson always cared for at least six lodgers and did their laundry and sewing as a matter of course.[38] Sara B., whose family lived in Bridgeport, remembered having to clean the rooms of six paying guests in their large house. Although Sara and her mother had to work hard, they met their trials with humor; her mother used to joke with Sara about being the "upstairs maid."

Sometimes a husband was unemployed, which meant that his wife had to find a way to bring in more income than could be earned from boarders. In 1911, New York's working wives, most of whom cared for lodgers, earned only 10 percent of their families' income.[39] The father of Frieda K. was a musician, and "when he worked it was wonderful." But all too often, he had no work or gambled away what money he made. So her mother managed to support herself and her daughter by embroidering blouses at home.[40] It was enough to keep them from going hungry. After Riva P.'s family arrived in New York in 1924, and her father could not get a job he considered suitable, her mother immediately went out to seek work, armed with a slip of paper with her name and address in case she got lost on the trolley. In Russia, she had trained as a milliner, and within a week, she had a job. Although the family at first lived with an aunt, within six months Riva's mother had saved up enough to enable them to move into their own apartment. This capable woman first took in a boarder to defray expenses and then found a job closer to home. Her husband failed in one business after another and eventually settled down as a waiter, so her steady income kept the family going. To earn extra money, she also worked in the evenings, making hats for friends and neighbors. Yet despite her long hours, she came home at midday to give her daughter lunch, and there was always a meal cooked for supper, even if she had to return to her job afterwards. Regardless of work to support the family, the needs of the home could not be ignored.

The mother of Marie Syrkin assumed the Eastern European role of the scholar's wife, but with an American twist. In Russia and Poland, Talmudic scholars usually had great prestige in the community but little money, and their wives considered it a privilege to work to support such worthy men. Marie's father held a similarly prestigeous but poorly paid position. He eked out an insufficient income by editing a Socialist-Zionist journal and brought in no money at all when he went off to Europe to attend a Zionist Congress. After he left, Marie's mother took a job in a millinery factory, but because in this country such work was considered a shameful loss of caste for the wife of an intellectual, Marie had to pledge not to tell her father or their friends what subterfuge paid the rent and fed the family.[41]

Many men, however, succeeded in establishing small businesses, and, as in Eastern Europe, wives often played an important role "helping out."[42] Here, too, women were sometimes the mainstay of the enterprise. The mother of Anna Kahan, who had never worked outside the home in Europe, put on an apron and plucked chickens in the small butcher shop she and her husband bought. "The main thing was plucking the chickens," Anna observed, "but he never did it. Oi veh! What a life!" Another Jewish daughter similarly observed that her mother had the real "head" for business and was the mainstay of the family butcher shop.[43] When the father of Elsie F. decided to try to make a living at peddling, his wife started stitching away making housedresses and frilly tea aprons so that he would have something to sell door-to-door. While Ethel B.'s father read his newspaper, her mother ran their small mattress store and through her frugality managed to tuck away over a thousand dollars in savings. When the depression struck and the business failed in the early 1930s, she had the money to start again.

Working in a family shop or at home gave women the flexibility to take care of their children as well. "Mother was a great housekeeper," Ethel recalled. "She was a baker, she did everything. She always managed. You came into my home and there was never a time when she didn't have marvelous food and cakes ready for company. She was just great!" Some women thrived on this kind of life, in which family and business meshed. Rose G., for example, remembered that her "mother loved it when she was in business. She felt needed and busy. She managed most of the laundry. My father did the writing when a person brought in shirts. And she'd sort it through. He wrote the ticket. And they had to mark it and send it to the steam laundry. My father handled the books. She was in the back, in the three-room apartment. She did the cooking and gave out the stuff to the customers. She was happy in the business because she was needed," Rose concluded, "like I am too."

If a wife was widowed, divorced, or deserted, she often had to support her family alone. A third of all women in this situation were employed.[44] Because women's work generally paid much lower wages than men's, this was difficult at best, particularly since such unfortunate women also had to care for their children. A few women did well on their own. Rose Soskin recalled, "When papa passed away, my mother decided to open up a fruit store, and she did pretty good. She liked to be independent."[45] But for most women, being the only family wage earner meant a rapid descent into poverty.[46] After Rose Schneiderman's father died at thirty-one, her mother weaned her newborn baby, placed her young sons in an orphanage, and, leaving Rose at home to care for the infant, took a job in a factory.[47] Frieda W., deserted by her husband, with no home and a child to feed, was forced to find domestic work where she would be able to keep her son with her. Alfred Kazin painted a vivid picture of the women who supported families by selling herring and pickles out of large, dark barrels in the market. From his childhood, he remembered their

> familiarly harsh, mocking cries and shouts. . . . Their shrewd open-weather eyes missed nothing. The street was their native element; they seemed to hold it together with their hands, mouths, fists and knees; they stood up in it behind their stands all day long, and in every weather; they stood up for themselves. In winter they would bundle themselves into five or six sweaters, then putting long white aprons over their overcoats, would warm themselves at fires lit in black oil drums between the pushcarts, their figures bulging as if to meet the rain and cold head-on in defiance.[48]

Struggling to care for a family was not easy. When her father died of tuberculosis, Jennie Herbst asked, "What was my mother to do? There were no jobs for women. She cooked at weddings, she plucked chickens, took in boarders. My oldest brother dropped dead three weeks after his wedding in 1911 when I was eight. What was my mother to do? She became a janitress in the *Talmud Torah* [Hebrew School] at 31 Tompkins Avenue, Brooklyn, scrubbing the classrooms and halls, making up the stoves to heat the offices. I wouldn't be a bit surprised if my own tuition in the *Talmud Torah* came gratis along with the apartment on the third floor. . . . Now you know why my mother had a bitter tongue."[49]

Bitter lives made for bitter tongues. Anzia Yezierska remembered her mother's resenting her husband's absorption in religious studies while she had to struggle to feed the family. Her mother "dried out her days fighting at the push-carts for another potato, another onion into the bag, wearing out her heart and soul and brain with the one unceasing worry—how to get food for the children a penny cheaper." She remembered her father, on the other hand, as "a Hebrew scholar and dreamer who was always too much up in the air to come down to such sordid thoughts as bread and rent." As a child, when young Anzia had asked her mother why they didn't have butter on their dry bread as a friend did, she shrieked, "Have you got a father a businessman, a butcher, or a grocer, a bread giver, like Masha Stein's father? You don't own the dirt under Masha's doorstep. You got a father a scholar. He holds himself all day with God; he might as well hang the beggar's bag on his neck and be done with it." At another time, she complained, "Woe is me! Your father works for God and his Torah like other fathers work for their wives and children." Yezierska understood that her mother's defeated attitude was the way she "accepted the crushing weight of life."[50]

Women who daily faced a constant struggle often had little time to devote to the emotional needs of their children. The writer and therapist Lillian Rubin remembered the grinding poverty of her life after her father's death, and her widowed mother's telling her angrily—or so it seemed to the child—"You're lucky you're not in an orphanage." Although she was terrified at the time, Rubin later understood her mother's frightening statement as a distorted expression of how much she cared.[51] For such harrassed women who had to work and make do with the little money they could earn, keeping the family together represented a deep manifestation of love.

Daughters sometimes resented mothers who had to take jobs outside the home and therefore had less time to spend with them. This was particularly true for children of middle-class families who believed that their mothers worked out of choice rather than necessity.[52] Sophie Ruskay remembered dreading the moment when her mother left for the family's shop. "To be sure, she would come back for lunch, but then only to leave us again. We never seemed to get used to it."[53] Riva P. and Janet A. swore that they, unlike their mothers, would stop working when their first child was born and always be there when the children came home from school. Riva recalled, "My mother was the only one of all my friends who worked. And the worst of it was when I opened the door at three o'clock and there wasn't anybody home. I vowed when I was very little that if I ever had children, I would never go to work unless it was a matter of bread." Janet had similar memories. "When I was little and I needed her for something," she recalled, "she was busy. And I didn't want my children to go through that." Yet in later years, both women understood their mothers' problems and the unreasonableness of their own early attitudes. "I held it against her that she never got up to make breakfast," Riva recalled. "The poor woman used to get up and run to work. But she came home to make me lunch every day, ran up four flights of stairs. And she would stand there with her hat, making me a hot lunch. She was a very good mother," Riva concluded. "How dare I resent that she didn't make me breakfast."

Even without the added burden of poverty, running a home properly was in itself a full-time job. Fannie C. described her mother's activities. "She was busy the whole day long," Fannie recalled,

> sending the children to school, her husband to work, making lunches, buying food at the market. She was an immaculate housekeeper, and

she used to sew beautifully. When I went to look for my first job I wore a dress that my mother had made. She made all my clothes. She sewed shirts for my father and my brother, and she knitted and crocheted and baked and cooked and hardly bought anything. And she used to do her own laundry, and her own ironing and her own windows. My mother was more than busy. By the time she got finished with the dinner dishes, she was glad to sit down and read the paper, or read a book.

Women's preservation of the Sabbath ceremony and holidays celebrated chiefly in the home assumed an importance in this country that it had lacked in Eastern Europe, where the synagogue was central to religion. Here, where economic pressures made religious learning apparently irrelevant to daily life, women's domestic practices became major rather than peripheral components in transmitting a sense of Jewish identification to children.[54] "My mother did everything herself, especially for Friday," Fannie recalled. "She began on Thursday. She would bake her own *challah*, her own cakes, and make her own gefilte fish and noodles." Daughters who retained these traditions did so mainly because they wished to follow their mothers' example. Sara B. remembered that until she died, her mother made *challahs* and gefilte fish and "did everything to enhance the *Shabbes*." And these high standards applied to all other holidays, which "she'd serve to the letter." Sara did the same. Mollie Linker also followed her mother's example. "I keep a strictly orthodox home," she asserted, "the dishes and everything. I feel like I'm obeying my tradition, from my father's and mother's side. And I think I like it too. . . . It's the heritage; it's embedded in me. . . . I feel that I want my grandchildren to remember me, saying 'My *bubbe* or Grandma did that,' just like my children remember what my mother did."[55]

Many daughters' memories of their mothers are intricately connected with some of the special food they prepared. Frieda K. recalled that her mother made "the most wonderful streudel; I'll never have that again. I wrote a poem about that, I really did—about how homesick I got for memories of my mother." Marie Jastrow remembered the cheap but delicious lung goulash her mother prepared when finances were tight, and the special Sunday treat of *palacsinta*—pancakes rolled with jam and bathed in sauce.[56] Hattie L. and her sister would reminisce about the lunch their mother cooked for them—"beans and barley and noodles—the reliable soup and a piece of *flanken* [meat]. We enjoyed it long after we were married and had children and grandchildren, and we spoke about the soup mother made, we remembered it. It was so beautiful." Other memories also centered about a mother's domestic skills and consideration. "I remember my mother sitting up nights and sewing," recalled Naomi L., "so that if a friend of mine was wearing a pretty dress, I should also wear a pretty dress." Rose Chernin reminisced with her own daughter about her mother, "the *zudhartkes* she took hot from the oven, the way she put down an apple on the table when I was studying."[57]

It was another important sign of a woman's competence to offer hospitality, no matter how poor the home, and since money was often in short supply, this was no small challenge. "In my mother's house, poor as she was," Rose Chernin recalled, "nobody went hungry. The pleasure it gave her to serve somebody a glass of tea. . . . The sweater she would knit for every occasion."[58] "We always had an open house," Fannie N. observed, "especially for family, that if they come over to my mother's they could always have a dinner, always a cup of tea, and everyone knew that she ran a very lovely and substantial home." Rose Pastor Stokes remembered the "company" that visited her parents' home and stayed all evening, arguing and singing, with her mother, who was "the life of these gatherings."[59]

Hospitality also extended to putting up a relative or friend in need, particularly one just arrived from the Old Country, who might remain for an indefinite period of time. Janet A. remembered her parents' house being filled with a constant stream of visitors who stayed with them, most often her father's friends who had been rabbis at home. "It was sort of an open house," she mused, "a very lively home." Such guests usually required a rearrangement of living conditions in their small apartment. Janet used to joke with her brother that she would have to get married before she had her own bed, because whenever they had a visitor, "It wasn't right that he should sleep on the couch, so I gave him my bed and I slept on the couch in the living room." Hannah F. remembered being similarly displaced. "We'd sleep in the kitchen for months," she recalled. "Why? Because a cousin was coming. She was an old maid, and my mother said she's got to stay until we married her off. So I remember my father's brother and his wife and three children moving in, and they took out everything from the dining room and they turned it into a bedroom, and we were in the kitchen." After they left, her mother's sister and brother arrived from Odessa and lived with them until he bought a farm in the Catskill Mountains.

But far from viewing the crowding and inconvenience negatively, these young women learned from their mothers' example to take great satisfaction in helping others. Hannah recalled, "Things like that were beautiful memories to me because it was sharing. I learned how to be understanding of other people's needs." Like Hannah, Janet observed that her mother "helped other people—not as an obligation—but because it was what they did." Anna R. asserted with pride that she took after her mother—a "people's person"—the kind of woman who "blooms through sustaining others."[60] Quite possibly, these daughters also learned that such activities, which made the home the focus of social life, enhanced their mother's status in the family.[61]

While family came first, sometimes daughters learned from mothers that helping others in need was its own reward. "I like to take care of people," Tanya N. observed. "Like my mother, I don't think it's my duty. I just like it." The widowed mother of Jennie Herbst, who worked as a janitress to support herself and her children, spent her spare time aiding new immigrants. "She was forever on her way to Ellis Island to *abhole* [bring home] someone," Jennie recalled,

> and as the youngest, I was dragged all over. Our house was full of *aufshtel-bettels*, folding beds for any number of them. She placed the girls as domestics in Jewish families she investigated, the boys went to work in the sweat shops. She watched over them, sewed their trousseaus, and delivered their babies. There was a "feather" bank in our house; she saved soft down for pillows and quilts for their trousseaus. There were feather parties on the oil-cloth covered kitchen table on Saturday nights with much song and laughter.

Although her mother had a hard life and a bitter tongue, her daughter remembered her as "a great lady. An *aishes chayil* [woman of valor]. A battler. Wherefore," she concluded, "I am today."[62]

Hattie L. also proudly ascribed her own character to her mother's example. "My mother became a real social worker," Hattie recalled,

> and that's what she left with me. I don't know how she did it, she didn't even speak English, but she was allowed in everywhere. She went to the Connecticut mental hospital, and this will stand in my mind as long as I live. She used to take us along, my sister and I. And there was a young boy who became depressed because he lost his job. Well, she went to the doctors and the doctor admitted that it was just a mild depression, and if he had a job and a place to live that he would be all right. So she asked the boy what kind of work he did. He said he repaired shoes, and if he could get a job, he could leave the hospital and earn a living.

So she took us along and went from house to house, and she collected two dozen pair of shoes. And she went and rented a front store and paid a deposit. And she signed him out of the hospital. And when the landlord heard that he was coming out of the institution, he came—I was in the house when he knocked on the door. He told my mother, "Here's the deposit back." She said, "I will pay the rent."

Well, by the time I graduated from school, he had his own shoe store, he had a wife, and he had two children. And he used to come and kiss my mother's hand. And he said he'd never forget her.

With her mother's encouragement, Hattie became a psychiatric nurse. She had learned from her mother the satisfaction of a life spent in helping others. "My mother didn't have a television," she recalled, "she didn't even have the radio. I say to my children, 'What did my mother have? Nothing! But she had her work, though. She had real gratification.'"

Few of these mothers could advise daughters how to be Americans— how to speak properly, dress, or behave—for in this country as in the cities of Russia or Poland, the culture of young people was diverging from that of their parents.[63] What young immigrant women *could* learn from their mothers, though, were the basic values and attitudes that would affect their lives once the initial desire to "fit in" with American society was satisfied. Regardless of the country they lived in, young girls of every ethnic group learned from their mothers what it took to manage a home properly. They saw their mothers shopping, baking, cooking, cleaning, sewing, caring for children, managing the family's money, and sometimes earning it themselves. They learned how to do the emotional housework of dealing with the psychological needs of husbands and children. Daughters saw their mothers doing whatever had to be done to assure the smooth functioning of their households and knew that they eventually would have to perform the same tasks.

Most daughters emphasized the importance of this role their mothers played in the family's life. Although they themselves became Americanized and usually worked steadily before marrying, they did not assume that a homebound mother was less important to the family economy than a wage-earning father. In fact, the highest compliment a daughter could pay a mother was that she was "a good manager," a function that carried over from Eastern Europe to the United States, and that meant doing whatever was necessary to hold the family together.[64] "Managing" encompassed everything from housekeeping and caring for the children to taking in boarders, doing piecework, and controlling the family's expenditures—the key to most married women's authority throughout industrial society at that time.[65] Such wives often led their families "onward to a bank account and competency," according to Abraham Cahan. "She it is who carries the family purse, purchases every article in the family wardrobe and deposits the family savings in a bank of her own selection."[66]

These women's sense of competence, pride, and strength within the home stemmed from the ability to do this job well,[67] and daughters spoke admiringly of their skills. Marie Jastrow wrote that her mother "always patched, covered, manipulated and made do with what she had on hand." To save money, she even managed to fabricate an ice box out of a washtub and a corrugated cardboard box. Marie remembered her mother's "agonizing" over spending ten cents that might be better saved for a "rainy day."[68] Managing might mean bargaining with a local storekeeper to buy a winter coat for a child a few cents cheaper, or better still, it could mean exchanging children's outgrown clothing with neighbors. It might mean buying a pair of shoes two sizes too large to provide for growth and stuffing the toes with newspapers, or taking up hems on oversized coats to keep them from dragging on the ground. It might mean temporarily pawning a wedding ring or a featherbed when money ran out between a husband's paydays.[69] Like Marie's mother, the mother of Rose G. derived a sense of satisfaction from making "every penny count." "She used to say," Rose recalled, "'My little bags will outlive other people's big sacks of money.' Because she watched every cent—she was very good at it." Like Rose, Ethel B. believed that her mother's talents held the family together. She was "terrific at business, a great housekeeper, a baker, she did everything. She really managed!" During the depression, when the father and brother of Janet A. were unemployed, her mother "never gave us the feeling that we weren't going to eat. I don't know how she managed," Janet observed, "I really don't know." Rita S. also marvelled at her mother's skill in marshaling the family's meager resources. "She was able to make two pennies out of one," Rita recalled. "I don't know how she did it!" The smooth functioning of the household thus depended on a woman's ability to "manage," and daughters appreciated that skill and prided themselves on taking after their mothers. Rose L. observed that "any money my husband had, he gave it to me— thank God, like my mother, I was always a good manager."

A girl's relationship with her mother generally was more complicated than that with her father.[70] An older woman might attempt to relive her own experiences through her daughter who in turn could view her mother as either a role model to emulate or a negative example to escape. Immigration affected this relationship only insofar as it added a new element to the

strains developing in all early twentieth-century industrial societies between traditional parents and children wanting to enjoy the new freedom
available for young people. Thus, unmarried young women sometimes had
an ambivalent relationship with mothers who saw that their children were
exceeding them in education, in adjustment to America, and in possibilities
for a satisfying life. While most mothers took pride in such accomplishments, an element of rivalry might lead a woman to withhold from her
daughter the finer points of baking or cooking, since this was the only
arena in which she excelled.[71] It might lead a daughter to reject her
mother's "old-fashioned" ideas, fearful she might discover these undesirable traits in herself.

Although the relationship between mother and daughter could be difficult when a girl was in her teen years, frequently it changed for the better
once the young woman married.[72] After a daughter had established her
own identity and moved out of her parents' home, the desire to distance
herself from her mother was no longer an issue, and seeing her mother's
characteristics emerge in her own behavior and attitudes became less
threatening. The possible tensions arising from a young girl's desire to date,
buy clothing, or lead a relatively independent life disappeared, for the
daughter now faced concerns similar to those of her mother: how to
manage a home, deal with a husband, and raise children. A common
interest in household activities, baby-sitting, or even domestic problems
often helped to forge new ties between Jewish mothers and daughters, as
it did among women in other ethnic groups as well.[73] At this point, if
the relationship was basically sound, young women could accept their
mothers as models. Even if they sought to follow a different path, daughters
were still aware of mothers' influence in shaping their own attitudes: "My
life," observed Rose Chernin, "you can only understand if you know my
mother."[74]

Young women could also learn values from fathers. Although Tanya N.
clashed frequently with her father, he nevertheless taught her how to enjoy
life regardless of worldly success. "Because my father was a failure in
business, he had no money at all," she recalled. "And this I remember. My
father only worked one or two days that week. He had only eight dollars.
And he called mama. He said, 'It's not going to pay the grocer and it's not
going to pay the butcher. It can pay only part of what we owe and we will
still remain in debt. Come and meet me in New York and we'll go to a
restaurant and drink wine.' Now that," Tanya concluded with obvious
approval, "is a typical Russian value." Rita S. learned from her father to view
life optimistically. "He was a very bright man, very outgoing," she remem-

bered, "and he was always smiling and he was always in a good mood. I don't think he was ever depressed. He'd get up in the morning and he'd say, 'It's a gorgeous day,' and it was like his life was just beginning. It was the most beautiful thing." The father of Lisa and Rose H. taught his daughters to have confidence in themselves. He was an Anarchist, and on Friday nights, instead of the Sabbath ritual, he would tell them stories of the Russian Revolution, including tales of women activists. "From that," they observed, "we got the idea that we could do things in life."[75]

Young women could pick up negative values from their fathers' behavior as well. Despite his love for her, Riva's father inadvertently taught her to distrust men. "I was a little afraid of marriage," she admitted. "My father was a philanderer. He had a lot of girlfriends, and I thought that all men were that way."

From mothers, however, daughters assimilated a whole system of values, reinforced by continuous observation. Many women internalized their mother's way of affecting family decisions, of helping other people, of running a home and raising children.[76] Mollie Linker recalled that her mother, the "backbone" of the family, had taught by example how to bring up children—"not to curse or raise the voice"—and, Mollie insisted, she was "the best teacher."[77] "You follow your mother's way," Rose S. agreed. "The way she taught you, you think it was great, and that's the way you bring your own children up." Sometimes the similarities between their attitudes or mannerisms and those of their mothers took women by surprise. Rose G. remembered as a child making fun of her mother praying for her children. "Now," she observed with amusement, "I'm doing the same thing." Some daughters attributed an acceptance of life's tribulations to a mother's example. A friend once asked Tanya N.'s mother where she got all the sunflower seeds she liked so much. "I'll tell you," she replied. "When I scrub the floor, I also plant seeds between the boards. And in the summertime, I have sunflowers." "She was always imaginative," recalled Tanya. "From my mother, I got a good sense of humor. Even when things were bitter, she never gave up."

Most women did, in fact, express positive views of their mothers. "My mother approved of everything I did," observed Frances F., trying to explain the basis for their close feelings. Sara B., speaking of the nine years her mother had spent under her roof, said, "I always felt that my mother was a *tsirung* in the house, something very beautiful and decorative." Minna S., instead of marrying, lived at home and cared for her mother devotedly until her death. "Even now," she mused, "I never forget her. I feel an aura of love around me because of her." Ethel B. recalled that her mother, whom she described as a "matriarch," constantly told her children "what to do and how to do it, and she didn't approve of what I did. We were really different from one another," Ethel observed, "but still very close. The bond between my mother and myself was always very strong. We spoke at least twice a day if we didn't see each other, to the very end." After her mother's death, Rose S. married—not to gain a husband, but in the futile hope of finding in her new mother-in-law a replacement for her beloved mother, her "best friend."

Relationships could remain distant, though, if a daughter felt unloved or if she rejected her mother as part of the heritage she wanted to shed. In a few families, daughters used mothers as negative role models. One woman, an oldest daughter who had to forego an education and care for younger children without any appreciation, branded her mother's methods and attitudes "primitive" in comparison to her own "civilized" views.[78] Rose Chernin, seeing her mother destroyed by a constant battle for survival, resolved to lead a different and better life. "I would lie awake at night and remember those fists beating at her, breaking her down, destroying her," Rose remembered. "And I knew it would not be me. . . . I would see to it. Always I struggled never to be like mama. Never like that poor, broken woman."[79]

Even when daughters had not been close to mothers as children or young women, later years and their own experiences gave them a different perspective. Women who believed mothers had not loved them or treated them properly explained that their mothers' lives had been too bitter or harried to permit the luxury of love. "My mother happened to be a selfish woman," observed Rose G., who then went on to explain that her mother "had no real childhood" and suffered great deprivation. Jennie Herbst recalled her mother's "caustic and sarcastic retorts" that often made her young daughter cry. "Love was never talked about," she remembered, "nor ever was there a gesture or intimation that such a thing existed between mother and child." Yet after Jennie grew up and married, she thought about her mother's life "with pity and commiseration."[80] Although their values may have differed from those of their mothers, such daughters were in time able to understand those differences without rejecting the parent.[81]

Perhaps one reason for this tolerance is that many mothers had also accepted the values or behavior of their children, though they may not have shared them. Although Mildred L. rejected her mother because of her foreign ways, when this simple, devout woman learned that her troubled daughter was attending a Christian Science church, she told her, "If it's doing you good, then it has to be good, and I want you to have it." The mother of Marie F. "learned to adjust" when her daughter insisted on becoming an opera singer, and even moved to Chicago to help with her career. Louise C., who fled a life of poverty in Eastern Europe, discovered new connections with her mother through their letters. Louise particularly remembered the day she left for the hospital to give birth to her first child. "I had a letter at eight o'clock in the morning," she recalled. "My mother wrote me to have courage to give birth. In spite of the fact that you were an ocean apart," she observed, "the umbilical cord was never really cut. The tie was there."

Mothers could offer little useful advice to daughters on how to behave as young single women, but they set important examples in understanding how to approach life, care for a family's physical and psychological needs, and relate to people. Daughters learned how to "manage," how to act as mediators and play an important role in running families behind the facade of paternal authority. And once they married, many daughters would use these skills to help their own families survive in difficult times. As members of a generation that emphasizes self-fulfillment, we might not easily understand the satisfactions of those who lived their lives for and through others. It seems clear, though, that these immigrant daughters were profoundly affected by mothers' examples of service and self-sacrifice, and, like their mothers, if efforts were rewarded by an appreciative family, they learned to achieve satisfaction from such a life.

8

. . . .

Opportunities
and Obligations

Even if my parents didn't give me much, I still would have wanted to have that responsibility because if they didn't give me much then it was because they couldn't give me much. . . . My parents depended on me. My brother really enjoyed his life—and I had the responsibilities.

—Fannie C.

. . . .

At the end, my mother lived with her youngest daughter. She was the one that was attached to her most. She was four years old when she came to the United States. And here my mother saw how they treat children, with ice cream cones and orange juice, and how they respect children, and how they speak to them. And she learned.

—Ruth R.

. . . .

13. An immigrant brother and sisters.

Collection of Diana Shapiro Bowstead

*Coming here, I immediately went
to school, I had the opportunity.
Whereas my sister, who was much
older, had to go to work. . . . I was
the youngest and she was the
oldest. It makes all the difference
in the world.*

—Marie F.

In the world of the fairy tale, all good people live happily ever after. But in the demanding industrial society immigrant families faced in the first three decades of the century, hard choices had to be made as to who would benefit from the opportunities available in the United States. The most obvious determinant of a child's role was the economic condition of the family. If poverty oppressed a household, most able-bodied family members had little option but to work. Less obvious, but no less important, were the sex and age of a child in relation to her or his brothers and sisters, for children often differed widely in the obligations they shouldered and the opportunities they gained through the sacrifices of others.

Many parents who came to America knew that their lives would be hard, but hoped to find consolation in the success of their children—a favorite Jewish saying is *nakhes fun di kinder*, or "gratification from the children." However, definitions of "success" varied widely. Traditionally, hopes for a son had centered about religious learning or a lucrative business career, while a daughter was expected to marry and raise a family. This system was already under attack, particularly in the urban centers of Eastern Europe, and many daughters as well as sons were seeking a secular education, some with the support of their parents. Thus the longing of many girls for an education in the United States did not represent a new expectation as much as it did an old dream that was more easily fulfilled in this country.

Yet even if education was free and open to all, it did not mean that all could take advantage of it. As one troubled mother wrote to the *Forward*, "Even when the schooling is free, who will support the family?"[1] Few families could afford to send all children to school rather than work. When a father's income was insufficient, the older children of both sexes almost inevitably worked while the younger ones, who learned English with an ease that was the pride and envy of older siblings, went off to join their peers in the public school.[2] "My younger sister is American-born," observed Minna S., "and I'm from the other side. She understood more." Sometimes sons attended school[3] while daughters worked, although among the Jews age just as much as sex determined whether a child could study or had to take a job.

For older girls in particular, if the family needed their income, full-time schooling was simply an unaffordable luxury. Regardless of the education they had received in Europe, most had no option but to enter the garment shops or work at some other low-paying job. Rae K. recalled, "I came from the Ukraine where I was an educated girl, a teacher myself, and to come here and not know the language, not be able to go to college—it was terrible!" This was a common refrain. "We were the lost generation," observed Fannie K., who came to America at the age of twenty. "If we were born here, who knows what we could have been?"

The older sister of Naomi L., in her early teens, begrudged the fact that she had to forego an education for the factory, while Naomi did not, and Tanya N. felt the same way about her younger sister. Rahel Mittlestein's older sister could not return to high school after emigrating because she had to work to support her mother and younger sister. She spent her life as a worker and resented her sister's college education.[4] The older sister of Rita S. was also disappointed at having to work in a shop after the family left Russia, but, Rita observed, "It was very nice for me because I was one of the lucky ones. I could go to school—I didn't have to work." Hattie L., who came here at six, had a similar story. While she attended school, her two older sisters went to work in a factory. "There was nothing else they could do," she concluded. Hannah F., the "baby" of four sisters, was the only one able to "take advantage of the United States and what it offered." Younger children considered themselves lucky to have come here early enough in their lives to attend school. "I was one of the fortunate ones," observed Marie F., and this was a sentiment echoed by many.

Sometimes, older children who had come too late to get an education transferred their unfulfilled desires to younger brothers or sisters. "My sister Jenny was very disappointed when she came," Rita recalled. "She was a beautiful girl and she thought that all the men of America are just waiting for her. But she had to go to work in a shop and she hated it. She even stopped eating." Her sister coped by living vicariously through Rita. "I could go to school and I was like the queen in that house. My sister really loved me. She was like my mother." Rose Cohen, who had to work when she came here in the 1890s, used to watch children on the way home from school. "In their white summery dresses and with books under their arms," she wrote, "they appeared to me like wonderful little beings of a world entirely different from mine. I watched and envied them. But I often consoled myself with the thought, 'When our children come they too will go to school.'"[5] Lena Kimberg and her oldest brother worked to support the family after their father became ill, and Lena also took comfort in the thought that the younger children could remain in school, for, like Rita's sister, she felt as if they were as much her own as her mother's.[6] Many women attended high school, and Miriam M. even finished law school, in part because older siblings worked and insisted that they continue to study. They were aware of the sacrifices of older brothers and sisters, of the limited horizons imposed on them regardless of talent or intelligence. Marie F. spoke of the talents of her "brilliant" sister, who was forced to lead a stunted life. "She was the oldest and I'm the youngest," observed Marie, who became an opera singer. "It made all the difference in the world."

As in Eastern Europe, or with girls of any ethnic group, an older daughter was expected to care for younger siblings. This might have been even more burdensome in this country, for in Europe, a grandmother might have acted as surrogate mother, but here there were fewer grandmothers.[7] Tanya N. remembered that when she was little more than a child herself, she had to bathe her younger brothers and wash their heads with kerosene after an outbreak of head lice in school. When her mother was ready to give birth again, Tanya had complete charge of the children. She recalled the annoyance of attending to their bodily needs. "They had to go to the bathroom," she recalled. "So I took them to the curb. But when I noticed that they were wetting their knickerbockers, I guided their 'penees.' I was a 'penee' guide for two kid brothers. They stood at the curb and pissed, and I kept their 'penees' from wetting their pants." Tanya had her fill of premature mothering. After she married, she told her husband that she had no desire to have children of her own—she already knew what it was to be a mother. Rose G. had a similar story to tell. "I had to take care of that little brother who was five years younger than me," she remembered. "Oi! I had no freedom. And when I was in school, if something happened, I'd think, 'Oh God, I hope it isn't my brother.' So when I found it wasn't him, I'd thank God." Florence B. also became a child-mother to her brother. "I was fourteen years older than my youngest brother Sam," she recalled, "and I undertook the responsibility of bringing him up. He was brought home from the hospital when he was ten days old, put on the bed, and I stayed up all night watching him to make sure he wouldn't fall off. And from then on, I became his—he ended up on the psychiatrist's couch not knowing who was his mother. His real mother was forty-five when he was born, with long gray hair, and he was partly ashamed of her, I think. Me he loved."

Whether or not they had a paying job, girls were expected to assist with the housework. "I always used to help my mother," recalled Fannie G. "I never let her wash a floor." Miriam M. remembered her mother's doing the family wash while she did all the ironing. Her youngest sister "was sort of the privileged one," and didn't have many household obligations. If a mother did piecework in the home,[8] daughters usually helped them. Frances F. would go to a nearby factory and get embroidery for her mother to complete. Her mother taught her what to do, and "after school," recalled Frances, "we would both sit at the frame, she on one side and I on the other, and stitch, stitch, stitch." Mildred Hecht remembered her life in Eastern Europe as being easier. In America, she had to work in a shop during the week and do the housework and wash clothes for the family on Sundays. "All the conveniences" of living here, she observed wryly, "weren't so convenient."[9]

If there was no mother in the home, the oldest daughter would inherit the entire burden. When she was only twelve years old, Rose Cohen had to work as a "feller" in a garment shop and keep house for her father as well. One night a week she cleaned, another she washed, and often she was too tired to eat before falling asleep.[10] Rebecca August also emigrated at twelve years of age and worked in a shop as well as caring for a household. While she labored ten or twelve hours a day making button holes to save to bring over her mother and six other children, she still had to shop, clean, cook, and do the wash for her father, her brother, and a boarder.[11] Sophie Ruskay's mother told her that she had "never had a childhood like other children," for she was the oldest and her mother died when she was eleven. She had to leave school and take complete charge of the housekeeping and two younger siblings.[12] Like all these women, Pauline H., who came here at fourteen to live with her father and brothers, was expected to maintain the household by herself. Her brothers worked with her father, and none of them helped with the chores. "It came hard on me," she recalled,

> because it was much too much. I had to cook for four people. I cried, oh, did I carry on. I wanted to go back. And I couldn't go to work, I couldn't do anything at all. I was tied down to the house. I had three men to take care of. They made me work for a big person. Myself, I was always busy. Take a kid and make her a *balabusteh* for a whole apartment. That was very hard. I had to make up the stove too. And there was no steam. I had to shine the stove too. I had to make the *Shabbes*. That was a lot of responsibility. It was very strange to me, because now I'm only with men. And I used to cry an awful lot—no mother, she wouldn't come.

"I had the dirty end of it," Pauline concluded, "'Cause I had to please my father and my brother." Many young women felt overworked by early responsibilities. "I had no freedom," asserted Rose G., echoing the statements of others, "no childhood at all."

Even if children were too young to have a full-time job, they frequently had to do what they could to help bring money into the house. Rose G. remembered her chore of sweeping out the laundry that her family owned. Mildred L., the oldest of three children, was only ten when her parents sent her to work in a local butcher shop. "My parents let me work there," she recalled, because "they were glad that I was bringing in a few pennies. And I used to bring my lunch. But I never went to the bathroom. I was afraid to leave the box and go there. I was afraid that somebody might follow me. That's the God's truth. And I used to die, I couldn't wait until I got home. I figured to make those few dollars, it was wonderful, that I could do something. But I wouldn't go into that bathroom." Frances F. helped her father sell greeting cards from a pushcart. It was her job "to go from store to store and ask for a permit, ask for permission to sell cards in front of their store, at the curb." Every day, when Frances came home from school, she went to join her father and help him sell. "Some of the shop owners would say no, and turn away roughly," she recalled, "and my spirits would fall." Anna R., another oldest daughter, helped her parents with their small businesses. When they had a shop selling food and soda, Anna or one of her parents would tend the store for fourteen hours a day. "We had relays between the three of us," she recalled. Later, they bought a fish store. "My father used to go out to the fish market at two o'clock in the morning," Anna related, "and the fish would come. Then my mother was up, and my father was relieved. And then I was getting older, I was nine years old. You see, I was a mensch [a fine person] already. I was strong physically. I was busy all the time, relieving. Before I went to school and then when I came back from school, I had to relieve my father so he could go to sleep."

Besides being able to attend school, youngest daughters frequently escaped the domestic burdens of the eldest. They generally had only minor household chores, and there were no infant siblings for them to care for. As the youngest, they were often spoiled by parents or older sisters. "I never had to do any housework because I was the baby," observed Hannah F., "but my three sisters each had their chore." Naomi L. remembered that although her sister later resented having to work while Naomi attended school, she nevertheless had a new dress ready every time there was an assembly. Miriam M. remembered her youngest sister as the privileged child who had the toys Miriam had been denied. Sara B. believed her younger sister "had more advantages than any of us because she was the baby."

Often, parents' changing attitudes meant that they would have different relationships with younger children than they did with the older ones. Louise C., who left her home in Russia because of poverty and her father's repressiveness, learned from her mother that he was less severe with the younger children than he had been with the first four. Dora W. explained that the parent-child relationship in her family, described in Chapter 6 from the children's point of view, was different for her than for her older siblings because her father had mellowed and become less restrictive when she was growing up. Her older brother and sister had been forced to fight for their privileges, while she was permitted more freedom without a struggle. Part of this change she attributed to her father's age, but part was also due to the respect she believed her father had for his more Americanized child. "I felt that my parents felt I was important, that I knew more about America than they did, and therefore my father did not dictate to me the way he could to my sister or brother." Gussie M. also believed that her mother's changing attitudes accounted for the close relationship she had with her youngest daughter. In their village of birth, children had been expected from their earliest years to labor for the family, with little reward or thanks—a system similar to that of working-class families throughout the Western world in the nineteenth century, where parents considered children as "their own flesh, blood and labor supply."[13] Gussie's own life, as the oldest daughter, had been one of thankless, unremitting toil. When they came to America, however, Gussie's mother saw how people treated children—"with ice-cream cones and orange juice, and how they respect children, and how they speak to them. And she learned."

If a family could not afford to emigrate together, older children often took on the burden of coming alone to the United States and working to save up the money to send for their parents and siblings. When the father of Yetta Altman died in Poland, his twelve-year-old daughter emigrated to America to work in a garment shop by day and care for her cousin's children in the evenings. "I should only make a living for my mother and the kids," she remembered thinking, and managed to save enough to bring them over.[14] If parents did not want to emigrate, daughters would send money to make their lives easier. "I worked to help out my folks," observed Sonia O., "and to go to Russia to visit. What did I need the money for?" Hilda S. remembered the difficulty she and her sister had in managing to put aside enough for their own food and rent,

> because we had to fix an apartment for my mother when she came here, get furniture and all that. And it was a peculiar thing that nobody helped us in Europe. Everybody that was left there, no sooner did you go to America, automatically you became rich. So I had to send money to Uncle so-and-so and Aunt so-and-so, and to this one and that one. My aunt that we lived with was a noble person. Not smart, but very good natured. When we used to bring the pay home— let's say I got eighteen dollars—so she used to say, "Well, five dollars we'll send to your mother, five dollars we'll send to Uncle so-and-so." I said, "Wait a minute, what are we going to live on?" She said "We'll live on air." So if I didn't put any money away, we had nothing to live on.

Once parents had arrived here, a daughter's work had to continue if her father could not get a decent job. Other goals had to be held in abeyance, sometimes permanently. Bella Hyman had wanted to become a nurse, but she had to work in a garment factory to bring her parents over. Bella managed to sublimate unfulfilled desires in union activity, which she viewed as "another kind of school."[15] It was not unusual for young women to put off getting married because parents needed their income. When a child married, financial responsibilities to parents ended and the obligations of others remaining at home increased.[16] "My younger brother married early, before I did," explained Tanya N. "I was the only one left to help my father financially." Ethel B. and her fiancé "went together" for five years because her family could not do without her paycheck. "Everything that I earned went into the home," she recalled. Anna R. postponed marriage for several years until she could bring over her parents and three brothers and sisters. "In three years," she related with pride, "the whole family was here. But *I* was the one to bring the rest of them over, because I made more money than all of them." She told her boyfriend, "This is the only way to do it—to bring first my family and then to get married."

These continual obligations could exert a heavy toll. Hilda S. had to choose between continuing with night school or her job, and family obligations determined her decision. After working all day and attending Washington Irving High School at night for two years, the pace began to tell. "Not only did I work eight hours," she recalled, "I worked ten hours, Saturdays and Sundays. And then I got sick. I lost a lot of weight, and the doctor said that I had to stop either work or school. Since I couldn't stop work—I had people depending on me—I stopped school. I feel very sorry about it. And you never start again. But I was money hungry. I had to make the money to bring four people here." Anna Kahan believed that her years of hard work to save the money to pay for her parents' and brothers' passage permanently destroyed her health. "I was a healthy child," she observed, "and they killed me. This life killed me. All I took on myself. Of course, I saved the family. But they killed me."

Such daughters obviously took on responsibilities beyond their years. Yetta Altman came to America at twelve and began working in the garment industry to bring over her family. "When I was here I knew I had to go to work," she stated, "I didn't come here for pleasure, you know. I was twelve years old but I wasn't twelve. Compared to a child here, I was twenty. I don't know when I was a child."[17] One sixteen-year-old girl who had worked since she was eleven returned to Russia to arrange to bring her parents and their seven other children to the United States. At Ellis Island she answered all the officials' questions with confidence.[18] Tanya N. was also sixteen when she decided that her family needed a more spacious apartment. Her mother had just had her fifth baby, and Tanya went out to look for a larger place with a bath. She and a younger brother found an apartment with a rent they could afford—fourteen dollars—"but there was no bathtub. So we made a deal with the landlord that we would give him fourteen and a half dollars a month if he would remove the washtub and put one bathtub in its place." One eleven-year-old daughter habitually did all the writing necessary for the charitable bureaus that helped her mother, and another, whose mother was janitor of a tenement, conducted all the necessary interviews with Board of Health officials, street cleaners, and other authorities.[19]

Although many young women sacrificed for their families, often they were proud of what they had done if parents valued their labors. Young women who grew up in poor households often developed family-centered values that emphasized obligation rather than self-fulfillment.[20] "I don't know whether it was blood or duty," observed Fannie C., "but I felt a great deal of responsibility toward my parents. I sort of felt that I owed them something. Even if my parents didn't give me much, I still would have wanted to have that responsibility because if they didn't give me much then it was because they couldn't give me much. I was always a secure child," Fannie concluded. "I always felt that my parents loved me dearly."

Like Fannie's parents, middle-class families in Europe and America, particularly urban ones, were by this time treating young children *as* children rather than as an economic investment.[21] This did not mean that daughters no longer had obligations to the family, but rather that their efforts could be appreciated rather than simply taken for granted. Four-teen-year-old Pauline H. not only kept house for her father and brothers but also had the adult responsibility of managing the family's money, as a mother would do. "But these things didn't come hard to me, because I was not just a child," she observed with pride. "They used to say, '*a yunge kind un an alte kopf*' [a young child and an old head]." Anna Kahan remembered her mother's gratitude to her for bringing the rest of the family to America. "This is my daughter's miracle," she used to tell her. "You did it for us!" The father of Fannie N. made her feel similarly important. Although in Europe her father had been sorry when she was born a girl, he kept telling her, "I wish I had another one like you!"

If family members took the efforts of daughters for granted, however, a young woman understandably might come to resent them.[22] Elizabeth Hasanovitz wrote of a friend who worked and saved to bring over her brothers and sisters and then continued working so that they had the opportunity to attend school. But all the thanks she got was their mockery of her foreign ways and inability to speak the language she enabled them to learn. "Having profited by her sacrifices" Hasanovitz wrote, "and gained through her what she had coveted for herself but had never been able to obtain—an education—they looked down on her because she had not their superficial knowledge of American customs, language and cheap styles. They deemed that she lacked culture and refinement because . . . their understanding of Americanism was limited to speaking English, wearing high pompadours and powdering their noses."[23] Clearly, such unfortunate women later regretted surrendering their own dreams for the sake of a thankless family.

But if parents or siblings were grateful for a daughter's or sister's sacrifices in working in the home or taking a job, these exertions often provided a source of fulfillment and were not considered a chore. "When I was a child," recalled Sara B., "there wasn't anything that was too hard for me to do in the house." Her mother, though, made such labors worthwhile. "When she came home she used to say to me that I have 'golden hands.' So you can imagine what my mother meant to me." Fannie C. also remembered her mother's consideration. "I always used to help with the dishes at night," she observed. "But she happened to be the kind of mother that if she knew that I had homework, she would rather I do the homework than help her. But," she concluded, "I always managed to help." In general, the closer the bond, the more willingly did daughters assist their mothers.

This relationship also helped determine a daughter's attitude toward giving her wages to the family. Most immigrant sons and daughters who worked outside the home took jobs to help parents, and some were even the sole support of families.[24] In most Western nations, this was expected of working daughters,[25] and statistics indicate that girls contributed to a greater extent than their brothers.[26] Social workers invariably mentioned that it was a widespread practice for young working women to turn over unopened pay envelopes to mothers, while brothers generally kept at least some of their salaries for themselves.[27] Daughters were also less likely than sons to move out and stop contributing altogether. Dora W. remembered that although she and her brother both gave wages to their mother, her brother "was able to manipulate it so that he could keep something for himself." The brother of Naomi L., a "unionist," moved into his own apartment and left the burden of caring for their parents on his sisters. When the father of Frances F. fell ill, she supported the household because her two working brothers did not.

Although mothers often lavished affection on their male children, many appreciated daughters for the companionship and help they could give. One woman, after having several sons, finally gave birth to a daughter. She was delighted to have a girl, she later told one of her sons, after being surrounded for so long by "all you betassled creatures." Mildred Hecht, a factory worker who had only sons, longed for a daughter. "It's hard to work and then come home and find the house dirty and cold," she complained. "I get so disgusted sometimes I feel like crying. . . . Men don't understand it and leave everything on my shoulders, making stove, fixing wood in cellar. If I had a daughter, she would help more. Girls help their mothers."[28]

Boys seemed to have easier lives than girls. Although they too might leave school at a young age to work, their childhood years were relatively free of family obligations. Few attended daylong Hebrew schools,[29] as they would have in Eastern Europe, nor were they expected to help with the cooking, cleaning, and younger children, as girls were. "My brother really enjoyed his life," recalled Fannie C. "I had all the responsibilities." Despite the protectiveness of the Jewish mother toward her sons, Jewish sons were still, like most other boys, allowed more freedom than girls.[30] Many boys joined gangs, to the consternation of their mothers and sometimes to the envy of their sisters, who were denied such liberty.[31] In Michael Gold's semiautobiographical novel, *Jews without Money*, a sister envied her young brother when a coach driver let him come along to a funeral. "Girls were never taken on these rides by the coach drivers," Gold observed. "My sister always wanted to go, but couldn't. . . . She cried now as I teased her, and . . . she grew very jealous of my good luck."[32] While the boy did as he pleased, his mother worked, and his sister did most of the housework, watched a baby brother, and nursed their sick father. Like many Jewish girls, "Esther was not driven to the housework: she herself saw its necessity and did it with sunny cheerfulness," wrote Gold. "She wished to help my mother. She wished to help everybody; she was precociously kind."[33] Not all sisters felt kindly toward their brothers. Rose G. did all the cleaning in her mother's house and clearly resented her brothers' freedom. "I worked so hard," she recalled. "And my two brothers slept in one bed. So in order to get one of them out, I had to wash the bathtub and get his bath ready for him. I had to get that big mattress off the bed and clean the springs. And I was such a little thing, but no one helped me with the cleaning."

Girls' perceptions of their mothers' chores were more precise than the descriptions recorded by sons, as one might expect from the different roles mothers played in the lives of their male and female children. For a boy, his mother's kitchen was a refuge where he was a coddled guest, while for a girl it was a school and workshop where there were always chores to do. In the

14. A brother and sister.

Collection of the author

memories of sons, in America as in Eastern Europe, a mother's performance of her duties takes on a vague, almost mystical quality, as in Sholem Asch's *The Mother*, where in an impoverished family, "Sarah Rifke turns to her magical cooking pots to provide for her family. She could milk her pots as though they were cows. They never denied her anything. She gave them cold water and the pots yielded yesterday's carrot soup anew. . . . When the pots heard mother sigh it was as though she had repeated a secret incantation over them with which she adjured them to supply the pitifully meager bit of nourishment which was all she demanded for her large brood."[34] Alfred Kazin similarly described his mother's world through the romanticized haze that comes of being a guest at the table rather than a participant in the preparation. When his mother got ready for the Sabbath, he wrote, "by sundown the curtains had been drawn, the world put to rights. Even the kitchen walls had been scrubbed and now gleamed in the Sabbath candles. On the long white tables were the company dishes." In her son's eyes, Kazin's mother accomplished her tasks without effort, almost magically: "When my father came home from work she had somehow mysteriously interrupted herself to make supper for us, and the dishes cleared and washed, was back at her machine."[35] Girls knew that it was their mothers' efforts rather than "magic" that put food on the table.

The relationship of sons to their parents also differed from that of their sisters. The stereotypical, smothering "Jewish Mother" of the post–World War II novel, if it bore any relation to reality, reflected the attitudes of some sons.[36] Daughters might have felt overworked, but they seldom felt "smothered" by their mothers. Just as fathers were often more indulgent with their daughters and demanding of their sons, mothers frequently spoiled sons and expected more of daughters in the way of day-to-day help.[37]

This is not to imply that sons had an easier time psychologically. Just as mothers might see their own early potential reflected in the lives of their daughters, fathers could hold their sons to the same standard. While a father might eventually accept a daughter's American ways, often a son's insistence on following his own path could create a major conflict. Because of the greater flexibility of mothers, they often accepted the Americanizing trends brought into the home by their daughters, but fathers and sons clashed more easily, each insisting on the correctness of his views.[38] Sometimes mothers had to choose between the values of their sons and those of their husbands,[39] whereas after daughters married, their interests did not differ greatly from those of their mothers. Furthermore, a mother's expectations of her daughter were more easily achieved. Although many mothers encouraged their daughters to attend school and perhaps become teachers, the vast majority of Jewish girls could fulfill their mothers' goals by marrying and having children. Sons were the repository of grander hopes.[40] Mothers often pushed them to study and work to "make it" in the American system by becoming successful businessmen, or possibly professionals—a way of justifying the sacrifices made by the family.[41] The burdens of such expectations could be very high indeed. Thus, while the physical demands made on daughters were larger, sons were often subjected to greater psychological pressures. Furthermore, a daughter's success could be achieved within the context of her parents' value system, while often a son, to achieve the success his mother sought for him, might paradoxically have to abandon the values of his parents.

Within a family, daughters often believed that their mothers displayed more love for their brothers. This favoritism was generally accepted as normal and was often shared by an older sister. Tanya N., for example, was proud of her brothers' college educations yet resented the fact that her American-born sister was able to attend college while Tanya had to work. Dora W. observed that her mother saved most of her affection for her son, yet she didn't envy her brother, "because I loved him dearly too." In the family of Frances F., a mother's preference for her son failed to cause resentment because Frances took almost as much pride in his accomplishments as did her mother. However, in both these families, the girls outstripped their brothers in accomplishments. One wonders what their attitude would have been if they had had to surrender their opportunities for schooling or a good job to benefit an ungrateful brother. A study of three generations of ethnic women in Pittsburgh reveals that Jewish immigrant women were aware of and resented their parents' preferential treatment of their brothers and subsequently brought up their own daughters with more fairness. First-generation Italian women, on the other hand, had probably so internalized parents' values that they consciously recalled little discrimination and raised their daughters in the same restrictive way.[42] Italian daughters, for example, almost universally took pleasure in sacrificing to help their brothers achieve success.[43]

Although age as much as sex determined the fate of children, with the younger ones having more access to school, often a daughter would be expected to subordinate her ambitions to make sure that her brother could remain in school. In the family of Jennie H.'s husband, a sister worked after high school graduation to put her older brother through college with the understanding that when he graduated, he would do the same for her. But after getting his degree, he decided to marry and went back on his promise. She never completed her education and resented it for the rest of her life. Such sacrifices did not result in resentment, though, if a daughter felt that her effort was valued, or if she had transferred her own ambitions to a brother. Rose G. paid for her brother's college education as a matter of course. If the money hadn't gone to pay his tuition, Rose observed, it would have gone to her mother. "I didn't realize that I was doing anything big," she concluded. "I knew that was what I had to do." Frances F., who along with her older brother had to work to help the family, hoped that a younger brother would get the education denied to her. "He was anxious to please his sister," she recalled, "because he was as much attached to me as I to him. I was his second mother. I was very eager that he do it," she observed. "I was hoping that if I couldn't get the kind of education I wanted, I wanted at least my brother to get it. Well," she concluded, "I was disappointed. He dropped out."

Daughters rather than sons cared for parents in old age, and many seem to have derived particular satisfaction from ministering to elderly mothers. Although Jewish girls, and indeed most girls, were socialized to assume such obligations, there is little question that they could achieve gratification from fulfilling what they perceived as a filial responsibility.[44] The mother of Rose S., after being widowed, lived in turn with each of her daughters, all of whom urged her to remain, but she refused to stay with her son and his wife. Hannah F. and her three sisters also fought over what they considered the privilege of providing a home for their mother, but again, the brothers were not involved. An occasional daughter even gave up the thought of marriage to continue caring for parents.[45] Frieda K. decided to remain single because her younger brothers had married and could no longer contribute to their parents' support. "They had their own lives," she observed. Frieda remained the sole support of her mother and sick father. Yet she did not consider it a burden. "I loved my mother very much," she affirmed. "For my mother I would have done anything."

Sons would visit and contribute financially to the care of an elderly parent, but this was the extent of their obligation. Since sons often were raised to believe that their interests were paramount, they would generally continue as adults to assume a limited role in looking after aging parents. Jewish sons were expected to repay their mothers and fathers not by caring for them in declining years, but by being successful and passing on these advantages to their own children. One Yiddish proverb goes, "When a father helps a son, both smile; when a son helps his father, both cry."[46] No such proverb relates to the obligations of daughters to parents. A brother's responsibility for a sister was even more limited. One dying mother told her devoted daughter that after her death she would be alone—a prophecy that became true—because her brother "is a man and will go his own way."[47]

Daughters, not sons, learned from their mothers to take satisfaction from acting as caretakers in the family. Rose S. told how her mother had taught by example. "When my grandfather died," Rose related, "my grandmother's three daughters knew that they had the responsibility to their mother. So my grandmother went to live with one of her daughters and lived there for six months, and she didn't like it. So she went to the second daughter. I mean, there was no question—one of the daughters had to do that. There was one son, but she didn't want to go to the son because there was a wife, and she felt freer with her daughters. So she went to the three daughters and finally came back to the first daughter, and that's where she spent sixteen years until she died." Rose remembered her grandmother's dying in their home because her mother refused to consider taking her to a hospital. When her own mother developed cancer, the same issue came up. Her mother did not want to spend her remaining time in an alien atmosphere. "She had learned a few words of English, but not very much. So she said, 'How can I stay in a hospital, if I cannot tell the nurse what I want?' We told her to ring the bell. She says, 'After I ring the bell, then what? I want to go home.' So I spoke to my brothers," Rose recalled,

and I said, I'm willing to stay home and take care of her. That's what we decided. I gave up my job and I just stayed home with her, and it took a whole year. The understanding with my brothers was that if she gets very bad, they are going to pay either for a nurse during the day or night. They didn't expect me to be on duty twenty-four hours a day. So I said, "All right. I'll let you know just when I'm ready for help." And I never did, because what I did was move my bed into my mother's room. And I slept there with her, and I had a person used to come in and let me go do my shopping. And the rest of the time for a whole year, I stayed home, and it was twenty-four hours a day. My brothers made it their business every couple of months to come in for a day or two to see how things were. And that was it.

Rose remembered, as a child, her mother's closing the eyes of her dead grandmother, and she felt privileged to do the same for her own mother. "Something remained with me," she mused. "That was my grandmother, and this is my mother. So honestly, I didn't feel that it was a sacrifice." Like Rose, Miriam M. gave up her job to be with a dying mother. For a year, she visited her in a nursing home every day. "It was no sacrifice," Miriam insisted, for she had done this not out of obligation, but because of the example her mother had set before her. "It was a natural thing to do," she explained, "because she was always so sweet and self-effacing." Her mother had even given up a chance of remarrying after her husband died because a stepfather might not be kind to the children. Sometimes the mother-daughter relationship was cemented late in life by this apparent role reversal—a daughter caring for her mother. Frieda M. observed, "My mother was never important to me until I had to take care of her. And then," she explained simply, "she was."

Immigrants thus learned quickly that the streets of America were not paved with gold, and families had to make difficult decisions if they were to survive.[48] These strategies implicitly sacrificed the well-being of some for the benefit of others, although ideally, family members who profited would eventually assist those who had held their own goals in abeyance. Parents resigned themselves to a life of toil so children might advance, sisters went to work young so brothers could remain in school, and older children entered the factories and sweatshops to enable younger siblings to avoid the same fate. Often the rewards of successful family members failed to trickle down to those who had made the sacrifices, but among many daughters, a mother's appreciation seemed adequate compensation. Like most women, Jewish girls, and older daughters in particular, placed family obligations before personal gratification.[49]

The experiences of assisting parents hardly differentiate the lives of Jewish girls from those of other young women in the late nineteenth or early twentieth centuries.[50] All daughters were expected to help with chores in the home or give their wages to parents if poverty forced them to join the work force. Every chronicler of the immigrant experience has mentioned the apparent role reversal when children who learned English quickly assisted their less fluent parents. It is quite possible, though, that the *value* placed upon these services by parents and other siblings, but especially by mothers, provided a source of satisfaction and strength. These traditional, family-oriented values, shared by both generations of women immigrants, may also have aided a daughter's ability to reconcile her European background with America and to bridge the transition from child to adult.

9

Education: Dream and Reality

I always wanted education. I never got it. And even when I came here, I never got it. For different reasons all the time. In night school, we read Shakespeare and I used to fall asleep. I needed "cat" and "rat," but we got Shakespeare. So I had trouble with English.

—Gussie M.

We were poor. I didn't have an orange until I was grown up. But my father had a thing about education. He said to all of us, "I can't give you beautiful things, but as long as you want to go to school, you can go to school."

—Frieda M.

Whatever I know—dressmaking, writing, reading, even Hebrew—I learned up in the air by people. I didn't get any education. I wanted, but I didn't have the opportunity.

—Jennie H.

15. Jewish immigrant women at night school on the Lower East Side.
New York City Board of Education Archives, Milbank Memorial Library, Teachers College,
Columbia University

For all those who came to America with little more than the clothes on their backs, economic necessity would shape their fates. The need to make a living precipitated most young Jewish immigrants into the garment factories or other low-paid jobs. But if class determined their work lives, culture gave them their dreams.[1] Many who labored ten and twelve hours a day in the shops still longed for the shining grail of education, denied them by government edict in Poland and Russia and as often as not beyond their grasp in America as well because of financial need. Few families did not have at least one member who yearned to go to high school, or even to college. A parent might invest hopes in one child, and if older brothers and sisters had to work in a factory or the family store, they saw to it that the youngest children remained in school. While the desire for an education may have been strong in Eastern Europe, the possibilities for achieving it were limited.[2] In New York, the free public school system, from elementary school to Hunter College and City College, made such a dream appear within reach.[3] And unlike in Russia, a secular education in America gave young people access to sought-after careers and jobs. Schooling was thus functional as well as culturally desirable.[4]

Young Jewish women who came to America in the years around World War I had arrived at a time when a high school education was becoming a possibility, and upon discovering that learning was not the prerogative of males alone, they took to the schools with a zest unmatched by other groups. Most of those who arrived as teenagers already had learned to read and write in Eastern Europe, where these skills had become acceptable for Jewish girls. Many of them hoped to continue their educations in America, but more important at first was to learn the prerequisites for jobs. Thus, vocational courses such as dressmaking, sewing, and hat-trimming, which were offered by the Board of Education, the Industrial School for Girls, and the Educational Alliance, were filled by young women seeking to develop job skills. Those who had already learned English might take typing or bookkeeping and aspire to positions with more status than that of factory worker.[5] One contemporary observer noted that Jewish girls alone "seem to understand the increased power which preparation gives. As a result [they] are everywhere crowding the high and commercial schools."[6] If they worked during the day, many managed to attend night school in the evenings.[7]

These young women wanted to learn English and become Americanized, but they also sought to attain a cultural ideal that often had eluded their grasp in the Old Country. "We were all ashamed of showing our ignorance," wrote Rose Cohen. "A girl who could not read and write would do anything to hide it. We were as much ashamed of it as we were of our poverty."[8] Rose L., who began to work full-time in her native Bialystok when she was twelve, attended school here for three months after immigrating at the age of fourteen. When her sister-in-law made her quit school to take a job, Rose recalled, "the desk was saturated with tears." In Europe, poverty had kept her from even thinking of going to school, but here, she wanted to continue her education. "I was older," she observed. "I had more sense." Girls who had learned how to read and write as children had more ambitious goals. Minna S. graduated from evening high school after she had had to leave day school to take a job as a bookkeeper. "I went to school for years and years at night taking courses," she recalled. "I was always school conscious. It seems I knew that I had missed something."

Like Rose L., most young immigrant women could not attain the goal of an advanced education because of the economic hardships of immigrant life. If they were able to attend school at all, only a few lucky ones could afford to remain until they reached fifteen or sixteen, when they usually graduated and then went to work. Many, though, left school for full-time jobs as young as nine or ten. Only a third of all children entering public school in New York in 1913 advanced as far as the eighth grade.[9] In the next year, the State Factory Investigating Commission found that 75 percent of women working in factories had left school before completing even these few years.[10] Anna Kahan had ended her education in Russia at ten to work as a milliner's assistant after failing to gain admission to the local state school. When she arrived in New York four years later, she got a job in a millinery shop and then immediately enrolled in night school and hired a tutor for twenty-five cents an hour to try to learn English quickly. Anna hoped to enter high school and then go on to college, but illness born of overwork defeated her hopes.

Other women who came here as young adults found that the long working day left little time to master English—the prerequisite to getting "a real education." Gussie M., who came here in 1912 at seventeen, attended night school for a time and found the experience frustrating rather than fulfilling. "We read Shakespeare," she recalled, "and I used to fall asleep. I needed 'cat' and 'rat,' but we got Shakespeare. So I had trouble with English." Rae K., an intense and dynamic woman at ninety-four, had a single interest in her young life—to get a college education despite the opposition of her father. As far as traditional skills went, she observed, "I couldn't boil water for kasha." She left Russia for America in 1908 to pursue her ambition. "I just had to go to college," she recalled with fervor, "it was my dream, it was my goal. I wanted to be a doctor, a lawyer, to teach languages! Everything!" But poverty and the English language defeated her. Having failed to achieve her dream, she said simply and with regret, "I'm unfinished."

The only way for most youthful workers to get any education was by attending evening school. As early as 1898, there were sixty-one evening elementary schools and four high schools run by the Board of Education.[11] Ten years later, there were 100,000 immigrants enrolled in elementary, high school, and Americanization classes, and 40 percent of the students in these classes were Jewish immigrant women or their daughters.[12] Two-thirds of the students attended classes specifically to learn English.[13] But it was difficult for working women to get a high school degree at night, especially if they chose to follow the rigorous course of study that prepared students for university entrance examinations. These advanced classes met five times a week, for three hours each session. Few young people who labored in the shops all day had that much energy or free time in the evening, and although registration was high, attendance in the high school courses was erratic.[14] Still, many Jewish women with more modest goals, after a long day at work or caring for a family, looked forward to going to school. Janet A.'s mother, for example, was so proud of graduating from elementary school at night that she went back and took the classes a second time. Frances F., who managed to complete high school at night, felt that she got as much education as she wanted there. Evening courses given by the Workmen's Circle or the Henry George School also attracted thousands of students to lectures on such academic subjects as literature, philosophy, and economics.

For the few who cherished hopes of attending college, a whole crop of evening preparatory schools sprang up on the Lower East Side. They were usually run by young Jewish men recently graduated from City College. Their purpose was to teach students enough to pass the state examinations qualifying them for entrance into the city colleges or professional schools. Thus, in addition to attempting to master English, many young people also struggled with the intricacies of algebra, economics, physics, or Latin. The courses were taught from seven to ten-thirty or eleven at night, and one graduate marveled at the pace. "I cannot tell you how we did it," he recalled. "I only remember that I would sit and puzzle over x's and y's from the time I got home at eleven o'clock until my eyes would give out; and at seven in the morning I would be back at the machine sewing shirts."[15] Yet somehow they managed. While she worked during the day, Miriam M. attended such a school four nights a week to enable her to gain entry to law school, which she also completed at night.

Many young women got their education among workers like themselves. Minnie Fisher made hats in a millinery shop and lived in a "commune" of young people who worked all day and attended the *Yiddishe Arbeiten Universitet* [Jewish Worker's University] at night. This school was founded by workers themselves, and it had dual goals. Its founders taught young immigrants about American language and culture, and they also sought to bring Jewish culture to the American-born and develop a sense of class consciousness among all students. At the university, Minnie observed, "knowledge itself was your diploma. The goal was to live with the rest of humanity, and to help yourself, and to help the other people, the workers in the shops." Other radical evening schools also appealed to workers. For a while, Minnie attended the Rand School, a Socialist institution, where many students were sent by their unions. It was there, she recalled, that "we started to understand capitalism" and "got our development along social lines."[16]

Men and women of other major ethnic groups did not share this intense desire for education, mainly because of differing conceptions of family welfare. Most Italian and Polish children would work to enable their parents to buy a house or land.[17] As the family prospered, the reasoning went, children would benefit as a part of that family. Individual goals or achievements counted for little unless they helped the family as a whole. Since the men generally earned their living with manual labor and the young women took on domestic or factory work, education seemed irrelevant to their lives. After sons and daughters had learned to read and write, parents usually took them out of school at a young age.[18] Children raised in homes with such traditional attitudes often shared their parents' views and wanted to leave the classroom and begin working. Early in the century, one social worker observed that a young Italian girl was "as eager to go to work as her parents are to have her. She takes it for granted that she should help in the family income. Carlotta gets a job not because she feels the need of self-support as an expression of individuality, or self-dependence, but because she feels so strongly the sense of family obligation."[19]

Sometimes, education itself was viewed with suspicion as a competitor for the child's allegiance that might jeopardize the basis of family life and accepted patterns of behavior.[20] These parents instinctively understood that children indoctrinated with American values in the schools might easily become estranged from their own culture. And if schooling was sometimes tolerated for boys in the interest of getting a better job, it was viewed as useless for girls, who were expected to learn all they needed to know from mothers.[21] One young French-Canadian girl who had loved her few years at school resented her father's taking her books away and telling her "it wasn't good" for her to read. In her family, all the girls had to go to work to support the brothers who remained in school.[22] Even if some mothers wanted their daughters to get an education, the girls could seldom be spared from helping them because so many of these women had to work outside the home.[23] It was only in the 1930s and 1940s, when better-paying clerical jobs in stores or offices were seen as viable alternatives to factory work, that Italian daughters began to complete high school.[24] But few were encouraged to attend college, for an education was still valued only insofar as it led to immediate economic rewards.[25]

Among Jews, the family was equally important, but the conception of family well-being was different. Jews in Eastern Europe had seldom been permitted to own land and thus did not consider property the ultimate security. There, as in America, unconscious family strategies relied instead upon investing in the future of male children so they could advance either by means of an education or by building up a small business. Because education was a strong cultural value among Jews, in America the desire of a son to attend school would not be opposed unless parents needed money badly or wanted him to enter the family business. Parents usually encouraged sons to do well at their studies, and Jewish boys remained in school longer than Italian or Irish boys and were less often held back.[26] Daughters, who would marry within a few years after leaving school, were expected to have little practical need for an education. But because families valued education generally, as long as older children were working, younger ones, even if they were girls, were in most instances permitted to remain in school. And since few Jewish mothers worked outside the home,[27] daughters were not the essential helpers they had been in Eastern Europe. Jewish immigrant children got a clear message from their parents—pursue secular education,[28] the more the better—and there no longer seemed much reason to limit this goal to boys. Lillian Wald took note of the great value placed by Jews on education—"an overvaluation, one is tempted to think, in view of the sacrifices which are made, particularly for the boys." But as early as 1915, she observed that "of late years the girls' claims have penetrated even to the Oriental [Russian] home."[29]

Although Jewish parents usually wanted to keep their children in school as long as possible,[30] economic need often required that older sons and daughters go out to work while in their early teens. Still, more Jewish boys than girls remained at their studies,[31] for family strategies generally determined that if the wages of only one child could be spared, it was more important for an older son than a daughter to get an education. Such families looked to the future. One social worker observed that the oldest daughter of a Russian family left school after her second year to permit her brother to attend college. The girl explained that she would have liked to continue, but for her brother an education was "a matter of life position," while for her it was not.[32] Since daughters were expected to marry, advanced schooling was not essential for their future. A boy's success depended upon his education, a girl's on her marriage.

But if financial circumstances improved for a family, so that it did not have to send some of its children to work, then sex scarcely mattered in determining who stayed in school. This usually benefited the youngest, American-born children in a family rather than the older ones who had emigrated with their parents. In a census bureau survey of Jewish immigrant men and women who were forty-five years and older in 1950, many of whom obviously had emigrated in their teen years, the men averaged 8.1 years of schooling and the women 5.8. These brothers remained in school longer than their sisters, but the number of years of education either sex achieved was low compared to that of their younger siblings. Among younger foreign-born Jews, twice as many boys and three times as many girls as in the older group graduated from high school. Children who came to this country at a younger age thus had a greater chance of receiving a high school education, and the difference in years of education between girls and boys is narrow. Among American-born Jewish men and women, many of whom were the younger children of immigrant parents, the difference is insignificant.[33] One might conclude that although sons were initially favored slightly if a family could afford to permit only one of its children to remain in school rather than work, younger children of both sexes had greater access to education than either their older brothers or sisters once financial stability was established. Age was therefore a more important consideration than gender in determining the amount of education a child could expect. American customs, economic circumstances, and the desire of daughters for education had eroded the traditional attitude that reserved advanced learning for males.

Despite the belief of many parents that girls did not need an advanced education, there was usually no real opposition if the family did not need their income.[34] The poverty of most immigrants initially meant that all older children had to work, but once a younger child entered the public school, attitudes quickly began to change. Although an orthodox man might arrive in this country assuming that his daughters required no education, Henrietta Szold observed that "before he knew it his girls had slipped into the public schools, and were being taught pretty much all his boys were learning. To his own amazement he found himself not half so rabid as before in opposing the 'custom of the Gentiles.'"[35]

Often, a parent was bewildered by a daughter's longing for more learning, but this seemed an insufficient reason for forbidding it. When Miriam G. graduated from high school at sixteen after being editor of her school's newspaper and yearbook, she wanted to go to college, but her father "was not too receptive to the idea. He didn't seem to think it was necessary." Nevertheless, Miriam attended pharmacy college. Other well-meaning fathers felt the same way. They could understand a daughter's wanting to get a middle-class job, but not an apparently useless college education. "My father couldn't understand why I should go to college," recalled Fannie C. "In those days [the 1920s], when a girl even graduated high school, it was unusual. Because almost all of my father's friends' daughters, they would go to business school for a year or two and get a bookkeeping job." Sometimes, a mother whose own desires for education had been frustrated was more sympathetic. Although Fannie's father opposed her desire for more education, her mother supported her because she knew that her daughter had always been eager to learn. The mother of Frieda K. persuaded her reluctant husband to permit their youngest daughter to attend high school because she wanted their daughters to "go as far as [they] could."

Although a mother or father might not understand a daughter's desire to attend college, many were supportive, and by the late 1920s, they generally wanted her to go to high school, for most parents instinctively understood that schooling was the route to status in America. Girls also tended to be better off in a family without sons, or with a father who did well economically. Hannah F., the youngest of four daughters, went to college with the full support of her parents. "My father was rich enough not to send us to work," Hannah observed. "So he said, 'Education, all you want.'" After 1920, children legally had to remain in school until they were sixteen, so parents also became accustomed to thinking of them as students rather than workers. Once economic security was achieved, the younger girls in a family and a few fortunate older daughters could get their wish for education. In the 1920s, Jewish girls attended high school and college in disproportionately higher numbers than young women of other ethnic groups.[36] By 1934, 52.1 percent of female college students in New York were Jewish.[37]

A few parents who did not need an additional wage earner still opposed their daughters' getting an education, and some young women seem never to have forgiven them for this attitude. Parents discouraged ambitious daughters from seeking a graduate or professional degree because of fears that too much education would make marriage impossible.[38] In the 1920s, when Helen Weinstein told her parents that she wanted to go to college, she remembered them confronting her with the statement, "You're a girl. And girls are very stupid. You stay where we are. What do you want? Why do you want to be different? You'll never be able to make friends."[39] Possibly their need for her help in running their resort in the country had something to do with this attitude. Helen began college anyway. Earlier in the century, the father of Leah Morton, an orthodox rabbi, had wanted his daughter to think of marriage rather than go to high school, probably because he believed she might be drawn away from a traditional life.[40] With her mother's support, however, Leah went to school and subsequently managed to justify her father's fears by marrying a non-Jewish man. Fannie Shapiro also turned away from her parents' religion because they opposed her attending high school. Fannie's mother, a religious woman, pushed her son to stay in school, but insisted that her daughter remain at home and help with household chores. Fannie got even by refusing to light candles on Friday nights and by purposely mixing up the meat and dairy dishes.[41] Sarah Zasuly got back at her father in a more productive way. A learned man, he "believed that the man counts, the woman doesn't, and I was more or less a revolutionary. The woman has to count." Sarah made herself count by attending the new free high school and college and becoming a school teacher.[42]

It was more usual for Jewish parents to want all their children to have an education. Contemporary observers wrote that "the poorest among them will make all possible sacrifices to keep his children in school."[43] The *Forward*, the most popular paper in the immigrant community, urged the education of girls as well as boys.[44] Frieda M., for example, came from a very poor home. "I didn't have an orange until I was grown up," she recalled. "But my father had a thing about education. He said to all of us, 'I can't give you beautiful things, but as long as you want to go to school, you can go to school.'" The mother of Rose S. insisted that her daughter learn English well because she was anxious for her to attend college. Hattie L.'s mother was also the "pusher for education" in her family, while her father contented himself with his religious books. Neither of these girls could afford to go further than high school, though, because the family needed their wages.

Despite the desire of many parents that their children be educated, economic necessity forced difficult choices on families. Hattie observed that although her mother wanted her daughters to stay in school, parents always wanted more for boys—"girls after high school education the parents didn't push." An older daughter, in particular, would go out to work if the family needed her wages. Tanya N., whose family emigrated in 1904, asserted, "It never occurred to my parents *not* to have educated children. We took it for granted that our parents would want us to be educated." Yet there was a difference between an older child and the younger ones. Tanya knew that she could not go to college. "After all," she noted, "I was the oldest. And my father thought a woman is a woman, she must marry, she must raise a family, and that's her career. He didn't see the possibility that he would educate all his children." So because the family needed their income, Tanya and her older brother went to work, while the three younger children—two boys and a girl—remained in school. "I couldn't help it," Tanya observed. "I had to work. So you can't regret something that you couldn't do, not through your own failing, but because you simply had to help support your family."

Although many young women made peace with having to work for a living rather than attending school, some retained a keen desire for knowledge.[45] Anna R., for example, always regretted being taken out of school in the fifth grade. "There's no use in living," she observed, "if you haven't got an education. Unless you have an education, you have a mind that isn't working. I was a maniac for education. It just meant everything to me." Anna went to work as a thread cutter in a shirtwaist factory, working ten hours a day, but she wanted to continue learning. At lunchtime, she took food orders from six women. One asked her to get some coffee for them all and a half pound of granulated sugar. "So I got the coffee," Anna recalled. "But when it came to 'granulated,' I didn't know how to spell it, and I put down 'grand lady sugar.' And [the woman who had ordered the sugar] said, 'This is not the way you write granulated.' And she spelled it for me, she wrote it down, and I looked at it, and I thought, 'My life can't be worth anything if I can't write "granulated" instead of "grand lady" sugar.' From that moment on, I went just all out in every possible way to learn—I never went anywhere without a little dictionary. And so," she concluded, "I went to work by day and went to school at night." Libraries and dictionaries were very important for girls who had to get some education on their own. Louise C. recalled, "I was very ambitious. When I was in school, I was a good student, and I used the library. I was very anxious to become educated to an extent that I could converse and read." Frieda W., who had no education at all in America, had to learn English by herself. "When somebody says to me a word," she described, "I took and I wrote it down." Fannie N., who completed her formal schooling in night school, was proud of her command of English. Although she would have preferred to continue her studies longer, she considered herself an educated woman. "I read the *Times*," she explained.

Some young women had grander expectations, and for them, losing the chance for an education could be a wrenching blow. Rose Chernin had to leave school young to take a job to help her mother. "But that work was eating up my life," she recalled. "I never thought of playing, my childhood was over, school was over. I was afraid I would forget how to read. Each night, before I went to bed, I made certain I read something. A page, two paragraphs. Only not to forget." Rose, however, got another chance for education. When she was given an early shift at her factory, Rose made an uncertain visit to a local college-preparatory high school. The principal encouraged her to attend, and new vistas opened for her. "I, Rose Chernin, go to college?" she marveled. "Think who I was. An immigrant girl, fourteen years old, a factory worker, without a future. But now I stood there. In the office of an American high school. I heard the possibility I might go to college."[46]

If young people came here early in the century, without parents, a college education was even more difficult to achieve. Rae K. had struggled unsuccessfully to be admitted to a university in her native Russia. In 1908, after emigrating to Chicago at twenty-two with a young sister, she lived temporarily with an older stepsister and went to work in a shirtwaist shop, but "education was always hammering in [her] head." She learned of an evening college-preparatory school and arranged to live in the kitchen and clean the school in return for tuition. The headmaster's wife found additional work for her to do sewing for friends over the weekends. Although she did well in the entrance examinations of a small, local college, she failed English. "School opened and everybody in my class went," she recalled, "but I didn't. For three days, I didn't sleep, I didn't eat. I couldn't imagine that I cannot go to school. So I picked up my courage and went to school and asked to see the dean." Because she had done so well in the other subjects, Rae managed to convince him to let her attend an English class and try to make up her deficiency. She then moved into an attic room with a family from her hometown who had come years before and whose daughter therefore knew English well. "When I had to write a composition," Rae recalled, "I knocked at her door to ask her how to say what I needed. I was thinking in Russian and had to translate it in English, and I didn't have enough words." She was able to have her little sister live with her now. And while her sister went to school, Rae got a job in a factory turning out collars. Both she and the child would work on collars taken home at night, and whenever there was a free moment, Rae wrote another composition in English.

After being accepted as a full-time student, however, she left the factory, and her sister had to return to their stepsister's house because Rae could no longer support her. When a teacher discovered that the young woman did without lunch because she had no money, he offered her a job helping his wife in return for room, board, and enough money for carfare. Before school, she made breakfast for the family, and when she returned home, it was time to prepare dinner and clean the house. "By the time I would get to school," Rae remembered, "I was just exhausted." Someone had told her about Hull House, the social settlement run by Jane Addams, and she was permitted to live there for a while. "I helped the cook in the morning—they wanted me to feel that I worked. So it was heaven!" Rae recalled. "I had everything. I could go to school." But "heaven" did not last long. "Already I was destitute. I was without clothes, without shoes, without anything, worn out. I used to go to school with open shoes, and I got sick and didn't say anything to anybody. The teachers were kind, but what could they do? You have to make a living. You have to have a job, and I couldn't work and go to school too. I just couldn't combine it, it was too much for me." Rae collapsed and spent three months in a sanitarium.

Rae wound up sewing and keeping house for other families to make a living for herself. She never got the education she longed for. Another friend had suggested sneaking into lectures at the University of Chicago, but Rae drew the line at trying to go to school piecemeal. "I mean, this isn't an education," she explained. "It's grab here and grab there. It isn't systematic, it's nothing. It's just sickening," she concluded, "when you want something so much, and you see people going to the University, and you are helpless." But if she could not learn, she could still teach. She and friends established a school to train young boys who wanted to return to Russia after the Russian Revolution, although the school was soon ended by raids from the attorney general's office.[47] Her great ambition had to be put aside.

Children who came to the United States young enough to start school here had an advantage, although they could have difficulties until they learned English. For example, on Tanya N.'s first day of school,

> my mother gave me a bagel and an apple which I brought to school with me. And my teacher was talking and I didn't understand a word she said. I got bored, so I bit into my apple and I bit into my bagel. And the teacher's face looked a little angry, so I thought something was

wrong, but I didn't know what was wrong. I just kept eating the apple. And after a few minutes the teacher went over to me, took me by the hand, walked me to a corner of the room, sat me up on a very high teacher's chair. I took my apple with me. She put a dunce cap on my head and the children began to laugh, so I began to laugh. I didn't know that it was a dunce cap. I learned later.

Tanya was entranced with the study of English. She learned to appreciate poetry even before she could understand the language by going to the library and reading nursery rhymes. "At first I didn't know what nursery rhymes were," she recalled, "but I just listened to sound, though I didn't know if I made the correct sounds because I didn't know those words, how they should be pronounced. But I kept reading them. What interested me was the meter—the meter was good. So it was like music. And I kept reading and reading them."

Although Tanya picked up English easily, it took years for her to feel comfortable with it. When her aunts arrived from Russia less than two years later, their night school teacher let her attend class with them if she acted as monitor. "I went to school in the morning and I was a monitor at night for the teacher of my aunts," she recalled. "I did that to hear more English, to learn it faster." When Tanya was in the sixth grade, she finally felt sure of herself with her adopted language. She had written a composition in which she used the words, "my attention was arrested by . . ." Her teacher, Mrs. Valentine, "was delighted! And she said to me, 'Now I am certain that you will speak English and understand it better than most young people.' She told me that and I never forgot it. And she said, 'You know that "arrested" has nothing to do with going to jail.' She could see that I was a reader and was beginning to understand words and their different usages and meanings. And then," Tanya concluded, "I got more confidence in myself."

Other women also credited a teacher with stimulating their love of learning and everything American. Mary Antin, newly arrived in America, received from a teacher her first book, a volume of Longfellow's poems. Antin called the teacher, who encouraged her writing, her first American friend.[48] Dora W. also benefited from a teacher who took extra pains with immigrant children who were avid to learn. Once she started school, Dora recalled,

I made very rapid progress. I was out of public school in five and a half years, mainly because I had such a dedicated teacher. She was an absolutely beautiful person. She changed the course of my life. She gave us everything that she had and more. I met her when I was in the third grade and I didn't leave her until I was in the fifth.

She recognized children who had aptitudes and she worked with us. And we made all those grades in six months. But not only that. She formed a club for us, these special girls at the Henry Street Settlement. And that is the place that introduced me to anything that was cultural and good in the United States.

The Henry Street Settlement prided itself on being an agent for the acculturation of such young immigrants.[49] There, as in the schools, girls learned American ways and brought them home to parents.

For such young women as Dora or Tanya, who came here young enough to take an elementary education for granted, the quest for knowledge went beyond learning to read and write English properly. Tanya regretted her lack of a college degree and attempted to acquire an education on her own. When she was nineteen, her aunt introduced her to a man who headed a group called the Self-Culture Club. "I found myself in a highly cultural environment," Tanya recalled. Every Sunday morning there would be "very important, interesting, gifted speakers, including the niece of the poet Walt Whitman. When the speaker was not up to my standards, I was disappointed." Tanya then joined the Brooklyn Philosophical Society. "I went to all of these things," she remembered. "I enjoyed them immensely. I enriched my own understanding. And I'm still doing the same thing when I read. That never stopped."

Public lectures like those Tanya attended attracted enormous crowds on the Lower East Side, and young Jewish working women had more freedom than women of other groups to attend such speeches and meetings in the evenings.[50] New York State's People's University sponsored lectures on almost every conceivable subject by popular speakers before more than five thousand audiences. These Adult Free Lectures offered talks to education-hungry immigrants on such varied topics as "The Times of the Roman Emperors," "How to Breathe," "Pictures from Hindu Life," and "Practical Electricity." In 1903–4, over a million people attended. Cooper Union's People's Institute offered a similarly varied and popular series of evening lectures; the Workmen's Circle, unions, the Socialists, the Zionists, and all manner of groups spoke to their mainly immigrant audiences about subjects as diverse as "Hegel's Dialectic" and "How to Be an American."[51] Anything considered at all "educational" or intellectually provocative brought out scores of ghetto residents. As one recent chronicler pointed out, to these young Jewish workers, "eager to swallow the world's culture at a single gulp, it hardly mattered whether a lecturer spoke on popular science or ancient history, German literature or Indian customs."[52] "Always and everywhere the same audience," observed the *Forward* in 1904:

> During the winter there are several hundred lectures. Big societies have series of lectures; the tiny ones have single, irregular ones. . . . There are thousands and thousands of Jews coming to be educated, which means that the most illiterate masses are being reached. . . . There are numerous young men and girls whom you can see at every talk. . . . They come to hear about socialism on East Broadway and about literature on Forsythe Street; about a play in Harlem, and even a lecture in Russian on Grand Street. Although they hardly know the language, it doesn't matter—they sit and sweat and listen.[53]

The newspaper was critical of the topics offered. "Our people," it complained, "are not getting what they need, but whatever is available."[54] But these lectures served an important purpose for immigrants hungry for knowledge and having no other way to get it. Jennie S., who at nineteen went alone from a poor town in Galicia to a shirtwaist factory in New York where she spent most of her life, took great pride in the fact that her friends considered her "an educated woman." Although she had no formal education, she explained, "I go to lectures, and I like to listen to the speaker when he speaks. I listen," Jennie concluded, "and I learn."

Education was the great dream of many young people who came to America from Eastern Europe. Even the daughters of illiterate parents grew up with a reverence for learning that had little if anything to do with job skills or earning a living. These young women came to America knowing that they would have to work to support themselves and their families. But they also wanted to enlarge their horizons and breach the barrier that had kept all but a few of them from entering the world of learning in Eastern Europe. Satisfaction with educational achievements depended largely on their aspirations. Some young women were proud and happy to complete high school, while others, like Rae, were embittered by their inability to achieve the college education they coveted. Women from poor families often were pleased simply to learn English and to attend the numerous lectures on the Lower East Side. This was more education than they ever expected to receive, and it was all free. While parents might not understand a daughter's desire for advanced education, after a family achieved financial security, the younger children might remain in school as long as they wished. The older ones, of course, had no such option, and whatever education they got came haphazardly during the few hours after the demands of the work day. If any of these older children remained in school, family strategies determined that an education was more important for a son, and many sisters struggled to see their brothers through high school or college.

The vast majority of these women had to wait another generation to see their ambitions fulfilled. Sarah Reznikoff remembered the frustrations of many who had to forego an education because of financial necessity. Once, when a cousin recently arrived from Russia cried at seeing the children coming out of school, Sarah remembered how she too had longed for an education. "We are a lost generation," she told him. "It is for our children to do what they can."[55] Anna R. never forgave her parents for taking her out of school after the fifth grade and determined that her own three daughters would have the education she lacked. All of them subsequently became professionals. Gussie M., who spent most of her life sewing ladies blouses, was delighted when her daughters completed college. "College—it's a pleasure! To me, the college was my ideal. I was longing for education to such a degree that this was my only goal in life. And since it didn't cost anything, they could go to college. This is what I dreamed of and this is what I have," she concluded, "and I'm still happy about it." Most women with children expressed greater pride in their education than their earning power, and almost all said that if they could do it over, what they would most want was more education. The children of this first generation went to school in greater numbers and remained there longer than the sons and daughters of any other contemporary immigrant group. And daughters made use of their education to enter the white-collar world of the salesgirl, secretary, and teacher at a higher rate as well.[56] Thus, although education remained beyond the reach of most women who came here in their early adult years, they determined that it would be the birthright of their children.

10

. . . .

Becoming a Person: Work and Independence

In Europe, how could you go to work? There was no place to work. Especially for girls it was very bad. But when I came here, I became very independent because I used to make a lot of money right away.

—Ruth R.

. . . .

I was the oldest. My father wanted me to go to work when I was seventeen. Work was success. As long as I was working at something that was paying a salary, my father wouldn't have to support me. . . . And I wanted to work to help out. I wanted to make money and have the things I wanted for myself in the way of clothes and such. I was always vain.

—Tanya N.

16. Young women at work in a garment shop.

Photographer: Lewis Hine. International Museum of Photography at George Eastman House, Rochester, N.Y.

If education was a dream for many girls, work was the reality, for families needed the money they brought home. But often a role as breadwinner gave young Jewish women unexpected importance and helped them, as Anzia Yezierska put it, "to become a person."[1] In an earlier time, this position could only be achieved by marrying and setting up an independent household. Now, with the opportunities of industrialism and the changing attitudes of parents toward a daughter's rights and obligations, the assumption of financial responsibilities frequently won for these young women the status of adults while they were still living under their parents' roofs.[2] This involved both heightened self-esteem as well as increased prerogatives—freedom to come and go as they wished, the right to keep some of the money they earned, and a voice in family decision-making.

Although beginning work did not in itself confer higher status, it led inexorably in that direction. Around the turn of the century, daughters were expectd to be single-mindedly devoted to family, and Jewish girls who wanted to keep some of their wages might face a struggle. In the 1890s, for example, Rose Cohen resented having to work and yet have no money of her own. She remembered that when she asked her father for spending money, he gave her a penny, and then beat her for contrariness when she handed it back.[3] Good daughters were supposed to give parents all their wages and receive back an "allowance" for carfare, lunches, and other necessities. Although there may have been tensions over spending money or social freedom, most young women accepted this role without question.[4] Dora Shapiro worked in a dress factory and had little interest in her job or wages because whatever she had went to her mother. "I didn't know the difference," she recalled. Sometimes, girls rebelled. Bea Gitlin at first gave every penny to her parents and got an allowance in return. But then, she "put [her] foot down and gave ten dollars a week and kept the rest." Fanny Helzer originally gave her whole salary to an older sister, but when they clashed over Fanny's desire to buy clothing, she went to live with a friend and kept the money for herself.[5] Yet even early in the century, observers noted that Jewish girls generally had more freedom in spending their earnings than Italian or German girls in the same shops.[6]

Twenty or thirty years later, although young women still contributed most of their wages to families, it seldom required an act of rebellion for them to withhold an amount for personal use. Many parents had begun to believe that children were entitled to some of the money they had earned for clothing or entertainment.[7] Now, when Jewish girls kept money for themselves, their mothers generally considered it proper behavior. This practice contrasted with Italian families, where as late as the 1930s and

1940s, despite some resistance, mothers expected daughters to turn over their entire paychecks.[8] As early as 1914, when Tanya N. started work, she kept part of her wages. "I wanted to make money and have the things I wanted for myself," she observed. "I was always vain." The amount a girl could withhold depended in large part upon the family's economic circumstances. When Fannie C. got a job, for example, she used some of the money she earned for her own needs. But when her father fell ill and could no longer work, everything went to her parents. "Even when I had to buy clothes," she recalled, "I would go to my parents and ask them for the money because I would give them my whole salary."

Yet regardless of the amount given, the way the money was presented to mothers marked a subtle change in the relationship between them and their daughters. "I just kept for myself what I needed," Fannie explained. "You know, expenses like carfare, lunches." Ethel B. repeated the same story. "I just told my mother, 'This is what I need,'" she recalled. "And when I had to buy clothing, I went out and bought it." In other words, Fannie and Ethel decided for themselves how much money they required for expenses and gave their mothers the rest. Many Jewish daughters decided in this manner how much to contribute to the family's coffers. When Janet A. began working, she gave twelve dollars of her salary of fifteen dollars a week to her mother. "I figured out how much I needed," Janet recalled, and she kept the three dollars for her own expenses. Anna Kahan used five dollars out of the twenty-five she earned. Although these young women kept relatively little, they themselves rather than a parent made the decision. Money offered in this way is given by choice, and it is therefore a kind of gift rather than an unthinking obligation automatically assumed by a daughter and expected by a parent. Some young women even went a step further: Gussie Kimball never told her parents how much she earned, but gave them five dollars out of her fifteen dollar salary for board.[9]

If a family was not dependent on a daughter's wage alone, mothers generally approved of their having spending money. Tanya N. remembered that her mother saw nothing wrong even when she spent some of her salary for a down payment on an absurdly expensive dress made of "kitten's ear silk" that she saw in a Fifth Avenue shop. Fannie N. and her sisters gave paychecks to their mother, who distributed money for expenses and put the rest into the bank. When Fannie married in 1935, her mother handed her a check for two thousand dollars, saying, "This is your money, and it belongs to you." Fannie had been the mainstay of the family for several years, and now that times were easier for them, her mother chose this way to thank her daughter. Mothers reciprocated for their daughter's help by trying to make their lives easier or more pleasant in little ways. A favorite soup, a freshly ironed dress, enough saved out of the housekeeping money for a new hat or pair of shoes—these were a mother's way of saying "thank you." Anna Kahan remembered her mother's insistence that she buy herself a treat. "You've got to get some clothes," she told her. "And we found a place, it was wholesale. We went there, and one dress was a beauty. It was three or four dollars. And the other dresses were two dollars each. She says, 'You should take a half a dozen.' I couldn't take that many, but I did take three. So I had plenty of dresses. But my mother had to tell me to do it."

Most daughters took pride in their contributions, in part because of the example of their mothers' selflessness. The desire to "help mama" was a common reason why women of all ethnic groups went to work.[10] When Sara B. left New Haven for New York at twenty-one for a job as a buyer of dry goods, she observed, "I was young but very serious, because my mother had a hard life and I always wanted to ease things up for her." Anna Kahan's father was only able to get a job making eight dollars a week, so Anna remained, while only sixteen, the major breadwinner in her family. "The twenty-five dollars a week I earned paid the rent," she noted, "so I could not afford to be out of work. When I lost one job, I went out right away to look for another." Fannie C. recalled, "When most bookkeepers were making twenty dollars, I was making thirty-five. My parents really depended on me." "We were a very cohesive family," observed Miriam M. "For instance, whoever worked, my mother got the money, and whoever needed, whether you worked or you didn't work, you got. If you needed shoes, you got shoes. The only person who didn't get what she needed was the mother. And when we got older we began to insist that she get those things first and then we'll get them." In Miriam's family, all contributed, and all received. Decisions were made by the mother, who denied only herself. "It was the respect to bring and give your mother the money" related Mollie Linker, who began working at sixteen. "It was the mother always there."[11]

Working outside the home was another way for young women to fulfill responsibilities to parents, just as a mother's "helping out" sometimes augmented the family's income in Eastern Europe or the United States. As with other immigrant daughters, this work usually reflected a commitment to family values rather than a quest for self-fulfillment.[12] Families were central to their lives, and if a father's income was insufficient, daughters almost automatically sought a job.[13] During the 1920s, fewer than half the working-class families were supported fully by the earnings of a husband or father, so other family members often had no option but to find work. "Whatever we had, we pooled," observed Miriam M. Among Jews, however, it was generally considered unacceptable for married women to seek outside employment, so children felt all the more keenly the need to supplement the family income. Furthermore, despite the American emphasis on individualism, responsibility to family became even more important after the depression struck.[14] "Work was success," observed Tanya N. "As long as I was working at something that was paying a salary, my father wouldn't have to support me. My mother was helping my father. If she could take care of a house and five kids, then I could work. And," she concluded, "I wanted to work to help out."

Although most young women learned from their mothers to be selfless in working to benefit the family, children might be less generous if mothers set a different example. Rose G., for example, remembered her mother as a selfish woman. "My mother got herself the best shoes," she remembered. "The children, she took us to a place where we got shoes on sale. I remember I wanted Dr. Brown's shoes and my mother wouldn't get them for me. She never got them for me." As a proper daughter, Rose still gave her money to her mother—"every penny" she insisted. "I felt I had to contribute," she recalled. Yet, she later mentioned that she kept back five dollars a week—twenty out of seventy-five dollars a month—which she spent on clothing and saved to go to secretarial school. Rose's brothers, who were students, contributed nothing. They used the money from part-time jobs for their own expenses.

Working for wages meant more to many Jewish girls than being able to assist parents, although this was usually essential.[15] It frequently meant thinking of themselves and being treated by parents as adults.[16] Rose Schneiderman, who became a union activitist, believed that her independence began when she started work as a capmaker and kept a dollar of her six-dollar salary instead of giving it all to her mother and letting her decide what to return for expenses.[17] This sense of independence did not mean that they sought to live apart from the family—quite the contrary, like most immigrant girls, young Jewish women with parents in America lived with them and respected their wishes. Most young working women remained closely bound to parents by traditional obligations and emotional ties.[18] Yet for these Jewish girls, work seemed to make a difference, and it was more than simply being out in the wider world and associating with other young women. One study comparing different ethnic groups demonstrated that while young Italian women identified mainly with parents and viewed themselves as passive, Jewish girls focused more upon jobs and described themselves as active agents with control over their own lives.[19] The Italian women did not consider work performance a confirmation of their worth, while the Jews did. Although family was important to both groups, it did not dominate the perceptions of Jewish women as it did the Italians. If holding a job alone made the difference in attitudes toward independence, then this first generation of young Italian women, who often worked side by side with Jewish coworkers, should have felt similarly independent. Perhaps the practical message of self-sufficiency Jewish mothers passed on to their daughters inadvertently encourged an independent spirit.[20]

Once young people assumed increased financial responsibilities, many parents started giving them more decision-making authority. For example, when Anna Kahan was only sixteen, she had a job making hats for twenty-five dollars a week in a small shop with pleasant conditions and a friendly forelady. "For the first time, I had no aggravation," she recalled, "for the first time I enjoyed my work, and it was a pleasure to go and a pleasure to come." But her father was sick and the family needed more money. A distant relative who had a "dirty little shop" came and offered her a job as a hat designer for thirty-five dollars a week. "I knew I'd have a harder time," Anna recalled, "but ten dollars a week more! I couldn't refuse." Yet her mother did not tell Anna to take the job. "You have to decide," she told her daughter. The girl knew that for financial reasons she had to accept the better-paid position, but again, the final choice was hers to make. The obligation was thus assumed by the daughter rather than imposed by the parent, as it may have been among parents in other immigrant groups for whom working did not elevate daughters to the status of adults.[21]

Sometimes daughters of authoritarian fathers began to demand increased freedom after taking a job.[22] When Fannie C. started work, she gained the courage to oppose her father's will. Within a year after he had refused to let her stay out late to attend her high school prom, she went to the country for a weekend with the man she would later marry, despite her father's protests. She had started work, she explained, and decided that there were things she wanted to do, regardless of his anger, and he would simply have to accept it. As with Dora W., who took a job on the Sabbath against her father's wishes, these fathers lost the fight and eventually accepted their daughters' new-found independence. Because Jewish parents depended on their children as guides to becoming American, one contemporary observer wrote, "The result is an unusual development of independent initiative on the part of the young Jewish shop girl."[23]

It was more common for daughters to discover that their assistance to the family had won them the status of adults without a struggle.[24] Naomi L. was surprised when her father agreed to let her go by train to visit a sister in California. "I thought he would say no!" Naomi recalled, "because in those years young girls didn't travel alone." Yet her father agreed to the trip without protest. "I think my father was kind of proud," Naomi observed. "He felt that he could depend on me." When the brothers of Sara B. decided to stop working in their parents' dry-goods store, Sara told her parents that she could carry on by herself. The seventeen-year-old girl did all the buying and ran the office until her parents decided to sell the business. Soon after, at nineteen, Sara left for New York and a career with the blessings of her mother and father. Frieda K., who worked as a bookkeeper, supported her mother, invalid father, and sister single-handedly, and whatever she chose to do was fine with her parents. Miriam G. left her family in Iowa at seventeen to go to Boston, with her parents' consent. When she started work there, her father sent her a letter and a check, which she proudly sent home. "I guess I was a very independent person," she mused.

Although earning money was in itself enough to give many young women a feeling of autonomy, the type of work they did and the degree of satisfaction they had in their jobs contributed to their feelings about themselves. Almost all women expected to work only a few years and then retire when they married. "I had marriage on my mind," recalled Ida Richter. "I thought to myself: 'I just want to work and get through and after a while to get married.'"[25] Yet, for these years, their work experience could be challenging, demeaning, satisfying, or sheer drudgery, depending upon the particular jobs and the expectations of the women who held them. They could provide a source of pride, a stimulus for radicalization, or a sense of frustration and degradation. Above all, their experiences in the world of work were crucial in shaping the personalities of these young women.

Probably the worst jobs were in domestic service, and although Jews tended to avoid such jobs, those with no skills sometimes had to become servants.[26] Many poor young women who had been domestics in Eastern Europe remained so here.[27] Mary Wasserman Nathan, who came to the United States around 1900, could not aspire to a job in a garment shop because she had never learned how to sew, so she began working as a maid for a New Jersey family. But her father made a fuss at what he considered shameful work and insisted, to her relief, that Mary leave the job.[28] When she was only fourteen, Rose Cohen worked as a live-in servant and slept on two old quilts and a pillow on a bed made of two chairs. But she was glad to have her wages of six dollars a month to give to her jobless father.[29] Living with relatives was no assurance of decent treatment. Louise C. got to this country by promising to work as a maid when an aunt in Milwaukee sent for her to take care of her house and six children. "She figured," Louise assumed, "Well, a nice girl, a strong girl. I'll have a maid in the house and it won't cost much." After a year with her aunt, she moved to New York and worked for a family as the only maid in a house with nine rooms. "I wasn't trained for it," she recalled. "It was too much work for me and I couldn't do it." Dora G., who was sent here at fourteen, had an even more difficult experience. Forced by abject poverty to leave her village in Eastern Europe, she came to relatives who put her to work at two jobs. "I was working at a butcher," she recalled.

> I was working in the kitchen, I was washing clothes, I was cooking, I was baking, I was ironing. For ten dollars a month. And then I got so homesick, I didn't want to eat, I didn't want to live no more. I say, "I want to go back home." So my uncle came, my father's brother, and he says, "Your papa didn't send you to America he should have you home. You know, you can't help at home. He's got younger ones than you that he has to feed."
>
> And I said that time to my aunt, "I can't work this hard no more. I want to go back home, and I don't want to stay here." By my aunt I'm a servant—she expected a baby and I used to help her with the work. Cleaning and cooking. For the butcher, I cleaned the counters and chopped the meat. He was a *landsman* [person who came from her town]. It was a second marriage and he liked to be with his wife. So I did the work. A young woman, a strong girl that he put to work for ten dollars a month. There was no hours. In the morning, as soon as it got light, I used to have to come down, make breakfast, make the fire. There was no gas, no electric. I had to go to the yard and get some boards from houses that were ripped down to start the fire.

No wonder that Dora grasped at any straw to escape this drudgery and married an elderly widower when she was fifteen.

Other jobs were equally wearing and ill-paid. Most women did not earn a living wage, and working conditions could be horrendous.[30] Frieda M. worked in a laundry. "That was a place," she recalled, "that you imagine hell is like—the laundry. The sound of those constant machines, the heat of the mangles, especially in the summer." Most laundries had little ventilation, and temperatures registered ninety-five degrees, even in the spring.[31] Yetta Altman remembered her work in a garment shop as "real slavery" for two dollars a week. She was only twelve, and all the more easily exploited. Her boss was "a monster" who wouldn't let his operators lift their eyes from the machines. When a factory inspector came around, he pushed the under-age Yetta into a back room until he left.[32] Factory work often left little time for anything else. "That time was slavery," recalled Frieda W. "Fifty-seven years ago when I came to America, it was slavery. We used to work until nine o'clock at night. We began at eight in the morning, sometimes seven-thirty. Slavery! I used to come home in the Bronx and it was half past ten already. How can I go to night school? How can I live even?" Although such women were glad to have work, they wanted more out of life. "No one questioned the necessity of working for a living," wrote Rose Chernin. "This was good fortune, the reason we came to America. But I didn't like it. I could not accept the factory for my life. I tried going to school at night but after ten hours in the factory I would fall asleep in my class. We always had to help mama at home. . . . From the moment I woke up, early, early in the morning, there was something to do."[33]

A young woman's expectations were important in determining how she viewed her job. Factory work was more than welcome to women like Ruth R. or Louise C., who remembered a background of poverty and hunger in Europe, but children who spent most of their lives in the United States expected more. Dora W. was in her second or third year of high school and hoped to attend college when her father became sick. "There was no way for me to go back to high school," she recalled,

> So I left and I went to work in a shop that took the quills off feathers. These feathers were used for stuffing pillows and such things. We had a little machine with a razor blade, I think, that sliced off the quill. And you put the quills in one place and the feathers in another place, until you had a certain number of ounces, and they paid you by the ounce. I think I must have made six dollars a week doing that.
>
> And I was with people, poor girls. I was terribly unhappy. They were uneducated, and I had had a bit of, a taste of education, and the better things in life. I used to come home and weep. I worked there for a year. And I said to my parents, "I must go back to school. I simply cannot live this way."

Dora was unable to identify with young immigrant women who had limited horizons. She managed to return to high school and worked taking care of a retarded child after classes.

Other women enjoyed working with their hands, but the factory tended to destroy any pleasure they may have derived from craftsmanship. Mildred Hecht, who had been a tailor in Russia, prided herself on her ability. "I liked it like a painter likes his work," she observed. "When I used to finish making a coat it was good and I would get much pleasure from it. I would look at it and feel good all over like I made a beautiful sculpture. . . . In America, when I went to work in a factory, I felt like a machine. Here is a bigger speed-up, hurry-up."[34] And in the busy season, one might have to work at this pace for more than sixty hours a week.[35]

Women could still take satisfaction from their ability to learn on the job. While some went to school to gain advanced skills, others, like Jennie H., picked them up in the factory. "A friend of my [future] husband's cousin took me up to a big factory for a job," she recalled,

> And they were making dresses. I used to baste everything and drape and pin. And when they used to pin the dresses, I basted, so the operator could sew it on the machine without pins. And there was a man who was a specialist on basting sleeves in. So he was out one day, and I walked over to that section and I started basting. I was curious about everything, so I basted in a pair of sleeves and then another pair of sleeves. The boss came over and looked at it, and he says, "Who basted those sleeves?" And I says, "I did." And I became a sleeve baster. I saw how he was doing it and I learned it from him and I was able to do it when he was gone.

"And they paid a good price for doing that," Jennie concluded with satisfaction. Fannie N., who went to work at fifteen in a factory making silk underwear, also took pride in her craftsmanship. "They used to give me a bundle of material and a bundle of lace and I had to make my own design," she recalled. "It was very artistic, very beautiful." Like Jennie and Fannie, most young women in need of a job found their way into the East Side's garment shops to work in the burgeoning dress and shirtwaist industry.[36] A factory might be attractive, particularly if it was near home and did not require girls to work on Saturday.[37] "When I had to work on the Sabbath," recalled Jennie, "I cried all the time."

Some trades, like hatmaking, could be gratifying because one saw the completed product of one's own labor. Frieda K., who worked in a fine shop, recalled that "some of the hats took three days to make. Everything was done by hand, and it was really an art." Anna Kahan also took pride in her skill as a milliner. "We did everything by hand," she echoed Frieda. "We even made the wire frames and sewed braid on them." After two jobs in unpleasant places, Anna found work in a "high-class" millinery shop. There they made "a beautiful line of hats," she recalled,

> and it didn't look like a factory at all. It looked like a salon with curtains, such a beautiful place. And we didn't sit at long tables with the lamps, with the green shades down. I had a little table for myself. And the madam came and gave me three hats. Less than a dozen!?

Only three hats. It was a beautiful sample and everything was cut right. And I sat down and I made the three hats. I enjoyed doing it, for the first time in four or five years.

I brought them in and she looked at them. She says, "You're a perfectionist." And she gave me another one. It was beautiful, with hand-made flowers. I remember it was made of shirred chiffon because it was in the summer, on a wire frame, one of those garden picture hats. It was an expensive line.

Despite the satisfaction, there was a catch. "They only paid twenty-five dollars a week," Anna recalled. "It was the highest they paid. The better the line, the less they paid." So when her father got sick, Anna had to take a better-paying job in an unpleasant factory.

As a family became secure financially, almost all Jewish married women remained at home, and more daughters could remain in school rather than going out to work. By 1911, only 1 percent of New York's Jewish housewives were officially employed outside the home, and the number of all Jewish women who worked for wages declined steadily between 1910 and 1925.[38] Those who worked sought more prestigious positions than the factory offered. With upward mobility, girls could complete high school and possibly even attend college, and families encouraged them to enter the white-collar worlds of the office, the department store, or the teaching profession. In 1905, fully 25 percent of employed Russian Jewish daughters worked as teachers, clerks, salespersons, or shopkeepers.[39] Only five years before, few young Jewish women had taught in the schools, but by 1914, some observers suggested that they had already replaced American-born and Irish women as the largest group among New York City teachers.[40] At the time, this was an overstatement, for few Jewish women had entered the school system before 1917, but by 1930, 44 percent of the new teachers were indeed Jewish.[41]

Women who came here young, went through the public schools and thus had no foreign accents to mark them, could realistically aim higher than the factory. Bookkeeping was considered professional work, and many girls took commercial courses in high school to prepare for this genteel position. Naomi L., after graduating from high school at sixteen, had no trouble finding a job with a leather goods firm. But timing was important. Minna S., who sought work during the depression, had more difficulty, although she had two years of high school. Without experience, she explained, she couldn't get a job, and without a job, she had no experience. Sometimes the depression put an end to dreams of quick upward mobility. Even with a diploma, it was seldom easy to find employment, and many Jewish families had to continue to rely on more than one wage earner.[42] Miriam M., while working during the day, put herself through high school, preparatory school, and law school at night. She graduated in the unfortunate year of 1929, when many lawyers without the disabilities of being Jews or women were having a hard time finding jobs. Besides, as Miriam observed, she was not willing, as some of her female classmates were, to "sleep around." Miriam scaled down her expectations to a more acceptable female role. After graduation, she would go every day to the Remington Typewriter Company to improve her typing. "I was sitting and practicing," she recalled, "and a man came and picked me out for a job, like he picked out on the auction block when they were selling slaves. I was very flattered," she concluded. It meant she had work.

Some young women found satisfactions in less usual work. Tanya N. had the good fortune to find a job during World War I in a newspaper clipping bureau. She later became an executive for the New York Society for the Deaf. Rita S. was hired as a model for Macy's and then became an assistant buyer in the cosmetics department. "I had a ball," she observed, "I loved it." Leah Morton also worked in a department store, as a personnel director.[43] Frances F., who was a dancer when she did not have to support her parents by working as a bookkeeper, took great pleasure in her art. Once, when she performed at a home for unwed mothers, she danced for the girls, and then she danced with them. "And they felt so happy, so important," Frances recalled, "to have danced with me. The simple pleasures I could give so readily." Hattie L., who also started as a bookkeeper, longed to be a nurse or a social worker—anything that would enable her to help people in need. She took numerous Red Cross courses and eventually became a psychiatric nurse, a position she held for eighteen years. "Then I had all the recognition and satisfaction I wanted," she observed.

Some young women found themselves trapped in a cycle of poorly paid and unsatisfying jobs. A teacher in Anzia Yezierska's story, "Soap and Water," aimed high and was therefore unhappy with what to others was a prestigious situation:

> Starvation forced me to accept the lowest paid substitute position. And because my wages were so low and so unsteady, I could never get the money for the clothes to make an appearance to secure a position with better pay. I was tricked and foiled. I was considered unfit to get decent pay for my work because of my appearance, and it was to the advantage of those who used me that my appearance should damn

me, so as to get me to work for the low wages I was forced to accept. It seemed to me the whole vicious circle of society's injustices was thrust like a noose around my neck to strangle me.[44]

For such positions, it was important to look like a middle-class American "lady."

Most women had fewer options. Jennie S., who came here alone in her teens and married late in life, spent most of her life working at one unsatisfying and ill-paying job after another. She always had difficulty earning enough to pay for food and rent. "I looked only to make a living," Jennie recalled. "I worked in ladies waists for two and a half dollars a week for six days a week, Sunday the whole day. Eh, you made a poor living." Women could be paid so little, because, as the Working Women's Society reported, "Men's wages cannot fall below a limit upon which they can exist, but women's wages have no limit, since the paths of shame are always open to her."[45] For some, prostitution was one way out. But the vast majority did not consider this a feasible alternative to the factory. Jennie continued to work on buttonholes and buttons. "When the needle hits the button, the button breaks and jumps in your eyes. It wasn't so good," she observed, "but it was better than not working." To escape the factory, she took care of a blind woman for a few years, but after she died, Jennie was back sewing on buttons.

Regardless of whether their jobs were in factories or offices, many young women were distressed by the coarseness and sexual advances of co-workers, bosses, and supervisors.[46] Polly Adler, the famed bordello opera-tor, attributed her descent into prostitution to being thrown out by a cousin after she was raped at seventeen by a foreman in her factory, became pregnant, and had to have an abortion. "I had lost my virginity, my reputa-tion and my job," the former madam observed. "All I had gotten was older."[47] Less extreme experiences could be equally traumatic for inexperi-enced young women. Rae K. left a job in one garment shop because the designers "were getting too cozy" with her. Anna Kahan remembered the operators in one shop "throwing dirty jokes at the girls, and this was going back and forth, and I was too delicate for it. I got headaches. I rushed myself and I stuck my fingers. Three of my fingers got infected." Elizabeth Hasanovitz lost an otherwise good job when the owner flirted with her and his furious wife told her to leave. At another shop, she was physically attacked.[48] Rose Cohen remembered the vulgar jokes and pinches of the men in the shops. When she came to the United States at twelve, the first English sentence she learned was "Keep your hands off please." Rose left one job because of the obscene stories of the men and was fired from another when she refused to sit on the boss's knee.[49] Gussie Agines also suffered from the abuse of her employer. "He tried to hug me," she recalled, "and I was so ashamed because I didn't know what to say or do. No man had ever kissed me except my father before."[50]

The status of the job or religion of the boss seemed not to matter. Naomi L. had to quit a position as a bookkeeper when the boss "began to get too personal, too friendly." Miriam M., who graduated from law school, remained mired in low-level jobs. "Some jobs where I was," she recalled, "if you didn't get on the couch with the boss, you didn't get on." Once, when she got a position assisting a Jewish lawyer who was a friend of her brother, "he had no hesitancy about making sexual advances to me. I would never tell my brother about it," she observed. "Well, maybe *now* I would have."

Frieda W. seemed unable to keep a job because of the unwanted attentions of her employers. Once, when she worked in a shirtwaist shop, her boss asked her to stay after hours "to finish up a sample." When everyone had left,

> the boss came over to me and says, "Frieda, I don't need the sample. I just want to have you for a sweetheart." I say, "Mr. Feld, I don't want to be a sweetheart to a man if I can't be his wife for real." He tells me, "You got to be!" I say, "No, I don't want." That was the first time. Then for a week, he didn't bother me again. But in another week, he starts again. He says, "If you don't be my sweetheart, then you don't work here." Goddamit, I got so mad, I told him, "The hell with you! And the hell with your job too!"
>
> That's already three jobs I had already bad experience with men. That's when I was young. No more now. Thank God!

Some young women found a focus for their lives in union work. Few became as totally immersed as Rose Schneiderman, who never married and discovered, when she became active in the union, "All of a sudden, I was not lonely any more."[51] Yet many found a new form of solidarity and strength in organizing, even if marriage a few years later put an end to their activity. Like many other women, Sara Plotkin had developed sympathy for the workers' cause in Eastern Europe: she had refused to dig potatoes for twenty-five kopecks a day, because she was small, when other girls got forty.[52] The revolutionary movement in Russia had imbued a whole generation of young women with the desire to fight for social justice, and they came to America bringing those beliefs with them.[53] One biographer suggested that the radicalism of the anarchist Emma Goldman could be traced

to her experience of anti-Semitism in Russia and to the ethical requirements of the prophetic strain in Judaism.[54] Regardless of the reason, Jewish
working women became famous for their rebelliousness and radical ten-
dencies. Hutchins Hapgood in 1902 described these "ghetto heroines . . .
willing to lay down their lives for an idea, or to live for one."[55]

Others learned the value of unionizing in this country, particularly after
the success of the shirtwaist makers strike of 1909–10, when 30,000 to
40,000 workers, mostly Jewish women, succeeded in forcing employers to
set up new wage standards in the industry.[56] Rose Chernin learned from a
social worker that there were different classes of people. "I found out," she
recalled, "that there were people struggling for a better system than capitalism. . . . To me, socialism was just common sense."[57] But even before this,
conditions in the shops led many young Jewish women to radicalism.
Rebecca August traced her transformation to a period in 1906 when she
was making buttonholes in men's suits for Hart, Schaffner and Marx shops.
She made a good living because she was very fast, but the boss "thought it
was an outrage for a girl to make twenty-five dollars," so he cut the rate for
piecework. Rebecca was infuriated and convinced the other young women
in the shop to agree not to accept the cut. As a result, she and her father
were fired. Whenever she got another job, after a week or two, she was laid
off. "I presume they were informed of who I was," she observed. Rebecca
later joined the Socialist Party and became a branch officer. In 1910, she
moved to Seattle and continued to be a union organizer. Because of her
success in winning an eight-hour day, the manufacturers got Rebecca
arrested, and she was held in immigration jail for two months on charges of
entering the country for immoral purposes.[58]

"It has to be in you that you should be attuned to something radical,"
observed Sonia O., who came here alone at nineteen and worked her whole
life in the garment industry. When organizers unionized her shop, she was
one of the first to join, and she wrote proudly to her father in Russia, "Don't
worry about me! I belong to a union now." Sonia became forelady in her
shop, and when they went on strike, she told the boss, "'If you don't settle
the strike, there's gonna be streams of blood here in the streets.' We were on
strike many, many weeks," she recalled. "And the police used to beat us up.
Oh, it was very hard. But that was life." Life was difficult, but gratifying.
These days, Sonia observed, people are more selfish and care little for the
welfare of their neighbors. "Now there is no shop and no factory," she
concluded, "and already I got social security. But I feel that we paid in
plenty. I felt, by God, that we immigrants contributed an awful lot to the
capital of America. And I feel that I'm a part of it."

Like Rose Schneiderman and Sonia, Fannie K. only developed an interest in her job when she began organizing each shop she worked in. Until she married, Fannie worked on underwear, then blouses and dresses. "The unions were big," she recalled, "but not so much strong and organized, and with open shops. So I enjoyed to go in and organize a union shop. And as soon as I did it, naturally the boss didn't like me, and he treated me so that I left. And I went to another place and it started all over again. It was the ILGWU," she remembered, "and I was always a shop leader." After she married, her husband had the chance to become a boss, she observed, but he would never betray the interests of the workers by becoming a capitalist.

Anna Kahan also developed a great sense of satisfaction when she and her co-workers decided spontaneously to stop work in their millinery shop. Such work stoppages were fairly common.[59] "One day," she explained,

we had a sample that took us at least an hour to make. And we had to wait an entire week to know what the boss would pay. And when he told us, it was fifty cents a hat. And what would we have at the end then? A dozen hats would be six dollars. And it took more than a day to make. And we started saying, "Look at this! Look at the price we are getting!" And then I said, "What are we going to do—are we just going to take it again and again?" I had a friend, and she said, "The only thing that we can do, we'll refuse to make it if they don't give us a raise." And then we talked with the other girls, and they said "Good, we'll refuse to make this hat. We'll stop working because all these prices are terrible—we'll complain about the other hats too."

And it was the height of the season. They had big orders. So this forelady came in and she said "What's going on here?" And we said "We are not going to do any work." She laughed it off and said, "Oh, go on. You'll change your mind." She went out for lunch, and she came back and we were still sitting. So she said, "What is this?" We said, "We are not going to work. You better go and tell Mr. Elmer about it." So her smile, her beautiful smile vanished, and she went in and she kept going back and forth. She gave us a little raise, back and forth, and we sat there, and we said "No." Finally, it took till about four or five o'clock we sat there. She came back, and they gave us a raise of fifty cents, actually double, on that bad hat, and others they raised a quarter. And I think now this was the first sitdown strike. We won the strike, and then we went back to work.

Whether young women left the labor force once they married or continued work, these early experiences invariably had an important effect upon their lives. For girls who lived with their parents, working often served the purpose of bridging the gap between childhood and adult status in the household. Along with the obligations they voluntarily assumed in helping to provide for the family came the rights and privileges of making decisions, keeping some of their earnings, and deciding how to spend free time. In most families, these changes were granted automatically after a teenage daughter took a job. If a father objected, the mother usually mediated, thus validating her daughter's claim to the rights of independent adulthood. It was not necessary for a daughter to marry and establish her own household before achieving recognition as a grown-up person.

Apart from this effect upon family relations, work also gave young Jewish women a sense of their own capabilities. In all but the most menial jobs, despite the long hours and general harshness of working conditions, most of these women seem to have learned something from their experience that increased self-esteem and confidence.[60] Girls from poor homes in Eastern Europe had the great and very basic satisfaction of being able to support themselves and assist their families. Factory workers took pride in their assertiveness in joining unions or in their ability to progress on the job; milliners could point to craftsmanship and creativity; bookkeepers were often pleased to be the first in their families to secure white-collar employment; saleswomen enjoyed being admitted to the all-American world of the department store. Although most of these young women may have left their jobs after marriage, the increased confidence they gained from working, in addition to their parents' recognition of them as adults, made it unlikely that they would revert to dependent roles once they decided to marry.

11

. . . .

Love and Marriage

Day and night and night and day,
And stitching, stitching, stitching!
Help me, dear God, may my handsome
*   one come along,*
and take me away from this toil.

—*Jewish folk song*[1]

. . . .

In my family I didn't count so much. My
money and my work—I was necessary. . . .
I never felt that I amounted to anything.
And my husband made me feel that I do.

—*Rose G.*

. . . .

I moved in with my friend without a
marriage license, without even thinking of
sex. . . . But he's a man and I'm a woman.
So little by little we got acquainted more
and more, and we finally decided to live
together for good. . . . I didn't go to a
rabbi. A rabbi has the function to tell me
whom I am to sleep with?

—*Sonia O.*

17. An immigrant couple, about 1910.

Collection of Audrey Kobrin Weinberg

Within a few years of starting work, the vast majority of young Jewish women married and began raising a family. Unlike most of their parents, these girls chose their own mates, usually with their mothers' and fathers' approval. Like the idea of a "chief rabbi," the marriage broker never really caught on in this country. Some of the earlier immigrants made use of the *shadkhen*, particularly before World War I. But the ability of young women to earn their own living ensured that they would not willingly marry someone they disliked because there was no other future for a single girl. As in Eastern Europe at this time, young Jewish women in cities had choices not available to their mothers. "I was independent," recalled Jennie S. of her refusal to marry an unappealing young man. "I didn't come to America to have to marry someone like him." Helen Rothman, who emigrated in 1910, refused to marry the man her parents selected for her and chose another.[2]

After the turn of the century, many parents who assumed this right found that their daughters were increasingly resistant. In 1900, one *shadkhen* complained to a journalist that young immigrant women "believe in love and all that rot . . . they learned how to start their own love affairs from the Americans, and it is one of the worst things they have picked up."[3] A young woman wrote to Rose Pastor Stokes's newspaper column in 1903 asserting that "it is every young woman's right to decide who shall be her life's partner. Who would tear that right from her and force her to a loveless marriage is—inexpressible."[4] As early as the 1890s, many parents saw the handwriting on the wall and knew that their right to select their daughters' husbands was limited. When Rose Cohen agreed to marry a young shop-keeper in a match arranged in this way and then found herself physically repelled by the man, her parents assured her that she did not have to go through with the wedding.[5]

Yet because marriage was the goal of almost all young women, and an "old maid" was an object of ridicule,[6] parents and other relatives devised acceptable methods for assuring that appropriately matched young people could meet and "fall in love." The *shadkhen* did not suddenly disappear, but his function changed. Marriage brokers were sometimes used like a modern "dating service," introducing prospective mates and then letting them decide whether they were interested in each other. The Yiddish theater was a popular place to arrange "accidental" meetings between marriageable young people. "*Shadkens* were often the excuse for urging a young man or woman to buy a ticket for the occasion," recalled Sophie Abrams-Flint, "so that possible mates could see you 'quite unexpectedly,' and more likely than not, the entire family of either or both sides was present to eye the prospect;

no item of wearing apparel was overlooked, and in the case of a young lady, she was sure to wear her best, furs by all means if one had them, and diamond rings and scarf pins were sported by the young men, as evidence of their affluence."[7] Often, relatives served as unofficial matchmakers. While Louise C. was living with her mother's sister in Milwaukee, she was introduced to a man her aunt considered a reasonable marriage prospect for a poor young girl. The man, a hunchbacked tailor, took Louise to the movies, but she would have nothing to do with him. Her aunt wrote reproachfully to Louise's parents that she had found a rich bachelor, but their daughter "did not behave like a lady." Soon after, Louise left for New York to get a job and seek a husband of her own choosing.

By about 1920, most young women were meeting men on their own, without a relative's supervision or a marriage broker's help. Like other working women, Jewish girls looked to peers more than parents in determining selection of a mate.[8] Unlike young women of the previous generation, whose lives revolved around the home, women who had grown up after World War I might spend a weekend day or evenings with friends, going on excursions to Coney Island or to movies. They were free to meet men at dance halls, clubs, picnics, meetings, and other social affairs.[9] Many young working women saved up for an annual vacation in the Catskills in hopes of attracting a wealthy suitor.[10] "Necking" with a boyfriend had become common.[11] In the eyes of young Jewish women, this was perfectly acceptable behavior regardless of whether their elders approved. Anna Kahan remembered an aunt remonstrating with her about relationships with young men. "She says, 'I saw you yesterday walking with six fellows. Everybody was looking at you.' I says, 'Well, what's wrong? We walked to the park.' 'You were the only girl there.' I said, 'I don't care. If they want to walk with me, they walk.' And that," she concluded, "was how it was." With parents and other older relatives uncertain of American customs, yet themselves wanting the children to become good Americans, the assertiveness of these young women was bound to win the day. It contrasted vividly with the situation of young Italian women who were chaperoned closely and expected to marry only men first approved by their families.[12]

But if parents lived in this country, dutiful daughters, even in the 1920s and 1930s, knew there were limits to their freedom to choose a husband. Miriam M. dated an Italian lawyer for several months. "I might have married him," she observed, "but I didn't encourage him in the least because it would have broken my mother's heart." Although some Jewish women married Italian men they had met in their shops,[13] parents considered a daughter's marrying outside their faith impermissible, whether or not they themselves were religious. Apart from this taboo, most young women were permitted to "date" men as long as suitors came to the house to be inspected.[14] Ethel B. recalled that all her young men had to call for her at home so her parents "could pass on them." On one occasion, she was asked out by the teller at her father's bank. "Then I asked him to come see my parents," she recalled, "and it turned out that he was a Christian. A very nice young man. He was from an excellent family—by today's standards, much above me actually. I didn't feel that way, but my father took his account out of that bank! And I had to explain to this young man that I couldn't see him any more." Sometimes parents still had the authority to veto their daughter's selection. When Mary Wasserman Natelson wanted to marry the son of a tailor, her father, a former rabbi, objected; Mary cried, but gave up her suitor.[15] But generally, mothers and fathers were not unreasonable in their demands, and daughters did not step over the forbidden line.

Despite a desire to select their own mates, many young women were unsure of how to behave in this freer atmosphere. Particularly for those who came here alone, and therefore felt more vulnerable, acceptable behavior with young men was something to feel out gingerly. A man met in one of the many dance halls could be either a prospective husband or a seducer,[16] for there was often a thin line between the conduct of a proper young woman and one who earned the reputation of being "loose"—an inappropriate marriage partner. Sex was still a great mystery to many Jewish girls, as it was to most young women at this time. What they learned came from peers who were frequently little better informed. "We were not educated to be prepared for life," observed Hannah F. "I was ignorant until my wedding day. I didn't know a thing. We thought if we just touched a man, we'd become pregnant. We had to find out everything for ourselves." Fannie Edelman learned from a girl in her shop that she would not become pregnant just by sitting next to a man. It was a liberating bit of knowledge. From then on, her life changed dramatically. She began to date men, and, she recalled, "I felt as if I was in seventh heaven."[17] Louise C., who was more knowledgeable about sex, had to determine just where to draw the line in relations with the young man she eventually married. "I wouldn't let him put his arms around me," she recalled,

I mean, it was a bitter experience to find out what love is. It was bitter because you just did not know where does the buck stop. How far is it permissible to give in to your feelings?

Something has to happen, and when it happens, my feeling was, either you're going to be smart or you're going to put an end to this. I told him, "Look, I can't see you no longer. I don't want you to come around and don't call me, and that's it. I don't know what will happen. I mean, how many times can you go down to the lake to make love in January?" So, I had to learn the hard way, and he had to learn the hard way.

And yet, I loved him, I was just crazy about him, and he was crazy about me. And he said, "No you won't. I want to marry you." And I'll tell you something. As ignorant as I was, and I was not ignorant, I would have told him eventually, "You want to have me and I want to have you, but it can't be outside of marriage." I would have told him. Well, it didn't come to that.

Jeanne S., who came to this country alone and worked her way through medical school, remembered the sexual quandary of her days as an intern. "I had boyfriends," she recalled. "You couldn't very well have intercourse with a boy, though. There was a great fear. We did not know how to take care of ourselves. Fear lived in my heart always, that I might get pregnant and not be able to continue, because I didn't have anybody to take care of me." Jeanne's ambition came before sex *or* marriage.

Dating was one thing, marriage quite another. Marriage for love was the ideal, but what did "love" mean? Ruth Katz gave a wise interpretation of the attitude of most of her contemporaries. "In this country, I think all my generation married for love. You think it's love, but when you're married for a while, life settles down more serious. It's not what you dreamt, but we make the best of it. One good thing about it is you get companionship."[18] Love meant different things to different women. And just as nineteenth-century German Jewish daughters had to convince themselves that they "loved" the spouses their parents had selected for them,[19] most young women in the modern age, as Ruth Katz observed, had to believe that they married for love. But they had other goals in mind as well. Some wanted to gain the freedom they lacked in their parents' homes. Yetta Brier stated baldly, "I got married for one reason, to get out of the house and become independent."[20] Becoming a bride also gave young women status in their families. Gussie Agines married early because she wanted to be "something special." Her brothers, she explained, had their business, but she had nothing besides her work in a factory.[21] Marriage was the only way for this young woman to be the center of attention. Rose G. married for the same reason. She liked the man who was courting her but was disappointed that he had no real education. But marriage made her feel important. "In my family I didn't count so much," she explained. "My money and my work—I was necessary. With him, nothing was necessary. Just to be loved. I never felt that I amounted to anything. And my husband made me feel that I do."

For young women without families in this country, marriage could be a way to escape loneliness. Louise C. missed her mother intensely and would have returned to Europe if her parents did not need her wages so badly. "I suffered very much by being separated from my parents," she observed. "And then when I met my husband, he had no one and I had no one." Rose S. also married to escape the loneliness she felt after her beloved mother died, hoping to replace her with her mother-in-law. "When I married into [my husband's] family," she explained, "what I wanted was to be able to sit near her or to hold her hand, to feel her warmth. You see, I lost my father, I didn't have my brothers here, and the only one who remained was mother, and then mother died. I felt close to this woman because she was my mother's friend." But Rose was disappointed both with her husband and her mother-in-law. "There was no warmth in his family," she observed. "She had had a hard life, and there was no warmth."

Sometimes, marriage was a way for young women to fulfill ambitions they had not managed to achieve on their own. If they had come to this country too late to become "real Americans" or get an education, marriage was another way to accomplish these goals. Mildred L., who sought to distance herself from an immigrant background, married her American-born husband after knowing him only a week. Fannie Shapiro had been unable to go to school herself, but when she met an educated, American-ized man, to her "that was the most important," and she thought that she "was getting a bargain."[22] Frieda W. also was flattered that her suitor was American. She recalled a friend's telling her, "See—a greenhorn, what *mazel* [luck]." Frieda continued, "I couldn't speak the language, I just came from across, and an American boy, such a beautiful boy, he's falling for me." Helen Weinstein married her husband because he was educated. "I thought," she recalled, "even if I'm not in love with him, this was it. I wanted a cultured person, distinguished—I don't want to marry someone who was not in my class."[23] Young women who grew up in this country and went to high school were able to take for granted, as these women could not, their education and status as Americans.

Some radical women chose mates they lived with out of wedlock. Sonia O. recalled, "I moved in with my friend without a marriage license, without even thinking of sex. We were roommates. But he's a man and I'm a woman. So little by little we got acquainted more and more, and we finally decided to live together for good. Without any contract." Parents, naturally, were not enthusiastic about such arrangements. When Sonia and her friend visited Russia in 1928, her father asked about her marriage. "Don't worry," she told him. "I didn't tell him a lie," she observed, "but I didn't tell him the truth. I didn't go to a rabbi. A rabbi has the function to tell me whom I am to sleep with?" she concluded with indignation. "What do you call that?" Gussie M., who met her future husband at their Socialist Party branch, recalled, "He wasn't even a husband when I started living with him. We were free people. I enjoyed my freedom. And my family approved of him. He was compatible with me, let's put it that way. And it was all right in my crowd. In somebody else's crowd, maybe it wasn't kosher." Usually, pregnancy resulted in a traditional marriage. The idea of "free love" seldom extended to having children born out of wedlock. "When I became pregnant," Gussie explained, "my uncle insisted on a regular wedding, and I did it for the child's sake. She or he would go to school, and what kind of name he'll have?"

Occasionally, young women had ambivalent feelings about marriage, or at least wanted to wait until they were older before settling down. Tanya N. was never sure that she wanted to marry because she did not want to have to raise children in poverty. Through the thin partition between their rooms, she remembered hearing the sounds of her mother's resisting her father's sexual entreaties, and she could never forget her mother's twelve abortions. Yet Tanya succumbed, and at twenty-seven married a man several years younger than herself. "You know why I married?" she asked. "I was still against marrying a man younger. But I married because I realized that a year from now I'll be an old maid! And I said yes, and no one was more surprised than I." Anna Kahan had decided not to get married until she was at least twenty-five, because she hoped to study and also to bring her family to this country. When she said no to proposals, her working-class suitors thought she was just waiting for a rich man to come along. They could not understand, Anna observed, that "I was a new modern woman. In those 1920s, I was for women's equal rights. And when a young man wanted to take me across the street and took my elbow, I said, 'Thank you, I can cross the street myself.' That was the spirit. I should have organized Women's Lib." Anna fell in love with a young engineer who felt he had too little to offer to propose marriage. "I wanted to keep my first love," she reminisced. "I still cry for it." Facing reality, Anna eventually married her employer.

Despite considerable freedom and the ability to earn their own living, marriage was still the ultimate goal of virtually all young Jewish women.[24] It was the only way they could rise out of the working class. Although most young women worked outside the home, their jobs usually paid insufficient wages to support them decently, and they hoped to marry a man who would be "a good provider." When they met such a man, young women were primed to "fall in love." Frieda M. recalled going to a wedding and meeting her future husband, who was the caterer.

> He asked me to dance with him. And he asked me to stay until he closed up the place. And when I heard that it was his place—I was ready. Because all our lives, my sister and I always figured to take care of our parents. I figured I'd make my father and mother rich. I always wanted someone with sufficient means. And I wanted to get married, but I couldn't just marry anyone. I was twenty-seven years old. In those days, it was very old. My mother was dying. None of her kids were married.

Like Frieda, many young women married to escape the factory and improve their status. When Rose Cohen, after her first week in America, saw how many hours her father worked, she asked him, "Father, does everybody in America live like this? Go to work early, come home late, eat and go to sleep? And the next day again, work, eat, and sleep? Will I have to do that too? Always?" Her father thought a while, then replied, smiling, "No, you will get married."[25] The labor activist Clara Lemlich described marriage as a young woman's only hope of getting free of the factory. "In the beginning," she wrote, "they are full of hope and courage. Almost all of them think that some day they will be able to get out of the factory and work up, but continuing work under long hours and miserable conditions they lose their hopes. Their only way to leave the factory is marriage."[26] Shopgirls would go without food and save their earnings to spend a week at a boarding house in the country where they might meet a prosperous young man to marry and relieve themselves of the anxiety over earning a living.[27] Marie F. described her sisters' marriages as making the best of limited options. "If they had come here at an earlier age, they could have accomplished much more," she observed. "As it was, they had to work, under terrible conditions, getting very little money. And when they met a young man who fell in love with them, they were very glad to get out of having to work as they did. They made a home, had children immediately, and were content with that."

Sometimes, there was no choice for a young woman but to marry, whether she wanted to or not. At the age of fifteen, Dora G. was forced to wed a widower who was seventeen years older than she and had three children. "I had to get married," she explained,

I couldn't live by the butcher, and I couldn't stay with my aunt. Because my uncle was a very religious man. And with the real religious, men can't sleep in the same room where a girl is sleeping. So they say, either he has to move, or I have to move.

So Mr. G. was there by my aunt and uncle all the time. And my aunt says, "He'll take care of you, he'll be very good to you. Do me a favor, don't make yourself any more hard work. You've had enough. You're never gonna go back home because you'll never have enough money saved to go there and you're a girl, and you're in this country, and you should have a man that'll take care of you." So I listened to my aunt, my father's sister.

I was so desperate. I didn't want to get married yet. And I didn't want to go to work any more by the butcher. So I didn't want to work and I didn't want to live no more and I had enough of life. In the end I stopped eating, and I kept on crying. I got run down and weighed about ninety pounds.

With no other option, however, Dora married her elderly suitor.

The success of a marriage did not seem to depend on whether a man and woman were "in love" when they married, or, with some exceptions, on whether a husband was "a good provider." Other factors were more important. Women active in the labor movement sought men with similar political views. As Gussie M. observed, it was important that she and her husband both belonged to the Socialist Party—"it was already deep in our life—the radical view. This was our thing." Kindness and intelligence, though, were the qualities most often cited as desirable in a husband. Ethel B. believed that, like her parents, she and her husband were "ideally mated," that they complemented and had great regard for each other. "He was kind and sweet and loving and gentle," Ethel observed. Beatrice Pollock also called her husband "a very gentle man" who lived up to her expectations. He was also highly educated—"a husband to be proud of."[28] Rose G. remembered her spouse as a "very, very smart man who spoke beautifully." Hilda S. described her husband as "goodness itself. Not a bad streak. Everybody tipped the hat for Meyer—for his knowledge, for his *menschlikeyt*—you can't translate this to English—something like a sense of humanity. Because he never had a bad word for anybody."

In emphasizing intimacy, sharing, and communication, these women, regardless of their actual economic status, resembled middle-class rather than typical working-class women, who wanted above all a husband who worked steadily and did not drink or beat them.[29] Louise C., who remained a factory worker almost all her life, had a clear idea of the kind of person she wanted to marry. "I wanted an honest, decent, intelligent man who would appreciate me as a woman," she stated. "And that's what my husband was." Fannie N., who also continued to work in a factory after marriage, sought an understanding husband who was smart and good-natured and had a sense of humor.

Perhaps one reason these working-class women seemed to have middle-class standards for marriage stemmed from child-rearing practices in Jewish homes. Among most non-Jewish working-class families, children were socialized to observe rigid gender distinctions. Boys learned that they were expected to be strong, active, assertive, and unemotional. The sons of middle-class families, on the other hand, learned that it was permissable to cry and show emotion; to be thoughtful, at times even passive; to be eager to learn; and to express feelings openly.[30] Many Jewish boys, regardless of their parents' origins, tended to be raised with such middle-class attitudes, for the Eastern European ideal of the Yeshiva student emphasized these characteristics, whereas working-class cultures generally associated them only with women. Similarly, Jewish girls were conditioned to value such traits. Although they were raised to pursue different objectives than their brothers, girls may have internalized a single standard for emotional life rather than the double standard common to most working-class women.

Some women married men they did not love, but all who did this insisted that they "fell in love" with their husbands after marriage because of their fine characteristics. Rose G., who would have preferred a husband with more education, recalled telling herself, "I married a man I wasn't even in love with, and now I know what love is! Because after I married him, I was crazy about him. He was so wonderful, so gentle and fine." Frieda M., who married a man "with sufficient means," began to love him only after they were married. "He was really exceptional," she explained, "the kindest human being you ever met in your life." Anna Kahan said of her husband, who had been her employer, "I loved him, but I didn't fall in love. It took time. He was kind and he was good." Like her father, "he was too good to other people—sometimes it wasn't good for me in the depression time. He used to bring me people from out in the street. And I used to feed them and put them to sleep on a cot."

Relations between husbands and wives seemed most harmonious when husbands valued their wives' views and family matters were decided jointly. As Rose Katz observed, "Whatever I have, we both worked for, both of us, and my husband always valued my opinion. He never done anything without consulting me."[31] Rose L. and her husband also got along well. "All the years we were married," she explained, "I can honestly say that we never had an argument over money. If there was money, there was for the both of us. If there wasn't, there wasn't for anyone." Mutual respect was another component of successful relationships. "My husband was very helpful," observed Ethel B. "We did everything together. I helped him, he helped me, so life really was not difficult." Mollie Linker recalled the importance of this quality in her own and in her parents' marriage. "I guess love comes with caring and doing things for each other," she observed.[32] Frances F. remembered her husband as "the most beautiful person in the world. He was a little bit like my father, insofar as he was also selfless." Yet Frances had not wanted to marry him because she felt that she needed a strong husband to influence her. Other women also recalled wanting a strong will in a husband, but they defined it in a curious way. Rita S. explained how this operated in her own and her sisters' families:

> We all had husbands that were the dominant ones in the family. We evidently looked for men who were the strong ones, who we thought were the strong ones. Basically, they weren't that strong. Basically, in the long run, it was we, the sisters, who took care of things in the family. But in smaller things in life, we let the husband rule. We didn't like fighting, so we'd give in to certain things, small things that were not that important. But there were other things we really wouldn't give in to.
>
> [One sister] married a man who had his weakness which she knew, and she could have been the one that ruled, but she didn't. She let him. She is the one that let him be the strong one in the family, because I think she knew that she is stronger than he is. But I think it was right for the man to *be* the man in the family—to build up his ego.

The parents of many of these women had similar relationships, where the wife insisted that her husband was the head of the family, but got her own way when she wanted to. As in their parents' homes, husbands of this younger generation of immigrant women were also accepted as "ceremonial leaders" of the household, because women believed their egos required it. Even when wives resolved problems in the home, the decision-making process often was disguised so that it appeared that husbands were the decisive figures. For example, when one of the daughters of Hilda S. asked to do something, Hilda would talk it over with her husband, and then tell the child to ask her father, who would always agree with his wife. Thus, like the mother of Fannie C. (see Chapter 7), Hilda made the decision but assured that her husband received the credit. And, also like their mothers, these women made sure that the children thought of their fathers as the heads of the family. "I looked up to him," observed Rose G., "and our children had to respect him above all. I remember if my husband would lie down, my children knew it was the worst sin to wake daddy up." This freely granted authority differed from relationships in typical working-class families, where regardless of a wife's wishes, her husband's word was law.[33]

It is not unusual for children to replicate aspects of their parents' relationship in their own marriage. A psychologist addressing this issue suggested that we are all deeply influenced by patterns unconsciously absorbed early in life that "live on in our heads." Because we are most familiar with the world created in our own families, we thus operate within a system internalized from childhood. What we have experienced seems the appropriate way to behave, and it takes a conscious act of will to act in any other way. Whether they wish it or not, the generations are interconnected in ways that are insufficiently appreciated.[34] Rose, Hilda, Fannie, and many other women indicated that the way they related to their husbands indeed emulated what they had learned as children in their parents' homes. These women's circumstances certainly differed from those of their mothers, but attitudes toward a spouse showed remarkable similarities.

A young Jewish woman learned from her mother to place her husband's needs before her own and to make his life easier through proper performance of housewifely skills. Tanya N., who described her mother as very modern and broadminded, remembered her traditional advice on marriage: "Tanya," she told her daughter, "you'll never know what happens in life. If you should be at such a point that you only have one sheet, give that one clean sheet to your husband. Your husband comes first." When parents had a clear division of labor, with husbands working to support the family while wives took care of home and children, women took particular pride in mastering their work and in keeping the domestic sphere for themselves. Fannie C. remembered that in her parents' house, neither her father nor her brother "took a glass from here and put it on the next table. And you know something," she continued, "I inherited that. As long as my husband was alive, I don't think he took himself more than a glass of water. I just don't like a man in the kitchen. I think if you would have asked my husband how to put a diaper on a child," she stated with pride, "he would have looked at you as if you were insane. I mean, whoever heard of it?" Her sense of competence seemed to compensate for the heavier work load at home.

Most of these women, like their mothers, also handled the family's finances. "Any money that my husband had," recalled Rose L., "he gave it to me. He says, 'You can keep it better than I do.' We always managed, because, thank God, I was always a good manager." This was particularly important during the depression, when many husbands worked intermittently and wives had to make do on meager resources and sometimes find some way to make money themselves. Here, too, their mothers' examples stood them in good stead.

Although women were socialized to believe that men do not belong in the kitchen, and that they shouldn't do "women's work," some working women felt differently. Gussie M. agreed that it wasn't customary for a husband to work around the house. When her husband was unemployed, though, he helped with the dishes after she came home from work and made dinner. "I thanked and complimented him," she recalled. However, she always remembered that his response was, "This I can only do when I don't work. But when I work I couldn't do it." Gussie observed with chagrin, "It impressed me so much that now he could help me, but if he works he couldn't do it. I could work and do everything else. So, this was ordinary. Not only in my house. All over." Women's control over the home was a two-edged sword. If they had to work to supplement or replace a husband's income, it usually meant a double responsibility. Some, like Gussie, resented it, and a few, like Rose Chernin, rebelled. Even though Rose lived with a man without marrying him, their relationship followed the same pattern as married couples. Radical beliefs, it seemed, stopped at the threshold. Rose's life seemed to her an unending cycle of working during the day in a store and finding dishes in the sink when she came home. One night, she felt she couldn't go on. "I was in the kitchen," she recalled. "I picked up a plate. 'No more, it's all over,' I shouted. I smashed the plate against the sink. Right away, I snatched up another. 'There's got to be more to life,' I shouted. I grabbed a cup. But that was enough. Two plates and a cup and I had my resolution. 'A woman,' I said, 'is not the same thing as a slave.'"[35]

Even if women could concentrate on caring for their families, rather than take on the double burden of housework and wage work, some were not satisfied, particularly if they always skirted the edge of poverty. Ruth R., who had emigrated to Palestine and then came with her husband to the United States, observed that there was a saying in Palestine when lively, active girls got married: "They are dead. Once you get married," she went on, "you settle down, and what is there? There is just the man goes to work, the woman takes care of the house, you have the baby. You go out in the street, you go to the park. You meet some women and they are talking like 'the baby today didn't want to eat this,' and 'yesterday the baby ate better.' It just isn't interesting." Unlike Ruth, Goldie Stone had a husband who supported her in style. Yet she was also frustrated by a life bounded by the walls of their home. "I was not satisfied," she related. "Something in me cried out for growth to flourish and succeed."[36] Goldie found herself in active volunteer work for Jewish institutions.

If their husbands could support them so they did not have to take a job, most women, like their mothers, found satisfaction in caring for home and family. The husband of Riva P. was proud of the fact that his wife never had to go out to work and was able to stay home and look after their daughter. Although Riva approved of careers for women and was pleased that they could now "be their own persons," she felt "That's not the most important thing. The most important thing in life, I think, is finding a true mate." Frieda M., who, like Riva, was fortunate in marriage, gave up her dream of becoming a writer once her first child was born. "It was either Ina or writing," she observed. "I decided I preferred Ina, because I realized that that was always what I wanted. I wanted a husband, a family. The only reason I wanted fame was to get a husband! That was the end of my writing."

If daughters had rejected their parents' lives, they took pains to ensure that their own marriages were different as well. "This man was to me everything my father had never been to my mother," observed Rose Chernin of her husband. "Always, we respected each other. I was proud of his education. . . . And he admired me for the way I could speak to people and organize. In our home there was, between the husband and wife, something never known in our family before."[37] Generally, affection between husbands and wives was more freely demonstrated than it was among their parents' generation. Rose G. recalled, "If I went out shopping, I'd leave a note, 'Lou, darling, I'm going to the butcher's. I love you.' One time I forgot to write, 'I love you,' and he said when I came back, 'Where's the "I love you"?' He was very affectionate." Riva P., who married when she was almost forty, observed that when she and her husband went out, "it was always like a first date. He was a good husband, a good father, a marvelous lover."

Some marriages, of course, did not work out. Elsie F. fell in love with a young man, but they parted and married other people. Her husband, a musician with a poor sense of responsibility, deserted Elsie and their son after eight years of marriage; her first boyfriend's wife had a mental break-down and spent her remaining years in and out of sanatoriums. Elsie and her early love met again accidentally in 1940 and discovered that their old feelings were still alive. But until his wife died and they could finally marry fifteen years later, they had only stolen minutes together. "Sometimes we just took a subway ride," Elsie recalled. "He used to visit his brother's summer cottage some weekends. And I couldn't wait for him to come home Sunday evening. I showered and dressed and went to meet the train at ten, eleven o'clock—whenever it pulled in. And just to be together for half an hour. During those fifteen years it was just spare moments that we were able to be together."

Just as women sometimes married men to rise out of the working class, a man might seek a wife to support him through college or in relative idleness.[38] The "artist" husband of Minna S. obviously thought he had a dependable meal ticket. She remained married to him for three years during whch she continued to work to support them. Minna doubted his feelings for her and blamed herself for failing to inspire him. Her husband was undependable financially and sexually, and despite her sister's opposition to a divorce, Minna left him. "As timid as I was," she observed, "I was also very independent, and when I had an idea in my head, there was nothing that could change it."

Frieda W., a poor, illiterate, recent immigrant who had the "good luck" to attract an American man, had the bad luck to marry him. Her husband lost interest in her once she became pregnant and was less "fun" to be with. When she was too nauseous to travel on the bus with him to Coney Island, she recalled, "He just went himself and he found other girls." The birth was a difficult one, and after that, she recalled telling him with passion, "I would rather die than have another child. No, no more!"

And the doctor called me in and he said to me, "Mrs. W., if you go and have another child, it's a sure death. You cannot have any more children." I told him and started to cry, "Doctor, if that would be up to me, I will never want to see a man in my life and I would never want to have any more children. What should I do? I've got a young man and he's a brute, he's not a gentleman. I'm afraid he'll kill me. What should I do?"

My husband came and the doctor talked to him. He didn't say nothing to the doctor. And the nurse called a taxi. I put up the baby in a blanket, and she helped me to go in the taxi, and she give me the baby on my legs. And my husband was sitting there on the left side, I remember it even today. As soon as the taxi start to go, you wouldn't believe it, what he said to me, you wouldn't believe. He says, "What do you think, I should stay with a *kranker*?" *Kranker* means sick, a misfit. Like a dead horse, a dead dog, a dead anything. "You think I gonna stay with you?" What should I tell him? I didn't say nothing.

Frieda's husband packed his bags and left soon after. "I wish I would never be married," Frieda stated. The men she met thereafter assumed that a woman deserted by her husband was either fair game for sexual overtures or else a poor specimen of womanhood. She remembered a foreman in a factory where she worked who told her, "It's no wonder your husband left you. From a good woman, a husband don't go away." "I got mad on him," Frieda recalled angrily. "He burned me up my heart." Frieda wanted nothing to do with men sexually after her husband left. She would have liked to have a man provide for her and her son, as long as he left her alone. "I wanted to get married with an old man who don't need no wife," she observed, "but it don't happen. Even old men they want a wife. They're worse than the young ones." Dora G., who was forced to marry a widower when she was fifteen and after his death married, in turn, two other men who failed to support her, felt much the same way about sex. "I'm surprised today when people say they're mad in love and they can't live without it," she asserted. "I never loved any of my husbands. I loved my children. That's all. Sex didn't mean to me nothing. It meant to me a very filthy life. I seen the pants next to the bed, already the child was in my belly."

These two women, from what would now be called deprived backgrounds, knew nothing about birth control. "I didn't know the tricks," Frieda commented. "I wasn't too smart." Although Frieda obviously disliked sex, fear of pregnancy compounded her attitude. Dora had to manage to support her three children, illiterate though she was, through a succession of marriages with men who became too sick to work. Abortion was the only method of birth control she knew. "I was smart," she observed. "Why do you think I had so many miscarriages? The miscarriages I didn't have to feed, I only had to feed the living children." Dora knew the awful risks involved. Only a year before one of her own "miscarriages," her sister had died having an abortion. Yet desperation drove Dora to end yet another unwanted pregnancy. She left her house, preparing food for several days in case she did not survive. As she tells it, only concern for the fate of her children pulled her through. She kept bleeding after the abortion and thought she was going to die.

I says, "*Kindelekh* [children], do me a favor, let me go. I see that I struggle too hard. My life is very sad. I was born by a very poor father and mother. I mean good for everybody, but what good is my life if I have to struggle that way?" So my niece bust out crying, she says, "I brought you here and I want you should live." I says, "Feige, [her niece] *ikh kin nikht lebn meyr* [I can't live any more]. Leave me go, just

leave me go." But then I thinks, "What will happen to my children?"
Times was very hard. I had a very hard life.

For many such poor women, ignorant of birth control, abortion was the
only way they knew to prevent having more mouths than they could feed.
The average Jewish immigrant family in the first decade of the century
included five children, and Emma Goldman, who worked for a time as a
midwife, wrote of the "fierce struggle of the women of the poor against
frequent pregnancies."[39] In the 1920s, fully half the clients of one birth
control clinic, all poor Jewish women on welfare, had already had abortions.[40] The local midwife or doctor on the Lower East Side often performed them out of compassion. Kate Simon remembers her mother's
being particularly fond of her youngest daughter, who had been born only
because the doctor refused to end another unwanted pregnancy. Her
mother had already undergone thirteen abortions, and she assured Kate
that this was by no means the neighborhood record.[41] Florence B. remembered being closest with her mother's last, unwanted child. Her mother had
complained loudly and frequently to neighbors that at forty-five, she did
not want another mouth to feed. Her mother knew about contraception,
because Florence had overheard her advising one of her son's girlfriends to
"take precautions." But her father refused to use it because he believed
orthodox law forbade it.

Women whose mothers had made them aware of abortion were usually
eager to discover other ways to prevent pregnancies. As we saw above,
Tanya N. had been scared away from marriage by memories of her mother's
abortions. "The reason that I looked down on marriage," she asserted, "was
that my mother had so many abortions."

> It was so cruel, so difficult. And my father was very inconsiderate
> because he refused to wear condoms. We used to wear chemises and
> things made of silk and since he wouldn't wear the rubber condoms,
> she used to make them out of silk. She was constantly sewing con-
> doms made out of my old chemises!
>
> My mother told me she had twelve abortions! And I saw one that
> she herself aborted. And that's how I learned really about how babies
> are born—or not born. She had done something to herself, and the
> baby fell out. My mother picked it up, put it into a glass of vinegar,
> and she said to me, "Here is the way babies look before they are born,
> when they are first conceived."
>
> My mother couldn't have been pregnant very long, it was a tiny

little thing. And yet there were little points where the fingers were and it was a boy, a little teeny boy.

"That was how I learned," she concluded. Tanya's mother had begged her husband to leave her alone, and when she became diabetic and developed a vaginal itch, this was a good excuse for prohibiting relations. But to take care of his sexual needs, she urged her husband to take as his mistress a widow from their hometown. As Tanya's father told her years later, he took the woman out but decided to remain faithful to his wife.

Tanya was careful to remain childless for the five years of her marriage. "I definitely did not want a child," she asserted, but she was afraid that her husband would hold it against her if she continued to refuse to have children. So she promised to start a family once they had saved a thousand dollars, hoping that he would change his mind before they reached this goal. "After all," she observed, "the Russians had a saying, 'Any peasant without boots can have children.' What's the big deal?!" Her husband's premature death settled the issue permanently.

Several women found out about contraception long after they were married, usually from a friend or neighbor. Many of them credited Margaret Sanger's birth control clinics with changing their lives.[42] Louise C. had one son in 1927, and another was born eighteen months later. "That was before I knew there was a Margaret Sanger," she observed. Soon after, she was pregnant again. Louise had a close friend who lived next door. "We could talk about everything," she recalled. "Her husband told my husband to 'use the fire escape' sometimes—that's the term he used for withdrawing." Ruth R. remembered how her mother suffered bearing many children, and she saw abortion and birth control as offering women freedom from constant pregnancy. Like many other working-class Jewish women, she learned from reading Sanger's birth-control pamphlet, *What Every Woman Should Know*, in Yiddish. Margaret Sanger, Ruth asserted, was the real pioneer. "It was the universal case that every woman suffered," she recalled. "My mother was not the only one," although "if a woman is a rich man's wife, she has no problems and is not interested in the others." Rose L. also pointed to Margaret Sanger as the savior of her marriage. She and her husband both had to work to support the two children they already had, and he "used to like to see us dressed *balabatish*—decent. He didn't like that the poverty should whistle off you. So he said, 'Look, we can't support three children. You can't make three pair of shoes from two.' All right, the food somehow you can manage. If you haven't got, you haven't got, that's all. So my husband didn't want another child—I couldn't go anyplace else. I wasn't a swinger. We didn't stop having sex. I used Margaret Sanger. I used her for twenty-three years. That was the best thing, the best thing to this day."

Like Rose, many women who might have afforded more children practiced birth control to be able to give more advantages to the ones they had.[43] Nina S. intended to have only one child in order to be able to give her such luxuries as education that she herself had been denied. Many of these women remembered the difficulties their own mothers had managing numerous pregnancies and trying to keep food on the table for constantly growing families. Like Tanya, who did not want to bring up children in poverty, they saw family limitation as an important method of assuring that their children could get the material comforts and education that they had been unable to achieve. And although they were dedicated to their children, this generation of women did not want the continual subordination to the needs of others that resulted from a large family.[44]

Knowledge of birth control methods traveled along the female grapevine. Rose learned of the possibility of preventing births from her mother, who in turn learned of it from women in their neighborhood.

> My mother had a ring. I think they said it was gold, and a man who said he was a doctor put it in her. Because she found out from the grocery woman across the street that it protects them from having babies. It did—it protected her. But it wasn't gold, and that woman died as a result, a young woman. So naturally my mother immediately had it removed. But she had a rust discharge for months. She was lucky to be alive! She was a very hardy woman—I think she had at least two abortions. I remember just vaguely, because I was too young, but she told me about it.

The poor women Rose knew had to depend upon themselves to prevent conception because their husbands refused to consider taking precautions. "The women had to protect themselves," Rose recalled, "the man, nothing." When Rose was about to get married, an Italian woman who lived in her building tried to give her some friendly advice. She remembered her saying, "Rosie, when you got married, don't be like me—stupid!" When Rose asked why, she told her, "My husband. When he wants, you gotta get up and get the douche ready and make hot water. And then he finish right away, and I say, 'Why don't you wear protection?' He says, 'I can't get sick— you're no whore!'" "So," Rose concluded, "that was life." Fortunately, most of these Jewish women's husbands proved as sensible as Rose's.

For women who were now free to dissociate sex from pregnancy, it could become an important part of a relationship rather than a cause for concern. Riva P. described her husband as "a wonderful lover," and Elsie F.'s long-lasting liaison with her married friend was very physical in nature. Tanya N. had a brief affair after the death of her husband with a man she had loved years before. His wife was away for several years in a tuberculosis sanatorium, and when she returned, the liaison ended. When they were both seventy-nine and his wife died, they finally began to live together. Minna S. regretted passing up a sexual relationship after her marriage ended. "Afterwards," she observed, "I realized what I had missed and I feel like how wrong I was. I had all these chances and I always had a one-track mind: I learned how to be a wife and not a mistress! It was terrible!"

This did not mean that these women would be more open about sex with their daughters than their mothers had been with them. The daughter of Mildred L., born in 1935, remembered her mother's few words about the subject. "Mother never mentioned anything remotely connected with sex," she observed.

> Never a word was spoken. The few things I found out, I found out in school. It was a terrible shock to me when I had my first menstrual period because I thought I was dying. By the time I got married the word sex had still never been mentioned. I thought it was funny at that time. And so the night before my wedding, I thought I'd have some fun with her. And I said to her, "Mother, don't you have anything to tell me? I mean, this is our last evening together, and tomorrow night, I'm going to be a married lady." So she says, "About what?" And I could see she was getting nervous. I said, "About sex, mama—sex!" So she said, "Oh sex. Oh, darling, what can I tell you. It's something to do!!" And that's been her whole pronouncement on that topic to this day!

The marriages of many of these women who came to America as children or young women bore striking similarities to those of their parents. True, they lived in a different environment, and this affected their expectations and options. They had greater freedom than parents to select their own mates, and the dating patterns they followed had little resemblance to what they would have encountered in Eastern Europe a generation earlier. But within the marriage itself, the relationship between husband and wife often reflected that of parents, and if it did not, it took an act of will to create a different home atmosphere. The characteristics prized—or viewed as lacking—in a father were consciously sought in a husband, and many patterns of decision making followed the ones young women had learned in their parents' homes.

These young women differed from their mothers, however, in their ability to limit their families without having to banish husbands from their beds. Sexual relations were thus freed from the constant fear of having another mouth to feed. Although some still resorted to abortion to keep from having children, by the mid-thirties, even most poor Jewish women were aware of birth control and used it to keep their families within manageable size. They knew that only in this way could they avoid the terrible decisions their parents had been forced to make about taking children out of school to send them to work. This generation of women determined that *their* daughters, as well as their sons, would get the education and other advantages that they had been denied by poverty.

12

. . . .

A Question of Bread

When I was in business about seven or eight years, my husband says, "Give it up." I said, "All right, but don't ever have me come to you for money." Because as little as I did, I was still independent. When I went into the egg business, it was a question of bread.

—Rose L.

. . . .

When I had my youngest child in 1932, I had to send my two children away to a home because I had no one here to help me. These are things that you live through. And this was the beginning of the depression. Where you had no funds, and you had no one, you had to learn to live by your wits.

—Louise C.

. . . .

18. A married woman working during the depression.

Lewis Hine, *Women at Work* (Dover Publications, 1981)

I really enjoyed working. Because regardless of what job I chose, I liked them, they liked me. . . . I did not think of it as a career. But it turned out to be a career, because I worked all my married life. . . . Why did I do it? Because I felt that my husband needed me there.

—*Fannie C.*

While most Jewish women hoped to retire from paid work after marriage, the expectations of many were frustrated by the onset of the depression. If a husband lost his job, his wife had to find a way to pay the rent and feed the family. With one out of four men unemployed at the height of the depression, such crises occurred frequently. Generally, women took a job only when necessity demanded and left when and if their husbands found steady work. Life was insecure, and women in such families drifted in and out of paid work as family needs determined.[1] As Gussie M. put it, "My husband made a living, sort of, unless he lost his job and I had to help out. Money didn't mean much to me," she observed. "I wasn't used to it, and as long as I paid my rent, bought the little groceries I needed, I was satisfied. So as soon as he found a job, I remained home to watch after my family." But this security seldom lasted long. "When the landlord had to come and I didn't have the rent," Gussie explained, "I had to go look for work again." For thousands of women like Gussie, "helping out" became a way of life.

Like Gussie, Louise C. spent her whole married life trying to earn enough money to keep her family together. "When you had no funds, and you had no one," she observed, "you had to learn to live by your wits." Louise's husband eked out a meager living as a waiter, and when their third child was born in 1932, she was forced to leave her older children temporarily in a Jewish federation home. She swore never to see her family broken up again. "It was the hardest part of my life," she declared, "to maintain the family, to keep them together."

After she returned from the hospital, Louise decided to take in sewing, which she had learned in Europe. Earlier, she had worked for a peddler, making pillowcases of leftover pieces of material. "I made my own curtains," she observed with pride. "I sewed them, I embroidered them, I put lace around them. And everybody in the community came to look at those curtains. They never saw such curtains." Homework had made a comeback during the depression, and Louise decided to do sewing at home. She answered an advertisement in the newspaper and went to a novelty showroom on Fifth Avenue and Thirtieth Street where she saw quilted clothes hangers, shoe tree covers, and such. After a brief trial, she was given material to take with her. "I went home," she recalled. "That night I didn't go to bed. I took care of my children. And I sat down and I made that night fifty hangers. I just couldn't believe it, the drive in me. It just goes to show, when you have something in you and know how to use what you have, that you can really get places." Louise worked for the firm for a few months. "They used to send me a gross of hangers with the material cut, with the trimming and thread to match. I used to put my kids to bed about seven, eight o'clock, and then I used to sit down and do my homework until midnight when my husband came home. They paid at that time six dollars a gross, which was a lot of money." But soon, the pay rate went down to $3.75, and "there was no money in it anymore."[2] She got a job cleaning a doctor's office, until the stress of trying to pay the rent and feed her family brought about a nervous breakdown.

Louise stopped work for a while, but her husband got sicker and his income became more sporadic. He now made a poor living as a messenger, and their son took an after-school job with United Parcel to help out. Louise decided to operate a laundry business, and she remembers this as the happiest period in her married life. The whole family was able to work together. "It was just unbelievable," she observed.

> We became a family. I opened up a hand laundry and I worked like a horse by myself and business was pretty good. And a store opened up around the corner, which was the main street—181st Street—and I took the store and moved in there. And everybody helped. We had an apartment—not far—and my husband was able to go home. He used to get up very early in the morning, open up the store. I went in later and I stayed at night. He used to come to the store and do the bookkeeping, he could pack the small bundles and give them out. So I did all the hard work. I used to take the wet clothes, and then the ironing. I used to have a woman come in to do it, and if they were no good, I sent them away and I'd do my own ironing. And I worked day in and day out. For eleven years I had the store. *And it was heaven on earth!*

Louise was one of many wives who had to work out of necessity and who hoped for little more than a steady job, no matter how hard, that assured them a modest income. If a husband brought in too little, staying home with the children was not economically feasible. Keeping the family from disintegrating was one of the few sources of satisfaction for such women. Rose L. was another who had to cope with a life of deprivation. "When I went into the egg business," she recalled simply, "it was a matter of bread." Her husband first took the route, but he told his wife that "he felt like a beggar" delivering eggs. With two children to feed, Rose was less proud. "It wasn't that easy," she observed. "And I still had young children. But I managed. My neighbor used to take care of the children." So Rose took the job and kept it for more than twelve years. After their children left home, her husband wanted her to stop work. "I can't help you," she recalled him saying, "and you can't do it yourself. You can't take a box of eggs with thirty dozen and carry it through the window. And put it into the car, and then to walk all the stairs, in bad weather." But Rose refused to stop because they needed the income. "Any money that my husband had, I had it," she recalled. "But he didn't have any."

Despite Rose's need to work, she obviously enjoyed the feeling of competence it gave her. Once, when her husband had asked her to give it up, she remembered replying, "All right, but don't ever have me come to you for money." "As little as I did," she observed, "I was still independent." Yet poverty dominated her life. Once, when Rose and her husband had the opportunity to buy a candy store, they went to her wealthier brothers to ask for a loan. "You think they loaned it to us?" she asked. "Maybe my whole life would have been different if they had loaned me that few dollars."

Rose S. also had to juggle the continual demands of work and family. "We were married a very short time," she recalled, "and then came the depression and my husband lost his job." After they had exhausted their savings, she worked in the millinery business. "I didn't have good jobs, or make a lot of money," she observed, "but I always had a job. If I didn't help out, we couldn't have managed at all." Rose had to wait ten years before having a child.[3] Her husband, an intermittently employed printer, brought in little money, so after their daughter was born, Rose managed to get work making hats at home.

> I used to get up in the morning and give Diana her breakfast and send her off to school. I lived about three or four blocks from school, so she used to come home for lunch, and that tied me up. I used to go in the morning and return one load of work and pick up the next load of work and come home with it. But I had to be home in time for lunch.
>
> And in the meantime, my husband was getting night jobs. So he'd come home at eight in the morning and he'd sleep late. And so I used to work in between. When I had work for a few days, I didn't have to go downtown. I used to work till Diana came home, and then I'd work another few hours and my husband would get up and I'd make him dinner. And this kept on for a number of years.

"My husband never wanted me to work," Rose concluded, "but it was always a necessity, so I had to."

Sometimes, though, a job taken through necessity turned into a satisfying career. "I worked before I was married, and after a while I worked after I was married," Jennie H. recalled, "because my husband didn't make a good living."

19. A working-class immigrant couple and their children during the depression.
Collection of Jack Olshen

He was a shipping clerk. And then in later years he learned in the fur line to be a nailer. He worked very hard, but all he was making was fifteen dollars a week. When I used to give birth to a child, they used to give him a dollar raise—big deal! When I worked, on what I was making, he could have eat and drink and clothing without working.

I worked not because I wanted to work but because it was an emergency when my husband got sick. What was I supposed to do— let the children starve? One time he went away to work, my husband, and he didn't leave a penny in the house. It was on a Friday. And downstairs lives a tailor. He calls up to me—a woman brought three dresses to fix. But one dress she wanted right away. I went upstairs and I fixed that one dress. And I took the money she gave me—at the time there were no refrigerators, and when the chicken woman was left with chickens after twelve o'clock, she used to sell them at half price. So I bought a chicken and something for dessert, and I bought *challah*. And I made a supper. When he came home, the table was set with the white tablecloth and the dishes and the children were there and it was *Shabbes*. So when he walked in, he got so red like beet. He says to me, "Jennie, where did you get money?" I said, "I stole it." He was so excited because he knew that when he left, there was no money.

Like Louise and Rose, Jennie had to manage to earn money while caring for her children at the same time. And when her husband was no longer able to work, her job had to come before all else. "I didn't work *Shabbes* at that time," Jennie recalled. "But when he got sick and couldn't work at all, I had to take a job, and a job as an alteration hand in stores you could only get by working on *Shabbes*. I cried one *Shabbes*, and I cried another *Shabbes*. And then like the story, in a few days you're used to the troubles." Jennie's husband died when her youngest daughter was eight years old, so she had to redouble her efforts. While her daughter was young, Jennie had a contract with a firm in Williamsburg to make bridal dresses in her home. Eventually, she had three young women working for her. "I used to work night and day," she recalled. "She used to ask me, my Tabbeleh [her daughter]. She says 'Mama, how do you do it? You work a whole night and then you work in the daytime.' Somehow, I was able to do it. When Tabby was big enough to be able to function herself, I used to take jobs in the factories. People used to envy me, when I used to come in the evening after a day's work, I was fresh as in the morning."

Jennie, Louise, and Rose seemed to derive a great deal of satisfaction and independence from their ability to earn their own living. But while Rose and Louise chose to remain widows after their husbands died, Jennie would have liked to remarry. After her younger daughter left home, she recalled, "it got very quiet and the house became empty. And I was lonely and I was looking for someone, very, very much. But I never found somebody that appealed to me like my husband." Despite her loneliness, because of her financial independence, she could afford to be choosy. "Maybe," she surmised, "if I were hungry for a dollar and I wouldn't be able to have what for to eat, maybe I would have accepted someone. But I didn't need that, because I was earning a living."

Unlike Jennie, Dora G. married three times hoping to find a husband who would support her and her growing family, only to be disappointed each time. She scaled down her expectations and went on working. Her last husband, a kindly man, got sick as the others did and couldn't make a living. "All right," she recalled, "I looked away from that too. So I had to keep doing things for myself anyhow." Dora had to earn enough to provide for her three children while laboring under a dual handicap. She had never learned a marketable skill, and because she was from a poor village and had had to work since she was ten years old, she had never learned to read. Yet she managed. "When I moved away from New York," she recalled,

> I took in my son-in-law's father. And I took in a lot of my *landsleit* [townspeople] for boarders. And because of my husband's papers, I got to be a citizen right away. And I used to go and help out a lot of people. You know, they needed to go to a doctor and he couldn't talk Slavish or Polish, or Hungarian or Russian, or Jewish. I used to go to get the citizenship papers with them. I used to go when they wanted to buy something—they couldn't talk. I tried to work myself through. I talked seven, eight, nine—if I want to tell you, I spoke ten languages. Any language besides Italian. Russich I know, Polish I know, German I know, Slavish I know, Hungarian I know—Hungarian I learned here in New Brunswick. And Yiddish is my mother's speech, and English is our country's speech.

Dora's knowledge of languages and her ability to assist new immigrants in working their way through the maze of officialdom helped her support her family.

These working-class women all had to manage to care for children while somehow maintaining the egos of husbands who had lost their roles as primary breadwinners. Husbands generally did not want their wives working for others. Ruth Katz remembered, "During the Depression when we lost everything, when my husband couldn't get a job, I went out and I got a job selling dresses. I came back and I told him that I'm going to work tomorrow and he says, 'Not as long as I live.' He wouldn't let me go," she concluded proudly.[4] In working-class families, a wife's employment was a symbol of defeat.[5] Success was achieved when a husband could support his family and a wife was able to remain at home with the children.

Some women, like Fannie G. or Frieda W., were even less fortunate than women married to "poor providers," for both were deserted by husbands who left them with young children to support. Fannie managed to make a living by operating an illegal still and selling "bootleg" liquor in her neighborhood. At least she could live with her parents. Frieda had no parents to turn to when her husband left shortly after the birth of their baby. With no money for rent, she was evicted from her apartment. Her brother and sister-in-law took her in and agreed to care for the child if Frieda went to work. Without skills, in the midst of the depression, the only job available was doing housework. Although Frieda wanted to take her child with her, she had to become a live-in maid and leave the boy with relatives. When he was eight, and she managed to get her own apartment, her son told her something that pointed up her own feelings of helplessness: "Mama, when I was with *Tante* [aunt] Dora, I was afraid to tell you, because she told me, if I tell you, she'll kill me."

> I said, "What happened? Tell me." She had two children, a boy, Morris, and a little girl, Sandra. On Sunday, for Morris she used to give a steak, and for Sandra a lamb chop, but for my boy, she used to make him a plate of soup with just a little bone in it. Then, he says, he starts to cry, "Aunt Dora, I want also a steak like you're giving Morris, a lamb chop like you're giving Sandra." She gives him a slap in his face! "Here you got a steak!" He was crying, but then she gives him another slap. "Here you got a lamb chop! And don't tell your mother, because if you'll tell your mother, I'll kill you!" That was my brother's wife. What could I do? I couldn't take him before I got a job and I made a little money.

For a while, Frieda had a neighbor watch her son after he came home from school, but one day he ran away and was hit by a truck. After he recovered, his mother sent him to a Jewish home for orphans in Pleasantville, where she visited on her day off. After three months, the child cried and begged her to take him home because he claimed that an older boy had attacked him sexually. Frieda took him back and struggled to care for him and earn a living. Several years later, Frieda found her husband and brought him to court to force him to help support the boy. But he never paid and her problems continued. The boy wound up in a reformatory. "What could I do?" she repeated, with all the powerlessness of poverty.

Most women at this time believed the man in the family should be the sole breadwinner, but this view represented an ideal rather than reality. Although only one wife in ten worked at any given time during the depression, the proportion of married women in the female work force increased gradually from 28.8 percent in 1930 to 35 percent in 1940.[6] Yet even at the lowest economic levels, only one married woman in four worked for wages.[7] Because family values opposed working wives, women tended to try to manage without taking jobs, and if they had no alternative but the factory, they left the work force as soon as finances permitted.[8] Husbands sometimes preferred to forget that their wives had to assume the role of breadwinner: one man in a WPA survey described his wife as leaving factory work when they married, when in fact she had continued to work intermittently throughout their marriage.[9] For most white Americans, a working wife placed a stigma upon husband and family.[10] This attitude assured that when married women did take jobs during the depression, they would view their labors with ambivalence. They often saw themselves as "standbys," rather than the chief breadwinners, and as such were prepared, as Rose L. was, to swallow their pride and take jobs their husbands scorned when the family's economic security was at stake.[11]

Yet if general family values exerted pressures to keep wives from working, ethnic values and traditions could ease the stress caused when Jewish women had to seek jobs. For example, a strong bond of affection and mutual understanding in marriage often cushioned the effects of adversity,[12] and these were precisely the traits that many Jewish women had sought and found in their husbands. Equally important, sometimes ethnic values that are compatible in one situation may conflict when applied to a new context, and the one proving most functional will win out. As one illustration, Cuban women who emigrated to the United States during the past twenty-five years came from a middle-class background and believed that women should remain in the home. But in this country, entry to the middle classes was only possible for these new immigrant families if wives entered the work force. Most married Cuban women took jobs and thus achieved the more important cultural goal by sacrificing the other, which had become disfunctional.[13]

Similarly, Jews emigrated with strong family values, combined with the belief that a woman working to support a scholarly husband could be proud of her role and was certainly no source of shame. In this country, families quickly learned that husbands were expected to support wives, and Jewish women usually remained at home after marrying.[14] Thus, while there was enough work for men, one value gave way before the desire to fit into the customs of this new land. Yet even though Jewish wives did not work in factories, many who emigrated around the turn of the century pitched in to help support the family by taking in boarders or doing homework. Daughters remembered, above all, their mothers' "managing" in hard times, when "managing" frequently meant earning enough money to keep the family together. And when the economic situation changed for this younger generation of women so that *their* husbands were denied the opportunity to support their families, it may have been easier for people with such a background to adjust to working wives.

A few middle-class Jewish women enjoyed working and continued after they were married, either because their jobs were particularly satisfying, or because they appreciated being able to find work when so many could not. Anna R., for example, considered herself lucky to have a job during the depression. When people complained, she would reply, "I can't understand. You go to Europe, where we came from, then you'll know what it means, difficulty. There was no problem at all," she observed of her life. "We was very happy." Miriam G. enjoyed the ambiance of the position she took "temporarily" at Macy's. "It wound up being a little more than temporary," she observed. "I liked it. I always did like figures. And I ended up in the comptroller's office, at a very interesting time. My boss was a Wellesley graduate living in the Village, and her costudent was Madame Chiang Kai-shek. I got advanced to head of the department. I always worked." Like Miriam, Marie F. married an artistic man supportive of his wife's desire to work. In Marie's case, her husband had to adjust to the demanding schedule his wife followed as an opera singer.

Miriam and Marie worked out of choice; women who were widowed or who had invalid husbands usually got a job because of necessity. As we saw in the Introduction, Nina S. sewed corsets and petticoats for her husband to peddle, and when his health deteriorated, she operated a dry-goods shop for many years. With two children to support, Mildred L. was forced to seek work at thirty-five, after her husband died and the small amount of insurance he left was exhausted. Because Mildred had spent so many years caring for her family, she was terrified about getting a job. As her daughter tells the story,

As strong as she was in the home, and would have literally killed herself for us, she was still a scared person, a timid soul, until she got

20. A middle-class immigrant couple and their children, about 1928.
Collection of Rita Riman

out and felt confident, about doing anything outside. She stayed within this little cocoon. And when jobs opened up for women when the war came, she wanted to go back to work. We needed the money, but she was too timid to even go on an interview.

So I got up and I got dressed and I got her dressed and *shmeared* her up [made her up]. And I said, "If it's the last thing you ever do, you're going to go, and you're going to finish a week. And then if you want to quit, I'll understand. But you are going to go!" I literally had to take her there, I put her in the door, and told the guard there at the employees' entrance of Sterns that I would come for her when she was done, and he was not to let her out before that time. Because I knew her, she'd sneak out.

The tale of Mildred's first day at work has a happy ending. Her supervisor was a helpful, understanding woman, and Mildred went on to become, in her daughter's words, "the best saleswoman they had." She worked in Sterns, then in Lord and Taylor, selling jewelry until she was almost eighty years old. "They don't usually keep them so long," Mildred observed, "but I was terrific, I really was. I loved my work." Like many women who went out to work,[15] Mildred became more self-reliant in the process.

Some middle-class wives sought jobs because they simply were tired of staying at home. Either they were childless or else the children were in school all day. Sara B. tried to fill time with cleaning her large house until her mother told her to go into business. "If you don't get yourself busy doing something," she remembers being told, "you're going to have a nervous breakdown." Sara "halfheartedly" applied for a job in a children's clothing shop, and found, to her delight, that she enjoyed the work. Her boss rewarded her competence with a quick raise. "He was very partial to me because he knew that I was very conscientious," she observed. "If it was my own business, I couldn't have tried harder." Ethel B. also discovered that remaining at home, after her children were older, had lost its appeal. "My interest in it petered out," she recalled, "and I just found time too heavy on my hands. And I went to work, first part-time and then full-time." When her husband died, she was particularly glad she had revived her bookkeeping skills. Without a job, she felt, "I would have gone out of my mind." Rita S. worked before and after her marriage at various department stores. She began in Macy's as a model and then became assistant buyer in the cosmetics department. Rita then remained home for several years trying to become pregnant, but when her efforts failed, she took a job with Bonwit-Teller, also in the cosmetics department. "I had a ball," she recalled. "I loved it."

Tanya N. worked with her husband in an organization that cared for the needs of deaf people. "I think most of our nights in bed were spent teaching me signs!" Tanya observed. She worked first as a volunteer and soon found enormous satisfaction in working with the deaf. "I realized that this job was so fascinating, so wonderful, so new, so fresh, so original," she observed. "It forced me to become imaginative and practical and down-to-earth. I didn't have to do anything but create and that was certainly very challenging and very wonderful. And every time I succeeded at something, I was the happiest woman in the world."

None of these women had to enter the labor market for economic reasons, but all preferred working to staying at home. And all had the support of husbands in the decision to return to work. However, these women were unusual. Generally, whether or not their families needed their income, there was only one avenue of work automatically acceptable for married Jewish women, and that was helping in a family enterprise. As in middle-class families in Eastern Europe or in their parents' families in America earlier in the century, a wife could take part in a family business without embarrassing a husband who viewed a working wife as evidence of a man's financial incompetence. When Ida Richter's husband refused to let her get a job, they opened a shop making children's clothing. He did the cutting, and she supervised the sewing staff.[16] This was permissible, but if she performed the same function for a "boss," her husband would have considered it degrading. Some women were cynical about this "double standard" applied to women's work. Lena Kimberg observed, "They said that only widows went out to work and it demeaned a man for his wife to go out to work, although if he had his own business his wife could work extremely long hours."[17] Mollie Linker explained the rationale: "If you had to help out in the store you were still home." Her father-in-law had told her years before that it was fine to stay in the family store, that it was "nicer" than going out to work.[18]

Women who worked with their husbands, however, usually appreciated the advantages of such a relationship. In their own eyes, being "in business" clearly had more status than "working." For some, it provided a justification for doing something they enjoyed without having to feel guilty about neglecting their families. Fannie C., for example, observed that she "really had fun" once she began to work. "Regardless of what job I chose," she recalled,

> I liked them, they liked me. I was always the youngest, they always
> made a big fuss over me. I was always a very efficient worker. I always

gave more than was expected. My employers always liked me, they always complimented me. And I made friends and I enjoyed it. But I did not think of it as a career.

But it turned out to be a career, because I worked all my married life until my husband died. I was with him in business, so it really turned out to be a career. For fifty-two years. But I thought of it as a job until I got married, and of course, when I got married, nobody worked. I was the only one in my circle that ever worked after marriage. Why did I do it? Because I felt that my husband needed me there. At that time I really became rather important to his organization. And also that my husband wanted me there.

Working in a family business was thus acceptable as an extension of her proper role as her husband's helpmeet.

Like their mothers, sometimes women who worked with their husbands had better business sense than the men did. In their small grocery store, Pauline H. did the ordering and had more ability to please customers than her husband. When the husband of Nina S. made the mistake of purchasing a large number of small-sized corsets to peddle to ample-sized Italian women, his wife saw his mistake immediately and came up with the idea of stitching three together to make them saleable. Anna R. also took the initiative in the knitting factory she and her husband owned. "My mind always went a mile a minute," she recalled. "And it was necessary because my husband was very conservative and I was the gambler of the family. I ran the factory and my husband was the accountant."

Another advantage of working in a husband's business or store was that it gave women flexibility in caring for their families. Their mothers had learned that doing homework and taking in boarders permitted them to sandwich in the needs of husbands and children between the demands of paid work. If daughters married before the depression, they might, like their mothers, take in boarders, as Mary Wasserman Natelson did in the 1920s.[19] But after immigration was cut off in 1924, fewer "greenhorns" were around to seek lodgings. This generation of women managed the same juggling act as their mothers by working for and with family. Janet A., for example, was able to work until a week before her first child was born. After she had children, she observed, "I would help my husband when he needed me. He'd either bring some work home, which I would do, or if he needed something special, if he was running behind, I would run down to the office for a few hours." Later, when Janet went to work for another firm, her family's requirements were paramount. "I lived on Eighty-fifth Street," she recalled, "and I worked on Eighty-seventh. Very convenient, and it suited my needs. If one of the children were sick I could run home. I could put things up in the morning and go home for lunch and take it out of the oven. It really worked out well, and they were very sympathetic to my needs where I worked."

All women who worked outside the home had to balance the needs of job and family, some with more success than others. Naomi L. went to work in Los Angeles as an income tax agent when her son was eight years old. One of the benefits of the job was the hours. Naomi could take her son to school in the morning and be home shortly after he returned. Unlike Naomi, Hattie L., a psychiatric nurse, had to continually rearrange her schedule of duties at home because of changing shifts in the hospital. Whenever she left for work, she would put a pot of vegetable soup or a pot roast on the stove and get everything ready for dinner. Her daughters would set the table and turn off the oven when the alarm rang to let them know the food was finished cooking. "They were very capable," Hattie observed. "You know, when you have to, I think you just do it."

This could well be a motif for the women of this immigrant generation: "When you have to, you just do it." Rose G. observed that "there were times when things were very hard. But I was economical like my mother and made things do." Rose T. echoed these sentiments. When her husband died at forty-one, she managed. "Like my mother did," she observed. "I didn't make very much, but it was enough." For many of these women, the line between working-class and middle-class was indistinct. Even when husbands had operated small businesses, the depression could wipe them out and send their wives back to the factory. Women who labored with their husbands twelve hours a day in a grocery or candy store may have had the satisfaction of working without a boss's supervision, but they hardly achieved a life of comfort. And the majority of wives who did not work for wages had a full-time job making do on the limited amount of money their husbands brought home.[20]

The fact that many married women had to work at some time during the depression affected their self-image as well as their roles within the family. Like all wives forced to work because of economic necessity, Jewish women entered the job market to help sustain their families.[21] But this change in traditional roles was bound to affect relationships as well. Although these wives were accustomed to handling the family's finances and having a large share in decision-making, their position was further enhanced by an increased economic role.[22] Mothers who worked during the depression or World War II often became more assertive within the home, and children usually viewed them as the dominant parent.[23] One study of women who held wartime jobs demonstrated that working had a great effect upon their attitudes. Like those in another study in Oakland, California, they wanted their daughters to get an education and be able to provide for themselves.[24] Daughters learned from their mothers' examples. The daughters of Jewish women who had worked during the depression were more likely to be in the labor force after the birth of their first child. This was particularly true among upper-middle-class women who could have afforded to remain at home.[25]

Jewish immigrant mothers were no different from women of other ethnic groups in ambitions for their daughters. They hoped their girls would marry well and not have to work. But like most women, including their own mothers before them, they wanted their daughters to be prepared for whatever life might bring. To Jewish mothers, such preparation invariably meant an education. As Hilda S. recalled, "We always told [our daughter], my husband and I, we don't care how long you want to go to school or where you want to go. But when you go to school you bring us something that would qualify you to do something. Not that we're going to send you out to make a living for yourself, but we always felt that it was important for a woman just as well as a man to have something to fall back on." The positive attitude toward education was reinforced by the economic insecurity of the depression.

Many of these women did not differentiate between daughters and sons as far as education was concerned. One study indicates that second-generation Jews were likely to give all their children, as opposed to sons alone, equally high status.[26] This seems to be true as well for first-generation women who immigrated at a young age. Jennie H., for example, was proud that *all* her children attended college. As she observed, "I raised my children I think very beautiful as a woman without any background or any education from way back. When one of my children would get sick, I used to go to school every day and bring them the homework, so when they come back to school they shouldn't be missing their work. And I used to bring them to school, and I was always participating when there was something—Open School Week I was always there. I was conscious of giving my children the best that I understood."

Like their mothers, many women made sacrifices for their children's educations. Mildred L., widowed at thirty-five, sold her engagement ring to pay for her son's medical school tuition. Rose T., whose husband died at forty-one, had a hard time supporting her family. "But I managed," she observed. "My son went through college; he's an attorney. I managed. I worked. I didn't make very much. But it was enough because everything was cheap. Bread was five cents a loaf—and I managed. My daughter also had a college education." Hattie L., the psychiatric nurse, explained, "I needed the money, and I wanted it too. And my two girls both have their masters degrees, one in music and one in education." Mothers often hoped their daughters would become teachers—a job that combined status with economic security. The sacrifice was worthwhile if children got the education their parents valued so highly. During the depression years, one out of five young Jewish women in New York attended Hunter College or Brooklyn College at a time when only 9 percent of non-Jewish women were enrolled.[27]

Sometimes, a woman supported her daughter's desire for higher education despite a husband's opposition. "I made the decision," recalled Frieda M.

> I mean, when it came to their education, Aaron didn't want Ina to be a lawyer. I wanted her to marry too. But she came to me. And she said, "You owe me. I'd like to study law." I laughed at her, and she said, "At least you can let me try." I said, "If you get in, I'll fight Daddy. But if I were you, I'd take up typing." But she wasn't good with her hands anyway. So she took the test and came out very well.
>
> She wanted to go and I felt it was an education, no matter what she does; it's very important. She didn't have to choose law. If she had chosen to be a doctor, I would have gone along with it—anything. It was the same with Doris. If they wanted schooling, they got it. They wanted it, and I could afford it at that time.

Gussie M., who never left the working class, cherished the same dream for her two daughters, although her husband was lukewarm at best. It was especially important that they get the advantages she had been denied. "I talked my daughter into taking piano lessons which I couldn't afford," she recalled, "and she was never a pianist. And little things that didn't amount to anything. To other people, they know they can't manage it and they don't. But to me, it was important." But, she went on, "school was more important than anything. After they finished college, it was finished, for my dreams."

Not all women encouraged daughters to attend college. Although Pauline H. was proud of her daughter's achievements in high school, and agreed to let her take a few courses in college, she was afraid that too much education would make her unwilling to settle down to marriage. "I was very much afraid that she was going to be an old maid. With her knowledge, with her education, with her looks, she was going to look for something higher than she could get. Years do not stay in one place, and if it's one thing, I do not want an old maid. Courses yes, but not for steady." When Pauline's husband became ill with cancer, she talked her daughter into marrying to rescue both of them from the economic insecurity she had combatted most of her life.

Once they had passed the uncharted period of adolescence and courtship, most women had to deal with the same issues that had confronted their mothers. Many experienced economic adversity and had to care for the egos of men whose ambitions were frustrated. They felt responsible for holding the family together and earning money if husbands were temporarily unemployed. While few originally had sought work for its own sake, earning a living often contributed to their own self-esteem. Most wanted their children to get a good education, but unlike their mothers, they did not have to make the painful decision to send some children to work so that others might stay in school. With jobs requiring education at a premium during the depression, it made sense to keep young people at their desks at least through high school. And like their mothers, they saw education as the best means of assuring the children a better life.

13

Looking Back

My husband died, my daughter left for medical school, and my son had just gotten married. And I was left alone. And my first reaction was, "For whom will I do anything?" Because I had either been my father's daughter, my husband's wife, my children's mother. I didn't know who I was. I had to find out who I was.

—Dora W.

I can live with myself, and I'm happy.

—Miriam G.

Whatever I've wanted to do, I've done.

—Ethel B.

21. An elderly immigrant woman.

Collection of Diana Shapiro Bowstead

W hile women of the younger immigrant generation were caring for families and trying to make ends meet, they were too busy filling the needs of others to wonder about the direction of their own lives. But with the passage of years, children grow up and husbands die. After being the center of the family for so long, most women eventually had to come to grips with losing the focus that had shaped their lives. Often widowed, with children dispersed, middle-aged and elderly women had to find a different purpose to give their lives meaning.

Once the children were on their own, new relationships had to develop. Some women from poor backgrounds, without financial resources, simply accepted the reversal of the mother-child tie and took pride in the fact that their offspring now cared for them. As the sister of Mary Wasserman Natelson said, after divorcing her philandering husband, "Better the worst marriage than none at all. See what my children are to me."[1] For women like Mary's sister or Dora G., it was enough that their children set them up in comfortable apartments and visited occasionally. Dora's children provided the economic security that had eluded her while they were young. "God was good to me in my children," she observed. Compared with the hardships her mother had suffered, Dora felt her own life of poverty had been easy.

Women who grew up in America tended to seek more of an emotional or intellectual relationship with children. "Diana lets me share her life," observed Rose S. "I don't understand everything she does, but it's very important to me." Dora W. took college courses to be able to understand her daughter, and Ethel B. was proud that her children chose to confide in her. "We talk a great deal, and they don't feel that I'm an old fogey." However, Ethel considered this relationship a "bonus," something a mother could not automatically anticipate, but had to earn. Such rapport seemed easier to achieve when mothers had attended high school or felt they could share their children's interests.

Mothers differed in their ability to let sons and daughters live their own lives. Jennie H., a religious woman, saw her older children abandon orthodoxy and her favorite child marry a non-Jew. Her response, at least in retrospect, was philosophical.

My son isn't religious, neither are the girls. How do I feel about it? You know, two men were walking together, so one says, "How are you?" And he says, "So-so." "So-so? Tomorrow it will be better." He says, "How do you know?" He says "You'll get used to trouble." The same thing is with me. I don't like it, to be very frank, but I got used to it and that's how it is. I can't make them over. What should I do? I still want to live. And I have it very good now. I'm alone and I live in a nice area. And I have nice friends, and my children are very nice, they respect me. But I let them do what they want to do, I can't help it. I did the best I could. They honor me and they respect me and they love me. But I can't teach them now, they're no longer babies.

At the other extreme was the attitude of Louise C. After struggling to hold her family together during the depression, Louise could not tolerate any hint of disruption. When her son came and told her that he wanted to marry, she found all sorts of reasons for him to postpone the wedding: he was still in the Navy, he had no money, he hadn't finished his education, and his mother was sick. His irate fiancée told Louise that she would not have to worry about doing anything for the wedding, and Louise exploded. She remembered telling the girl,

> What do you mean, I don't have to take care of one thing? Do you know what it meant to me to raise my son? Who are you, that you are going to come and take over, just like that? How do you know I'm ready to give him up, just like that? Don't you come and tell me that you're going to take over. I had no one here, no one to go to. We would have been only too glad, if we would have had our families here, to go to them and to do the right thing. But I wouldn't have had the nerve to go to a mother of my husband and tell her that "You don't have to do anything."

Because Louise had never gotten over a sense of loss at leaving her parents in Eastern Europe, she could not bear the feeling that her son might abandon his family responsibilities and, by implication, herself. Like some "Jewish mothers," she was unable to accept the idea that she could become a marginal rather than the central figure in her son's life. "I needed family so bad," she reminisced, "that it was a great void in my life, something I was always missing."

While few mothers were so possessive, relations with children were seldom free of some kind of ambivalence. Rae K., for example, asserted that her daughter loved her and telephoned every second day. Yet they had not had a good relationship before she married. "She was like me," Rae observed. "She needed to dance like I needed to go to college or like my father needed to learn." Despite the understanding of later years, Rae, like her father, alienated her daughter by insisting that she give up an unacceptable ambition for her own good. Without explaining, she commented, "I just can't go and stay with her now."

Neglect was a more common, if understated, complaint. Anna R., for example, was delighted that her children followed the family tradition and were "people's people," and she took pride in the educational achievement of her three daughters. Still, her pride was tinged with sadness, or even pique, as she sat in her Miami Beach room and observed that her children were so busy that they seldom had time to visit. Anna's feelings were not unique. Elderly Jews in a senior citizens' center in California demonstrated this ambivalence ritually. They claimed on the one hand that they had realized their most cherished ideals by raising children who were educated, successful, and devoted to their parents. On the other hand, they felt neglected by their children, sometimes cut off, and asked almost covertly, "Do we deserve this?"[2]

When children greatly exceeded parents in education, a gap too wide to be bridged by affection could easily develop between generations. One woman in the center told friends of her daughter's almost embarrassing concern. "Mamaleh," she recalled her saying, "you're sweet, but you're so stupid!" Basha's response reflected her simultaneous pride and sadness in having an educated daughter whose accomplishments served to distance her from her mother. "What else could a greenhorn mother expect," Basha asked, "from a daughter who is a lawyer?"[3] The very education that parents struggled to make possible for their children thus sometimes created cultural gulfs that inhibited communication.

While some women were supported by children in their later years, few lived with daughters, and most seemed to know that they would not receive the kind of personal care that many had given their own elderly mothers. Rose L. cherished her son's promise that she would never have to go to a home when she was too old to keep her own apartment. She was depressed after visiting a childless cousin who had to enter an old age home, and she viewed her son and daughter as the only insurance against this frightening prospect. Rose insisted many times, a bit nervously, that she had wonderful children who called her every day. Rose S. had fewer expectations. After telling of the care her mother and two aunts had given their own widowed mother, she observed, "We don't have that here nowadays, because the children can throw off the worry about their mothers or fathers. In an emergency they are going to be taken care of by the city. Somebody's going to cart them away to a home." With different life-styles and increased geographical mobility, many American-born children redefined their responsibilities to elderly parents.[4] Obligations once automatically assumed by daughters could be replaced by the impersonal care of the welfare state.

As they aged, these women had to cope with the physical limitations time had imposed upon them. Most of those who retained freedom of movement were grateful to be able to continue managing on their own. "Every morning when I get up," related Jennie H., who at ninety-three enjoyed good health, "I say a prayer to thank God that I'm alive. And I have my own place and can do for myself. This is my satisfaction," she concluded, "my independence." Others who had lost this cherished freedom found dependence on others, as Tanya called it, "infuriating," particularly if they had been accustomed to leading active lives. Jeanne S. raged against the fate that had deprived her of sight, essential for a doctor, and rendered her unable to perform the duties that had made life fulfilling. Naomi L., who had entered an "adult" home in her mid-seventies, came to regret her decision. "Everyone is so old," she observed sadly. Naomi's greatest source of pride had been the certainty that she could always take care of herself. In one of her last stories, Anzia Yezierska described an elderly woman, herself really, who could not remember where she had placed her glasses, and then misplaced as well the letter she had wanted to read. She is overcome with anger at being betrayed by the weakness of her own body. "In that moment of fury," she wrote, "I felt like kicking and screaming at my failing memory—the outrage of being old!"[5]

All middle-aged women had to reevaluate their lives after the death of a husband. "I used to think," recalled Rose G., "if my husband would die, I couldn't live either. I spent my life being a wife and mother, and then when my children were grown up and my husband died, I felt I was nothing. At the beginning the children were very good to me. And later on, they figure, it's time to take care of yourself. But that's the way of the world." Just as these women learned to deal with widowhood, many learned to find new meaning in their lives. Rose remembered talking to one woman when her own husband was hospitalized with only a week to live. The woman's husband had died, and she told Rose, "I thought I couldn't exist without him." Then she went on, "But I'm still here." Rose insisted, "my children are my life. And it's very important to me that they should be happy." Yet, with her children grown, her sense of self-worth was no longer defined by fulfilling their needs. At eighty-seven, she found that working in a family hardware store gave her satisfaction. "I thank God that I have my self-respect," she observed, "and the love I can remember. And that's about it. If I didn't go to work, I think I'd become a potato." After her own husband died, Hannah F. remained strong for the sake of the children, who looked to her for emotional support. "I felt I couldn't fall apart," she recalled. She chastized one self-pitying widow by urging her to emphasize the positive. "You're alive," she recalled saying. "It's the worse thing one can do, feel sorry for yourself." Hannah attributed this strength to her parents, remembering the steadfast way her mother and father overcame their problems. She was especially proud of taking over the business her husband had established and putting their sons through college.

One woman with a less satisfying marriage found that widowhood had brought an unexpected relief. Although she loved her husband, he had made her life "a series of disasters" that she continually had to cope with. He was a compulsive gambler, and she often had to take a job to pay his debts. "Now," she stated, "I have peace. I could never even *think* of marrying again!"

After a husband's death, many women particularly enjoyed relationships with others who shared their background. Jennie H. sometimes preferred friends to her children, who had gone their own ways and whose concern for her well-being reminded her too much of her own frailty. She refused to celebrate Jewish holidays with them, in part because they would have to drive to visit her, which she forbade them to do because of her orthodox beliefs, and in part because it was a way of asserting independence. She described her feelings:

> These people where I go every *Shabbes*, there is not another family like that anymore, anywheres. They're very fine. And you know, I feel, when I come into their house, I feel like a family from them. I feel like I'm one of them. Because they like me very much. I sometimes tell them "I like you better than my children." You know why I like them better? Because I go there twelve years. Never she has anything to tell me anything of anything. We just get along like smooth. And my children sometimes yell at me, "Don't do that, Don't do this." You know, they interfere with me. But I don't interfere with her and she don't interfere with me. We just have fine discussions on *Shabbes* together.

Satisfactions in later years are different from the ones experienced earlier in life. At ninety-five, Anna R. observed,

> I get up in the morning. I don't say my prayers. I say, "Thank God for giving me another day." When I go to sleep at night I take inventory of the day. What did I do that was right, what did I do that was wrong

that I could improve on the wrong and continue with the right. So I almost make a list in my mind what I should do.

While life was not always what I would have liked it to be, I always seemed to have the feeling that I had it better than somebody else. So I was never discouraged. Einstein once said that "the only things that are left in life are the things you give away." And that's always in my mind. So you gather those things together and you leave something behind that might benefit people. What I feel is just three words: you love, care, and share.

I look into my mind, and my grandmother is with me all the time. The things she did and how she did it. And what's more, my children know this, and they are of the same pattern. And you know everybody is an individual, but you can feel it's like an apple falling off the tree.

Anna felt fulfilled by her role in passing on to her own daughters the legacy of helpfulness she had learned from her grandmother.

Some women found different sources of gratification in their later years. Frieda K., who cared for her mother until she died when Frieda was thirty-two, enjoyed a freedom she had never known as a young woman. Although she regretted not marrying and having children, Frieda sat in her bright, cheerful apartment and talked about how good her life was. Her time was completely her own, and a small pension and Social Security benefits gave her financial independence. "I was the one that supported the family," she explained.

And now I'm really living it up! I'm having a ball! You know, this is senior citizen housing. And the rent is very nominal. It's wonderful, just wonderful. And I've got my Social Security, which is a godsend. I never had it so good! I live it up. I can do anything I want with my money and I treat everybody.

Frieda took particular delight in her nieces and nephews and in her ability to travel. Financial comfort gave her access to a world of experiences she had never expected. "The Queen Elizabeth is a palace," she recalled with awe. "It's like being on a different planet."

Helping people gave many women great pleasure. Family, of course, came first. Frances F., who remained childless, devoted much time to assisting her parents and brothers. "I always put everybody ahead of me— their desires, their needs came before my own. I filled their needs. I guess I'd hate myself if I didn't because I am a doer, I am a giver. I want to do, I want to give, I want to help. And I think the things that I got were more important than the things that I didn't get. And what I got is the love of my parents and of everybody around me." Frances was an optimist. Like three other women with similar attitudes, she summed up her life by recalling the Yiddish proverb of the wise man who told people to tie up their problems in bundles and lay them on the ground, and when they heard of the others' troubles, then each one ran to get back his own.

Most women extended this concern to others outside their families. Many found satisfaction in doing volunteer work for such Jewish women's organizations as Hadassah, the National Council of Jewish Women, or ORT (Organization for Rehabilitation through Training). Although they themselves may not have been aware of it, their attitude toward helping those less fortunate than themselves flowed unconsciously from the traditional Jewish obligation of *tsedakah*, often passed on through their mothers' example. Almost half of all Jewish women belong to organizations, while fewer than a third of women of other ethnic backgrounds belong to similar groups.[6] At ninety-three, Jennie H. continued to attend biweekly meetings of Mizrachi Women and enjoyed being able to contribute a few dollars to their charities. Sara B. took pride in her work as president of the United Order of True Sisters, a Jewish group that helps people afflicted with cancer. "There's good in everybody," Sara observed. "Sometimes they have a real potential, and you can help them to bring it out if you want to go to the trouble." Louise C. made a new beginning after her husband's death by becoming an activist on behalf of the aging. "I don't know where it came from," she said of her persistence, "but I have great will power." Dora G., who had never learned how to read, but who helped other immigrants get settled, was proud of the assistance she gave. "I accomplished a lot," she stated. "I helped a lot of people with their *tsores* [troubles], put them on their feet, and that was my happiness." Hattie L., the nurse, had great empathy for the psychiatric patients she cared for. "The feeling for people has to be in you," she mused. "Maybe it's nurtured from childhood on. I saw it all the time in my home. Part of it had to rub off."

If women had greater expectations of life, they were less satisfied. Fannie K., who had strong leftist political beliefs, never saw her hope for an equitable society fulfilled. "My interest was that people should live just right. Whatever is unjust, I'm against it. We all struggled and we were on our own. My husband and I in principle were against making money at others' expense. So we didn't have a rich life, but I don't complain. I only complain now, after my husband is gone." After thinking about what she had said, she explained, "In a way, we did have a rich life culturally, and with organization work." Yet one senses that she was a disillusioned woman.

A fulfilling career could take the place of children, although this was unusual in the immigrant generation. Women who carved out nontraditional niches for themselves tended to have a single-minded commitment to their professions. Jeanne S., who sacrificed marriage and family to become a doctor, felt that America had been good to her. Her cousins and aunt had been proud of her accomplishments, and she helped raise one niece with whom she remains close. "My patients like me. I never stood with my hand out for the four dollars or five dollars. I told them to come to my office. I was good to them, and they were very grateful." She had her patients' gratitude and her niece's appreciation. That was thanks enough. "I had a feeling I wanted to be something, somebody. And I did it! I became somebody!" Tanya N., whose husband died after five years of marriage, spent her working life as director of an agency serving the deaf. "All I knew," she related, "was that you have to work hard, and you have to enjoy what you do, and that was the important thing. To succeed you must enjoy what you do. It has to be. If you can create, you will be successful. This is what I learned early in life. If people wouldn't just do what other people do, they would be so much more interesting. And it's the only way to attract people, even if you're not so hot, even if you're less than perfect. But to be what you are makes one interesting. Phoniness is a real crime against yourself." Always striving to better herself, Tanya sought friends among well-educated people. "My friends cannot be my peers," she observed. "They must be my superiors. Otherwise I get nothing out of the friendship. If they continue to be my friends, then it means that I am meeting the challenge. I realized that from the way people seek me out that there must be a plus somewhere within me." With an uncharacteristic touch of modesty, Tanya suggested that she was an ordinary person who had inherited a fraction of her mother's "unusual wit, sense of humor, physical grace, and charm." Although she never had children, she felt that she could better appreciate and understand her nieces and nephews because "I wasn't bothered with my own." She had seldom gone on vacation without one of her sister's or brothers' children accompanying her. "I took over completely," she observed. But in her eighties, she felt neglected by them and bitter about the depredations of age.

There were other disappointments as well. Many women were unhappy that they had been unable to gain more education. Tanya was proud of her ability to learn by herself, although she regretted not having a college education. Ethel B. and Janet A., who, like Tanya, grew up in this country, also were sorry they had not attended college. Ethel suggested, "Had I been an American, I would have done it. But I was very shy and handicapped by that [being an immigrant]." Although Janet felt that she had become an educated person by taking courses, she missed the formality of a degree, and thought that she would have become a teacher rather than a book-keeper had she graduated from college. In general, those who had emi-grated as children with their parents after World War I had easier access to high school and could even consider the possibility of college. Women whose families were poorer, who came before the war, or who arrived here in their teen years had similar feelings about high school. As a young woman, Fannie K. had wanted to attend day school, but like many others during the depression, she had no option but to work.

Some women were able later in life to get the learning they had missed. For Marie F., after the death of her husband and then her only child, school filled a great void. Although she enjoyed her career as a singer and felt fulfilled by it, she missed the sense of "greater vision" she believed she had finally attained by taking college courses. When Dora W., an aware, articu-late woman, was widowed at about fifty, she decided to take courses to fill the gaps in her knowledge. All her life, she observed, she had served the needs of her parents, husband, and children, and now it was time to determine who she really was. "I had to learn a lot of things," she recalled. "I had to learn how to manage money. I had to learn a bit about investment and Wall Street, because I wanted to do it. I took courses in psychology because I wanted to find out something about myself, and above all, I wanted to be able to talk to my daughter. It was all important."

For most of these women, a formal education was valued highly, almost as a magical achievement that could vastly expand the range of possibilities in life. Hilda S. observed that although she was eighty years old, if she had such an education, she could "still go out and do something" with her life. Yet very few felt that the lack of learning had seriously blighted their lives. "I used to get moody," Hilda recalled,

And I used to say to my husband, "What did I ever do with my life? I didn't get an education, I didn't do anything." He used to be very quiet, then he said, "Look, you had two nice children. You gave them a nice education. They never gave you any trouble of any kind. You married them off and you have lovely grandchildren. What do you lack? How could you say, 'What did I do with my life?' You did a wonderful job." So *if* I was in a good mood, I'd say, "OK, I guess you're right." And if I wasn't I'd say, "What did I ever do? I was just lucky to have children that cooperated and grew up decent people."

Marie Jastrow best sums up their attitudes about education. "I always felt that I was deprived of something special in life," she observed. "But no regrets; I lived in a different era."[7]

Like Hilda, many women believed that children were their finest accomplishment. Those who remained childless usually regretted not having a family of their own. Jennie S., for example, was sorry she had married late in life. "Children is better than money," stated Jennie, who had neither. Saddest of all were the two women who each chose to bear only a single child during the depression, only to have their sons die in young adulthood. Almost predictably, both women sought solace in work and adult education.

Those who were comfortable economically in later years tended to look back on their lives with contentment. But what seemed more important than finances was a sense of the distance each had traveled in her own personal odyssey. Frieda W. was by far the poorest and least fortunate woman in this survey. In Russia, she had wandered from town to town during World War I, looking for her parents and trying to find enough to eat. As a new immigrant, Frieda had been attacked and raped by a young man she dated, her husband left her shortly after her son was born, and after years of working as a domestic and trying to provide for her child, he left home and never got in touch with her again. She was alone, not very healthy, living in a public housing project and subsisting on minimal Social Security payments. She did not own a television because she could not afford one. Yet she was thankful for what she had. "Thank God, I got a good reputation. I don't owe nobody not a penny. I own my own furniture, no one will take it back because of installments. I got a phone. And I got the center—they show movies there sometimes and I can watch television. Sometimes they take us for trips." When I asked her how she passed the time, she took out a scrapbook filled with pictures cut from magazines. She liked famous people, she explained, even if they weren't very nice. Her collection was eclectic—Einstein next to Joan of Arc and Catherine the Great along with the picture of a man who became a woman. "This is how I spend my time," she told me. Best of all, she now had enough to eat. "Sometimes I think I can never eat enough," she explained, "to make up for being so hungry when I was young."

Like Frieda, a few women who had had difficult lives insisted that overcoming obstacles had made them stronger. If their old age was comfortable, they were particularly satisfied. At ninety-three, living in a pleasant apartment paid for by her children, with an attentive granddaughter in the same building, Rae K. observed,

> You can't go through life just smoothly. You have to have obstacles. What could I have changed? I struggled until I came to this country and then I struggled again. I was alone. I went to college, but I couldn't finish. I was helpless. My life was very difficult, but I wouldn't have changed it. I don't know how I went through it, but I did. Then my husband passed away, young, so young. My daughter was eleven years old, and I had to bring her up. I did everything. I was a housekeeper and I was a seamstress. I worked in Washington during the war. I did everything, everything. But I have a wonderful old age now, I must say.

Gussie M. had lived through a pogrom and suffered from poverty in a Russian village. When she came to America as a young adult, she longed for an intellectual life and found it in the Socialist Party and in Yiddish literature. Gussie never strayed far from her immigrant origins and derived great satisfaction from the fact that her daughters had the college education she never felt she could aspire to for herself. None of her circle of friends achieved more than a working-class life. "I call my generation the 'lost generation,'" she observed, echoing the phrase repeated by many. "I would be something else, my husband would be a writer, there's no question. I have friends who would be entirely different than they are. But in their childhood, it was too long ago. We didn't have anything. And that's an old story. In the small towns, it was entirely different. And Jewish people had no opportunity for even a little schooling. So we didn't have it, that's all." Because of the poverty of her childhood, in particular her mother's hard life, Gussie considered herself lucky. "I don't think I would change anything," she observed. "Of course if I could have a nicer apartment or good clothes, I wouldn't reject it. But," she insisted, "I didn't suffer from it." There were few regrets for the paths not taken.

Of these women's attitudes one could do no better than remember the words Barbara Myerhoff used to describe the elderly Jewish women at the senior citizens center in Venice, California. They "communicated a quiet conviction and satisfaction with themselves, perhaps because they did what had to be done, did it as well as it could be done, and knew that without what they did there would be nothing and no one. This is not scant comfort," she wrote, "at looking back at one's lifework."[8] As Rose S. phrased it more simply, "It was a hard life, but I made the most of it."

In many ways, these lives were similar to those of all women in modern industrial societies. They concentrated on home and family, although when necessity demanded, they found a means to place food on the table and pay the rent. Even the few women who did not have children validated their lives in terms of service and relationships to others. Tanya N. told of the love and respect of hundreds of deaf people she had helped; Jeanne S., the doctor, of the patients she had cared for and the affectionate tie with her niece. If, in old age, there was no remaining relationship, women like Frieda W. emphasized their own unsuccessful attempts to maintain family connections. Their concept of self was intricately tied up with feelings about others, and many seem to have had difficulty redefining their lives once children and husbands were no longer in the home.[9]

Some recent psychoanalytic theorists have suggested reasons why women seem so different from men in this respect. They argue that girls, unlike boys, have no need to separate their identities from mothers, and thus emerge from childhood with a stronger basis than boys for experiencing the feelings of others as their own. Consequently, while men strive for, and judge themselves according to, an external standard of achievement, women define their identities through personal attachments and tend to focus upon intimate relationships.[10] Their sense of self is organized around creating and maintaining such connections, and they evaluate themselves by their ability to nurture and help.[11] These immigrant women, regardless of their work lives, fit into this model. All of them placed relationships first and derived great satisfaction from success in caring for others. They did what had to be done and took pride and comfort in this knowledge.

In addition to sharing such traits with women generally, these Jews shared certain specific characteristics with immigrant women of other groups. They all had to cope with the transition to life in an urban, industrial society different from the one left behind. All these women had to learn the signposts of life in a strange country and work out what of their old ways could be retained and what had to be discarded. Most young immigrants sought to shed the obvious signs of a foreign background without simultaneously surrendering what they valued most in that heritage.[12] Although one could learn how to speak or dress or behave from friends at school or at work, family relations were more resistant to change. With few guides on how to act within the intimate confines of the family, many young women, despite their desire to be Americans, nevertheless maintained as adults the attitudes they had learned in their parents' homes.[13] Immigrant mothers and daughters all had to deal with subtle changes in the relationship between parents who retained old-country customs and children who learned American ways quickly and contributed to the family's economy. And because most immigrant families were poor, at least at the beginning, all wives had to master the skills of managing the family's resources and learn to deal with the want and illness that frequently haunted their lives.

Despite the problems encountered by most immigrants, the particular cultural heritage of Jewish women shaped their reaction to these common experiences. Whether they lived in New York or other urban centers like New Haven, Portland, Chicago, Indianapolis, Providence, or Pittsburgh, there are striking similarities in the behavior of Jewish immigrants that differentiate their responses from those of women with other backgrounds. While many individual coping mechanisms were similar to those of other immigrants, the total picture that emerges is unique. In many of these cities, Jewish mothers in need of money took in boarders or worked in the family's grocery or dry-goods shop. They tended to share decision making with their husbands, and the family's social life invariably centered about the home. Young Jewish women who had to work were more eager to Americanize than other young immigrants. And although parents believed the education of girls less important than that of sons, their daughters still attended high school and college in far larger numbers than those of other groups.[14] Thus, wherever they settled after leaving Eastern Europe, Jewish women transmitted similar messages to their daughters.

The attitudes of the older generation of immigrant women made it easier for daughters to Americanize, yet not feel they were completely abandoning the ways of their parents. Most Jewish mothers tended to be more accepting than other immigrant women of the American manners children brought home from school and the workplace. Daughters learned from them to make the religious compromises that seemed necessary for a life as Americans in a new land. If a mother lighted a stove on the Sabbath, or abandoned the *sheitel* and the *mikvah*, even if she never left Eastern Europe, a daughter might eat nonkosher meat or work on Saturday without feeling she was less of a Jew. And although many mothers and daughters seldom saw the inside of a synagogue, the culture of Judaism colored their lives. Among the attributes of that culture was the high value placed on education. Many women whose own educations were limited nevertheless esteemed learning and hoped their daughters as well as their sons could go to school in the United States. This outlook, shaped in Eastern Europe but reinforced in the United States, meant that mothers generally would encourage daughters to stay in school if the family did not need their income. Class may have limited the options of this first generation of immigrants, but it had little effect on their dreams. If education was impossible for economic reasons, mothers and daughters alike transferred this goal to younger children in the family.

Another factor that assisted acculturation was the traditional attitude toward women's working to earn money. Because Jewish wives had frequently helped support their families in Eastern Europe, no stigma had been attached to it. In the United States, although married women generally did not seek jobs outside the home, young women did, and mothers seemed inclined to accept a daughter's working as a sign of adulthood. At best, this meant that a mother might take pride in her girl's work rather than simply see it as a way to pay the bills until she married. At the very least, it gained for daughters such privileges and rights as staying out in the evenings or keeping some of their wages for personal needs. This acceptance eased the transition for young women who wanted to become Americans and contributed as well to their sense of self-esteem.

Many women emphasized the significance of mothers in shaping their own attitudes. Mainly from mothers, sometimes from fathers, they absorbed a cultural heritage that prized initiative and education—traits that meshed well with the needs of the urban, industrial society in which they had sunk new roots. And equally important, once girls were grown, mothers often served as role models in determining patterns of family relations. Young women learned from them how to relate to husbands, children, and others—a skill which many valued as their most important attribute. Women who came to this country alone missed this connection with mothers, although as Louise C. observed, "the tie was always there." Perhaps with so few guides to appropriate behavior in America, immigrant daughters remembered the strains of feeling like strangers in a strange land and could thus appreciate, at least in retrospect, the problems and sacrifices of mothers in a way that children of affluence and stability seem less able to do. How they passed on this cultural heritage to their own daughters is an intriguing subject for further study.

Appendix

. . . .

Twenty-one of the women interviewed came from Russia, with thirteen born in the Ukraine, three each from Minsk Province and Lithuania, and two whose families had settled in Siberia. Seven were from Congress Poland, which was controlled by the Russian Czar. Nine came from Galicia and two from other areas in Austria. One had lived in Czechoslovakia and two in Hungary. The remaining women were not certain of their birthplaces, although they all came to the United States old enough to remember something of their lives in Eastern Europe. The economic backgrounds of the women divided them about equally between poor and middle-class. They lived in approximately equal numbers in villages, towns, and cities, but the differences between these labels are imprecise.

These women emigrated between 1896 and 1925, with the majority arriving between 1912 and 1924. Eight of their families originally settled in other countries—four in England—and later embarked on a second migration to the United States. Two women were born in the United States and were brought as babies for visits to relatives in Russia. They and their mothers were prevented from returning for many years by World War I and the Russian Revolution. When they arrived in this country, about half of the women were in their teens, three were older than twenty, and the rest were from five to twelve years old. Half emigrated with one or both of their parents, while the other half came alone. The average age of the women at the time of emigration was fourteen; for those who came alone, it was sixteen and a half. Half of those who emigrated without parents were going to a father or other relative already in the United States, and two were already married when they arrived here. All of them settled in or near New York, although a few lived at first in other areas and subsequently moved to the city.

In America, women's education depended on their parents' economic condition and their age at the time of emigration. Many of those who came in their teens or older years had no formal schooling in America, and three had little or no education in Europe either. Sixteen had some education in Eastern Europe, ranging from private tutors to *gimnazye* which two completed. Only two women who came here as children left school before the fifth grade. Twenty-two attended high school, but only six graduated. Six also took business courses. Three did some college work, although only one graduated. Three took professional degrees (for admission to schools of pharmacy and law, one did not need a college education), although only the doctor practiced her profession.

It is difficult to establish what class women belonged to, as their circumstances late in life sometimes differed from those when they were younger. Occasionally, children who had done well established a comfortable home for mothers who had struggled with poverty most of their lives. Sometimes I interviewed a woman in a setting other than her home and got only a sketchy sense of her economic condition. There are other limitations. Women who worked in factories were clearly working-class, although a married woman who did such work to supplement a husband's wage was clearly better off economically than a single woman who did "white-collar" office work. Many women with working-class backgrounds entered the middle class through marriage.

Despite these problems, it is reasonable to say that about half the women were working-class and half middle-class. The working-class women were those who worked "in the trades" or in domestic service, ran small shops, or had low-level white-collar jobs. Middle-class women did bookkeeping or other clerical work sporadically rather than regularly, worked in substantial family firms, or had no need to work outside the home.

The economic status of married women generally depended on husbands' jobs, and about three-quarters of the working-class wives had to seek employment fairly regularly, usually in factories or small shops. Women whose husbands earned an adequate income remained at home when their children were young, although one had household help and returned to her husband's business within two weeks of the birth of her child. These middle-class women often began to work in a family business by the time their children were in school. If they worked for another employer, they chose their jobs on the basis of the convenience with which they could continue to care for their family's needs, rather than how much money they could earn, which was the major consideration for poorer women.

All these women worked outside the home before marriage to help their families, many either in garment factories (eleven) or offices (twelve). All worked at some time after marriage, although middle-class women worked by choice and working-class women because of necessity. The poorer women tended to take jobs even when their children were young; those who worked by choice usually waited until children were in school. Among the working-class women, apart from the eleven who worked in garment factories, one ran a butter-and-eggs business; one ran a small grocery shop with her husband; one ran a dry-goods shop; one helped immigrants get settled; two were domestics, although only temporarily; two did laundry and kitchen work; three were milliners; and one was a silk weaver. Only two of this younger generation of immigrant women took in boarders. Two of the three milliners stopped working at their trades and entered the middle-class after they married. Most of the middle-class women worked in offices, ten of them as bookkeepers, four working with their husbands in a family business. Others performed the same functions in department stores. Two women were buyers, one of yard goods, another cosmetics. One was a librarian, one a tax auditor, another a psychiatric nurse, another a rent collector (until she married); two were salespeople, and one an executive for the New York Society for the Deaf. Two were artists—an opera singer and a dancer—but they also did bookkeeping and stenography when they needed to earn more money.

A high percentage of these women did not have husbands to rely upon. All but four of the women married, although one lived with a man for thirty-five years without marrying. But two women were deserted early in their marriages, one married in her sixties, seven were widowed before they were forty, and one got a divorce after only three years. So fourteen had to earn their own way for most of their lives. Of these fourteen, only four earned a comfortable living.

The married women had many fewer children than their mothers. In part because they wanted to give them more benefits, in part because of the economic problems of the depression, most of them—twenty-one—had only two children. Three each had four, five had three, and seven had a single child. Ten remained childless, three by choice. All their children exceeded them in education, although fewer sons and daughters of uneducated mothers completed college. About three-quarters of these children became professionals, ranging from lawyers to teachers. Only about one-fifth of the daughters remained at home after the birth of children.

As with class, an evaluation of religious practice tends to be subjective. Although forty of their mothers had maintained kosher homes, only about a third of the younger immigrant women did, and a few more lit candles on Friday night. Only one wore a *sheitel*. However, more than 80 percent celebrated the major Jewish holidays, and all considered themselves good Jews, even the one woman who also claimed to be an atheist. Only one woman married a non-Jewish man.

Late in life, the overwhelming majority of these women were widowed. At the time I interviewed them, only five had living husbands. Although most lived comfortable lives, five working-class women were poor in old age as well. These women lived in public housing on the Lower East Side or in the Bronx. Other relatively poor women lived in Brighton Beach and other parts of Brooklyn. Only one woman lived with her daughter, and only three were in old age or "adult" homes. The rest, despite ages ranging from seventy to ninety-four, remained in their own apartments. One, on the Upper East Side of Manhattan, still had her own mother living with her. One lived in an apartment in Queens, another in a garden apartment in a New Jersey town. Three had retired to different communities in Florida. The rest lived on the Upper West Side of Manhattan in fairly comfortable circumstances (I approached many of these women through a senior citizens center in this area). Fully half of them did volunteer work of some kind, usually with a Jewish women's organization such as ORT (Organization for Rehabilitation through Training), Hadassah, the National Council of Jewish Women, Mizrachi Women, or the United Order of True Sisters.

Notes

. . . .

Introduction

1. For example, Yans-McLaughlin, *Italian Immigrants*; Hareven, *Family Time*; Myerhoff, *Number Our Days*; Diner, *Erin's Daughters in America*.

2. In a seminal book on interview methodology, Rhoda Metraux observed that "in work with informants, it is desirable, at least initially, to keep the possibilities of the informant-interviewer relationship open and to accommodate the relationship as far as possible to the expectations of the informant" (Mead and Metraux, *Culture at a Distance*, p. 144).

3. On this point, see Bertaux and Bertaux-Wiame, "Life Stories," pp. 187–88.

4. See Bertaux-Wiame, "Study of Internal Migration," pp. 262–64; Chodorow, *Reproduction of Mothering*, chap. 2, p. 11.

5. E. P. Thompson, *English Working Class*, pp. 12–13.

Chapter 1: Women of the Shtetl

1. Ruth Rubin, *Voices of a People*, pp. 112–13.

2. Joseph, *Jewish Immigration*, pp. 57–61.

3. The most severe governmental decrees, the "May Laws" put into effect after the assassination of Czar Alexander II in May 1881, forbade Jews to settle in villages and gave villagers the right to drive out Jews already there; expelled Jews from cities like St. Petersburg, Moscow, and Kiev; limited drastically the number of Jews in secondary schools and universities; and prohibited Jews from entering the legal profession and participating in local government. The governmental strongman, Konstantin Pobednostsev, hoped to solve the "Jewish problem" by convincing a third of all Jews to convert and another third to emigrate, leaving the remainder to eventually die out. See, for example, Karp, *Haven and Home*, p. 112.

4. Ain, "Swislocz," pp. 86–87.

5. Zborowski and Herzog, *Life Is with People*, p. 66. Much of the information in this source is somewhat romanticized and tends to present the ideal situation as the real one.

6. Antin, *Promised Land*, p. 1.

7. Baron, *Jew under Tsars and Soviets*, pp. 98–99, 101; Zborowski and Herzog, *Life Is with People*, pp. 215–16.

8. According to the Russian census of 1897, 77.8 percent of the Jews lived in "urban" areas (usually more than 2,000 people). They were prohibited from living in small

villages, although large numbers lived in *miestechkow*—larger villages or towns serving the surrounding countryside as commercial centers. See Rubinow, "Jews in Russia," p. 4.

9. YIVO Manuscript Autobiography no. 293. Probably no more than 2 percent of Jews—the number engaged in agricultural pursuits—lived in such places. See Rubinow, "Jews in Russia," p. 500.

10. Jastrow, *Looking Back*, p. 40.

11. Zunser, *Yesterday*, p. 200.

12. This privileged, assimilated class probably numbered no more than 3 percent of the Jewish population. See Rubinow, "Jews in Russia," p. 576, and Kuznets, "Immigration of Russian Jews," p. 69.

13. Kramer and Mazur, *Jewish Grandmothers*, p. 61.

14. Howe and Greenberg, *Treasury of Yiddish Stories*, p. 6; Zborowski and Herzog, *Life Is with People*, p. 214.

15. For example, between World Wars I and II, in the Polish town of Stoczek, most men were workers, a third were businessmen, and no more than 1 percent were scholars. Rosenthal, "Social Stratification," p. 2. During the same period, it was estimated that 100,000 Jews in Poland were middle-class, 2,000,000 belonged to the petit bourgeoisie, 700,000 were workers, and only 300,000 were members of the professional and intellectual classes. Mendelsohn, *Jews of East Central Europe*, p. 27.

16. Cited in Antin, *Promised Land*, p. 37.

17. Cited in Schwartz, "Immigrant Voices," p. 3.

18. I. J. Singer, *World That Is No More*, p. 18.

19. Scott and Tilly, *Women, Work, and Family*, pp. 48–49.

20. Rubinow, in his classic "Jews in Russia," pp. 498–99, noted that over 15 percent of Jewish artisans were women, and the Russian census of 1897 indicated that women comprised 21 percent of the Jewish labor force. However, Baum argues that because of the categories employed, most shtetl women were probably not included in the count of the gainfully employed. See Baum, "What Made Yetta Work?," p. 32.

21. Chernin, *In My Mother's House*, pp. 22–23.

22. Abramovitch, "Rural Jewish Occupations," p. 205.

23. Reznikoff, "History of a Seamstress," pp. 22–23.

24. Saroff, *Stealing the State*, p. 3.

25. Ain, "Swislocz," pp. 106–7.

26. Scott and Tilly, *Women, Work, and Family*, pp. 52–53. Scott and Tilly noted that many widowers in Western Europe were on charity lists because they had great difficulty supporting themselves after their wives died.

27. Fischer, *Twentieth Century*, p. 7.

28. Rose Cohen, *Out of the Shadow*, pp. 10, 23–24.

29. Tcherikower, *Jewish Labor Movement*, p. 10.

30. Ain, "Swislocz," p. 95. The Russian census of 1897 indicates that the largest number of employed women, 113,740, worked in domestic service. See Rubinow, "Jews in Russia," pp. 498–99.

31. Morris Raphael Cohen, *Dreamer's Journey*, p. 6.

32. Kramer and Mazur, *Jewish Grandmothers*, p. 91.

33. Brier and Farkas, "Reminiscences," Immigrant Labor History Project.

34. YIVO Manuscript Autobiography no. 293.

35. Plotkin, *Full-Time Active*, p. 6; Morris Raphael Cohen, *Dreamer's Journey*, p. 11.

36. Rabach, "Women's Professions in Sonik," pp. 26–27.

37. Sholem Aleichem, *Great Fair*, p. 188.

38. Antin, *Promised Land*, p. 43.

39. Chernin, *My Mother's House*, pp. 22–23.

40. Kugelmass and Boyarin, *Ruined Garden*, p. 43; Saroff, *Stealing the State*, p. 9.

41. Ain, "Swislocz," pp. 101–6.

42. In Central Europe, for example, all women's work—sewing, weaving, etc.—was devalued by workers' guilds. See Quataert, "Shaping of Women's Work," p. 1147. In Russia, despite the absence of guilds, women's work was similarly considered less important than what men did.

43. Antin, *Promised Land*, pp. 52, 56.

44. Lazarus, *The Jewish Woman*, p. 244.

45. Hyman, "Reminiscences," Immigrant Labor History Project.

46. Chagall, *First Encounter*, pp. 239, 265, 232.

47. Kahan, "Diary of Anne Kahan" (January 23, 1915), p. 158.

48. Kramer and Mazur, *Jewish Grandmothers*, pp. 142–43.

49. I. J. Singer, *World That Is No More*, pp. 16–18; Isaac Bashevis Singer, *My Father's Court*, p. 44.

50. Women often were able to speak languages other than Yiddish in part because parents sometimes were more willing to send daughters than sons to local, secular, Christian schools. In 1897, for example, 35 to 40 percent of Jewish women had acquired a working knowledge of Russian. See Rubinow, "Jews in Russia," p. 581.

51. Edelman, *Mirror of Life*, pp. 19–20.

52. As late as 1931, 2,000,000 out of 3,250,000 Jews in Poland lived in shtetlach, defined by Rachel Ertel as towns containing 3,000 to 30,000 people. See Ertel, *Le Shtetl*, p. 16. Even if one defined shtetlach as smaller villages, 23.6 percent of Jews still lived in them at this time. Mendelsohn, *Jews of East Central Europe*, p. 20.

53. Kugelmass and Boyarin, *Ruined Garden*, pp. 32, 78–79.

54. Morris Raphael Cohen, *Dreamer's Journey*, pp. 17–18.

55. Nirenberg, "Folksongs," p. 3.

56. Antin, *Promised Land*, p. 103.

57. Sholem Aleichem, *Great Fair*, p. 148.

58. Tcherikower, *Jewish Labor Movement*, p. 11.

59. Grade, *Agunah*.

60. Jewish *law* did not prohibit women from engaging in scholarly activity but custom frowned upon it. Rabbi Eliezer had said that whoever teaches his daughter Torah teaches her obscenity. Cited in Hyman, "Other Half," p. 112.

61. I. J. Singer, *World That Is No More*, pp. 15–17, 30–31.

62. Isaac Bashevis Singer, *In My Father's Court*, pp. 141, 151–52.

63. Zborowski and Herzog, *Life Is with People*, p. 134.

64. Beck, *Many Faces of Eve*, pp. 13, 16.

65. Sholem Aleichem, *Great Fair*, p. 53.

66. Kugelmass and Boyarin, *Ruined Garden*, p. 122.

67. Wisse, *Schlemiel*, p. 48.

68. The Siddur, the major prayer book, was also translated into Yiddish, and when women went to the shul, they recited the same prayers as the men, but relatively few attended. The content of women's prayers was analyzed by Weissler, in "Women's T'khina Literature."

69. Zborowski and Herzog, *Life Is with People*, p. 59, 130; Howe and Greenberg, *Treasury of Yiddish Stories*, p. 23.

70. Myerhoff, *Number Our Days*, pp. 243–44.

71. For example, see Peretz, "Devotion without End"; Beck, *Many Faces of Eve*, p. 16.

72. Zborowski and Herzog, *Life Is with People*, p. 18.

73. This was important to women in many societies where the female sphere was separate from, and ostensibly inferior to, the male. See, for example, Rosaldo, "Women, Culture and Society," p. 39; Chodorow, "Feminine Personality," p. 63; Wolf, "Chinese Women," p. 162.

74. This tended to be true of most women. See Bernard, *Female World*, p. 9.

75. For example, in Grade's memoir, a woman comes to ask his mother's advice because her husband has taken a girl friend. *Mother's Sabbath Days*, pp. 125–28.

76. I. J. Singer, *World That Is No More*, p. 99.

77. Myerhoff, *Number Our Days*, p. 263.

78. Grade, *Mother's Sabbath Days*, pp. 36–39.

79. Myerhoff, *Number Our Days*, pp. 234, 235.

80. Chagall, *Burning Lights*, pp. 84–86.

81. Myerhoff, *Number Our Days*, p. 256.

82. Aries, "Old World and the New," p. 33. Anthropologists observed that "as a consequence of their subordinate status [women] were less regulated than men and therefore . . . were able to partake in all activities that were not expressly forbidden them." See Mindel and Habenstein, *Ethnic Families in America*, p. 354.

83. *Proverbs* 30:10–31.

Chapter 2: Family Relations in the Shtetl

1. This was equally true for Jews in Germany before the late nineteenth century. See Kaplan, *Marriage Bargain*, pp. 121–63. In Poland, among the peasants, both young people were given dowries to cement the new relationship between their families. The boy's family gave land, and the girl's money. Thomas and Znaniecki, *Polish Peasant* 1:117.

2. Brayer, *Rabbinic Literature*, p. 59.

3. Morris Raphael Cohen, *Dreamer's Journey*, p. 12.

4. I. J. Singer, *World That Is No More*, p. 99.

5. Ibid., p. 108.

6. Jewish parents did not share the fatalism of Catholic parents to whom marriage was an indissoluble sacrament. For example, when an abusive Italian husband who had emigrated sent for his wife to come and cook and wash for men in the iron mines he worked in, her mother told her, "You must go. However bad that man is, he is your husband—he has the right to command you. It would be a sin against God not to obey." Ets, *Italian Immigrant*, p. 160.

7. Zborowski and Herzog, *Life Is with People*, p. 295. This was generally true of women in many countries. See Scott and Tilly, *Women, Work, and Family*, p. 139. In Southern Italy, women dealt with all the practical aspects of life. As one woman put it, "We do whatever no one else has done. That's what we're taught; that's what we're supposed to do. Men work and talk about politics. We do the rest. . . . We decide, but we don't have to talk about it in the Piazza. Call that power if you want to. To us it's just killing work" (Cornelisen, *Women of the Shadows*, pp. 219, 227).

8. Kramer and Mazur, *Jewish Grandmothers*, p. 62.

9. This was true among the Russian nobility as well, where mothers were more apt to spoil their sons and fathers their daughters. Tovrov, "Mother-Child Relationships," p. 22.

10. Landes and Zborowski, "Eastern European Jewish Family," pp. 31, 37.

11. Fischer, *Twentieth Century*, p. 10.

12. Ruth Adler, *Women of the Shtetl*, p. 116.

13. Chodorow, *Reproduction of Mothering*, p. 140.

14. Hammer, *Daughters and Mothers: Mothers and Daughters*, p. xiv.

15. This attitude transcended class and ethnic boundaries. Tovrov wrote of this relationship among the Russian nobility that "a mother's intense sense of responsibility for her daughter inhibited tenderness and spontaneity. Though it should be loving, the mother-daughter relationship was primarily task-oriented, devoted to the daughter's training" ("Russian Nobility," p. 32).

16. Brayer, *Rabbinic Literature*, p. 50.

17. Kramer and Mazur, *Jewish Grandmothers*, p. 63.

18. Ruth Adler, "'Real' Jewish Mother," p. 38.

19. Wiesel, *Beggar in Jerusalem*, p. 65.

20. This kind of relationship was reflected in many stories of Y. L. Peretz. See Ruth Adler, *Women of the Shtetl*, p. 79.

21. Chernin, *In My Mother's House*, pp. 110–11.

22. Kramer and Mazur, *Jewish Grandmothers*, p. 109.

23. Ruth Adler, *Women of the Shtetl*, pp. 87–89.

24. Reznikoff, "History of a Seamstress," p. 30.

25. Berg, "Childhood in Lithuania," p. 271.

26. Kramer and Mazur, *Jewish Grandmothers*, p. 79.

27. Antin, *Promised Land*, p. 99.

28. I. J. Singer, *World That Is No More*, pp. 140–41.

29. Chagall, *Burning Lights*, p. 114.

30. Zborowski and Herzog, *Life Is with People*, p. 348.

31. Simon, *Bronx Primitive*, p. 21.

32. In one area of Eastern Europe, there was a ceremony called *Holocosh* marking the birth of girls. For this information I am indebted to Beatrice Silverman Weinreich.

33. Cited from Weissler, "Women's T'khina Literature."

34. Zborowski and Herzog, *Life Is with People*, pp. 308–9.

35. Zunser, *Yesterday*, pp. 56, 75.

36. Yezierska, *Bread Givers*, p. 9.

37. Lang, *Tomorrow Is Beautiful*, p. 5.

38. I. J. Singer, *World That Is No More*, pp. 141–42.

39. Ibid., p. 202.

40. Zborowski and Herzog, *Life Is with People*, p. 310; Zunser, *Yesterday*, p. 75.

41. See, for example, Landes and Zborowski, "Eastern European Family," p. 31.

42. Kramer and Mazur, *Jewish Grandmothers*, p. 144.

43. Isaac Bashevis Singer, *My Father's Court*, p. 83.

44. Antin, *Promised Land*, p. 34.

45. Kahan, Unpublished manuscript diary (June 12, 1915), p. 108.

46. E. P. Thompson, *English Working Class*, pp. 332–33.

47. Reznikoff, "History of a Seamstress," pp. 24–25; Saroff, *Stealing the State*, p. 4; Farber, "Reminiscences," Immigrant Labor History Project.

48. See, for example, Asch, *Mother*, pp. 9–10, or Kazin, *Walker in the City*, pp. 66–67.

49. Kramer and Mazur, *Jewish Grandmothers*, pp. 24–25.

50. YIVO Manuscript Autobiographies nos. 266 and 293.

51. Saroff, *Stealing the State*, p. 3.

52. YIVO Manuscript Autobiography no. 266.

53. Nirenberg, "Folksongs," p. 3.

54. Simon, *Bronx Primitive*, p. 21.

55. Sholem Aleichem, *Great Fair*, p. 225.

56. Byer, *Transplanted People*, p. 23.

57. Rosenthal, "Deviation and Social Change." The most traditional families were less likely to emigrate. As a result, the women I interviewed tended to come from the somewhat less religious families.

Chapter 3: Changing Times

1. Kahan, "Diary of Anne Kahan" (February 27, 1915), p. 170.

2. For reasons, see Baron, *Jew under Tsars and Soviets*, pp. 44–45; Rischin, *Promised City*, pp. 23–31; Abramovitch, "Rural Jewish Occupations," pp. 220–21.

3. Tcherikower, *Jewish Labor Movement*, pp. 22, 13.

4. Baron, *Jew under Tsars and Soviets*, p. 84.

5. After the dismemberment of Poland in the late eighteenth century, Russia confined

the Jews it had inherited along with its new territory to these twelve western provinces of Russia. After the Congress of Vienna in 1815, Russia also gained control of that part of Poland that had previously been absorbed by Prussia, hence the name Congress Poland. By the late nineteenth century, half the world's Jewish population lived in the crowded cities of the Pale.

6. Dubnow, *Jews in Russia and Poland*, 2:157.

7. Joseph, *Jewish Immigration*, pp. 73–74.

8. Kaplan, *Jewish Feminist Movement*, p. 119.

9. In 1897, the Russian census indicated that 40 percent of all Jews lived in towns of 100,000 or less. See Tcherikower, *Jewish Labor Movement*, p. 73.

10. Baron, *Jew under Tsars and Soviets*, p. 112.

11. Zunser, *Yesterday*, pp. 14–15.

12. In 1911, 200,797 Jewish children attended Jewish schools in Russia and Poland, while 126,976 attended general schools, as opposed to 29,526 in such secular schools in 1886. See Baron, *Jew under Tsars and Soviets*, p. 118.

13. Sometimes young men studied in a state school, sometimes in a secular Jewish school. See Ain, "Swislocz," pp. 88–95.

14. See, for example, Covello, *Heart Is the Teacher*, p. 16, on the situation of Italian girls.

15. Baum, Hyman, and Michel, *Jewish Woman in America*, p. 61.

16. Berg, "Childhood in Lithuania," p. 271.

17. In 1899, only 36.8 percent of Russian Jewish women were literate. See Kuznets, "Immigration of Russian Jews," pp. 113–14.

18. Antin, *Promised Land*, p. 111.

19. Ayalti, *Yiddish Proverbs*, p. 95.

20. Engel, *Women of the Intelligentsia*, p. 105.

21. Ibid., pp. 158–59.

22. Ibid., pp. 51–52.

23. Zunser, *Yesterday*, p. 75.

24. Kahan, "Diary of Anne Kahan" (May 30, 1915), p. 190.

25. Saroff, *Stealing the State*, p. 3.

26. Schneiderman, *All for One*, p. 11.

27. Antin, *Promised Land*, p. 75.

28. Saroff, *Stealing the State*, p. 5.

29. In 1897, 29 percent of Jewish women were literate, as opposed to 49.4 percent of the males. Still, this was higher than the Russian rate of 29.3 percent for males and 13.1 percent for females. Rubinow, "Jews in Russia," pp. 576–77.

30. Byer, *Transplanted People*, pp. 21–22.

31. Kahan, "Diary of Anne Kahan" (May 30, 1915), p. 190.

32. Antin, *Promised Land*, p. 34.

33. Reznikoff, "History of a Seamstress," pp. 23–24.

34. Kugelmass and Boyarin, *Ruined Garden*, p. 44.

35. I. J. Singer, *World That Is No More*, p. 118.

36. Zborowski and Herzog, *Life Is with People*, p. 372.

37. A booth constructed for the harvest festival of Sukkoth, in which family members eat their meals for the duration of the holiday.

38. Chagall, *Burning Lights*, p. 103.

39. By 1897, younger women were considerably more literate than the previous generation: 44 percent of women from ten to twenty-nine years old could read, while fewer than 23 percent of women between forty and fifty-nine were literate. Among other reasons, the mass movement into the larger towns gave them more access to schools. See Rubinow, "Jews in Russia," pp. 576–77.

40. Kahan, "Diary of Anne Kahan" (May 30, 1915), p. 191.

41. Reznikoff, "History of a Seamstress," p. 28.

42. Antin, *Promised Land*, pp. 26–27.

43. Ruth Rubin, *Voices of a People*, pp. 78–79.

44. Roskies, "Yiddish Popular Literature," pp. 853, 856.

45. Ain, "Swislocz," pp. 67–68.

46. For reasons, see Rosenthal, "Deviation and Social Change," pp. 178, 180. Paradoxically, marriage for love was also becoming more acceptable among the Russian aristocracy. See Tovrov, "Mother-Daughter Relationships," p. 20. This transition was probably taking place in other countries as well as among the poor. For example, on Italian peasants, see Miriam Cohen, "Workshop to Office," pp. 45–47.

47. Zunser, *Yesterday*, pp. 82–83.

48. This was true of girls in German Jewish families as well. See Kaplan, *Marriage Bargain*, pp. 121–22.

49. Kramer and Mazur, *Jewish Grandmothers*, p. 23.

50. Reznikoff, "History of a Seamstress," pp. 60–67.

51. See Sholem Aleichem, *Tevye Stories*.

52. Brayer, *Rabbinic Literature*, p. 59.

53. Oral history is from collection of James P. Shenton.

54. This was true among workers in the new factories in other countries as well. See Kaplan, *Marriage Bargain*, p. 151.

55. Reznikoff, "History of a Seamstress," pp. 34–35.

56. Chagall, *Burning Lights*, pp. 197, 203.

57. Kahan, Unpublished manuscript diary (September 4, 1915), p. 185.

58. The idea of romantic love was a familiar theme in nineteenth-century German literature. See Robertson, *Experience of Women*, pp. 71–72. Such books were read in secularized, liberal Jewish families where a knowledge of German was considered a hallmark of education.

59. Kramer and Mazur, *Jewish Grandmothers*, pp. 144, 108.

60. This was generally true in middle-class families throughout Europe in the nineteenth century. See Robertson, *Experience of Women*, p. 15, chap. 7.

61. Kahan, "Diary of Anne Kahan" (February 27, 1915), p. 170.

62. Joseph, *Jewish Immigration*, pp. 42, 43, 45.

63. For the economic condition, see Rubinow, "Jews in Russia," p. 572; Tcherikower, *Jewish Labor Movement*, p. 73; Baron, *Jew under Tsars and Soviets*, pp. 94–95.

64. Women and children were most likely to work in the poorest areas. Thus, their labor was 42.4 percent of the work force in northwest Russia, but only 20.2 percent in the south. Women and girls alone comprised 17.7 percent of the total. See Rubinow, "Jews in Russia," pp. 546, 524.

65. These were the occupations of more than 80 percent of all women workers reporting occupations. Ibid., p. 525; Glanz, *Eastern European Jewish Woman*, p. 17.

66. Baron, *Jew under Tsars and Soviets*, p. 97.

67. Rischin, *Promised City*, p. 27; Baum, Hyman, and Michel, *Jewish Woman in America*, p. 74.

68. Reznikoff, "History of a Seamstress," p. 39.

69. Brier, "Reminiscences," Immigrant Labor History Project.

70. Women generally earned about half the wages of men doing similar work, and sometimes less. At a time when a normal Jewish family's yearly budget was estimated at 300 rubles, women working in the typical tobacco factories of Vilna or the wool factories of Bialystok earned from 1½ to 2½ rubles a week, or 78 to 130 rubles a year. Hours for a seamstress could range from fourteen to eighteen a day, particularly in the busy season. See Rubinow, "Jews in Russia," pp. 546–48, 526–27, 529–33.

71. On this point, see E. P. Thompson, *English Working Class*, p. 414.

72. Byer, *Transplanted People*, p. 52.

73. Chernin, *In My Mother's House*, p. 29.

74. This was the attitude of middle-class Jews, but it was also becoming a goal of working-class women throughout Western Europe as well. See Roberts, *Woman's Place*, p. 52.

75. Baum, Hyman, and Michel, *Jewish Woman in America*, p. 78; Rischin, *Promised City*, p. 45.

76. Lapidus, *Women in Soviet Society*, pp. 37–38.

77. Between June 1903 and June 1904, the Bund won 87 percent of the 109 strikes it called. Sometimes results were dramatic, as when female bakers won a reduction in their work day from nineteen to twelve hours. See Rubinow, "Jews in Russia," pp. 549–51.

78. Kramer and Mazur, *Jewish Grandmothers*, p. 82.

79. This was not the more famous labor leader. See Rose Cohen, "Reminiscences," Immigrant Labor History Project.

80. Farber, "Reminiscences," Immigrant Labor History Project.

81. Ain, "Swislocz," pp. 95–100.

82. Kramer and Mazur, *Jewish Grandmothers*, p. 126.

83. Fischer, *Twentieth Century*, p. 12.

84. Kahan, "Diary of Anne Kahan" (January 14, 1915), pp. 153–54.

85. Plotkin, *Full-Time Active*, p. 5.

86. Saroff, *Stealing the State*, p. 8.

87. Kramer and Mazur, *Jewish Grandmothers*, p. 127.

88. Altman, "Reminiscences," Immigrant Labor History Project.

89. Bristow, *Prostitution and Prejudice*, p. 93.

90. In the Russian Census of 1897, 200,000 Jews, or about 3 percent, claimed Russian rather than Yiddish as their native tongue and thus constituted a second generation of assimilated Jews. See Rubinow, "Jews in Russia," pp. 576–77; Kuznets, "Immigration of Russian Jews," p. 69.

91. Cited in Dawidowicz, *Golden Tradition*, p. 168.

92. Ibid., p. 124. Lilienblum lived from 1843 to 1910.

93. Kahan, "Diary of Anne Kahan" (May 8, 1915), p. 182. No work was supposed to be performed on the Sabbath, so cooking was forbidden.

94. Lang, *Tomorrow Is Beautiful*, p. 9.

95. Gogomil Golitz, cited in Lazarus, *Jewish Woman*, p. 248.

96. Rosenthal, "Deviation and Social Change," pp. 178–80.

97. YIVO Manuscript Autobiography no. 92.

98. Baron, *Jew under Tsars and Soviets*, p. 159.

99. German policy was to exploit the local population to feed not only soldiers, but the German homeland as well. See Baron, *Jew under Tsars and Soviets*, p. 160.

100. Kahan, Unpublished manuscript diary (July 29, 1915), p. 141.

101. Kramer and Mazur, *Jewish Grandmothers*, pp. 36–37.

102. Harris, "Reminiscences," Immigrant Labor History Project.

103. Lang, *Tomorrow Is Beautiful*, p. 12.

104. Simon, *Bronx Primitive*, p. 18.

105. Studies indicate that this process of increased self-reliance also took place in America during World War II when women had to take their first jobs. See, for example, Campbell, *Women at War with America*, p. 212; Gluck, "Interlude or Change."

106. Kramer and Mazur, *Jewish Grandmothers*, pp. 92–93.

107. Kahan, "Diary of Anne Kahan" (January 27, 1915), p. 160.

Chapter 4: Leaving Home

1. Kahan, "Diary of Anne Kahan" (February 5, 1915), p. 164.

2. For example, during November 1918 through January 1919, pogroms and anti-Jewish excesses were committed in one hundred towns and villages. See Heller, *Edge of Destruction*, p. 50.

3. Morris Raphael Cohen, *Dreamer's Journey*, pp. 23–24.

4. Bloom, "Saga of America's Russian Jews," p. 5.

5. Saroff, *Stealing the State*, p. 10.

6. Kramer and Mazur, *Jewish Grandmothers*, pp. 50–55.

7. Only one-twentieth of the Jews of Russia lived outside the Pale. See Rischin, *Promised City*, pp. 23–24.

8. Seven percent of the Eastern European Jews emigrated to other destinations, mostly in Latin America.

9. After 1890, most families were able to emigrate together because some members had gone over before and saved money. Between 1899 and 1903, only 12.9 percent of Jewish heads of family entering Ellis Island had thirty dollars or more, less than the average sum for most immigrants. See Tcherikower, *Jewish Labor Movement*, p. 143.

10. Schneiderman, *All for One*, p. 11.

11. Schlissel, *Women's Diaries*, pp. 28–30.

12. Jastrow, *Looking Back*, p. 28.

13. Cited in Brownstone, Franck and Brownstone, *Island of Hope*, p. 79.

14. Hyman, "Reminiscences," Immigrant Labor History Project.

15. Kahan, "Diary of Anne Kahan" (February 5, June 27, 1915), pp. 164, 205.

16. Ibid., pp. 368–69.

17. Hasanovitz, *One of Them*, pp. 9–11.

18. A Woman's Bureau survey of the time suggests that this was a frequently mentioned reason given by women of different ethnic groups for coming to America. See Smith, "Remaking Their Lives," p. 135.

19. Ruth Rubin, *Voices of a People*, p. 84.

20. Reznikoff, "History of a Seamstress," pp. 60–67.

21. Pesotta, *Bread upon the Waters*, p. 9.

22. Edelman, *Mirror of Life*, pp. 22–23.

23. Byer, *Transplanted People*, pp. 52–53.

24. We do not know how many young women came alone because immigration statistics did not clarify whether they traveled by themselves or as part of a family.

25. Kuznets, "Immigration of Russian Jews," p. 93.

26. Six hundred thousand left in the last two decades of the nineteenth century, and 1,800,000 in the first two decades of the twentieth, with 95 percent of these Jews emigrating from Eastern Europe. See Karp, *Golden Door to America*, pp. 14, 15. Seventy-five to 80 percent of the emigrants went to the United States, 10 percent to Europe, 10 to 15 percent to Asia, Palestine, and South Africa. See Kuznets, "Immigration of Russian Jews," p. 48.

27. Between 1908 and 1925, remigration rates exceeded 50 percent for Rumanians, Magyars, Italians, Russians, and Poles. For Jews, it was 5 percent. Ibid., p. 15.

28. Wischnitzer, *To Dwell in Safety*, pp. 100–120.

29. In the period between 1899 and 1910, 56.6 percent of Jewish emigrants were male, 43.4 percent female. See Joseph, *Jewish Immigration*, pp. 128–29, and Karp, *Golden Door to America*, p. 15 for statistics. The rate of Irish women had exceeded that of Irish men, but they came as older, single people; only 5 percent were children. For an explanation of Irish immigration statistics, see Diner, *Erin's Daughters in America*, p. 31.

30. Forty-five percent of Jews reported having no occupation. See Joseph, *Jewish Immigration*, p. 141.

31. Other groups averaged 12.3 percent children. Ibid., pp. 128–29, 156.

32. Each Jewish worker had to support 1.8 persons, non-Jews 1.3 persons. See Kuznets, "Immigration of Russian Jews," p. 100.

33. See Joseph, *Jewish Immigration*, pp. 146–48, 192–94. The overall Jewish rate of illiteracy among immigrants between 1908 and 1912 was 26.7 percent, slightly above the general immigrant average of 26 percent. The rate for males fourteen and over was 19.7 percent, as opposed to 36.8 for females in the same age group. The older a woman was, the less likely she was to read and write; in Russia, among men and women sixty years old and older in 1897, 54.3 percent of men were literate, and only 14.9 percent of the women. However, the rate of Jewish literacy was greater than that of the people Jews lived amidst. Among those over twenty living in the Pale in 1897, 49.6 percent of the Jews and 24.4 percent of the non-Jews were literate. For immigrants entering the United States, the following rates of illiteracy were recorded: for Poles, 35.4 percent; for Lithuanians, 48.9 percent; for Russians, 38.4 percent; and for Ruthenians, 63.4 percent. Ibid. See also Rubinow, *Jews in Russia*, pp. 577, 579; and Kuznets, "Immigration of Russian Jews," pp. 80, 81.

34. Rose Cohen, *Out of the Shadow*, p. 160.

35. Because of malnutrition and overcrowding in urban centers, the death rate among Jews from typhoid jumped in Vilna, for example, from 20.4 for 1,000 inhabitants in 1914 to 68.2 in 1917.

36. The bandits were a well-known group called the *Balachowicz*. See Kramer and Mazur, *Jewish Grandmothers*, p. 159.

37. Rose Cohen, *Out of the Shadow*, p. 56.

38. Liebman, "Religion of American Jews," p. 234.

39. Weinberger, *People Walk*, pp. 5–6.

40. Rose Cohen, *Out of the Shadow*, p. 79.

41. Weinberger, *People Walk*, p. 78.

42. Bristow, *Prostitution and Prejudice*, pp. 25, 97, 137.

43. Kaplan, *Jewish Feminist Movement*, pp. 108, 111.

44. For several such warning songs, see Ruth Rubin, *Voices of a People*, pp. 334–35.

45. Because steamship lines had to transport back to Europe, at their own expense, those immigrants who failed any of the examinations at Ellis Island, they set up their own examination centers at European ports to make sure that only those healthy enough to pass would be permitted to travel on their ships.

46. Antin, *Promised Land*, pp. 174–75.

Chapter 5: Reunions and New Beginnings

1. Cahan, "Yekl," in *Imported Bridegroom*.

2. Sanders, *The Downtown Jews*, pp. 356–59.

3. Hapgood, *Spirit of the Ghetto*, pp. 80–81.

4. Cited in Schwartz, "Immigrant Voices," p. 352.

5. Rose Cohen, *Out of the Shadow*, pp. 69, 78.

6. Chernin, *In My Mother's House*, p. 37.

7. Friedman, "'Send Me My Husband,'" p. 6.

8. In an abstract of the census of 1905, 96.6 percent of all Jews on the Lower East Side lived in households with a nuclear kin-related core. See Gutman, *Work, Culture, and Society*, p. 77.

9. See, for example, Schwartz, "Immigrant Voices," p. 577.

10. This transition took place in Jewish immigrant communities in England as well. See, for example, Burman, "Jewish Women in Religious Life."

11. Howe, *Margin of Hope*, pp. 4–5.

12. Boarders played an important role in family dislocation. The most common reason for a wife's desertion was involvement with another man, usually a boarder. See Friedman, "'Send Me My Husband,'" pp. 4, 6.

13. For such examples of Bintel Brief letters, see Howe and Libo, *How We Lived*, pp. 88–90; Karp, *Golden Door to America*, pp. 143–47; Metzker, *Bintel Brief*, pp. 32–33, 104, 106, 162–63; Glanz, *Eastern European Jewish Woman*, p. 70.

14. Cahan cited in Howe and Libo, *How We Lived*, p. 99.

15. Morris Raphael Cohen, *Dreamer's Journey*, pp. 68–69; Silberman, *Certain People*, p. 73; Tcherikower, *Jewish Labor Movement*, p. 135.

16. Bressler, "Study of the Bintel Brief," pp. 565–68. Although some of the Bintel Brief letters were actually written by the editor, Abraham Cahan, the issues reflected the concerns of the immigrant community. Quotation by Israel Friedlander in *Survey* magazine, cited in Elizabeth Ewen, "Land of Dollars, 1890–1920," p. 97.

17. Lederhendler, "Jewish Immigration to America."

18. Rischin, *Promised City*, p. 79.

19. Cited in Howe, *World of Our Fathers*, p. 72.

20. Cahan, *Rise of David Levinsky*, p. 95.

21. Hasanovitz, *One of Them*, p. 310.

22. Rose Cohen, *Out of the Shadow*, p. 73.

23. Liebman, "Religion, Class, and Culture," p. 231.

24. Rischin, *Promised City*, pp. 146–47.

25. Cited in Schwartz, "Immigrant Voices," p. 578. See also Tentler, *Wage-Earning Women*, pp. 87–88. In a 1925 Philadelphia Survey, only 11 percent of women interviewed worked because they wanted to. For most, it was necessary for survival. Stuart Ewen, *Captains of Consciousness*, p. 123.

26. This disruption was a common theme in immigrant memoirs. See Howe, *World of Our Fathers*, p. 74.

27. For living conditions, see Rischin, *Promised City*, pp. 86–88.

28. Kramer and Mazur, *Jewish Grandmothers*, p. 129.

29. Rosen, *Maimie Papers*, p. 4.

30. Tcherikower, *Jewish Labor Movement*, p. 117.

31. Joselit, *Our Gang*, pp. 15, 46, 48.

32. Wald, *House on Henry Street*, p. 225.

33. Mensch, "Social Pathology."

34. Rosen, *Maimie Papers*, p. 193.

35. Simon, *Bronx Primitive*, pp. 110–11.

36. Ruskay, *Horsecars and Cobblestones*, p. 44.

37. Melech Epstein, *Jewish Labor*, pp. 104–5.

38. Oral histories are from collection of James P. Shenton.

39. For example, Liebman asserts that most Jews who left Eastern Europe were the least rooted in the textual religious tradition, and that they generally associated religion with the cultural life-style of Eastern Europe and did not differentiate between religion and culture. See "Religion, Class, and Culture," pp. 229–30. As early as the 1890s, a contemporary observer noted that "the observances of the faith are so entwined with the everyday atmosphere of the home as to make the Jewish religion and the family life one, a bond in sanctity. In this sense, the synagogue is the home, and the home the synagogue" (Mary M. Cohen, "Jewish Religion in the Home," p. 116).

40. Weinberger, *People Walk*, pp. 20, 123.

41. Carolyn Ware, *Greenwich Village*, p. 225.

42. Morris Raphael Cohen, *Dreamer's Journey*, p. 67.

43. Ibid., p. 232.

44. Two-thirds of New York's Jewish families bought kosher meat. See Silberman, *Certain People*, p. 173.

45. Rose Cohen, *Out of the Shadow*, p. 106.

46. YIVO Manuscript Autobiography no. 92.

47. As early as 1899, Abraham Cahan commented on the "fashion" of even working men's sending their wives and children to farms in Greene or Ulster counties. See Rischin, *Grandma Never Lived*, pp. 270–72.

48. Gurock, *When Harlem Was Jewish*, pp. 36, 43.

49. Ibid.

50. Fischer, *Twentieth Century*, p. 14.

51. Rose Cohen, *Out of the Shadow*, p. 151.

52. Abrams, "Reminiscences," Immigrant Labor History Project.

53. Ruth Rubin, *Voices of a People*, pp. 346–47.

54. Yezierska, *Hungry Hearts*, p. 56.

55. As early as 1902, Abraham Cahan wrote of the spirit among the standing room ticket holders. See Rischin, *Grandma Never Lived*, pp. 316–18.

56. Peiss, *Cheap Amusements*, p. 89.

57. Ibid., p. 15.

58. Even among teenage children who emigrated as part of a family group, these young people formed their own groups with interests different from those of their parents. This was true in many other immigrant groups as well. See, for example, Thomas and Znaniecki, *Polish Peasant*, p. 77.

59. See Tentler, *Wage-Earning Women*, pp. 33, 64–65.

60. Kramer and Mazur, *Jewish Grandmothers*, p. 12.

61. Hasanovitz, *One of Them*, p. 24.

62. Peiss, *Cheap Amusements*, p. 60.

63. Fischer, *Twentieth Century*, p. 17.

64. Cited in Mitchell, *Mishpokhe*, p. 35.

65. On this point, see Smith, *Family Connections*, p. 143.

66. Glanz, *Eastern European Jewish Woman*, p. 86. Women generally were not accepted as members, but insisted on the formation of ladies' auxiliaries. *Landsmanshaftn* appealed primarily to the less sophisticated Jews from the shtetls rather than the larger towns of Eastern Europe, who wanted to retain many of their old world traditions and beliefs. As many as one million out of the two million Jewish immigrants at some time belonged to one of these local organizations. See Weisser, *Brotherhood of Memory*, pp. 4, 82, 65–66, 248–77.

67. Ibid., pp. 19, 20–30, 80.

68. Smith, "Remaking Their Lives," p. 151.

69. Mitchell, *Mishpokhe*, pp. 156–57, 172–73.

Chapter 6: Becoming Americans

1. Historians of the family have noted that an important determinant of relations is the difference between the life course of the family and those of individual members. See, for example, Elder, "Family History and the Life Course," p. 300.

2. This was true of Jewish families who emigrated to England as well. See Burman, "Jewish Woman as Breadwinner," p. 33.

3. Cahan, *Rise of David Levinsky*, p. 97.

4. In Pittsburgh, a study indicates that among immigrant families Jews also had the lowest rate of speaking their European languages in the home. Krause, *Grandmothers, Mothers, and Daughters*, p. 29.

5. Cited in Seller, "'Women's Interests' Page.'"

6. Reznikoff, "History of a Seamstress," p. 98.

7. Cahan, *Imported Bridegroom*, p. 42.

8. Cited in Glanz, *Eastern European Jewish Woman*, pp. 104–5.

9. Ibid., p. 104.

10. Rose Cohen, *Out of the Shadow*, p. 153.

11. John Higham observed, "If the immigrant were a woman, shut up in the home, and condemned to learn a new language and new ways from her children while pledging her own happiness to them, the strains of assimilation might become tragically intense" (*Send These to Me*, p. 92).

12. Cahan, *Imported Bridegroom*, pp. 37, 57.

13. Kramer and Mazur, *Jewish Grandmothers*, p. 130.

14. Antin, *Promised Land*, pp. 246–47.

15. Jastrow, *Looking Back*, pp. 37–38, 167, 171; *Time to Remember*, p. 134.

16. This was also true of immigrant women in other ethnic groups. See Krause, "Urbanization without Breakdown," pp. 293–94.

17. Yezierska, *Hungry Hearts*, pp. 198–99.

18. Kramer and Mazur, *Jewish Grandmothers*, p. 98.

19. Cahan, *Rise of David Levinsky*, pp. 242–43, 254–55.

20. During the earlier period of immigration, ending about 1890, the Baron de Hirsch Fund census of the Lower East Side indicated that fewer than a third of heads of households spoke English. Cited in Riis, "Children of the Poor," p. 102.

21. Only 14 percent of the first generation of Jewish men were not involved in Jewish community affairs, which Mindel and Habenstein consider as one index of orthodoxy. See *Ethnic Families in America*, pp. 258–59.

22. Glanz, *Eastern European Jewish Woman*, p. 16.

23. Simon, *Wider World*, p. 109.

24. Cited in Brownstone, Franck, and Brownstone, *Island of Hope*, p. 265.

25. Weinberger, *People Walk*, p. 20.

26. Feingold, *Zion in America*, p. 138. In Chicago in 1911, the third largest immigrant group represented in cases of wife or child abuse were Russians (behind Germans and Irish). See Pleck, "Challenges to Traditional Authority," p. 504. Still, one should not make too much of the relatively high divorce rate of Jews, for the other major New York ethnic groups—Italians, Germans, and Irish—were almost all Catholic.

27. Friedman, "'Send Me My Husband,'" p. 4.

28. Mensch, "Social Pathology."

29. In one reformatory, 14.5 percent of the Jewish prostitutes interviewed claimed to have been forced into prostitution after the desertion of their husbands. Friedman, "'Send Me My Husband,'" pp. 1, 7.

30. Bernard Cohen, *Sociocultural Changes*, pp. 91–92.

31. Berrol, "Public Schools and Immigrants," p. 39. This attitude contrasted with that of Italian families who opposed the Americanization of their children. Leonard Covello wrote, "The child finds himself in two cultural worlds and friction is unavoidable if he is compelled to participate in both cultures. He is not happy in either of them; for at home he is constantly reprimanded for adopting American manners, tastes and conduct" (Covello, *Heart is the Teacher*, p. 336).

32. Kessner, *Golden Door*, p. 204. Among newly arrived Jewish families, 33 percent spoke English in the home as opposed to 22 percent of Italians. After ten years, 46 percent of Jews as opposed to 35 percent of Italians had adopted English.

33. Silberman, *Certain People*, chap. 2 passim.

34. Cited in Brumberg, *Going to School*, p. 7.

35. Berrol, "Public Schools and Immigrants," p. 37.

36. Karp, *Eastern European Jewish Woman*, pp. 65–66.

37. Kimberg, "Reminiscences," Immigrant Labor History Project.

38. Some educators believed that children must be explicitly shorn of their ethnic background if they were to become proper Americans. See, for example, Weiss, *American Education*, p. xiii; Ravitch, *Great School Wars*, p. 176.

39. Moore, *Home in America*, pp. 90–91.

40. Cited in Brumberg, *Going to School*, pp. 76–77, 127–28.

41. This is still true of the children of Russian Jewish immigrants, although their

situation is quite different. For example, Rina Scharfstein, the ten-year-old daughter of two engineers, refuses to eat Russian food or read books in her native language and insists that she has forgotten Russia. She takes pride in the fact that people can't tell she is Russian-born. "They treat me like a normal person," she said with obvious pride. *The New York Times*, July 4, 1986, p. 18.

42. Riis, "Children of the Poor," pp. 112–13.

43. Kazin, *Walker in the City*, p. 22.

44. Covello, *Heart Is the Teacher*, p. 44.

45. What went on in the schools was therefore a mystery to most parents. See Brumberg, *Going to School*, p. 136.

46. For the rift between parents and children, see Melech Epstein, *Jewish Labor*, p. 355. This tension between the traditional attitudes of parents and the individualistic ideals of children raised in America existed among most immigrant groups. See, for example, Thomas and Znaniecki, *Polish Peasant*, pp. 78–79.

47. Antin, *Promised Land*, pp. 270–71.

48. Cited in Elizabeth Ewen, "Immigrant Women in the Land of Dollars," p. 107.

49. Rischin, *Promised City*, p. 145.

50. Schneiderman, *All for One*, p. 35.

51. Blau, "Strategy of the Jewish Mother," p. 176.

52. Rose Cohen, *Out of the Shadow*, p. 254.

53. Burko, "American Yiddish Theater," pp. 92–93.

54. Steinberg, "Jewish Education," pp. 8–9; Rudavsky, "Jewish School Organization"; Moore, "Jewish Ethnicity and Acculturation in the 1920's," p. 100.

55. Ninety percent of Jewish women immigrants older than fourteen learned English, as opposed to 34.7 percent of women in other ethnic groups. See Manning, *Immigrant Woman*, p. 28.

56. Yezierska, *Bread Givers*, p. 156. See also Tentler, *Wage-Earning Women*, pp. 67–72.

57. See, for example, Eisenstein, *Give Us Bread*, p. 52.

58. See Ewen and Ewen, *Channels of Desire*, pp. 86–97. In 1919, New York had over 340 movie houses, and working-class families spent twice as much attending them as the middle class. Stuart Ewen, *Captains of Consciousness*, p. 146.

59. Ewen and Ewen, *Channels of Desire*, pp. 99–102.

60. Yezierska, *Hungry Hearts*, p. 132.

61. Peiss, *Cheap Amusements*, pp. 31, 186.

62. Ewen and Ewen, *Channels of Desire*, p. 214.

63. Antin, *Promised Land*, p. 321.

64. Morton, *I Am a Woman*, p. 16.

65. Elizabeth Ewen, "City Lights," pp. S49–50; Elizabeth Ewen, "Land of Dollars: 1900 1920," pp. 106 07; Schwartz, "Immigrant Voices," p. 696.

66. Yezierska, *Bread Givers*, pp. 172, 206.

67. Michel, "Rotted Cord." Michel pointed out that immigrant mothers were unable to provide their daughters with role models here, but she assumed that what was true in youth was equally valid throughout women's lives (p. 275).

68. Rose Cohen, *Out of the Shadow*, pp. 260–73.

69. Yezierska, *Children of Loneliness*, p. 122.

70. Cited in Howe and Libo, *How We Lived*, p. 139.

71. Cited in Silberman, *Certain People*, p. 174.

72. This was a common problem in immigrant families among sons and daughters. See, for example, Covello, *Heart Is the Teacher*, p. 31.

73. Kramer and Mazur, *Jewish Grandmothers*, p. 131.

74. Yezierska, *Hungry Hearts*, pp. 208–9.

75. Yezierska, "The Fat of the Land," in *The Open Cage*, pp. 208–9; Hasanovitz, *One of Them*, p. 81.

76. On the importance of the department store to immigrant girls, see Leach, "Culture of Consumption," p. 335.

77. Michel, "Rotted Cord," p. 278. Feminist psychoanalytic theory supports the theory that the nature of the mother-daughter relationship differs from the bond between mother and son in that girls identify for a longer time with a mother, while boys fairly early perceive themselves as being different. Thus, they would feel less threatened by a mother's personality traits. See Chodorow, *Reproduction of Mothering*, pp. 97, 109.

78. Herberg, *Protestant, Catholic, Jew*, p. 30.

79. Yezierska, *Children of Loneliness*, p. 122; Hasanovitz, *One of Them*, p. 67.

80. Yezierska, *All I Could Never Be*, p. 194.

81. Yezierska, *Children of Loneliness*, p. 122.

82. Cited in Yezierska, *Red Ribbon on a White Horse*, p. 72.

83. See, for example, Liebman, "Religion, Class and Culture."

84. Jastrow, *Looking Back*, pp. 117–20.

85. Morton, *I Am a Woman*, p. 76.

86. Some of these books are Yezierska's *Bread Givers*, Asch's *Mother*, and Raphaelson's *Jazz Singer*. See Bienstock, "Changing Image," pp. 176–77.

87. On this point, see Weisser, *Brotherhood of Memory*, p. 274.

88. Glanz, *Eastern European Jewish Woman*, p. 58.

Chapter 7: Mothers, Fathers, and Daughters

1. Elizabeth Ewen, *Land of Dollars: Life and Culture*, pp. 126–27.

2. Gutman, *Work, Culture, and Society*, p. 63; Hyman, "Consumer Protest." In 1910, women in Providence also banded together and forced Kosher meat dealers to lower the price of beef. See Smith, "Remaking Their Lives," pp. 227–28, and *Family Connections*, pp. 156–57.

3. Kessler-Harris, *Out to Work*, p. 126.

4. YIVO Manuscript Autobiography no. 92.

5. See Kessler-Harris, "Organizing the Unorganizable," p. 147.

6. Simon, *Bronx Primitive*, p. 48.

7. Smith, "Italian Mothers, American Daughters," p. 217.

8. Kazin, *Walker in the City*, pp. 55–57.

9. Bressler, "Study of the Bintel Brief," pp. 569–70.

10. Ruskay, *Horsecars and Cobblestones*, p. 73.

11. For a survey of these attitudes in novels, see Bernard Cohen, *Sociocultural Changes*, pp. 116–17.

12. Byer, *Transplanted People*, pp. 86–87.

13. Simon, *Wider World*, p. 71.

14. For the types of relationships in families, see Manser and Brown, "Household Decisions," p. 5.

15. Corinne Azen Krause discussed this mechanism in her paper on Italian, Jewish, and Slavic women at the "Conference on Cultural Diversity among American Families," in Washington, D.C., in February 1978.

16. This was a typical relationship. Although the father always had the final word, "he might be advised, coached or opposed in private" by his wife. See Schlesinger, *Jewish Family*, p. 11.

17. WPA interview, cited in Schwartz, "Immigrant Voices," pp. 586–87.

18. On this point in Italian immigrant families, see Miriam Cohen, "Workshop to Office," p. 52; and Covello, *Heart Is the Teacher*, p. 210.

19. Myerhoff, *Number Our Days*, p. 247. Myerhoff used this term to describe the relationship between men and women in the governance of a senior citizens' center. The men held the important leadership positions, while women did all the work and kept things running.

20. For a description of the various types of social power exercised by husbands, see Wandersee, *Women's Work*, pp. 108–9.

21. For an explanation of such decision making, see Lamphere, "Strategies," pp. 99–100.

22. Jastrow, *Time to Remember*, p. 79.

23. Elizabeth Ewen, "City Lights," pp. 85–86.

24. Lerner, "American Feminism," p. 9.

25. See, for example, *Breadgivers*.

26. YIVO Manuscript Autobiography, cited in Kessler-Harris, *Out to Work*, p. 127.

27. Rose Cohen, *Out of the Shadow*, pp. 94–95.

28. This was true of Jewish women in Providence, Rhode Island as well. See Smith, *Family Connections*, p. 50.

29. Irving Howe, for example, wrote that "for the Jewish wife, the transition seems to have been a little easier [than that of the husband]" (*World of Our Fathers*, pp. 172–73). This was true for most immigrant wives as well. See Tentler, *Wage-Earning Women*, p. 147

30. For an explanation of this psychological perception, see Branca, "New Perspective," p. 147.

31. Many ethnic, working-class wives typically had to seek work when their husbands were unemployed. See Kleinberg, "Study of Urban Women," p. 22. Married

women's work is difficult to document, because women who worked part-time usually regarded themselves as housewives, as would women who worked intermittently. The census has no specific categories for women's work done in the home—caring for children, taking in one or two boarders, working in a family store. Furthermore, many immigrant women may have purposely given census takers the impression that they did not work, fearing legal reprisals. However, the 1909 Immigration Commission survey indicated that 32.5 percent of Jewish women aged sixteen and over were employed, a number lower than that of any other ethnic group except the Irish. See Schwartz, "Immigrant Voices," pp. 163, 589. In Providence, 31 percent of Jewish immigrant wives earned some income. See Smith, *Family Connections*, p. 47.

32. Kleinberg, "Study of Working Women," p. 23.

33. Kessner and Caroli, "Immigrant Women at Work," p. 26.

34. Modell and Hareven, "Malleable Household," pp. 167–68. One estimate is that 25 percent of Jewish households in New York had boarders. See Miriam Cohen, "Workshop to Office," p. 109. Another estimate is that at any one time, 25 to 50 percent of industrial working-class households contained boarders. See Strasser, *Never Done*, p. 151.

35. Miriam Cohen, "Workshop to Office," p. 109. It is difficult to determine the precise number of women who took in boarders, because the 1940 census defined women as boarding or lodging housekeepers only if they cared for five or more boarders. Thus, the census of 1910 described only 14,844 women in such a category. See Baum, "What Made Yetta Work?," p. 37.

36. Jastrow, *Looking Back*, pp. 110–11.

37. Kessner, *Golden Door*, p. 101; Pleck, "Mother's Wages," p. 372.

38. YIVO Manuscript Autobiography no. 240.

39. Tentler, *Wage-Earning Women*, p. 138.

40. Because homework generally was illegal by the second decade of the century, married women often concealed such work from census takers, and it is difficult to estimate how many helped support their families in this way. See Miriam Cohen, "Workshop to Office," p. 105; Kessner, *Golden Door*, pp. 76–77.

41. Cited in Howe and Libo, *How We Lived*, pp. 282–83.

42. This also helps explain why more Jewish married women in New York than other cities told census takers they did not work outside the home. In Philadelphia, before 1910, many Jewish married women worked in Jewish-owned factories to enable their families to save up enough money to establish a small business. See Klaczynska, "Why Women Work," pp. 83–84. It is unclear just how many women worked with their husbands in this way. See Baum, "What Made Yetta Work?," p. 32.

43. Cited in Schwartz, "Immigrant Voices," p. 643.

44. This was true in 1900 as well as 1930. See Tentler, *Wage-Earning Women*, p. 165.

45. Kramer and Mazur, *Jewish Grandmothers*, p. 42.

46. In 1914, when a family income of $800 for a family of four was viewed as a minimum for survival, fifty-three Manhattan widows without working-age children

averaged less than $400 a year in income. See Tentler, *Wage-Earning Women*, pp. 169–70.

47. Schneiderman, *All for One*, p. 26.

48. Kazin, *Walker in the City*, pp. 30–31.

49. Jennie Herbst to Beatrice Weinreich, September 18, 1984.

50. Yezierska, "Mostly about Myself," in *Children of Loneliness*, pp. 9, 20; *Red Ribbon on a White Horse*, pp. 38–39.

51. Lillian B. Rubin, *Worlds of Pain*, p. 46.

52. In Jewish working-class families as well as working-class families generally, children usually knew that their mothers had to take jobs and accepted it better. See, for example, Lillian B. Rubin, *Worlds of Pain*, p. 27.

53. Ruskay, *Horsecars and Cobblestones*, p. 15.

54. I am indebted to Rickie Burman for development of this argument, which she applied to immigrant Jewish families in Manchester, England. See Burman, "Jewish Women in Religious Life."

55. Kramer and Mazur, *Jewish Grandmothers*, p. 101.

56. Jastrow, *Looking Back*, pp. 57, 114.

57. Chernin, *In My Mother's House*, pp. 179–80.

58. Ibid., pp. 179–80.

59. Howe and Libo, *How We Lived*, p. 125.

60. Howe used this phrase to describe his own mother. See *Margin of Hope*, p. 7.

61. See, for example, Rosaldo, "Woman, Culture and Society," p. 46.

62. Jennie Herbst to Beatrice Weinreich, September 18, 1984.

63. See, for example, Michel, "Rotted Cord," p. 275.

64. An Italian immigrant woman, cited in Miriam Cohen, "Workshop to Office," p. 323; also see p. 194 on the importance of this function in Italian families. For Polish families, see Bodnar, Simon, and Weber, *Lives of Their Own*, p. 94.

65. On this point, see Bodnar, *Transplanted*, pp. 81–82 on immigrant households, and Scott and Tilly, *Women, Work, and Family*, pp. 106, 142–44, 205 on European families.

66. Rischin, *Grandma Never Lived*, p. 403.

67. Scott and Tilly, *Women, Work, and Family*, pp. 6, 106, 142–44, 205, 209.

68. Jastrow, *Looking Back*, pp. 67, 77.

69. Ibid., pp. 92, 112.

70. Neisser, *Mothers and Daughters*, pp. 20, 41.

71. Landes and Zborowski, "Eastern European Family," pp. 36–37.

72. This is generally true in mother-daughter relationships in industrialized society. See Scott and Tilly, *Women, Work, and Family*, p. 193; and Neisser, *Mothers and Daughters*, p. 170.

73. This is true of women in all societies and all times. For example, Joyce Carol Oates said of a character in one of her recent novels, "Marya goes through a period of feeling genderless, which is an experiment for women in our era. Then the trajectory is

back toward the mother and family that's been left behind. She realizes she is her mother's daughter. It's one of the currents in a woman's life." *New York Times Book Review*, March 2, 1986, p. 7. On Jewish women specifically, see Bromberg, "Mother-Daughter Relationships," pp. 32, 210. Among Italian women, see Theophano, "Tomato Sauce," pp. 586–87.

74. Chernin, *In My Mother's House*, p. 29.

75. Oral history is from the collection of James P. Shenton.

76. After marriage, young women generally tend to assume, often unconsciously, their mother's methods of keeping house, dealing with neighbors, etc. See Neisser, *Mothers and Daughters*, p. 179.

77. Kramer and Mazur, *Jewish Grandmothers*, pp. 98–99.

78. Ibid., p. 14.

79. Chernin, *In My Mother's House*, pp. 15, 39.

80. Jennie Herbst to Beatrice Weinreich, September 18, 1984.

81. Bromberg, "Mother-Daughter Relationships," p. 35.

Chapter 8: Opportunities and Obligations

1. Metzger, *Bintel Brief*, p. 50.

2. In *Family Time*, pp. 5–7, 166–67, Hareven discusses the ways such individual transitions relate to family needs and family timing.

3. This was the typical pattern. See Schwartz, "Immigrant Voices," pp. 613–15.

4. Ibid., p. 615.

5. Rose Cohen, *Out of the Shadow*, p. 90.

6. Kimberg, "Reminiscences," Immigrant Labor History Project.

7. Schwartz, "Immigrant Voices," p. 587.

8. This was unusual, for after the first decade of the century, Jewish women generally did not do homework. See Willett, *Employment of Women*, p. 84.

9. Cited in Schwartz, "Immigrant Voices," p. 604.

10. Rose Cohen, *Out of the Shadow*, p. 115.

11. YIVO Manuscript Autobiography no. 266.

12. Ruskay, *Horsecars and Cobblestones*, pp. 68–69.

13. Ryan, *Cradle*, p. 26.

14. Altman, "Reminiscences," Immigrant Labor History Project.

15. Cited in Elizabeth Ewen, "Land of Dollars: 1890–1920," p. 289.

16. On this point, see Ankarloo, "Family Formation," p. 123.

17. Altman, "Reminiscences," Immigrant Labor History Project.

18. Glanz, *Eastern European Jewish Woman*, p. 61.

19. Ibid., p. 65.

20. On this point, see Hareven, *Family Time*, p. 108; Wandersee, *Women's Work*, p. 116; and Bromberg, "Mother-Daughter Relationships," p. 239.

21. Scott and Tilly, *Women, Work, and Family*, p. 107.

22. Some examples of such resentment can be seen in Elizabeth Ewen, "Land of Dollars: 1890–1920," pp. 126–27; Schwartz, "Immigrant Voices," p. 615; and Hasanovitz, *One of Them*, p. 42.

23. Hasanovitz, *One of Them*, pp. 42–43.

24. The average annual income of Russian Jewish families in 1909 was $525—well below what was considered essential for subsistence. See Miriam Cohen, "Workshop to Office," p. 70. After the fire in the Triangle Shirtwaist Company factory, the Women's Trade Union League published a summary of the budgets of sixty-five of the victims. Fifteen contributed almost their whole salary to their families, nineteen were the main support of their parents, and twenty-one sent much of their money to relatives in Europe. Cited in Eisenstein, *Give Us Bread*, p. 25.

25. Scott and Tilly, *Women, Work, and Family*, pp. 108, 111, 115.

26. A Department of Labor Survey indicated that sons gave an average of 83 percent of their wages to parents, while daughters gave 95 percent. Since sons earned more, however, their total contribution was higher. Cited in Schwartz, "Immigrant Voices," pp. 610–12.

27. Ibid., pp. 117, 137. In one survey, 86 percent of young Italian women gave their unopened pay envelopes to their mothers, although many sons contributed little or nothing. "Of course they don't give all they make," observed one Italian woman. "They're men and you never know their ways." Even when sons did turn over their pay envelope, they received a larger allowance than their sisters. See Odencrantz, *Italian Women in Industry*, pp. 21, 175–76.

28. Schwartz, "Immigrant Voices," pp. 610–12.

29. In 1916, there were only two Yeshivoth (Jewish high schools) in the United States, and only 24 percent of Jewish elementary school children received a Jewish education. See Liebman, "Religion, Class, and Culture," p. 231.

30. Girls are generally held to a more exacting code of filial obligations, while boys are permitted more opportunities for independent action. See Komarovsky, "Analysis of Sex Roles," pp. 295–96.

31. Tcherikower, *Jewish Labor Movement*, pp. 127–28.

32. Gold, *Jews without Money*, p. 198.

33. Ibid., p. 199.

34. Asch, *Mother*, p. 10.

35. Kazin, *Walker in the City*, pp. 52, 53, 66–67.

36. Bienstock, for example, observed, "Towards the mother the child feels most grateful, and consequently, most guilty. Recalling the ruthless way in which he left her behind to pursue the American dream, he defends himself by converting her into a monster of motherhood." "Changing Image," p. 190. Ruth Adler, on the other hand, emphasized the tension between the dual needs of a child for growth and independence on the one hand, and protection and nurture on the other. Thus, a mother's accessibility in the home might engender resentment in a young boy who feels himself stifled. "'Real'

Jewish Mother," p. 40. See also Wolfenstein, "Jewish Mothers," esp. pp. 522, 531. For a psychoanalytic interpretation of the different relationships between mothers and sons, see Chodorow, *Reproduction of Mothering*, pp. 166–67.

37. See, for example, Landes and Zborowski, "Eastern European Jewish Family," pp. 31–32.

38. Glanz, *Eastern European Jewish Woman*, p. 58.

39. Bienstock, "Changing Image," p. 177.

40. Alexander suggested that as the father often proved incapable of coping with America, the son became the focus of hopes for the family's future welfare. He thus often took his father's place in the mother's affection and had to bear the burden of having to become successful. *Age of Unreason*, pp. 197–201.

41. Silberman observed that because Jews believe that redemption occurs within history, it encourages a belief in the future and lends itself to the willingness of parents to sacrifice their well-being to advance their children's prospects. Thus children, particularly sons, are viewed as an extension of the parents and are loved for their accomplishments. *Certain People*, pp. 137, 138, 140.

42. Krause, *Grandmothers, Mothers, and Daughters*, pp. 51–53.

43. Miriam Cohen, "Workshop to Office," p. 181.

44. Bromberg, "Mother-Daughter Relationships," p. 239. Among Italians, oldest sons were supposed to assume responsibility for dependent parents, but despite this formal obligation, daughters were more likely to be involved in their care. One Sicilian proverb suggested, "He who has female children has both sons and daughters, but he who has male children has neither sons nor daughters" (cited in Smith, "Remaking Their Lives," p. 129, and *Family Connections*, p. 87). This care of mothers by daughters cuts across all ethnic lines and still exists. See, for example, Abel, "Adult Daughters."

45. For example, see Smith, "Remaking Their Lives," pp. 168–69.

46. Silberman, *Certain People*, pp. 142–43.

47. Bender, "Looking Back," p. 34.

48. In many immigrant families, collective survival rather than individual mobility was the overriding goal. See, for example, Schwartz, "Immigrant Voices," pp. 153–55; Hareven, *Family Time*, p. 108.

49. Wandersee observed that "women's tendency to place family first, ahead of career and job, may even have made their adaptation to industrialization smoother than that of men, for it minimized the psychological risk-taking that has been so often thrust upon men." *Women's Work*, p. 122.

50. See, for example, Scott and Tilly, "Women's Work."

Chapter 9: Education: Dream and Reality

1. Kaestle and Vinovskis observed that culture could stimulate people to achieve goals at odds with their economic self interest. They observed that "because life requires sustenance, the closer an individual gets to rudimentary subsistence, the more salient

will become straightforward economic strategies, and the more potently these will overrule competing inclinations such as an abstract value placed on education or sanctions against women's work. But given the range of human diversity . . . some individuals . . . will doggedly pursue a course opposed to their economic self-interest because they are imbued with a cultural commitment" (Kaestle and Vinovskis, "School Entry and School Leaving," p. 76).

2. Those who emigrated after 1900 often had more experience with public schools, particularly those who came from the Austro-Hungarian Empire, where school attendance was compulsory and free. See Brumberg, *Going to School*, p. 47.

3. The schools were unprepared for the massive influx of immigrant children between 1899 and 1914. Before 1898, New York lacked any public high schools, and by 1914, Manhattan and the Bronx had a total of only five. So few children actually went beyond the eighth grade. Until 1903, New York City required only four years of schooling, but even when the legal age for leaving school was raised to fourteen, most young students left school after the sixth grade. See Berrol, "Economic Mobility," pp. 259–61; and Dinnerstein, "Advancement of American Jews," p. 50. In 1890, 4 percent of fourteen- to seventeen-year-old children were in public high schools. This had risen to 28 percent by 1920 and to 47 percent by 1930. Edson, "Immigrant Perspectives," p. 2.

4. See, for example, Brumberg, *Going to School*, pp. 42–43.

5. Glanz, *Eastern European Jewish Woman*, pp. 25–27; Baum, Hyman, and Michel, *Jewish Woman in America*, p. 124.

6. Cited in Kessner, *Golden Door*, p. 91.

7. This zest for education has been documented in Manning, *Immigrant Woman*, p. 27. Although Jews represented only a small percentage of Philadelphia's inhabitants, Manning demonstrated that seven-tenths of a group of women enrolled in night school in that city were Jewish. See also Berrol, "Immigrants at School," pp. 61, 63, 97, 99.

8. Rose Cohen, *Out of the Shadow*, p. 251.

9. See Brumberg, *Going to School*, p. 113.

10. Tentler, *Wage-Earning Women*, p. 93.

11. Berrol, "Compensatory Education," p. 210.

12. Baum, Hyman, and Michel, *Jewish Woman in America*, p. 129.

13. Berrol, "Compensatory Education," p. 211.

14. Berrol, "Education and Economic Mobility," p. 263; Berrol, "Compensatory Education," p. 212.

15. Cited in Howe and Libo, *How We Lived*, pp. 204–6.

16. Fischer, *Twentieth Century*, pp. 20–25.

17. Bodnar, Simon, and Weber, *Lives of Their Own*, pp. 153–54; Bloch, "Changing Domestic Roles," pp. 6–7.

18. Edson, "Immigrant Perspectives," pp. 218–19. On Poles and education, see Bodnar, Simon, and Weber, *Lives of Their Own*, pp. 93, 43. On Italians, Gambino, *Blood of My Blood*, pp. 252–56, and Kessner, *Golden Door*, pp. 85, 95–96.

19. Cited in Pleck, "Mother's Wages," p. 493.

20. Berrol, "School Days," pp. 208–10; Covello, *Heart is the Teacher*, pp. 312, 321; Yans-McLaughlin, "Memory and Consciousness."

21. See, for example, Kessner and Caroli, "Immigrant Women at Work," p. 24; Covello, *Heart is the Teacher*, p. 292; LaGumina, "American Education," p. 69; Bodnar, "Slavic-American Family," pp. 82–83. This attitude would change in the 1930s, when, as more white-collar jobs opened up for girls, Italian parents began to appreciate the value of a high school education for their daughters, and more Italian girls than boys remained in school. This would be true for Jewish girls as well. See Miriam Cohen, "Workshop to Office," pp. 282–87; "Educational Strategies," pp. 453, 457.

22. Hareven and Langenbach, *Amoskeag*, pp. 267–68.

23. Miriam Cohen, "Educational Strategies," p. 447.

24. Ibid., pp. 453, 460; Miriam Cohen, "Workshop to Office," pp. 282, 287.

25. Strom, "Italian-American Women," p. 197.

26. On this point, see Carolyn Ware, *Greenwich Village*, pp. 139, 222, 323; and Ravitch, *Great School Wars*, p. 178.

27. See Kessner, *Golden Door*, pp. 76–77.

28. For example, see Seller, "Immigrant Children," pp. 198–99.

29. Wald, *House on Henry Street*, p. 97.

30. This contrasted with the parents of German and Italian girls in the same shops whose parents took them out of school as early as the law allowed. See Willett, *Employment of Women*, p. 87. Estimates of Jewish public high school student enrollment in Manhattan in 1918 ranged as high as 53 percent of the total of 85,000. See also Brumberg, *Going to School*, p. 3.

31. A 1950 census study indicated that 20 percent of foreign-born male Jews over forty-five at least had completed four years of high school, while only 12 percent of Jewish women of this age had this much education. Cited in Miriam Cohen, "Workshop to Office," p. 251. In 1920, only 27 percent of all young people remained in school, with equal numbers of males and females. See Tentler, *Wage-Earning Women*, p. 95.

32. Ibid., p. 103.

33. Forty-four percent of twenty-five- to forty-four-year-old foreign-born males graduated from high school, whereas 36 percent of women in this age group did so. The median years of schooling for this male group was 10.9; for the women, 9.7. This is a narrower gap than for the older group, in which the males had a median of 8.1 years of schooling and the women 5.8. Among native-born children, in contrast, the gap between male and female education is narrower still. Males in the younger age group averaged 12.7 years of schooling, and 72 percent had at least completed high school, whereas women averaged 12.4 years of school, and 69 percent of them had graduated from high school. Miriam Cohen, "Workshop to Office," p. 251.

34. During this early period, many Italian families actively opposed an education for their daughters because girls did not need such skills, and, as one Italian mother said, the schools wanted to take her children away from her. See Berrol, "Public Schools and Immigrants," p. 39.

35. Cited in Brumberg, *Going to School*, p. 69.

36. Dinnerstein, "Advancement of American Jews," p. 47.

37. Marcus, *American Jewish Woman*, p. 132.

38. Cynthia Fuchs Epstein, "Women and Professional Careers."

39. Weinstein, "Reminiscences," Immigrant Labor History Project.

40. Morton, *I Am a Woman*, pp. 15–16.

41. Kramer and Mazur, *Jewish Grandmothers*, pp. 5–6, 14.

42. Cited in Brumberg, *Going to School*, pp. 146–47.

43. Cited in Kessner, *Golden Door*, p. 97.

44. Baum, Hyman, and Michel, *Jewish Woman in America*, p. 126.

45. For example, see Kessner and Caroli, "Immigrant Women at Work," p. 27.

46. Chernin, *In My Mother's House*, pp. 39–40.

47. Probably raids organized by Attorney General A. Mitchell Palmer in 1919 as part of the "Red Scare." The boys were taught to read and write Russian, as well as mechanical skills.

48. Antin, *Promised Land*, p. 216.

49. Wald, *House On Henry Street*, pp. 180–93.

50. Hyman, "Culture and Gender," p. 160; Seller, "Education of the Immigrant Woman," p. 324.

51. Berrol, "Compensatory Education," pp. 216–17; Brumberg, *Going to School*, pp. 148, 166.

52. See Howe, *World of Our Fathers*, pp. 238–40; Dinnerstein, "Advancement of American Jews," p. 49.

53. Cited in Howe and Libo, *How We Lived*, p. 287.

54. Ibid.

55. Reznikoff, "History of a Seamstress," p. 99.

56. Kessner and Caroli, "Immigrant Women at Work," p. 27; Kessner, *Golden Door*, p. 98. A 1910 survey showed that there were more Jewish students above the age of sixteen in school than those of any other immigrant group. At City College, 73 percent of the student body was Jewish; at Hunter, 44 percent. See also Glanz, *Eastern European Jewish Woman*, p. 66. By 1934, 52.1 percent of all female students in the city colleges of New York were Jewish. Marcus, *American Jewish Woman*, p. 132.

Chapter 10: Becoming a Person: Work and Independence

1. Yezierska, *Hungry Hearts*, p. 132.

2. See, for example, Modell, Furstenberg, and Hershberg, "Transitions to Adulthood," p. 9; Branca, "New Perspective," p. 140; Hareven, *Family Time*, pp. 74–75; and Tentler, *Wage-Earning Women*, p. 61.

3. Rose Cohen, *Out of the Shadow*, pp. 94–95.

4. See for example, Kessler-Harris, *Out to Work*, p. 126; Tentler, *Wage-Earning Women*, pp. 88–89; Bodnar, Simon, and Weber, *Lives of Their Own*, pp. 94–97.

5. From Immigrant Labor History Project, cited in Elizabeth Ewen, "Land of Dollars: 1890–1920," pp. 130–33.

6. Willett, *Employment of Women*, pp. 87–88.

7. This was true throughout industrialized society. See Scott and Tilly, *Women, Work, and Family*, pp. 186–87; Tentler, *Wage-Earning Women*, p. 92. Miriam Cohen indicates that Italian daughters still gave their whole paycheck to their mothers. See "Workshop to Office," p. 180.

8. Strom, "Italian-American Women," p. 197; Smith, "Italian Mothers," p. 213.

9. Kimball, *Gitele*, pp. 24–25.

10. Tentler, *Wage-Earning Women*, p. 91.

11. Kramer and Mazur, *Jewish Grandmothers*, p. 96.

12. On this point, see Wandersee, *Women's Work*, p. 1; Eisenstein, *Give Us Bread*, p. 6; Scott and Tilly, *Women, Work, and Family*, p. 108. One contemporary observer noted that young Italian women work because "the family relies on her to do her part." See Odencrantz, *Italian Women in Industry*, p. 179.

13. On this point, see Eisenstein, *Give Us Bread*, pp. 117, 124, 119.

14. On this point see Wandersee, *Women's Work*, p. 116.

15. Kessner and Golab, among others, have demonstrated that the paid labor of wives and daughters was often essential to sustain the immigrant family because of the seasonal or intermittent nature of men's work. See Kessner, *Golden Door*, p. 71; and Golab, "Industrial Experience."

16. For example, among the mill workers Hareven studied, "commencement of work was a rite of passage, separating the grown-ups from the kids. . . . Holding down a job did not necessarily convey independent adulthood. . . . But work in the mill did confer a degree of independence, particularly to younger women. . . . It also gave them a sense of managing their own lives, albeit a limited one." See Hareven, *Family Time*, pp. 74–75.

17. Schneiderman, *All for One*, p. 43.

18. See Eisenstein, *Give Us Bread*, pp. 6–7.

19. Yans-McLaughlin, "Memory and Consciousness." Social workers emphasized this difference as well. See Pleck, "Mother's Wages," p. 473.

20. On this point, see Kessler-Harris, "Organizing the Unorganizable," p. 8.

21. The evidence presented by Yans-McLaughlin or Covello on Italian family life, for example, indicated that the necessity of sending an Italian daughter out to work did not in any way give them more rights or decrease family control over their lives. This effect was emphasized by Virginia Yans-McLaughlin in a paper comparing the attitudes of Jewish and Italian first- and second-generation garment workers in 1978. See also Covello, "Social Background," pp. 203–4, 357, 359.

22. Harris, *Out to Work*, p. 126.

23. Willett, *Employment of Women*, pp. 87–88.

24. For example, see Tentler, *Wage-Earning Women*, p. 109.

25. Kramer and Mazur, *Jewish Grandmothers*, p. 131.

26. On the dislike of Jewish women for domestic work, see Katzman, *Seven Days a Week*, pp. 11–12, 69, 172, 272.

27. Only about 12.5 percent of Jewish girls, as opposed to up to 40 percent of other immigrant groups, worked as servants. See Glanz, *Eastern European Jewish Woman*, p. 20; and Baum, "What Makes Yetta Work?," p. 37.

28. YIVO Manuscript Autobiography no. 240 (Written in 1928).

29. Rose Cohen, *Out of the Shadow*, pp. 172–73.

30. In 1915, it was estimated that a wage of $9 a week was essential for room and board alone. Yet department store clerks, the highest paid group studied, earned an average of $7.75 per week. See Tentler, *Wage-Earning Women*, p. 18.

31. Ibid., p. 41.

32. Altman, "Reminiscences," Immigrant Labor History Project.

33. Chernin, *In My Mother's House*, pp. 38–39.

34. Cited in Schwartz, "Immigrant Voices," p. 391.

35. Willet, *Employment of Women*, pp. 73–74.

36. In 1913, 56.5 percent of workers in these industries were Jewish, and 70 percent of the Jews were women. In 1900, 53.6 percent of *all* employed Jewish women worked in the garment industry. See Kessler-Harris, "Organizing the Unorganizable," p. 161.

37. Rischin, *Promised City*, p. 61.

38. This compared with 36 percent of Italian wives who worked. See Baum, Hyman, and Michel, *Jewish Woman in America*, pp. 161–62; Miriam Cohen, "Workshop to Office," p. 120.

39. Kessner and Caroli, "Immigrant Women at Work," p. 27.

40. Glanz, *Eastern European Jewish Woman*, pp. 22, 66–67.

41. Brumberg, *Going to School*, p. 138; Moore, *At Home in America*, pp. 95–96.

42. See, for example, Smith, "Remaking Their Lives," p. 102.

43. Morton, *I Am a Woman*, pp. 172–73.

44. Yezierska, "Soap and Water," in *Hungry Hearts*.

45. Cited in Riis, *Other Half*, p. 177.

46. Tentler, *Wage-Earning Women*, p. 47; Eistenstein, *Give Us Bread*, p. 28.

47. Cited in Marcus, *American Jewish Woman*, pp. 690–97.

48. Hasanovitz, *One of Them*, pp. 100, 109.

49. Rose Cohen, *Out of the Shadow*, pp. 85, 87–88, 128–29, 274–75.

50. Cited in Elizabeth Ewen, "Land of Dollars: 1890–1920," p. 393.

51. Schneiderman, *All for One*, p. 34. See also Kessler-Harris, "Organizing the Unorganizable," p. 146.

52. Plotkin, *Full-Time Active*, p. 7. See also Glanz, *Eastern European Jewish Woman*, p. 91.

53. See, for example, Elizabeth Ewen, "Land of Dollars: 1890–1920," pp. 403–4.

54. Cited in Sochen, *Consecrate Every Day*, p. 34.

55. Buhle, *Women and American Socialism*, pp. 106–7, 123–24; Hapgood, *Spirit of the Ghetto*, p. 78.

56. Paradoxically, the wages institutionalized differentials between male and female workers: the highest paid, skilled women workers received less than the lowest paid, unskilled men. Eighty percent of the workers in the industry were women, 75 percent

between the ages of sixteen and twenty-five, and 65 percent of these were Jewish. On the strike, see Glanz, *Eastern European Jewish Woman*, p. 51; Levine, *Women's Garment Workers*, pp. 144–54; Epstein, *Jewish Labor*, pp. 388–90.

57. Chernin, *In My Mother's House*, p. 42.

58. YIVO Manuscript Autobiography no. 266.

59. Tentler, *Wage-Earning Women*, pp. 78–79.

60. On this point, also see Krause, "Urbanization without Breakdown," p. 294.

Chapter 11: Love and Marriage

1. Cited in Ruth Rubin, *Voices of a People*, p. 290.

2. Elizabeth Ewen, "Land of Dollars: 1890–1920," p. 343.

3. Marcus, *American Jewish Woman*, p. 504.

4. Cited in Eisenstein, *Give Us Bread*, p. 132.

5. Rose Cohen, *Out of the Shadow*, p. 226. On this changing function of the *shadkhen*, see Baum, Hyman, and Michel, *Jewish Woman in America*, p. 221.

6. See the same letter to Rose Pastor Stokes's column in 1903. Cited in Eisenstein, *Give Us Bread*, p. 132.

7. YIVO Manuscript Autobiography no. 92.

8. Scott and Tilly, *Women, Work, and Family*, pp. 188–89. This was not true of young Italian immigrant women, who were closely supervised by parents, brothers, or other male relatives. See Strom, "Italian-American Women," p. 194.

9. Glanz, *Eastern European Jewish Woman*, p. 74.

10. For a vivid description of this scene, see Cahan, *Rise of David Levinsky*, pp. 403–24.

11. This was true among the daughters of Jewish immigrant families in the 1920s, although it was unacceptable behavior among young Italian women. See Carolyn Ware, *Greenwich Village*, p. 149.

12. In a sample of twenty-two young Italian women in 1930, only three had ever been out alone with any man other than the one she married. See Carolyn Ware, *Greenwich Village*, p. 405. See also Strom, "Italian-American Women," pp. 194–95.

13. Glanz, *Eastern European Jewish Woman*, p. 82.

14. For example, see the "Reminiscences" of Mary Abrams, who emigrated in 1910. Immigrant Labor History Project.

15. YIVO Manuscript Autobiography no. 240.

16. See Perry, "'General Motherhood of the Commonwealth.'"

17. Edelman, *Mirror of Life*, pp. 24–25.

18. Kramer and Mazur, *Jewish Grandmothers*, p. 147.

19. Kaplan, *Marriage Bargain*, p. 123.

20. Cited in Elizabeth Ewen, "Land of Dollars: 1890–1920," pp. 343–44.

21. Ibid., p. 350.

22. Kramer and Mazur, *Jewish Grandmothers*, p. 13.

23. Weinstein, "Reminiscences," Immigrant Labor History Project.

24. One social worker observed that marriage was the "chief ambition" of the Jewish working woman. See Sochen, *Consecrate Every Day*, p. 14.

25. Rose Cohen, *Out of the Shadow*, p. 74.

26. Cited in Eisenstein, *Give Us Bread*, p. 21.

27. See Hasanovitz, *One of Them*, p. 247.

28. Kramer and Mazur, *Jewish Grandmothers*, p. 113.

29. For a description of working-class women's aspirations, see Lillian B. Rubin, *Worlds of Pain*, pp. 93–94. For an explanation of these differences between middle-class and working-class families, see Komarovsky, *Blue-Collar Marriage*, pp. 144–47, 335–36.

30. For an explanation of these differences, see Lillian B. Rubin, *Worlds of Pain*, pp. 125–26; and Komarovsky, *Blue-Collar Marriage*, pp. 76, 149.

31. Kramer and Mazur, *Jewish Grandmothers*, p. 148.

32. Ibid., pp. 99–100.

33. Lillian B. Rubin, *Worlds of Pain*, pp. 98, 112–13.

34. Scarf, "Intimate Partners," pp. 46, 47.

35. Chernin, *In My Mother's House*, p. 63.

36. Stone, *My Caravan of Years*, p. 120.

37. Chernin, *In My Mother's House*, p. 92.

38. See Abraham Cahan, "Get a Girl, Young Man," in Rischin, *Grandma Never Lived*, pp. 219–20.

39. Goldman, *Living My Life*, 1:185.

40. Petchesky, *Abortion*, p. 53.

41. Simon, *Bronx Primitive*, p. 70.

42. Sanger established her first clinic in 1917 in an ethnic neighborhood and printed circulars in Yiddish and Italian. In 1925 alone, her clinic saw 1,655 patients. See Gordon, *Woman's Body*, pp. 231, 263.

43. On this point, see Petchesky, *Abortion*, pp. 54–56.

44. On this point, see Sklare, *America's Jews*, pp. 82–83; and Gordon, *Woman's Body*, pp. 323–24.

Chapter 12: A Question of Bread

1. This is true of working-class families now as well. See Lillian B. Rubin, *Worlds of Pain*, p. 168.

2. With more women seeking piecework, the rates generally dropped. See Tentler, *Wage-Earning Women*, p. 23.

3. The birthrate fell during the 1930s because of economic hardship, improved knowledge of birth control, and probably also a decline in sexual relations because of the tensions of these hard times. See Susan Ware, *Holding Their Own*, pp. 7–8.

4. Kramer and Mazur, *Jewish Grandmothers*, pp. 148–49.

5. Tentler, *Wage-Earning Women*, pp. 139, 141.

6. Kessler-Harris, *Out to Work*, pp. 256, 258–59.

7. Wandersee, *Women's Work*, p. 82.

8. Susan Ware, *Holding Their Own*, p. 14.

9. Schwartz, "Immigrant Voices," p. 584.

10. Wandersee, *Women's Work*, p. 83; Komarovsky, *Blue-Collar Marriage*, pp. 70–73.

11. See, for example, Hareven, *Family Time*, p. 78.

12. See, for example, Elder, "Family History," p. 105.

13. Prieto, "Cuban Women," pp. 107–11.

14. Kessner, *Golden Door*, p. 76.

15. Campbell, *Women at War with America*, p. 212.

16. Kramer and Mazur, *Jewish Grandmothers*, p. 133.

17. Cited in Elizabeth Ewen, "Land of Dollars: 1890–1920," p. 349.

18. Kramer and Mazur, *Jewish Grandmothers*, pp. 100–101.

19. YIVO Manuscript Autobiography no. 240.

20. For example, see Susan Ware, *Holding Their Own*, p. 2.

21. On this point, see Wandersee, *Women's Work*, p. 104.

22. This tended to be true for all ethnic groups studied. On this point, see Elder, "Children of the Great Depression," p. 37; Scott and Tilly, *Women, Work, and Family*, p. 204.

23. See, for example, Elder, "Great Depression," p. 37; Gluck, "Age, Generation and Change."

24. Ibid.; Bennett and Elder, "Family Economy," p. 169.

25. Elder, "Family History," pp. 105–6.

26. Schlesinger, *Jewish Family*, p. 22.

27. Markowitz, "Daughters of Immigrants."

Chapter 13: Looking Back

1. YIVO Manuscript Autobiography no. 240.

2. Myerhoff, *Number Our Days*, pp. 106–7.

3. Ibid., pp. 2, 92–93.

4. This is true of the children of most ethnic groups, as well as the offspring of native-born stock. On this point, see Schwartz, "Immigrant Voices," pp. 689–90.

5. Yezierska, *The Open Cage*, p. 246.

6. Cited in Sochen, *Consecrate Every Day*, p. 72.

7. Jastrow, *Time to Remember*, p. 89.

8. Myerhoff, *Number Our Days*, p. 268.

9. Carol Gilligan has explored this attitude in *Different Voice*, pp. 171–73.

10. Chodorow, *Reproduction of Mothering*, pp. 159, 167.

11. Gilligan, *Different Voice*, pp. 17, 48. On the continuing importance of this charac-

teristic of women, see "Infirm Relatives' Care: A New Woman's Issue," *The New York Times*, November 13, 1986, pp. C1, C6.

12. On this point, see Higham, *Send These to Me*, p. 12.

13. For example, see Yans-McLaughlin, *Family and Community*, pp. 18, 186; Hareven, *Transitions*, p. 347.

14. For Portland, see Toll, *Ethnic Middle Class*, pp. 72–75, 118; for Pittsburgh, see Selavan, *My Voice Was Heard*, p. 92, and Krause, *Grandmothers, Mothers, and Daughters*; for Indianapolis, see Endelman, *Jewish Community of Indianapolis*, pp. 77, 84, 86; for New Haven, see Schwartz, "Immigrant Voices"; for Providence, see Smith, *Remaking Their Lives*; and for Chicago, see Sochen, *Consecrate Every Day*, pp. 15, 21.

Glossary of Yiddish Terms

· ·

The system of transliteration followed is that used by the YIVO Institute for Jewish Research. However, if words are spelled differently in common English usage or in citations from written work, that spelling is retained and the YIVO spelling included in parentheses.

Abhole. Bring home.

Agunah (Agune). Deserted wife.

Aishes chayil (Eyshes Khayl). Woman of valor.

Aufshtel-bettels (Oyfshtel-betlekh). Folding beds.

Balebatish. Properly, refined.

Balabusteh (Baleboste). Fine housekeeper.

Bar Mitzvzah (Bar mitsve). Confirmation ceremony at age thirteen marking a boy's manhood.

Besmidrash (Beys-medresh). Place for religious services and prayer.

Bintel Brief (Bintl briv). Column of letters to *Jewish Daily Forward* and replies.

Bris (Heb. *Brith*). Circumcision ceremony at birth of a boy.

Bubbe (Bobe). Grandmother.

Bund. Jewish social democratic workers' party.

Challah (Khale). Braided white bread eaten on the Sabbath.

Cheder (Kheyder). Boys' elementary Hebrew school.

Daven (Davn). To pray.

Dorf. Village.

Dybbuk (Dibek). A condemned soul that takes possession of the body of a living person.

Eynikl. Granddaughter.

Gefilte fish. Fish ball, often prepared for the Sabbath and holidays.

Gimnazye. Russian secondary school.

Goldene Medina (Goldene Medine). Golden Land (America).

Goy (pl. Goyim). Non-Jew(s).

Gorgl. Neck (usually of fowl).

Hasid (pl. Hasidim. Yid. Khosid, Khasidim). Member(s) of a pietist sect of Orthodox Jews.

Haskalah (Haskole). Movement for enlightenment which spread from Germany to the Jews of Eastern Europe in the eighteenth and nineteenth centuries.

Kaddish (Kadesh). Prayer for the dead.

Kasha (Kashe). Buckwheat groats.

Kashruth (Kashres). Dietary laws.

Kest. Right of newly married couples to live with the bride's family.

Kiddush (Kidesh). Prayer over cup of wine at beginning of the Sabbath.

Kikhlekh. Cookies.

Kind (pl. Kinder). Child (children).

Kosher. Pure, ritually clean.

Kugel (Kugl). Pudding, usually made of noodles or potatoes.

Kvass (Kvas). Liquor or cider, usually homemade liquor.

Landsman (pl. Landslayt). Person from the same town or area.

Landsmanshaft (pl. Landsmanshaftn). Society of immigrants from same area or town in Eastern Europe.

Liebe (Libe). Love.

Matzoh (Matse). Unleavened bread eaten during week of Passover.

Mazeltov (Mazltov). Good luck.

Melamed. Elementary-level Hebrew teacher.

Mensch (Mentsh). Literally, a man, meaning a good person.

Menschlikeyt (Mentshlekhkeyt). Humaneness.

Mikvah (Mikve). The ritual bathhouse where a woman purified herself after menstruation.

Mitzva (pl. Mitzvot. Yid. Mitsve). Good deed(s).

Pekl tsores. Pack of troubles.

Pesach (Peysekh). Passover.

Pogrom. Anti-Semitic riot and massacre.

Pratsh. Wooden paddle for beating laundry.

Rabbi (Rebe). Teacher and leader of the congregation.

Rosh Hashanah. Jewish new year.

Seder (Seyder). Special meal and ritual for first two nights of Passover.

Shabbes (Shabes). Sabbath.

Shadkhen (Shadkn). Matchmaker.

Sheitel (Sheytl). Wig worn by married women.

Shlep. To drag along.

Shtetl, pl. Shtetlach (Shtetlekh). Town(s) with a large Jewish population.

Shul. Synagogue.

Sukkah. Booth decorated with branches and vegetables in which family eats during the week of the harvest festival of Succoth.

Streudel (Shtrudl). Pastry, usually filled with fruit or cheese.

Talmud. Commentaries on the Bible.

Talmud Torah. Elementary Hebrew school.

Tante. Aunt.

Tfiln. Prayer phylacteries worn by men wrapped around forehead and arm.

Treyf. Nonkosher, ritually unclean.

Tsedakah (Tsdoke). Righteousness by performing acts of charity.

Tsene-Urena. Women's Bible, written in Yiddish.

Tsirung. Ornament, jewel.

Tsores. Troubles.

Yarmulke (Yarmelke). Skullcap.

Yeshiva. Upper-level Jewish school for Talmud study.

Yikhes. Status, or pedigree, based on family lineage and/or learning.

Yom Kippur. Day of Atonement.

Zudhartkes (Sukharkes). Oven-toasted bread, similar to zwieback.

Bibliography

. . . .

Manuscript Collections

Immigrant Labor History Project, City College. Tamiment Institute, New York University Library, New York. A collection of untranscribed oral histories of immigrant workers in the early garment trades industry.

Kahan, Anne. "The Diary of Anne Kahan: Siedlce, Poland, 1914–1916." Translated from Yiddish by the author of the diary. An unpublished, longer version of the diary excerpted in *YIVO Annual of Jewish Social Science* (18). YIVO Institute for Jewish Research, New York.

Shenton, James P. A collection of oral histories of immigrants, in possession of the collector, New York.

YIVO Manuscript Autobiography Collection. YIVO Institute for Jewish Research, New York.

Books and Articles

Abbott, Edith. *Women in Industry*. New York: D. Appleton & Co., 1910.

Abel, Emily K. "Adult Daughters and Care for the Elderly." *Feminist Studies* 12 (Fall 1986): 479–97.

Abramovitch, Hirsh. "Rural Jewish Occupations in Lithuania." *YIVO Annual of Jewish Social Science* 2–3 (1947–48): 205–21.

Adler, Rachel. "The Jew Who Wasn't There: Halakhah and the Jewish Woman." In *On Being a Jewish Feminist*, edited by Susannah Heschel, pp. 12–18. New York: Schocken Books, 1983.

Adler, Ruth. "The 'Real' Jewish Mother." *Midstream* 23 (October 1967): 38–40.

———. *Women of the Shtetl: Through the Eyes of Y. L. Peretz*. Cranberry, N.J.: Associated University Presses, 1980.

Ain, Abraham. "Swislocz: Portrait of a Jewish Community in Eastern Europe." *YIVO Annual of Jewish Social Science* 4 (1949): 86–114.

Alexander, Franz. *Our Age of Unreason*. Philadelphia: J. P. Lippincott, 1951.

Ankarloo, Bengt. "Marriage and Family Formation." In *Transitions: The Family and the Life Course in Historical Perspective*, edited by Tamara Hareven, pp. 113–33. New York: Academic Press, 1978.

The Annual Report of the Commissioner-General of Immigration for 1910. Washington, D.C.: Government Printing Office, 1911.

Antin, Mary. *The Promised Land*. Boston: Houghton Mifflin Co., 1969 (originally published in 1912).

Ariès, Philippe. "The Family and the City in the Old World and the New." In *Changing Images of the Family*, edited by Virginia Tufte and Barbara Myerhoff, pp. 29–41. New Haven, Conn.: Yale University Press, 1979.

Asch, Sholem. *The Mother*. New York: G. P. Putnam's Sons, 1937.

Ayalti, Hanan J., ed. *Yiddish Proverbs*. New York: Schocken Books, 1949.

Baron, Salo W. *The Russian Jew under Tsars and Soviets*. New York: Macmillan Co., 1964, 1976. Reprint. New York: Schocken Books, 1987.

Baum, Charlotte; Hyman, Paula; and Michel, Sonya. *The Jewish Woman in America*. New York: Dial Press, 1975.

———. "What Made Yetta Work? The Economic Role of Eastern European Jewish Women in the Family." *Response* 18 (Summer 1973): 32–38.

Beck, Evelyn Torton. *The Many Faces of Eve: Women, Yiddish, and I. B. Singer*. Working Papers in Yiddish and East European Jewish Studies no. 16. New York: YIVO Institute for Jewish Research, 1975.

Bender, Esther. "Looking Back." *National Jewish Monthly* 92 (November 1977): 28–34.

Bennett, Sheila K., and Elder, Glen, Jr. "Women's Work in the Family Economy: A Study of Depression Hardship in Women's Lives." *Journal of Family History* 4 (Summer 1979): 153–76.

Berg, Rebecca Himber. "Childhood in Lithuania." In *Memoirs of My People*, edited by Leo Schwartz, pp. 269–82. Philadelphia: Jewish Publication Society of America, 1943.

Bernard, Jessie. *The Female World*. New York: Free Press, 1981.

Berrol, Selma. "Education and Economic Mobility: The Jewish Experience in New York City, 1880–1920." *American Jewish Historical Quarterly* 65 (March 1977): 257–71.

———. "From Compensatory Education to Adult Education: The New York City Evening Schools, 1825–1935." *Adult Education Quarterly* 26 (Summer 1976): 208–25.

———. "Immigrants at School: New York City, 1898–1914." Ph.D. dissertation, Columbia University, 1967.

———. "Public Schools and Immigrants: The New York City Experience." In *American Education and the European Immigrant: 1840–1940*, edited by Bernard J. Weiss, pp. 31–43. Urbana: University of Illinois Press, 1982.

———. "School Days on the Old East Side: The Italian and Jewish Experience." *New York History* 62 (April 1976): 201–13.

Bertaux, Daniel. "From the Life History Approach to the Transformation of Sociological Practice." In *Biography and Society: The Life History Approach in the Social Sciences*, edited by Daniel Bertaux, pp. 29–45. Beverly Hills, Calif.: Sage Publications, 1981.

———, and Bertaux-Wiame, Isabelle. "Life Stories in the Bakers' Trade." In *Biography and Society: The Life History Approach in the Social Sciences*, edited by Daniel Bertaux, pp. 169–90. Beverly Hills, Calif.: Sage Publications, 1981.

Bertaux-Wiame, Isabelle. "The Life History Approach to the Study of Internal Migration." In *Biography and Society: The Life History Approach in the Social Sciences*, edited by Daniel Bertaux, pp. 249–65. Beverly Hills, Calif.: Sage Publications, 1981.

Bienstock, Beverly G. "The Changing Image of the American Jewish Mother." In *Changing Images of the Family*, edited by Virginia Tufte and Barbara Myerhoff, pp. 173–91. New Haven, Conn.: Yale University Press, 1979.

Blau, Zena Smith. "In Defense of the Jewish Mother." In *The Ghetto and Beyond*, edited by Peter I. Rose, pp. 57–68. New York: Random House, 1969.

———. "The Strategy of the Jewish Mother." In *The Jews in American Society*, edited by Marshall Sklare, pp. 165–87. New York: Behrman House, 1974.

Bloch, Harriet. "Changing Domestic Roles among Polish Immigrant Women." *Anthropological Quarterly* 49 (January 1976): 3–10.

Bloom, Solomon. "The Saga of America's Russian Jews." *Commentary* 1 (February 1946): 1–7.

Bodnar, John. "Schooling and the Slavic-American Family, 1900–1940." In *American Education and the European Immigrant, 1840–1940*, edited by Bernard J. Weiss, pp. 78–95. Urbana: University of Illinois Press, 1982.

———; Simon, Roger; and Weber, Michael. *Lives of Their Own: Blacks, Italians, and Poles in Pittsburgh, 1900–1960*. Urbana: University of Illinois Press, 1982.

———. *The Transplanted: A History of Immigrants in Urban America*. Bloomington: Indiana University Press, 1985.

Branca, Patricia. "A New Perspective on Women's Work: A Comparative Typology." *Journal of Social History* 9 (Winter 1975): 129–53.

Brayer, Menachem. *The Jewish Woman in Rabbinic Literature: A Psychohistorical Perspective*. Hoboken, N.J.: Ktav Publishing Co., 1986.

Bressler, Marvin. "Selected Family Patterns in W. I. Thomas' Unfinished Study of the Bintl Brief." *American Sociological Review* 17 (1952): 563–71.

Bristow, Edward J. *Prostitution and Prejudice: The Jewish Fight against White Slavery, 1870–1939*. New York: Oxford University Press, 1982.

Bromberg, Eleanor Mallach. "Mother-Daughter Relationships in Later Life." Ph.D. dissertation, School of Social Work, Columbia University, 1982.

Brownstone, David; Franck, Irene; and Brownstone, Douglass. *Island of Hope, Island of Tears*. New York: Rawson, Wade, 1979. Reprint. New York: Penguin Books, 1986.

Brumberg, Stephan F. "Born in Brooklyn: The Origin of the High Schools of New York City." Paper presented at the Annual Meeting of the American Educational Research Association, April 1986, San Francisco.

———. *Going to America, Going to School: The Jewish Immigrant Public School Encounter in Turn-of-the-Century New York City*. New York: Praeger, 1986.

Buhle, Mari Jo. *Women and American Socialism, 1870–1920*. Urbana: University of Illinois Press, 1983.

Burko, Faina. "The American Yiddish Theater and Its Audience before World War I." In *The Legacy of Jewish Immigration*, edited by David Berger, pp. 85–96. New York: Brooklyn College Press, 1983.

Burman, Rickie. "The Jewish Woman as Breadwinner: The Changing Value of Woman's

Work in a Manchester Immigrant Community." *Oral History* 10 (1982): 27–39.

_____. "The Role of Jewish Women in Religious Life, c. 1880–1930." Unpublished paper.

Byer, Etta. *Transplanted People*. Chicago: Lider Organization of Chicago, 1955.

Cahan, Abraham. *The Rise of David Levinsky*. New York: Harper & Row, 1960 (originally published in 1917).

_____. *Yekl, The Imported Bridegroom and Other Stories*. New York: W. W. Norton, 1970 (originally published in 1896 and 1898).

Campbell, D'Ann. *Women at War with America: Private Lives in a Patriotic Era*. Cambridge, Mass.: Harvard University Press, 1984.

Caroli, Betty Boyd; Harney, Robert F.; and Tomasi, Lydio F. *The Italian Immigrant Woman in North America*. Toronto, Canada: Multicultural Historical Society of Ontario, 1978.

Chagall, Bella. *Burning Lights*. New York: Schocken Books, 1946.

_____. *First Encounter*. New York: Schocken Books, 1983.

Chernin, Kim. *In My Mother's House*. New Haven, Conn.: Ticknor & Fields, 1983.

Chodorow, Nancy. "Family Structure and Feminine Personality." In *Women, Culture, and Society*, edited by Michelle Zimbalist Rosaldo and Louise Lamphere, pp. 43–66. Stanford, Calif.: Stanford University Press, 1974.

_____. *The Reproduction of Mothering: Psychoanalysis and the Sociology of Gender*. Berkeley, Calif.: University of California Press, 1978.

Chudakoff, Howard P. "The Life Course of Women: Age and Age Consciousness, 1865–1915." *Journal of Family History* 3 (Fall 1980): 274–92.

Cohen, Bernard. *Sociocultural Changes in American Jewish Life as Reflected in Selected Jewish Literature*. Rutherford, N.J.: Fairleigh Dickinson University Press, 1972.

Cohen, Mary M. "The Influence of Jewish Religion in the Home." In *Papers of the Jewish Woman's Congress*, pp. 115–21. Philadelphia: Jewish Publication Society of America, 1894.

Cohen, Miriam. "Changing Education Strategies among Immigrant Generations: New York Italians in Comparative Perspective." *Journal of Social History* 15 (Spring 1982): 443–66.

_____. "From Workshop to Office: Italian Women and Family Strategies in New York City, 1900–1950." Ph.D. dissertation, University of Michigan, 1978.

_____. "Italian-American Women in New York City, 1900–1980: Work and School." In *Class, Sex and the Woman Worker*, edited by Milton Cantor and Bruce Lurie, pp. 120–43. Westport, Conn.: Greenwood Press, 1977.

Cohen, Morris Raphael. *A Dreamer's Journey*. New York: Arno Press, 1975 (originally published in 1949).

Cohen, Rose. *Out of the Shadow*. New York: George H. Doran Co., 1918.

Cornelisen, Ann. *Women of the Shadows*. Boston: Little, Brown and Co., 1976.

Covello, Leonard. *The Heart Is the Teacher*. Reissued as *The Teacher in the Urban Community*. Totowa, N.J.: Littlefield, Adams & Co., 1970.

————. "The Social Background of the Italo-American School Child." Ph.D. dissertation, New York University, 1944.

Dawidowicz, Lucy, ed. *The Golden Tradition: Jewish Life and Thought in Eastern Europe*. Boston: Beacon Press, 1964. Reprint. New York: Schocken Books, 1986.

Diner, Hasia. *Erin's Daughters in America: Irish Immigrant Women in the Nineteenth Century*. Baltimore: Johns Hopkins University Press, 1983.

Dinnerstein, Leonard. "Education and the Advancement of American Jews." In *American Education and the European Immigrant*, edited by Bernard J. Weiss, pp. 44–60. Urbana: University of Illinois Press, 1982.

Dubnow, Simon. *History of the Jews in Russia and Poland*, vol. 2. New York: Ktav Publishing Co., 1916–20.

Edelman, Fannie. *The Mirror of Life*. New York: Exposition Press, 1961.

Edson, C. H. "Immigrant perspectives on Work and Schooling: Eastern European Jews and Southern Italians, 1880–1920." Ph.D. dissertation, Stanford University, 1979.

Eistenstein, Sarah. *Give Us Bread but Give Us Roses: Working Women's Consciousness in the United States, 1890 to the First World War*. Boston: Routledge and Kegan Paul, 1983.

Elder, Glen H. "Children of the Great Depression." In *Transactions: The Family and the Life Course in Historical Perspective*, edited by Tamara Hareven, pp. 17–64. New York: Academic Press, 1978.

————. "Family History and the Life Course." *Journal of Family History* 2 (Winter 1977): 276–304.

————. "History and the Life Course." In *Biography and Society: The Life History Approach in the Social Sciences*, edited by Daniel Bertaux, pp. 77–115. Beverly Hills, Calif.: Sage Publications, 1981.

Endelman, Judith. *The Jewish Community of Indianapolis: 1849 to the Present*. Bloomington: Indiana University Press, 1984.

Engel, Barbara A. "Mothers and Daughters: Family Patterns and the Female Intelligentsia." In *The Family in Imperial Russia*, edited by David L. Ransel, pp. 44–59. Urbana: University of Illinois Press, 1978.

————. *Mothers and Daughters: Women of the Intelligentsia in Nineteenth-Century Russia*. New York: Cambridge University Press, 1983.

Epstein, Cynthia Fuchs. "Women and Professional Careers in a Decade of Change." Paper presented at YIVO Conference on "Second Generation Jews," November 1981.

Epstein, Melech. *Jewish Labor in the United States of America: 1882–1914*. New York: Ktav Publishing Co., 1969.

Ertel, Rachel. *Le Shtetl: La Bourgade Juive de Pologne*. Paris: Payot, 1982.

Ets, Marie. *Rosa: The Life of an Italian Immigrant*. Minneapolis: University of Minnesota Press, 1970.

Ewen, Elizabeth. "City Lights: Immigrant Women and the Rise of Movies." *Signs* 5 (Suppl., Spring 1980): S45–S65.

————. *Immigrant Women in the Land of Dollars: Life and Culture on the Lower East*

Side, 1890–1925. New York: Monthly Review Press, 1985.

———. "Immigrant Women in the Land of Dollars, 1890–1920." Ph.D. dissertation, State University of New York, Stony Brook, 1979.

Ewen, Stuart. *Captains of Consciousness: Advertising and the Social Roots of the Consumer Culture.* New York: McGraw-Hill Book Co., 1976.

———, and Ewen, Elizabeth. *Channels of Desire: Mass Images and the Shaping of American Consciousness.* New York: McGraw-Hill Book Co., 1982.

Feingold, Henry. *Zion in America.* New York: Hippocrene Press, 1974.

Ferraroti, Franco. "On the Autonomy of the Biographical Method." In *Biography and Society: The Life History Approach in the Social Sciences,* edited by Daniel Bertaux, pp. 19–27. Beverly Hills, Calif.: Sage Publications, 1981.

Fischer, Minnie. *Born One Year Before the Twentieth Century: An Oral History.* New York: Community Documentation Workshop, 1976.

Friedman, Reena S. "'Send Me My Husband Who Is in New York City': Husband Desertion in the American Jewish Immigrant Community, 1900–1926." *Jewish Social Studies* 44 (Winter 1982): 1–18.

Gambino, Richard. *Blood of My Blood: The Dilemma of the Italian-Americans.* New York: Anchor Press/Doubleday & Co., 1974.

Gilligan, Carol. *In a Different Voice: Psychological Theory and Women's Development.* Cambridge, Mass.: Harvard University Press, 1982.

Glanz, Rudolph. *The Jewish Woman in America: Two Female Immigrant Generations, 1820–1929.* 2 vols. Vol. 2, *The Eastern European Jewish Woman.* New York: Ktav Publishing Co., 1976.

Gluck, Sherna Berger. "Age, Generation and Change: The Impact of Women's World War II Experience." Paper presented at the International Conference on Women's History and Oral History, Columbia University, November 1983.

———. "Interlude or Change: Women and the World War II Work Experience." *International Journal of Oral History* 3 (June 1982): 92–113.

Golab, Caroline. "The Impact of the Industrial Experience on the Immigrant Family." In *Immigrants in Industrial America: 1850–1929: The Huddled Masses Reconsidered,* edited by Richard Ehrlich, pp. 1–32. Charlottesville: University of Virginia Press, 1977.

Gold, Michael. *Jews without Money.* New York: Avon Books, 1965 (originally published in 1930).

Goldman, Emma. *Living My Life.* Edited by Richard and Anna Maria Drinnon. New York: New American Library, 1977.

Gordon, Linda. *Woman's Body, Woman's Right: A Social History of Birth Control in America.* New York: Penguin Books, 1977.

Grade, Chaim. *The Agunah.* Translated by Curt Levant. New York: Menorah Publishing Co., 1974.

———. *My Mother's Sabbath Days: A Memoir.* Translated by Channa Kleinerman Goldstein and Inna Hecker Grade. New York: Alfred A. Knopf, 1986. Reprint. Schocken Books, 1987.

Grele, Ron, ed. *Envelopes of Sound*. Chicago: Precedent Publishing Co., 1975.

Gurock, Jeffrey C. *When Harlem Was Jewish: 1870–1930*. New York: Columbia University Press, 1979.

Gutman, Herbert G. *Work, Culture, and Society in Industrializing America*. New York: Vintage Press, 1977.

Hammer, Signe. *Daughters and Mothers: Mothers and Daughters*. New York: New American Library, 1976.

Hapgood, Hutchins. *The Spirit of the Ghetto*. New York: Schocken Books, 1966 (originally published in 1902).

Hareven, Tamara. *Family Time and Industrial Time: The Relationship Between the Family and Work in a New England Industrial Community*. New York: Cambridge University Press, 1982.

―――. *Transitions: The Family and the Life Course in Historical Perspective*. New York: Academic Press, 1978.

Hareven, Tamara, and Langenbach, Randolph. *Amoskeag: Life and Work in an American Factory City*. New York: Pantheon Books, 1978.

Hasanovitz, Elizabeth. *One of Them*. Boston: Houghton Mifflin Co., 1918.

Heller, Celia S. *On the Edge of Destruction: The Jews of Poland between the Two World Wars*. New York: Columbia University Press, 1977. Reprint. New York: Schocken Books, 1980.

―――. "Poles of Jewish Background: The Case of Assimilation without Integration in Interwar Poland." In *Studies on Polish Jewry, 1919–1939*, edited by Joshua Feldman, pp. 242–76. New York: YIVO Institute for Jewish Research, 1974.

Herberg, Will. *Protestant, Catholic, Jew: An Essay in Religious Sociology*. New York: Doubleday & Co., 1955.

Higham, John. *Send These to Me: Jews and Other Immigrants in Urban America*. New York: Atheneum Press, 1975. Reprint. Baltimore: Johns Hopkins University Press, 1984.

Howe, Irving. *A Margin of Hope: An Intellectual Biography*. New York: Harcourt Brace Jovanovich, 1982.

―――. *The World of Our Fathers*. New York: Harcourt Brace Jovanovich, 1976. Reprint. New York: Schocken Books, 1990.

―――, and Greenberg, Eliezer, eds. *A Treasury of Yiddish Stories*. New York: Viking Press, 1953.

―――, and Libo, Kenneth, eds. *How We Lived: A Documentary History of Immigrant Jews in America*. New York: New American Library, 1979.

Hyman, Paula. "Culture and Gender: Women in the Immigrant Jewish Community." In *The Legacy of Jewish Immigration: 1881 and Its Impact*, edited by David Berger, pp. 157–68. Brooklyn, N.Y.: Brooklyn College Press, 1983.

―――. "Immigrant Women and Consumer Protest. The New York City Kosher Meat Boycott of 1902." *American Jewish History* 71 (September 1980): 91–105.

―――. "The Other Half: Women in the Jewish Tradition." In *The Jewish Woman: New Perspectives*, edited by Elizabeth Koltun, pp. 105–13. New York: Schocken Books, 1976.

Jastrow, Marie. *A Time to Remember.* New York: W. W. Norton, 1983.

————. *Looking Back: The American Dream through Immigrant Eyes.* New York: W. W. Norton, 1986.

Joselit, Jenna Weiszman. *Our Gang: Jewish Crime and the New York Jewish Community, 1900–1940.* Bloomington: Indiana University Press, 1983.

Joseph, Samuel. *Jewish Immigration to the United States: From 1881 to 1910.* New York: Columbia University Press, 1914.

Kaestle, Carl F., and Vinovskis, Maris A. "From Fireside to Factory: School Entry and School Leaving in Nineteenth-Century Massachusetts." In *Transitions: The Family and the Life Course in Historical Perspective,* edited by Tamara K. Hareven, pp. 135–85. New York: Academic Press, 1978.

Kahan, Anne. "The Diary of Anne Kahan." *YIVO Annual of Jewish Social Science* 18 (1983): 142–371.

Kaplan, Marion A. *The Jewish Feminist Movement in Germany: The Campaigns of the Judischer Frauenbund, 1904–1938.* Westport, Conn.: Greenwood Press, 1979.

————. *The Marriage Bargain: Women and Dowries in European History.* New York: Harrington Part, 1985.

Karp, Abraham J., ed. *Golden Door to America: The Jewish Immigrant Experience.* New York: Viking Press, 1976.

————. *Haven and Home: A History of the Jews in America.* New York: Schocken Books, 1985.

Katzman, David. *Seven Days a Week: Women and Domestic Service in Industrializing America.* New York: Oxford University Press, 1978.

Kazin, Alfred. *A Walker in the City.* New York: Harcourt, Brace & World, 1931.

Kessler-Harris, Alice. "Organizing the Unorganizable: Three Jewish Women and Their Union." In *Class, Sex, and the Woman Worker,* edited by Milton Cantor and Bruce Laurie, pp. 144–65. Westport, Conn.: Greenwood Press, 1977.

————. *Out to Work: A History of Wage-Earning Women in the United States.* New York: Oxford University Press, 1982.

————. "Problems of Coalition Building: Women and Trade Unions in the 1920's." In *Women, Work and Protest,* edited by Ruth Milkman, pp. 110–38. Boston: Routledge and Kegan Paul, 1985.

————. "Where Are the Organized Women Workers?" In *A Heritage of Her Own,* edited by Nancy F. Cott and Elizabeth H. Pleck, pp. 343–66. New York: Simon & Schuster, 1979.

Kessner, Thomas. *The Golden Door: Italian and Jewish Immigrant Mobility in New York City, 1880–1915.* New York: Oxford University Press, 1977.

————, and Caroli, Betty Boyd. "New Immigrant Women at Work: Italians and Jews in New York City, 1880–1915." *Journal of Ethnic Studies* 4 (Winter 1978): 19–31.

Kimball, Gussie. *Gitele.* New York: Vantage Press, 1960.

Klaczynska, Barbara. "Why Women Work: A Comparison of Various Groups, Philadelphia, 1910–1930." *Labor History* 17 (Winter 1976): 81–95.

Kleinberg, Susan J. "The Systematic Study of Urban Women." In *Class, Sex, and the*

Woman Worker, edited by Milton Cantor and Bruce Laurie, pp. 20–42. Westport, Conn.: Greenwood Press, 1977.

Komarovsky, Mira. *Blue-Collar Marriage*. New York: Vintage Books, 1962.

―――. "Functional Analysis of Sex Roles." *American Sociological Review* 15 (August 1950): 508–16.

Kramer, Sydelle, and Mazur, Jenny, eds. *Jewish Grandmothers*. Boston: Beacon Press, 1976.

Krause, Corinne Azen. *Grandmothers, Mothers, and Daughters: An Oral History Study of Ethnicity, Mental Health, and Continuity of Three Generations of Jewish, Italian, and Slavic-American Women*. New York: American Jewish Committee, 1978.

―――. "Urbanization without Breakdown: Italian, Jewish, and Slavic Women in Pittsburgh, 1900–1945." *Journal of Urban History* 4 (May 1978): 291–306.

Kugelmass, Jack, and Boyarin, Jonathan, eds. *From a Ruined Garden: The Memorial Books of Polish Jewry*. New York: Schocken Books, 1983.

Kuznets, Simon. "Immigration of Russian Jews to the United States." *Perspectives in American History* 9 (1975): 35–126.

LaGumina, Salvatore J. "American Education and the Italian Immigrant Response." In *American Education and the European Immigrant, 1840–1940*, edited by Bernard J. Weiss, pp. 61–77. Urbana: University of Illinois Press, 1982.

Lamphere, Louise. "Strategies, Cooperation, and Conflict among Women in Domestic Groups." In *Woman, Culture, and Society*, edited by Michelle Zimbalist Rosaldo and Louise Lamphere, pp. 97–112. Stanford, Calif.: Stanford University Press, 1974.

Landes, Ruth, and Zborowski, Mark. "Hypothesis Concerning the Eastern European Family." In *The Psychodynamics of American Jewish Life*, edited by Norman Kiell, pp. 23–66. New York: Twayne Publishing Co., 1967.

Lang, Lucy Robins. *Tomorrow Is Beautiful*. New York: Macmillan Co., 1948.

Lapidus, Gail Warshofsky. *Women in Soviet Society: Equality, Development, and Social Change*. Berkeley: University of California Press, 1978.

Lazarus, Nahida Ruth. *Nahida Remy's The Jewish Woman*. Translated by Louise Mannheimer. New York: Block Publishing Co., 1923 (originally published in Cincinnati, Press of C. D. Brechtel, 1895).

Leach, William R. "Transformations in a Culture of Consumption: Women and Department Stores, 1890–1925." *Journal of American History* 71 (September 1984): 319–42.

Lederhendler, Eli. "Jewish Immigration to America and Revisionist Historiography: A Decade of New Perspectives." *YIVO Annual of Jewish Social Science* 18 (1983): 391–410.

Lerner, Elinor. "American Feminism and the Jewish Question." Work in progress.

Liebman, Charles S. "Religion, Class, and Culture in American Jewish History." *Jewish Journal of Sociology* 14 (December 1967): 227–42.

―――. "The Religion of American Jews." In *The Jew in American Society*, edited by Marshall Sklare, pp. 223–52. New York: Behrman House, 1974.

Lifschutz, E. "Selected Documents Pertaining to Jewish Life in Poland, 1919–1939," in

Studies on Polish Jewry, 1919–1939, edited by Joshua Feldman, pp. 277–94. New York: YIVO Institute for Jewish Research, 1974.

Levine, Louis. *The Women's Garment Workers: A History of the ILGWU*. New York: B. W. Huebsch, 1924.

Manning, Caroline. *The Immigrant Woman and Her Job*. Washington, D.C.: Government Printing Office, 1931.

Manser, Marilyn, and Brown, Murray. "Bargaining Analyses of Household Decisions." In *Women in the Labor Market*, edited by Cynthia B. Lloyd, Emily S. Andrews, and Curtis L. Gilroy, pp. 3–26. New York: Columbia University Press, 1979.

Marcowitz, Ruth Jacknow. "The Daughters of Immigrants as College Students: Their Role as Student Activists during the 1930's." Paper presented at the annual meeting of the Organization of American Historians, New York, N.Y., 1986.

Marcus, Jacob R. *The American Jewish Woman: A Documentary History*. New York: Ktav Publishing Co., 1981.

———. *The American Jewish Woman, 1654–1980*. New York: Ktav Publishing Co., 1981.

Mead, Margaret, and Metraux, Rhoda, eds. *The Study of Culture at a Distance*. Chicago: University of Chicago Press, 1953.

Mendelsohn, Ezra. *The Jews of East Central Europe between the World Wars*. Bloomington: Indiana University Press, 1983.

Mensch, Jean Ulitz. "Social Pathology among Jews in New York: Desertion and Prostitution in the Immigrant Community." Paper presented at the annual meeting of the Organization of American Historians, New York, NY., 1986.

Metzker, Isaac. *A Bintel Brief*. New York: Ballantine Books, 1971. Reprint. New York: Schocken Books, 1990.

Michel, Sonya. "Mothers and Daughters in American Jewish Literature: The Rotted Cord." In *The Jewish Woman: New Perspectives*, edited by Elizabeth Koltun, pp. 272–82. New York: Schocken Books, 1976.

Mindel, Charles H. and Habenstein, Robert W., eds. *Ethnic Families in America: Patterns and Variations*. New York: Elsevier, 1976.

Mitchell, William E. *Mishpokhe: A Study of New York City Family Clubs*. New York: Mouton, 1978.

Modell, John, and Hareven, Tamara K. "Urbanization and the Malleable Household: An Examination of Boarding and Lodging in American Families," in *Family and Kin in Urban Communities*, edited by Tamara Hareven, pp. 164–86. New York: New Viewpoints, 1977.

Modell, John; Furstenberg, Frank, Jr.; and Hershberg, Theodore. "Social Change and Transitions to Adulthood in Historical Perspective." *Journal of Family History* 1 (Fall 1976): 7–32.

Moore, Deborah Dash. *At Home in America: Second Generation New York Jews*. New York: Columbia University Press, 1981.

———. "Jewish Ethnicity and Acculturation in the 1920's: Public Education in New York City." *Jewish Journal of Sociology* 18 (December 1976): 96–104.

Morton, Leah Stern. *I Am a Woman—and a Jew*. New York: J. H. Sears & Co., 1926.

Myerhoff, Barbara. *Number Our Days*. New York: E. P. Dutton, 1979.

Neisser, Edith. *Mothers and Daughters: A Lifelong Relationship*. New York: Harper and Row, 1967.

Nirenberg, Mariam. "Folksongs in the East European Tradition." Introduction to record album. New York: YIVO Institute for Jewish Research, 1986.

Oakley, Ann. *The Sociology of Housework*. New York: Pantheon Books, 1974.

Odencrantz, Louise C. *Italian Women in Industry*. New York: Arno Press, 1977 (originally published 1919).

Ornitz, Samuel. *Haunch, Paunch, and Jowl*. New York: Boni and Liveright, 1923.

Peiss, Kathy. *Cheap Amusements: Working Women and Leisure in Turn-of-the-Century New York*. Philadelphia: Temple University Press, 1986.

Peretz, Isaac Y. "Devotion without End." In *Selected Stories of Isaac L. Peretz*, edited by Irving Howe and Eliezer Greenberg. New York: Schocken Books, 1974.

Perry, Elisabeth I. "'The General Motherhood of the Commonwealth': Dance Hall Reform in the Progressive Era." *American Quarterly* 37 (Winter 1985): pp. 718–33.

Pesotta, Rose. *Bread upon the Waters*. New York: Dodd, Mead & Co., 1944.

Petchesky, Rosalind P. *Abortion and Woman's Choice: The State, Sexuality and Reproductive Freedom*. Boston: Northeastern University Press, 1984.

Pleck, Elizabeth H. "A Mother's Wages." In *A Heritage of Her Own*, edited by Nancy Cott and Elizabeth Pleck, pp. 367–92. New York: Simon & Schuster, 1979.

———. "Challenges to Traditional Authority in Immigrant Families." In *The American Family in Social-Historical Perspective*, 3d ed., edited by Michael Gordon, pp. 504–17. New York: St. Martin's Press, 1983.

Plotkin, Sara. *Full-Time Active: An Oral History*. New York: Community Documentation Workshop, 1980.

Prieto, Yolanda. "Cuban Women and Work in the United States: A New Jersey Case Study." In *International Migration: The Female Experience*, edited by Rita J. Simon and Caroline Brettell, pp. 95–112. Totowa, N.J.: Rowman and Allanheld, 1986.

Quataert, Jean H. "The Shaping of Women's Work in Manufacturing: Guilds, Households, and the State in Central Europe, 1648–1870." *American Historical Review* 90 (December 1985): 1122–48.

Raback, Berl. "Women's Professions in Sonik." *Yiddishe Shprache* 24 (June 1964): 26–27.

Ransel, David, ed. *The Family in Imperial Russia*. Urbana: University of Illinois Press, 1978.

Ravitch, Diane. *The Great School Wars, New York City, 1805–1973: A History of the Public School as Battlefield for Social Change*. New York: Basic Books, 1974.

Reznikoff, Sarah. "Early History of a Seamstress." In *Family Chronicle*, by Charles, Nathan, and Sarah Reznikoff, pp. 7–100. New York: Universe Books, 1971.

Riis, Jacob A. *The Children of the Poor*. New York: Arno Press, 1971 (originally published in 1892).

———. *How the Other Half Lives*. New York: Sagamore Press, 1957 (originally published in 1890).

Rischin, Moses, ed. *Grandma Never Lived in America: The New Journalism of Abraham Cahan*. Bloomington: Indiana University Press, 1985.

———. *The Promised City: New York's Jews, 1870–1914*. Cambridge, Mass.: Harvard University Press, 1962.

Roberts, Elizabeth. *A Woman's Place: An Oral History of Working-Class Women, 1890–1940*. Oxford: Basil Blackwell, 1984.

Robertson, Priscilla. *An Experience of Women: Pattern and Change in Nineteenth-Century Europe*. Philadelphia: Temple University Press, 1982.

Rosaldo, Michelle Zimbalist. "Woman, Culture, and Society: A Theoretical Overview." In *Woman, Culture, and Society*, edited by Michelle Zimbalist Rosaldo and Louise Lamphere, pp. 17–42. Stanford, Calif.: Stanford University Press, 1974.

Rosen, Ruth, ed. *The Maimie Papers*. New York: Feminist Press, 1977.

Rosenthal, Celia Stopnicka. "Deviation and Social Change in the Jewish Community of a Small Polish Town." *American Journal of Sociology* 60 (September 1954): 177–81.

———. "Social Stratification of the Jewish Community in a Small Polish Town." *American Journal of Sociology* 59 (July 1953): 1–10.

Roskies, David G. "Yiddish Popular Literature and the Female Reader." *Journal of Popular Culture* 10 (Spring 1977): 852–58.

Rubin, Lillian Breslow. *Worlds of Pain: Life in the Working-Class Family*. New York: Basic Books, 1976.

Rubin, Ruth. *Voices of a People: The Story of Yiddish Folk Song*. New York: Thomas Yoseloff, 1963. Reprint. New York: McGraw-Hill Book Co., 1973.

Rubinow, I. M. *Economic Condition of the Jews in Russia*. New York: Arno Press, 1975 (originally published in *Bulletin of the Bureau of Labor* 15, no. 72 [September 1907]).

Rudavsky, David. "Trends in Jewish School Organization and Enrollment in New York City, 1917–1950." *YIVO Annual of Jewish Social Science* 10 (1955): 45–80.

Ruskay, Sophie. *Horsecars and Cobblestones*. New York: A. S. Barnes & Co., 1948.

Ryan, Mary. *The Cradle of the Middle Class: The Family in Oneida County, New York, 1790–1865*. New York: Cambridge University Press, 1981.

Sanday, Peggy R. "Female Status in the Public Domain." In *Woman, Culture, and Society*, edited by Michelle Zimbalist Rosaldo and Louise Lamphere, pp. 189–206. Stanford, Calif.: Stanford University Press, 1974.

Sanders, Ronald. *The Downtown Jews: Portraits of an Immigrant Generation*. New York: New American Library, 1967.

Saroff, Sophie. *Stealing the State: An Oral History*. New York: Community Documentation Workshop, 1983.

Scarf, Maggie. "Intimate Partners: Patterns in Love and Marriage." *Atlantic Monthly*, November 1986.

Schlesinger, Benjamin. *The Jewish Family*. Toronto: University of Toronto Press, 1971.

Schlissel, Lillian. *Women's Diaries of the Westward Journey*. New York: Schocken Books, 1982.

Schneiderman, Rose. *All for One*. New York: Paul Eriksson, 1967.

Schwartz, Laura. "Immigrant Voices from Home, Work, and Community: Women and Family in the Migration Process, 1890–1938." Ph.D. dissertation, State University of New York, Stony Brook, 1983.

Scott, Joan A., and Tilly, Louise A. *Women, Work, and Family*. New York: Holt, Rinehart & Winston, 1978.

————. "Women's Work and the Family in Nineteenth Century Europe." *Comparative Studies in Society and History* 17 (1975): 36–64.

Selavan, Ida Cohen, ed. *My Voice Was Heard*. New York: Ktav Publishing Co., 1981.

Seller, Maxine. "The Education of Immigrant Children in Buffalo, New York." *New York History* 62 (April 1976): 183–99.

————. "The Education of the Immigrant Woman: 1900–1935." *Journal of Urban History* 4 (May 1978): 307–30.

————. "The 'Women's Interest Page' of the *Jewish Daily Forward*." Unpublished paper.

Sholem Aleichem. *The Great Fair: Scenes from My Childhood*. New York: Noonday Press, 1955 (originally published in 1916).

————. *Tevye the Dairyman and The Railroad Stories*. New York: Schocken Books, 1987.

————. *Tevye's Daughters*. New York: Crown Publishers, 1949.

————. *The Tevye Stories and Others*. New York: Pocket Books, 1965.

Silberman, Charles E. *A Certain People: American Jews and Their Lives Today*. New York: Summit Books, 1985.

Simon, Kate. *Bronx Primitive: Portraits in a Childhood*. New York: Viking Press, 1982.

————. *A Wider World: Portraits in an Adolescence*. New York: Harper & Row, 1986.

Singer, Isaac Bashevis. *In My Father's Court*. New York: Farrar, Straus & Giroux, 1962.

Singer, Israel Joshua (I. J.). *Of a World That Is No More*. New York: Vanguard Press, 1970.

Sklare, Marshall. *America's Jews*. New York: Random House, 1971.

————, ed. *The Jews: Social Patterns of an American Group*. New York: Free Press, 1958.

Smith, Judith Ellen. *Family Connections: A History of Italian and Jewish Immigrant Lives in Providence, Rhode Island, 1900–1940*. Albany, N.Y.: State University of New York Press, 1985.

————. "Italian Mothers, American Daughters: Changes in Work and Family Roles." In *The Italian Immigrant Woman in North America*, edited by Betty Boyd Caroli, Robert F. Harney, and Lydio F. Tomasi, pp. 206–21. Toronto, Canada: Multicultural History Society of Ontario, 1978.

————. "Remaking Their Lives: Italian and Jewish Immigrant Family, Work, and Community in Providence, Rhode Island, 1900–1940." Ph.D. dissertation, Brown University, 1980.

Sochen, June. *Consecrate Every Day: The Public Lives of Jewish American Women, 1880–1980*. Albany, N.Y.: State University of New York Press, 1981.

Steinberg, Bernard. "Jewish Education in the United States." *Jewish Journal of Sociology* 21 (June 1979): 5–35.

Stone, Goldie. *My Caravan of Years.* New York: Block Publishing Co., 1945.

Strasser, Susan. *Never Done: A History of American Housework.* New York: Pantheon, 1982.

Strom, Sharon Hartman. "Italian-American Women and Their Daughters in Rhode Island: The Adolescence of Two Generations, 1900–1950." In *The Italian Immigrant Woman in North America,* edited by Betty Boyd Caroli, Robert F. Harney, and Lydio F. Tomasi, pp. 191–204. Toronto, Canada: Multicultural History Society of Ontario, 1978.

Tcherikower, Elias. *The Early Jewish Labor Movement in the United States.* New York: YIVO Institute for Jewish Research, 1961.

———. "Jewish Immigrants to the United States, 1881–1900." *YIVO Annual of Jewish Social Science* 6 (1951): 157–76.

Tentler, Leslie Woodcock. *Wage-Earning Women: Industrial Work and Family Life in the United States, 1900–1930.* New York: Oxford University Press, 1979.

Theophano, Janet Schwarz. "It's Really Tomato Sauce but We Call It Gravy: A Study of Food and Woman's Work among Italian-American Families." Ph.D. dissertation, University of Pennsylvania, 1982.

Thomas, William I., and Znaniecki, Florian. *The Polish Peasant in Europe and America,* edited by Eli Zaretski. Urbana: University of Illinois Press, 1984 (originally published in 1918).

Thompson, E. P. *The Making of the English Working Class.* London: Victor Gollancz, 1963.

Thompson, Paul. "Life Histories and the Analysis of Social Change." In *Biography and Society: The Life History Approach in the Social Sciences,* edited by Daniel Bertaux, pp. 289–306. Beverly Hills, Calif.: Sage Publications, 1981.

———. *The Voice of the Past: Oral History.* New York: Oxford University Press, 1978.

Toll, William. *The Making of an Ethnic Middle Class: Portland Jewry over Four Generations.* Albany, N.Y.: State University of New York Press, 1982.

Tovrov, Jessica. "Mother-Child Relationships among the Russian Nobility." In *The Family in Imperial Russia,* edited by David L. Ransel, pp. 15–43. Urbana: University of Illinois Press, 1978.

Wald, Lillian D. *The House on Henry Street.* New York: Henry Holt & Co., 1915.

Wandersee, Winifred D. *Women's Work and Family Values, 1920–1940.* Cambridge, Mass.: Harvard University Press, 1981.

Ware, Carolyn. *Greenwich Village, 1920–1930.* Boston: Houghton Mifflin Co., 1935.

Ware, Susan. *Holding Their Own: American Women in the 1930's.* Boston: Twayne Publishers, 1982.

Weinberger, Moses. *People Walk On Their Heads: Jews and Judaism in New York.* Translated and edited by Jonathan D. Sarna. New York: Holmes and Meier, 1982 (originally published 1887, New York).

Weiss, Bernard J. *American Education and the European Immigrant: 1840–1940*. Urbana: University of Illinois Press, 1982.

Weisser, Michael R. *A Brotherhood of Memory: Jewish Landsmanshaftn in the New World*. New York: Basic Books, 1985.

Weissler, Chava. "Women's T'khina Literature." Paper presented at the Jewish Theological Seminary, November 15, 1984.

Wiesel, Elie. *A Beggar in Jerusalem*. New York: Random House, 1970.

Willett, Mabel Hurd. *The Employment of Women in the Clothing Trade*. New York: AMS Press, 1928 (originally published 1902).

Wischnitzer, Mark. *To Dwell in Safety: The Story of Jewish Migration since 1800*. Philadelphia: The Jewish Publication Society of America, 1948.

Wisse, Ruth. *The Schlemiel as Modern Hero*. Chicago: University of Chicago Press, 1971.

Wolf, Margery. "Chinese Women: Old Skills in a New Context." In *Woman, Culture, and Society*, edited by Michelle Zimbalist Rosaldo and Louise Lamphere, pp. 157–72. Stanford, Calif.: Stanford University Press, 1974.

Wolfenstein, Martha. "Two Types of Jewish Mothers." In *The Jews: Social Patterns of an American Group*, edited by Marshall Sklare, pp. 520–34. New York: Free Press, 1958.

Yans-McLaughlin, Virginia. *Family and Community: Italian Immigrants in Buffalo: 1880–1939*. Ithaca, N.Y.: Cornell University Press, 1977.

————. "Memory and Consciousness among Jewish and Italian Garment Workers." Paper presented at the International Conference on Oral History and Women's History, Columbia University, New York, November 19, 1983.

Yezierska, Anzia. *All I Could Never Be*. New York: Brower, Warren & Putnam, 1932.

————. *Arrogant Beggar*. Garden City, N.Y.: Doubleday, Page & Co., 1927.

————. *Bread Givers*. New York: Braziller, 1925.

————. *Children of Loneliness*. New York: Funk & Wagnalls, 1923.

————. *Hungry Hearts*. Boston: Houghton Mifflin Co., 1920.

————. *The Open Cage*. New York: Persea Books, 1979.

————. *Red Ribbon on a White Horse*. New York: Charles Scribner's Sons, 1950.

————. *Salome of the Tenements*. New York: Boni & Liveright, 1923.

Zborowski, Mark, and Herzog, Elizabeth. *Life Is with People: The Jewish Little-Town of Eastern Europe*. New York: International Universities Press, 1952. Reprint. New York: Schocken Books, 1962.

Zunser, Miriam Shomer. *Yesterday*. New York: Stackpole Sons, 1939.

Index

. . . .

SCHOCKEN BOOKS
OF RELATED INTEREST

WOMEN AND JEWISH LAW:
AN EXPLORATION OF WOMEN'S ISSUES IN HALAKHIC SOURCES
By Rachel Biale, 0-8052-0810-0, paper

"A rare book in Jewish women's studies, combining a scholarly review of Halakhah with the presentation of a thoughtful feminist opinion."
—Washington Jewish Weekly

THE MEMOIRS OF GLÜCKEL OF HAMELN
Translated with Notes by Marvin Lowenthal, 0-8052-0572-1, paper

"The personal diary of an extraordinary seventeenth-century German-Jewish woman."   *—Urban and Social Change Review*

ON BEING A JEWISH FEMINIST: A READER
Edited and with an Introduction by Susannah Heschel, 0-8052-0745-7, paper

"With this book, women who wish to be both feminists and religious Jews begin to find their authentic voice."   *—Rosemary Ruether*

THE JEWISH WOMAN: NEW PERSPECTIVES
Edited by Elizabeth Koltun, 0-8052-0532-2, paper

In discussing aspects of a woman's life within Judaism, this collection will prove indispensable in re-evaluating the role of the modern Jewish woman.

LOVE AND TRADITION: MARRIAGE BETWEEN JEWS AND CHRISTIANS
By Egon Mayer, 0-8052-0828-3, paper

"The most extensive study of intermarriage to date. . . . An important study of an issue critical to American Jews."   *—Library Journal*

HANNAH SENESH: HER LIFE AND DIARY
Introduction by Abba Eban, 0-8052-0410-5, paper

"Her life is an offering, her words a poem, her story an inspiration."—Elie Wiesel